Fidel in the Cuban Socialist Revolution

Studies in Critical Social Sciences Book Series

Haymarket Books is proud to be working with Brill Academic Publishers (www.brill.nl) to republish the *Studies in Critical Social Sciences* book series in paperback editions. This peer-reviewed book series offers insights into our current reality by exploring the content and consequences of power relationships under capitalism, and by considering the spaces of opposition and resistance to these changes that have been defining our new age. Our full catalog of *SCSS* volumes can be viewed at https://www.haymarketbooks.org/series_collections/4-studies-in-critical-social-sciences.

Series Editor
David Fasenfest (Wayne State University)

Editorial Board
Eduardo Bonilla-Silva (Duke University)
Chris Chase-Dunn (University of California–Riverside)
William Carroll (University of Victoria)
Raewyn Connell (University of Sydney)
Kimberlé W. Crenshaw (University of California–LA and Columbia University)
Heidi Gottfried (Wayne State University)
Karin Gottschall (University of Bremen)
Alfredo Saad Filho (King's College London)
Chizuko Ueno (University of Tokyo)
Sylvia Walby (Lancaster University)
Raju Das (York University)

Fidel in the Cuban Socialist Revolution

Understanding the Cuban Revolution (1959–1961)

José Bell Lara
Tania Caram León
Delia Luisa López García

Translated by
Charles McKelvey

Haymarket Books
Chicago, IL

First published in 2019 by Brill Academic Publishers, The Netherlands.
© 2019 Koninklijke Brill NV, Leiden, The Netherlands

Published in paperback in 2020 by
Haymarket Books
P.O. Box 180165
Chicago, IL 60618
773-583-7884
www.haymarketbooks.org

ISBN: 978-1-64259-370-9

Distributed to the trade in the US through Consortium Book Sales and Distribution (www.cbsd.com) and internationally through Ingram Publisher Services International (www.ingramcontent.com).

This book was published with the generous support of Lannan Foundation and Wallace Action Fund.

Special discounts are available for bulk purchases by organizations and institutions. Please call 773-583-7884 or email info@haymarketbooks.org for more information.

Cover design by Jamie Kerry and Ragina Johnson.

Printed in United States.

10 9 8 7 6 5 4 3 2 1

Library of Congress Cataloging-in-Publication Data is available.

Dedicated to the Cuban people

Contents

Preface   XI
Translator's Note   XIV

Introduction   1

Historical Context   3

PART 1
1959: Year of Liberation

Introduction to 1959: "Year of Liberation"   15

Call to Revolutionary General Strike   19

The Revolution Begins Now   20

To Speak the Truth Is the First Duty of All Revolutionaries   27

We Are Revolutionaries Making a Revolution, Revolutionaries in Power!   34

To Live on Our Knees, Why?   42

This Law Initiates an Entirely New Stage in Our Economic Life and a Magnificent Future Awaits Our Country   45

The Cuban People Is an Invincible People   51

In Cuba, There Is a Democracy Where the People Discuss Their Problems Directly   88

The Entire Nation Stands without Fear   92

The Working Class and the Cuban Revolution   97

We Have Kept Our Promises to the People   105

PART 2
1960: Year of Agrarian Reform

Introduction to 1960: "Year of Agrarian Reform"   123

The Revolution Converts Barracks into Schools   126

The Future of Our Country Necessarily Has to Be a Future of Men of Science and Thought   129

The Choice Is *Patria o Muerte*   132

Democracy Is This   139

The Slogan for the People Is: *Venceremos!*   149

Latin America Does Not Have the Right to Make a Revolution   152

Women, the Decisive Factor in the Revolution   163

Declaration of Havana   167

Speech in the General Assembly of the United Nations   173

We Are Going to Establish a System of Collective Revolutionary Watch   197

The Moncada Program Has Been Carried Out   201

PART 3
1961: Year of Education

Introduction to 1961: "Year of Education"   213

The Revolution Is a Struggle to the Death between the Future and the Past   217

What the Imperialists Cannot Forgive   226

Communiques from the Battle at Playa Girón   241

At Playa Girón, the Country for All Has Triumphed   247

Glossary   277
Bibliography   293
Index   299

Preface

Fidel in the Cuban Socialist Revolution is the result of research conducted by a team of three professors of the Cuba Program of the Latin American Faculty of the Social Sciences (Facultad Latinoamericana de Ciencias Sociales, FLACSO for its initials in Spanish) of the University of Havana: Dr. José Bell Lara, Dra. Tania Caram León and Dra. Delia Luisa López García. They constitute the FLACSO-Cuba Cuban Revolution Research Group, which for fourteen years has worked together on three projects: *Memoria Documental de la Revolución Cubana 1959–1965*, which received the award of the Cuban Academy of Sciences in 2014, *Memoria Documental de la Revolución Cubana 1966–1970*, in progress, and *Cuba: National Liberation and Socialist Transition*.

This book focuses on one of the most extraordinary socio-political processes of the Western Hemisphere: a socialist revolution of national liberation, emerging in the periphery of the capitalist world-economy, and only a few kilometers from the world-system's hegemonic core power.

In only three years (1959–1961), Fidel Castro and the revolutionary leadership, as rapidly as circumstances permitted, made advances in providing for the basic needs of the Cuban people, which had been accumulating a deficiency for years. There were few available strategies for attaining such advances. The most extensive and productive lands as well as the limited means of production and services were in the hands of foreign and domestic owners, both intimately tied to the ideology of free trade. Commodities proceeded to and from the United States on which the country was economically, commercially, and financially dependent. In order to advance in a continuous form, the revolutionary government had to break these ties and declare the full sovereignty of the nation over its territory.

Fidel was capable of discerning from the beginning that the Moncada program, proclaimed in his October 16, 1953 self-defense known as *History Will Absolve Me*, could not be implemented without anti-capitalist measures. He did not hesitate in proposing them and carrying them out, even though he fully understood the political and even the military costs to the nation that would result. Decisive anti-capitalist measures gave rise to a direct confrontation with the U.S. government, which, however, even before the nationalizations were carried out, had already decided on the destruction of the Cuban Revolution.

These initial years were very complicated. Within the country, an intense class struggle was unleashed, that well beyond the external hostility towards the Revolution included some initially within the Revolution. Those who failed to understand the justice and the purpose of the revolutionary laws and measures fell away and some passed to the ranks of traitors. During so many years of neocolonialism, particular interests wove a pro-USA ideological net, based on bourgeois democratic values, which was utilized intelligently by imperialist agencies with the intention of subverting the Revolution from within.

What is most clear is that it is impossible to write the history of the Cuban Revolution without Fidel Castro. He exercised his leadership through a permanent interaction with the people as a true popular educator. With simple words and clear examples, he explained for hours and hours the reasons for the measures that the Revolution was taking, in plazas full of people or in television appearances. Fidel's pedagogical discourses became a tool for the socialization of the political power and the consciousness of the Cuban masses.

Such power of communication was immortalized by Che Guevara in 1965 in *Socialism and Man in Cuba*: "Fidel is the master of it. His particular style of integration with the people must be seen to be appreciated. In Fidel's speeches before great public concentrations of people, there can be observed something like a dialogue of two tuning forks, whose vibrations provoke new vibrations in the speaker. Fidel and the mass begin to vibrate in a dialogue of glowing intensity, until reaching climax in a sudden ending, crowned by our shout for struggle and victory."

We begin with a historic introduction, providing the English-speaking reader with some background knowledge of colonial and neocolonial Cuban society before the triumph of the Revolution in 1959. The text consists of a selection of the most important speeches, television appearances, and other public discourses of Fidel Castro during the period 1959 to 1961, with footnotes that provide clarification of words and events. The volume is organized by years, and each is preceded by a description of the events during the year. In addition, a glossary is included with more precise definitions and mini-biographies of persons that are alluded to in the historic introduction and in the texts of Fidel. At the end of the book is a bibliography consisting of the works consulted by the authors in the development of the historic introduction.

The work would not have been possible without the interest expressed by Dr. Ricardo A. Dello Buono, Professor of Sociology at Manhattan College in New York City, at the Conference of the Association of Humanist Sociology (AHS) held in Havana in November 2017. On that occasion, a work session that included Professor David Fasenfest of Wayne State University, Editor of the journal *Critical Sociology* led to definitive results. It was agreed that the authors would undertake a selection of Fidel's speeches that would be particularly appropriate for English-speaking readers. To ensure an effective reach to global readership free of any political obstacles, it was agreed that the project would be brought to fruition in collaboration with the prestigious publishing house of Brill in The Netherlands.

The work culminated in a dedicated, delicate, and complex labor of translation into English by Dr. Charles McKelvey, Professor Emeritus of Presbyterian College in South Carolina, who has studied the Cuban revolutionary project over a period of decades. In the judgment of the authors, Dr. McKelvey has internalized the essence of a true translation: expressing in the codes of his mother language the particular texts that he is interpreting, sometimes departing from the strictly literal and perhaps linguistically exact replication in order to facilitate comprehension of revolutionary thought and reality. In the Translator's Note, he explains further the approach adopted in his invaluable work.

Fidel in the Cuban Socialist Revolution is dedicated to the sixtieth anniversary of the Cuban revolutionary triumph and its leader Fidel Castro. In the context of a world agitated by a proliferation of objective and subjective conflicts in which a seemingly invulnerable bourgeois ideology has expanded on a planetary scale, this work seeks to make a modest contribution towards illuminating its real character.

Translator's Note

As I worked on the translation of this volume, I met regularly with the authors and we collectively made decisions concerning difficult questions that emerge in a work of linguistic interpretation. Translating into English the speeches of Fidel Castro from 1959 to 1961 involves particular challenges. In the first place, the political and ideological context of the words of Fidel is different from that of the English-speaking peoples of the global North. Therefore, the translation continually involved two moments: a first moment of interpretation, understanding the meaning of the words in the political-ideological context in which they are expressed; and a second moment of *re*interpretation, expressing that understanding in a different cultural, political, and ideological context, perhaps in a different terminology, but faithful to its original meaning.

Secondly, Fidel for the most part did not write out his speeches and his spoken words were transcribed by the stenographic department of the Cuban revolutionary government. The spoken word, uttered in a form that effectively communicates, often is indifferent to the accepted grammatical structures of the written word. Paragraphs and sentences often are not clearly defined and the articulation can have a complex grammatical structure. Accordingly, I made the judgment in some cases that comprehension would be enhanced by expressing the words literally in English, with all their details and complexities. In other cases, however, I judged that understanding would be most facilitated by a reformulation of the words, in a form faithful to the original meaning. In this book, there are ample examples of both literal, detailed translation and faithful reformulation.

We have also decided to leave some words in their original Spanish. These words are frequently used in Cuban public discourse and their literal meaning in English has a somewhat different connotation. They include the following:

Compañero literally means partner, teammate, roommate, coworker, or colleague. In Latin American social movements, it connotes "companion in the struggle." It could be translated as "comrade" in the Cuban context but as a legacy of the Cold War, such a translation would have an image that invites some degree of distortion.

Comandante, literally "commander," "major," or "commanding officer," has a connotation in Cuba different from a military rank, as a result of the fact that the rank became associated with column leaders or officers assigned to important tasks in the revolutionary guerrilla struggle of 1956–1958. Some *"comandantes"* became legendary and their title permanent.

TRANSLATOR'S NOTE

Fidel used the slogan *Patria o Muerte* on March 5, 1960, at a speech pronounced during the funeral of the victims of the explosion of the ship "La Coubre," a target of counterrevolutionary sabotage. The slogan could be translated as "Country or Death" or "Homeland or Death;" it was intended to convey that every Cuban revolutionary is prepared to make all necessary sacrifices, including sacrificing his or her life.

Venceremos could be translated as "We shall overcome" or "We will be victorious". Fidel declared *"Venceremos"* to be the slogan of the people on June 7, 1960, maintaining that, in the long run, the people will be victorious.

The Spanish is retained in the book in common Latin American slogans. *Sí*, ("yes"), regularly used in the slogan *"Cuba, Sí,"* a proclamation of support for revolutionary Cuba; and *Viva!*, "Long live," as in *Viva Cuba!*, or *Viva Fidel!*

In certain political contexts in Latin America, the Spanish word *pueblo* (people) refers to persons with a common identity and common political culture. Accordingly, a concept has emerged of a nation that is formed by "a people;" and in multi-cultural nations, there are various "peoples." Similarly, there is common reference to "the peoples of Latin America" and "the peoples of the world." Although the plural "peoples" is used rarely in English, and some consider it grammatically incorrect, I generally use it to translate *"pueblos,"* in order to be faithful to the Latin American meaning and intention.

Following the custom of Cuban revolutionaries and the Latin American Left of the time, Fidel uses the word "monopolios" (monopolies) to refer to what we today call transnational corporations. I have translated it as monopolies, in accordance with the usage of the time.

In the period 1959 to 1961, Fidel was speaking prior to changes in language stimulated by the international women's movement. For the most part, Fidel's traditional language has been respected and retained. The reader should understand that when Fidel used the word *"hombres"* (men), in most contexts he meant men and women, and not men to the exclusion of women. Similarly, *"hijos"* (sons) should be interpreted as sons and daughters; and *"hermanos"* (brothers), as brothers and sisters. As is seen in some of the selected texts, Fidel was a groundbreaking advocate of the principle of full equality for women and the full participation of women in the revolutionary project. His use of traditional language reflected the usage of the time.

The nearly universal custom in written works is to refer to historic persons by their surname only, except for the initial reference to the person. Accordingly, many published writings outside of Cuba refer to the man who gave the speeches that form this book as Castro. But this is never done in Cuba. Sometimes, in the initial reference or in formal occasions or moments, he is referred to as Fidel Castro or Fidel Castro Ruz. In Cuba, however, he is never referred to as Castro and nearly always as "Fidel." I find myself unable to depart from this Cuban custom.

Charles McKelvey

Introduction

This book is a result of a research project, "Cuba: national liberation and socialist transition," which was conducted over the course of ten years by three professors in the Cuba Program of the Latin American Faculty of the Social Sciences of the University of Havana. The project included, among other themes, the promotion of greater understanding of the thought and work of Fidel Castro between the years 1959 and 1961, by means of a selection of his speeches and television appearances. The focus was not on biographical matters; rather, the intention has been to show the qualities of Fidel Castro's leadership in the Cuban revolutionary process.

Although we share an understanding that peoples and not persons make history, we nonetheless recognize that the role of Fidel Castro in the transformation of Cuban society during the second half of the twentieth century has been especially significant. He demonstrated a capacity to advance the revolutionary process, presenting himself dynamically in the evolution of its events, in a context that was nearly always adverse.

The reader will find that the interpretations of the authors in this book are offered only in specific places. For example, the *Historic Context* provides an analysis of relevant aspects of Cuban society since its constitution as a Republic, including the antecedents of the insurrectional process, the triumph of January 1, 1959, and the revolutionary transformations that were carried out in the period under study. In addition, the points of view of the authors are found in the *Introductions* for each one of the years 1959, 1960, and 1961. Here, we seek to provide the reader with a greater knowledge of the events not treated in the documents selected for the book due to space considerations.

The development of this project has included the following considerations:

1. The need for access to original documents in the complex process of identifying, analyzing, and interpreting the events that led to the Cuban Revolution and the role of Fidel Castro in them, with recognition of the need for other methodological approaches as well.
2. The possibility that, by means of analysis of the original documents, investigators, students, and serious readers could interpret for themselves the circumstances and the political and ideological climate of profound class struggle during the first three years of the Revolution when Fidel Castro carried out the principal tasks of revolutionary leadership.
3. The majority of the documents have not been reproduced following their original emission, giving usefulness to having them in a single volume.

4. The speeches have been compared with the sources and the original wording has been respected; only minimal changes have been made to facilitate understanding. Footnotes have been included to aid readers who are not familiar with the Cuban Revolution or with Cuban euphemisms employed in the various speeches.
5. The majority of the included speeches of Fidel Castro had to be edited by the authors due to their length. In his character of popular educator, Fidel repeated time and again his considerations and arguments to the people, in order that they would achieve a deep understanding of the momentous events which they were living, during a period in which revolutionary consciousness was still incipient.
6. A Glossary has been included that provides a brief sketch of the personalities and institutions most relevant to the period studied and to which the speeches allude.

Access to these documents permits us to conclude with confidence that the measures taken by the Cuban Revolution between 1959 and 1961, which ultimately realized the rebellious spirit of Moncada[1] by means of the road to socialism, were not, paraphrasing Mariátegui,[2] *an exact replica or a copy, but a heroic creation.*

---

[1] See glossary.
[2] See glossary.

Historical Context

Between 1959 and 1961, in a process without precedent, the Cuban Revolution fulfilled its duty of anti-imperialist social change and national liberation. It ceaselessly undertook profound anti-capitalist transformations, becoming the first socialist revolution of national liberation in the West. In order to understand this process, one must have some awareness of the basic components of pre-revolutionary Cuban society, including the events that led to the revolutionary outcome. Moreover, the revolutionary process must be understood in an international context.

Background

The Constitution of 1901 established the legal foundation of the Republic of Cuba. On this foundation, Cubans attempted to advance from a colonized society, which had lasted for four hundred years, to a formally independent society organized as a modern republic. Developed according to the standards of the U.S. political process, the Constitution of 1901 designed a centralized republic, with liberal representative democracy, to a high degree presidential, and with a classic division into executive, legislative, and judicial powers. Thus, the Republic of Cuba was established as a modern state, although with a foreign appendix, the Platt Amendment,[1] which made it integrally dependent on the United States. This dependency was reinforced by the 1903 Treaty of Reciprocal Commerce, which granted preferential customs duties to merchandise originating from the United States.[2]

From the day of the proclamation of the Republic until 1934, Cuba was politically, economically, and socially a U.S. protectorate in practice, dominated by a sugar oligarchy that was organically tied to Northern financial capital. Born as a neocolonial bourgeois republic, it was the first state in the world to hold such a condition.[3] It was a republic submerged in an abyss of

---

1   See glossary.
2   In 1934, another even more onerous treaty was signed.
3   Neocolonies form part of the periphery of the world-system; their social structures are adapted to the function that has been assigned to them in the system. Neocolonialism was developed in the former colonies during the twentieth century, when direct control over them no longer was necessary.

corruption, in which politics was synonymous with lucrative business and social mobility.

The first thirty years of the bourgeois republic (1902–1933) were characterized by a political system based on the oligarchic predominance of wealthy and related families, whose affiliation was divided between two political parties, the Liberals and the Conservatives, that rotated in power. On the payroll and in the directorships of both parties were found former members of the Liberation Army, plantation owners, property holders, merchants, doctors, lawyers, as well as persons of little resources and former gangsters. There were varied ideologies, such as autonomists, annexationists, anarchists—with racists found throughout the mix. Among the ranks of the conservatives were found figures of liberal thought as well as men of ultraconservative ideology. At the level of the neighborhood, municipality, and province, the prevailing norm was loyalty to a local leader.[4]

The Cuban people were frustrated by an independence postponed, but they were not resigned to it. Beginning in the 1920s, voices were raised, and popular movements were organized against imperialist[5] penetration and oligarchical domination, including movements by students and intellectuals. As a result, in 1933, the Machado[6] dictatorship was overthrown by popular mobilization. Mass mobilizations and demonstrations as forms of public protest had great importance in Cuba, and they can be traced to the first years of the colonization. The rebellions organized by indigenous communities, slaves, and tobacco growers in the eighteenth century as well as the wars of independence in the nineteenth century were all mass movements against foreign domination. When the Republic was installed, the mass movements proliferated, against the Platt Amendment and against the extension of powers by Estrada Palma[7] and Gerardo Machado, and for the overthrow of the latter. During the second dictatorship of Batista, the mobilizations and mass demonstrations in the cities and towns were constant, both before and during the revolutionary armed struggle organized to overthrow it.

---

4 Julio Carreras, cited in Guanche, 2004, 97.
5 Imperialist policies were initiated by the government of the United States at the end of the nineteenth century. They consisted of the adoption of measures necessary to ensure access to the raw materials, labor, and markets of other countries. Such measures included interventions in internal affairs, military action, and the imposition of beneficial commercial treaties.
6 See glossary.
7 See glossary.

The Revolution of 1930[8] marked the transition from the oligarchical republic, established in 1902, to a bourgeois democratic republic, which lasted until the triumph of the revolution in 1959. Cuban society experienced many sociopolitical changes between 1934 and 1958. New political parties emerged, such as the *Cuban Revolutionary Party (Authentic)*, with a social reformist orientation; and the *Party of the Cuban People (Orthodox)*, which had ample popular support for its moralist positions. *The Communist Party* had been founded in 1925, and it had dedicated itself to winning influence among the masses of workers throughا strategy of advocating support for their economic demands and by forging the unity of the workers' organizations.

In 1934, the Platt Amendment was repealed as a result of the anti-imperialist combativeness of the Cuban people. Working-class organizing efforts culminated in the formation of a single unified labor organization that had an important influence in labor-capital relations. Other parties and political movements emerged, reflecting the aspirations of change of a protagonist middle class. After the Revolution of 1930–1933, the nation-state, civil society, and bourgeois democracy were growing in strength, such that by 1940, with a new correlation of internal and external political forces, the convoking of a Constitutional Assembly was possible and a new constitution was adopted.[9]

At the same time, U.S. financial capital had consolidated neocolonial "real exploitation,"[10] which implied the assurance of relations of dependency, with the constant connivance of the local dominant bourgeoisie. Beginning in 1934, the Cuban sugar-based economy entered a period of stagnation and many

---

8   The Revolution of 1930 culminated in 1933 with the short-lived government of Ramon Grau San Martín, which was the only government of the neocolonial republic not recognized by the United States.

9   The Cuban Constitution of 1940 has been considered one of the most progressive constitutions of the era, although the bourgeoisie created obstacles to the implementation of its most far-reaching demands, such as the elimination of large-scale landholdings. After the Batista *coup d'état* of March 10, 1952, one of the demands of the popular movement was the restitution of the 1940 Constitution.

10 In *Capital*, Karl Marx established two historic forms of exploitation of the workers by the owners of the means of production. He called them the formal exploitation and the real exploitation of work to capital. Such concepts permit us to make a comparison between the two historic forms of exploitation exercised by the capitalist mode of production and the two forms of exploitation to which the underdeveloped countries have been subjected by the core countries. In formal exploitation, which pertains to the pre-monopoly stage of capitalism, the metropolitan centers exercise direct control over the colonies. In contrast, real exploitation is rooted in the conversion of the colonies into neocolonies on the basis of the penetration of monopoly capital into the productive sphere of the neocolonies, which implies the absorption of their resources and their labor in the process of capital accumulation and profits, which are transferred to the core of the system.

considered that the economic structure had fallen into permanent crisis. The social situation of the period was deplorable: unemployment, underemployment, lack of medical and educational services, generalized poverty in the countryside and the cities, in contrast with areas of ostentatious wealth in the capital, accompanied by a high degree of economic and political corruption.

In addition, the concentrated and excluding character of Cuban dependent capitalism created a small sector of privileged workers and a great mass of salaried low-income workers with high rates of unemployment, underemployment, precarious employment, and poverty. The principal industry of the country, that of sugar, only provided employment during three months of the year.

Regarding the social conditions of underdevelopment, there were an insufficient number of hospitals, schools, teachers, and housing, and the alimentation of the people was deficient, among other misfortunes. Sectors of the middle class were living in conditions of social instability, and under the threat of the deterioration of their incomes.

In essence, the Cuban social panorama during the first fifty-six years of the neocolonial Republic was constituted by an ample gamut of social classes and sectors that shared a common situation characterized by low standards of living, economic instability, and social misfortune.

Against Batista and Beyond

In the face of this complex scenario, popular demands pointed to the need for a new national direction. *The Cuban Revolutionary Party (Authentic)* won the presidential elections of 1944, but its two administrations (1944–1952) were characterized by an extraordinary level of corruption. A sector of this Party established the *Party of the Cuban People (Orthodox)*. The Orthodox Party was led by Eduardo R. Chibás, whose central anti-corruption slogan was "Shame against money." Chibás committed suicide in 1951, when he was not able to demonstrate a plot of corruption. But his preaching caught on, above all among the youth, such that the Orthodox Party was nearly certain to be the winner in the presidential elections planned for June 1952. The *coup d'état* carried out by Batista—on March 10, two months before the presidential elections—brought to an end the neocolonial republican constitutional order and enthroned a repressive and pro-imperialist military dictatorship.

Denunciations of the *coup d'état* were immediate. University and secondary school youth organized a public vigil for the assassinated Constitution, and demanded its restitution. Once again, mass demonstrations were launched, this time on the campus of the university where thousands gathered at the large stairway that marks the entrance to the university, as well as throughout the country. The young lawyer Fidel Castro sent a legal demand to the Supreme Court, claiming the unconstitutionality of the military regime. But the Court did not respond. Soon it became evident that little remained to be done in the venue of protests and mobilizations of denunciation.

The legendary assault of July 26, 1953 on the Moncada Barracks in Santiago de Cuba and the Carlos Manuel de Céspedes Barracks in Bayamo by a group of youths under the direction of Fidel Castro precipitated the turning point in the struggle for definitive liberation. This armed action marked the initiation of a change of epoch for Cuba. In *History Will Absolve Me*, a speech made before the Court in defense of the actions of Moncada, Fidel Castro defined the people as the subject of the Revolution that would be formed in the process of struggle.[11] In addition, he described an ample spectrum of socioeconomic sectors exploited by Cuban underdeveloped capitalism.

The Cuban Republic of 1902 to 1959 was not a pseudo-republic, but a true neocolonial bourgeois republic. The Cuban state was characterized by a government of bourgeois law, with multiple, competitive parties; it therefore was "democratic." This peculiar constitutional order was contravened during the periods of the dictatorial governments of Gerard Machado [1925–1933] and Fulgencio Batista [1934–1937 and 1952–1958], but both were elected to presidential terms.[12] In pre-revolutionary Cuba, thirteen presidential general elections were held, as were fifteen partial elections for mayors, governors, and

---

11 Fidel stated, "When we speak of the people we do not mean the comfortable and conservative sectors of the nation, who welcome any regime of oppression, any dictatorship, any despotism, prostrating themselves before the master of the moment until they grind their foreheads into the ground.... We understand by people, when we are speaking of struggle, to mean the vast unredeemed masses, to whom all make promises and who are deceived and betrayed by all; who yearn for a better, more dignified and more just nation; who are moved by ancestral aspirations of justice, having suffered injustice and mockery generation after generation; and who long for significant and sound transformations in all aspects of life, and who, to attain them, are ready to give even the very last breath of their lives, when they believe in something or in someone, and above all when they believe sufficiently in themselves" (Castro, 1993, 53).

12 Machado was elected in 1926 and reelected in 1928. Batista was elected for the 1940–1944 term. Aside from his carrying out of terror in order to eliminate the revolutionary wave of 1935, and his role as a strongman of the neocolonial Army until 1940, Batista's *coup d'état* of 1952 gave rise to an oppressive dictatorship that cost thousands of lives among Cuban youth. The government of the United States never described the Batista regime as a violator of human rights; to the contrary, the regime was presented as one of the pillars of democracy in Latin America, and Batista himself was recognized as a loyal ally of the United States in the region.

legislators. The legislative power functioned nearly all the time and the judicial branch never ceased operating. Thirty-three parties were politically active at the national level; even in the period of the second Batista dictatorship, no less than fourteen political parties coexisted with the regime.[13]

Those rebel youths who in 1952 launched a confrontation with an inhumane dictatorship began with the intention of restoring the constitutional order and the lost democracy. In the course of struggle over many years, however, the great majority of them were becoming increasingly aware that it was necessary to change the structures of Cuban society, so that tyrannies would never again emerge.[14]

The armed insurrection was organized with revolutionary strategy and tactics. Undeterred by temporary reverses, it expanded throughout the island, combining distinct forms of struggle. The guerrillas became a Rebel Army, liberating geographical zones of the country while integrating and unifying all of the revolutionary forces. Ultimately, the insurrection defeated the dictatorship militarily and it likewise destroyed the maneuvers of the United States to impede its triumph.

Popular consciousness had conserved the memory of an affront that had occurred in 1898, which constituted a symbol of the inconclusive, anti-colonial revolution. After thirty years of struggle for liberation, when the Liberator Army already had defeated the Spanish army,[15] the United States intervened in the war on the basis of an obscure incident;[16] and after winning against the Spanish with the aid of the Cubans, the United States occupied the country. One of the last military campaigns of that brief war resulted in the defeat of the Spanish in the area of the city of Santiago de Cuba, with the decisive participation of Cuban troops directed by General Calixto García;[17] but the Cuban Liberator Army[18] was not permitted to enter the city as part of the conquering forces.[19]

---

13   Martínez, 1987, 93.
14   Cf. Ernesto Che Guevara, *Lo que aprendimos y lo que enseñamos*, Patria. Órgano oficial del Ejército Rebelde «26 de Julio», Las Villas, año I, n° 2, 1° de enero de 1959 y *Notas para el estudio de la ideología de la Revolución Cubana* Revista Verde Olivo, 8 de octubre de 1960.
15   That this was the situation is revealed—according to J.J. Remos—by a Spanish opinion, that of Commander Victor Concas, who in his book, *La Escuadra de Cervera*, published in Madrid in 1898, expresses: "The war already was lost when the United States began taking part as another nation of much less importance." (See Remos, 1952, 422–23).
16   The explosion of the U.S. battleship *Maine*, docked in the port of Havana, was considered by the United States to be a Spanish attack, on the basis of which the U.S. Congress declared war on Spain.
17   See glossary.
18   Also known as the *Mambi* army.
19   In 1898, U.S. General Shafter prevented the entrance of the Cuban Liberator Army into Santiago de Cuba, in accordance with the terms of surrender accepted by Spain. The

Therefore, on January 1, 1959, Fidel Castro declared, *"This time the liberators will enter Santiago de Cuba."* He was not turning to a simple rhetorical phrase, but was expressing the sentiment of an entire people that it was retaking a piece of its incomplete history. In 1959, the rebels entered Santiago de Cuba and all the cities of the country. The rebellion had triumphed.

The International Situation

With the end of the Second World War, a wave of social and revolutionary changes occurred throughout the world, with its effects being felt in the core as well as in the periphery of capitalism. These developments created a crisis for the colonial system of imperialism. Newly independent nations were emerging in Africa and Asia as a result of anti-colonial struggles, in some cases by means of arms.

Notable among these events were the proclamation of the Republic of Vietnam; the independence of the Philippines, India, Indonesia, Burma, Syria, and Lebanon; the defeat of French colonialism in Dien Bien Phu; the triumph of the Free Officers Movement in Egypt and of a progressive military movement in Iraq, placing the Baghdad Pact in crisis. In Africa, various independent nations emerged that led the United Nations to declare 1960 as the Year of Africa. The international environment stimulated the appearance of the Conference of Bandung, declaring a positive neutrality in the Cold War, as well as the creation of the Organization of Solidarity of the Peoples of Asia and Africa.

In the 1960s, social conflicts also emerged in the United States, most notably the struggle of African Americans for civil rights, the most radical manifestation of which was the Black Power Movement, with many different organizations, such as the Black Panther Party. The protests against the war in Vietnam were massive and university students played an important role in them.

This liberating international context paradoxically was the epoch of the peak of US hegemony after emerging triumphant from the Second World War. In this international situation, the Cuban popular and autonomous revolution attained its overwhelming triumph on January 1, 1959. It then took decisive action by emitting new laws that responded to the longings for redemption of the popular sectors. These actions drastically altered the country, transforming the rebellion into full-scale revolution. In synthesis, these changes were as follows:

Spanish preferred a victorious procession by the "Americans" rather than the Cuban liberationist forces, who in practice already had defeated the powerful Spanish Army when the United States decided to intervene in the war.

During 1959, the Revolution:
- Constituted a revolutionary government representing popular interests.
- Destroyed the apparatus of bourgeois neocolonial domination.
- Democratized the society, displacing the oligarchy from power.
- Charted an independent foreign policy, without ties or restrictions, which meant the full exercise of its national sovereignty.
- Began to create a new state apparatus and new governmental organisms.
- Set out to eradicate illiteracy.
- Introduced a national system of social security with universal coverage.
- Initiated a profound cultural revolution, creating the National Publishing House and the Institute of Art and Cinematographic Industries, investing in access for all people to various areas of culture.
- Annulled the onerous concessions previously made to foreign companies.
- Reduced the rates for electric and telephone services; the price of medicines; and the price of housing rents.
- Initiated a profound Agrarian Reform, eliminating large landholdings, both national and foreign.
- Established the Revolutionary Militias for the popular defense of the revolution throughout the country.
- Launched an integral reform of teaching that would give rise to the national system of education with universal access, with the intention of elevating the education of the entire population.

During 1960, the Revolution:
- Created mass organizations, including the Federation of Cuban Women, Committees for the Defense of the Revolution, the Association of Small Farmers, and the Organization of Pioneers of Cuba; and strengthened the revolutionary mission of previously existing organizations, such as the Federation of University Students and the Cuban Confederation of Workers.
- Initiated the creation of a national system of health with universal coverage.
- Nationalized the large U.S. monopolies.
- Nationalized the large companies of the Cuban bourgeoisie.
- Carried out an Urban Reform that enabled millions of families to acquire housing.

During 1961, the Revolution:
- Eradicated illiteracy in the entire country and created a system of scholarship to ensure that the poorest would have access to all levels of education.
- Publicly declared the socialist character of the Revolution in the presence of militia battalions that were prepared to defend the country from an impending U.S. backed invasion.

- Conquered militarily, in less than seventy-two hours, an invading force that had been organized, trained, armed, and transported to Cuban territory by the United States and its Central American allies, thus defeating the largest covert operation that had ever been carried out against a Latin American nation.
- Unified the three revolutionary organizations that had struggled against Batista into the Integrated Revolutionary Organizations.[20]

With the socialist revolution of national liberation, Cuba attained its real independence, its sovereignty, and its full identity as a nation, demonstrating that a definitive struggle for de-neocolonization and major social transformations is not possible without rupturing the bourgeois limits of dependency and advancing the struggle toward socialism.

---

20 This process was full of contradictions, as a result of the sectarianism of the secretary of the organization, Anibal Escalante, previously a member of the Popular Socialist Party (the previous Communist Party). In 1962, Fidel Castro denounced publicly this sectarian deviation, and he would begin the formation of the United Party of the Socialist Revolution over new and revolutionary bases, until it was integrated into the Central Committee of the Communist Party of Cuba in 1965.

PART 1

1959: Year of Liberation

Introduction to 1959: "Year of Liberation"

General Eulogio Cantillo,[1] chief of the Joint General Staff of the armed forces of the dictatorship had agreed in communications with the revolutionary leadership to the total surrender of the Army and the prevention of the flight of Batista. However, in a last attempt to impede the triumph of the insurrection, and with the total connivance of the United States, Cantillo carried out a *coup d'état*.

Fidel Castro reacted quickly. At 11:30 on January 1, he spoke on *Radio Rebelde*, denouncing the maneuver, refusing to recognize the governmental junta created by the *coup* leaders, calling all the people to a general strike, and ordering continuation of military operations until total victory be secured. He dispatched Camilo Cienfuegos[2] and Che Guevara[3] to advance to the capital: the former, to Columbia,[4] and the latter, to La Cabaña,[5] the two principal fortresses of Havana at that time.

Events developed with extraordinary swiftness. The Rebel Army occupied Santiago de Cuba and the principal cities while a general strike paralyzed the country. In a memorable address of January 1–2, Fidel Castro affirmed: "*This time the revolution will not be frustrated.*"[6]

Accordingly, not only was there vindication with respect to the historic insult that remained in the memory of the Cuban people. It was now emphasized that, this time, it was indeed a matter of a revolution, announcing the beginning of the end of the frustrations derived from an independence robbed by the United States since its intervention in 1898[7] in the war of Cubans against Spain.

However, the complex circumstances of the insurrectional process and its triumph required the establishment of a revolutionary government of mixed social class composition. Accordingly, several members of the government were identifiable figures proceeding from the revolutionary struggle; but others were reformers and/or members of the local bourgeoisie. The presence of

---

1 See glossary.
2 See glossary.
3 See glossary.
4 See glossary.
5 See glossary.
6 Cited from a speech of January 2, 1959. See Instituto de Historia, 1983, 1:3.
7 See above.

reformist and bourgeois figures contributed to a dysfunctionality that characterized the post-insurrectionary government during the first forty-five days of its existence.

On February 16, 1959, Fidel Castro assumed the position of Prime Minister. From the first moment, he began the progressive radicalization of the government—not without conflicts and contradictions—until it became, at the end of the year, an apparatus in which revolutionary forces were predominant.

The telling documents of the year 1959 include the calling of a general strike to impede the *coup d'état* plotted by Cantillo, Batista, and the U.S. imperialists; and selections from the speeches of Fidel Castro on January 1–2 in Santiago de Cuba, on January 8 in Columbia at the time of his entrance into Havana, on February 16 on his taking of possession of the charge of Prime Minister, and on May 17 during the enactment of the Agrarian Reform Law.

In a speech pronounced on January 1, Fidel declared the victory of the Rebel Army and announced the treachery of General Cantillo, with whom he had had conversations in order to attain the surrender of the Army of the dictatorship and to avoid the flight of Batista, and the attempt to frustrate the popular triumph by means of a *coup d'état*.

Following the speech, Fidel Castro traversed the entire country in what was called the Caravan of Freedom, stopping in the principal provincial plazas to speak to the people, who were congregated to hear and see the victorious leader with their own eyes. The speech pronounced by Fidel on his arrival to the capital on January 8, delivered in what was then Columbia military camp, Office of the Joint General Staff of the Batista Armed Forces, was of great importance. He denounced before the people the improper behavior by one of the groups participating in the insurrection, which was potentially dangerous for the course of the revolution.

The naming of Fidel by the revolutionary government to the charge of Prime Minister on February 16 was a decisive moment in the radicalization of the Revolutionary Government. It led to various measures, including the Agrarian Reform Law on May 17, which defined the radical anti-neocolonial character of the Revolution. Fidel's speeches during the ceremonies for the taking of possession of the charge of Prime Minister and for the signing of the Agrarian Reform Law are included in this volume.

Also included are speeches that demonstrate the commitment and capacity of Fidel Castro to overcome the internal and external conditions and circumstances—nearly always adverse—to which the revolutionary process was being subjected, in order to bring about, in the words of Martí,[8] the conversion of the dreams of yesterday into the laws of tomorrow.

---

8   See glossary.

A very delicate moment was precipitated by the betrayal of President Urrutia. Fidel Castro analyzed this difficult national and personal scenario in a broadcast on national television, the text of which is also included in Part 1.[9] Among other things, it brings to light the ideological motivations behind the preparations for the overthrow of the Revolution from the United States. Fidel renounced his position of Prime Minister in order to be able to make a public denunciation of the presidential betrayal, in a gesture of significant political and revolutionary consequences. The people were firm in asking his return to the charge of Prime Minister in various platforms, including the mass demonstration of July 26. His address on this occasion is one of the most important documents of the year.

Another complex situation of 1959 was the relationship between the revolution and the leadership of the workers' movement, one of the necessary bastions of the revolutionary process. In 1949, Eusebio Mujal,[10] tied to the Authentic Party and the government of Prío,[11] had assumed control of the Confederation of Cuban Workers (CTC),[12] which led to widespread and high levels of corruption among the supposed leaders of the federated unions. Ten days after *the coup d'état* of March 10, he was placed at the service of the dictatorship, including the carrying out of repressive actions.

During the first months following the revolutionary triumph, the correlation of forces in the interior of the leadership of the CTC did not assure the eradication of the "Mujalistas" and their Mafia-like methods of union direction. In this context, it was decided to convoke the Tenth Congress of the CTC, with the principal objective of initiating revolutionary change in that organization. During the Congress, it was clear that there still existed factions with aspirations far removed from the revolutionary process demanded by the working class. In his speech at the closing ceremony, Fidel Castro confronted the situation with the courage that he always displayed, undercutting the counterrevolutionary maneuvers.

In December, with the celebrated trial of the traitor Huber Matos,[13] Fidel Castro declared that the objectives and the goals carried out by the Revolution up to that moment were not communist, as external enemies as well as those within Cuba had begun to assert. He observed that, since the March 10 *coup*, he

---

9   The text previously has been published only in a pamphlet following the television broadcast.
10 See glossary.
11 See glossary.
12 See glossary.
13 See glossary.

had clearly expressed the objectives and goals of the Revolution in his speeches and writings in the press, and of course, in *History Will Absolve Me*.

In all of these speeches, one can discern the decisive role of Fidel in combatting all attempts to denigrate revolutionary actions by means of multiple manipulations in the mass media. Above all, his effort to educate the people is evident, with the intention that they would become a protagonist in a full revolution of national liberation that would sweep away the structures of oppression inherited from the past.

Call to Revolutionary General Strike

To the people of Cuba and especially to all workers:[1]

A military junta, in complicity with the dictator, has taken power, in order to ensure his flight and that of the principal assassins, with the intention of stopping the revolutionary impulse and robbing victory from us.

The Rebel Army will proceed with its overwhelming campaign, accepting only the unconditional surrender of the military garrisons.

The people of Cuba and the workers ought to prepare themselves immediately for a general strike on January 2, in support of the revolutionary arms, in order to guarantee the total victory of the Revolution.

Seven years of heroic struggle, with thousands of martyrs whose blood has been shed in all the fields of Cuba, are not going to function to enable those who yesterday were accomplices, responsible for the dictatorship and its crimes, to continue governing Cuba.

Cuban workers, led by the worker section of the July 26 Revolutionary Movement, should today assume direction of all the mujalist[2] unions and organize the factories and centers of work in order to initiate tomorrow at dawn the paralysis of the entire country.

Batista and Mujal have fled. But their accomplices have remained under the control of the Army and the unions.

No to a coup d'état aimed at betraying the people. That would prolong the war.

The war will not be over until Columbia[3] has surrendered.

This time, nothing and no one will impede the triumph of the Revolution.

CUBANS:

For Freedom, democracy, and the full triumph of the Revolution.

TO THE REVOLUTIONARY GENERAL STRIKE IN ALL THE NON-LIBERATED TERRITORIES

---

1 Speech on *Radio Rebelde*, Palma Sorianos, January 1, 1959. *Periódico Revolución*, July 26, 1962, p. 8.
2 See glossary.
3 Military garrison in Havana.

The Revolution Begins Now

People of Santiago;[1]
 Fellow patriots of all of Cuba:
 Finally, we have arrived to Santiago. The road has been hard and long, but we have arrived.
 It was said that today at 2:00 in the afternoon they were waiting for us in the capital of the Republic. I was more surprised than anyone was, because I was surprised by the treacherous coup, rigged this morning in the capital of the Republic.
 Besides, I was going to the capital of the Republic, that is, the new capital of the Republic, because Santiago de Cuba will be the capital, in accordance with the wishes of the provisional President, in accordance with the desires of the Rebel Army, and in accordance with the desires of the people of Santiago de Cuba, who deserve it. Santiago de Cuba will be the provisional capital of the Republic!
 ...
 The Revolution begins now. The Revolution will not be an easy task. The Revolution will be a hard enterprise, full of dangers, especially in this initial stage. In what better place to establish the government of the Republic than in this fortress of the Revolution, so that it is known that this is going to be a government solidly backed by the people in this heroic city and in the foothills of the Sierra Maestra, because Santiago is in the Sierra Maestra. In Santiago de Cuba and in the Sierra Maestra, the Revolution will have its two best fortresses.
 ...
 It was agreed with General Cantillo that the uprising would be carried out at 3:00 in the afternoon on the 31st. It was declared that the support of the armed forces to the revolutionary movement would be unconditional. The President would designate the revolutionary leaders and the charges that the revolutionary leaders would assign to the military officers. An unconditional support was offered.
 The plan was agreed to in all of its details: the military garrison of Santiago de Cuba would rebel at 3:00 in the afternoon on the 31st; immediately various rebel columns would penetrate the city, and the people, with the

---

1 Selections from a speech delivered in *Parque Céspedes*, Santiago de Cuba, on January 1, 1959. *Versiones Taquigráficas, Consejo de Estado*. The selections from the speeches and television broadcasts have been made by the authors.

military and the rebels, would fraternize immediately, emitting to the country a revolutionary proclamation inviting all honorable military personnel to join the movement.

It was agreed that the tanks in the city would be placed at our disposition, and I offered, personally, to advance toward the capital with an armored column preceded by the tanks. The tanks would be delivered at 3:00 in the afternoon, not because it was thought there would be combat, but in order to prevent it, in the event that the movement would fail in Havana, and there would be need to move our vanguard as near as possible to the capital. In addition, to prevent excesses in the city of Havana.

...

It would be good for the people to know of the communication that I exchanged with General Cantillo, and if the people are not tired ("No!"), I can read the letter.

After the agreements made, when we already had suspended the operations on Santiago de Cuba (already our troops were near the city on the 28th, and already all the preparations for the attack on the Plaza had been made), in accordance with the agreement, we had to carry out a series of changes, to abandon the operations on Santiago de Cuba and to march our troops to other sites, where it was thought that our safe movement could not be assumed. When all our movements were completed and the columns were prepared to march on the capital, I received a note a few hours before from General Cantillo, which said:

"*The circumstances have much changed, making favorable a national solution,*" in the sense that he wanted for Cuba. It was strange, because after analyzing the important factors, I was not able to see more favorable circumstances. The triumph was assured, and it was strange that he would say, "*The circumstances have changed favorably.*" The circumstances included the fact that Batista and Tabernilla[2] were in agreement, and this assured the coup.

"*I recommend that you do nothing in these moments and wait for the developments in the next weeks, before January 6.*" Of course, the prolonged indefinite truce, while they prepare everything in Havana.

My immediate response was: "*The content of the notes departs completely from the agreements made; it is ambiguous and incomprehensible, and it has led me to lose confidence in the seriousness of the agreements. Hostilities remain suspended until tomorrow at 3:00 p.m., which is the date and the hour agreed to by the Movement.*"

---

2 See glossary.

Then a very curious thing occurred. In addition to the note, which was very brief, I informed the chief of the Plaza of Santiago de Cuba, through his messenger, that if hostilities break out because the agreement was not carried out, we would be compelled to attack the Plaza of Santiago de Cuba, in which case there would be no other solution than the surrender of the Plaza. Thus, we would demand the surrender of the Plaza, if the hostilities break out and an attack on our part were initiated.

...

This is where the conversations were when ... Coronel Rego, chief of the Plaza of Santiago de Cuba, and I were surprised by the coup d'état in Columbia, which departed completely from the agreement.

And the first thing that was done, and the most criminal thing that was done, was to let Batista, Tabernilla, and the others responsible to escape. They let them escape with millions of pesos. They let them escape with 300 or 400 million pesos that they have robbed.

...

What did we do when we knew of the coup, which we heard through *Radio Progreso*?[3] Already at that hour, guessing what was being hatched, I was making some declarations when I heard that Batista had left for Santo Domingo. And I thought: Could it be an error? Could it be a lie? So I sent for verification when I heard that really Mr. Batista and his cronies had escaped, and even better, that General Cantillo said that that flight was thanks to the patriotic motivations of General Batista, the patriotic motives of General Batista(!) who resigned in order to prevent the shedding of blood. What do you think of that?

...

And they did not name President Urrutia,[4] who is the president proclaimed by the Movement by the all the revolutionary organizations. They called upon a gentleman who is nothing less than the oldest of all the judges of the Supreme Court, all of whom are fairly old, and above a gentleman who has been President, until today, of the Supreme Court of Justice that does not have justice in any form.

In every respect, the coup at the Columbia military garrison was a counterrevolutionary action. In every respect, the intentions of the people were ignored. In every respect, it was suspicious. And immediately Mr. Piedra said that he was calling the rebels to a peace commission that he was going to invoke, and we should calmly leave our arms and leave everything, and that we should go there to pay respect to Mr. Piedra and Mr. Cantillo.

...

---

3   Cuban radio station located in Havana.
4   See glossary.

I ought to make clear that if in Santiago de Cuba a bloody battle did not break out, it was due, in great part, to the patriotic attitude of the Army coronel José Rego Rubido,[5] the commanders of the frigates "Máximo Gómez" and "Maceo," the chief of the naval district of Santiago de Cuba, and the official that was assuming the role of the chief of police. They all—and it is just that we here recognize it and thank them for it—contributed to avoiding a bloody battle and to turn the counterrevolutionary movement of this morning into the revolutionary movement of this afternoon.

We had no option but to attack because we were not able to permit the consolidation of the Columbia coup, and therefore, we had to attack without waiting. When our troops were prepared to move toward their objectives, Coronel Rego traveled in a helicopter to locate me; the chiefs of the frigates made contact with us; they placed themselves, unconditionally, at the order of the Revolution.... I then called a meeting of all the army officers of the Plaza of Santiago de Cuba, of which there are more than 100.

...

I met with those military officers, and I spoke to them of our revolutionary sentiment.... There are two kinds of military officers—we know them well—: the officers like Sosa Blanco, Cañizares, Sáncjez Mosquera, Chaviano,[6] who engage in criminal activities and the murdering of many unfortunate peasants. But there were military officers that were honorable in the conduct of their campaigns; there were military officers that never assassinated anyone, nor burned a house.... Such military officers did not rise in the ranks; those that ascended were the criminals, because Batista always was in charge of rewarding crime.

...

United with the officers of the Navy, of the police, and of the Army, it was agreed to not recognize the rigged coup in Columbia and to support the legal government of the Republic, because its counts with the support of the majority of our people, which is that of the Doctor Manuel Urrutia Lleó. Thanks to that attitude much blood was saved; thanks to that attitude, in truth there has been brewing in the afternoon of today a true revolutionary military movement.

...

I want to declare that today, this night—this morning, because it is nearly day—the illustrious magistrate, Doctor Manuel Urrutia Lleó, will take possession of the presidency of the Republic. Does Doctor Urrutia have the support

---

5 See glossary.
6 See glossary.

of the people? The President of the Republic, the legal President, is he who has the support of the people, and that is Doctor Manuel Urrutia Lleó.

...

None of the positions or ranks that have been conferred by the Military Junta of the early morning have validity today; all of the appointments to positions by the Army are null and void—I refer to the appointments made this morning. Whoever accepts a position designated by the treacherous Junta of this morning will be assuming a counterrevolutionary attitude, however it calls itself, and in consequence, will be in violation of the law.

This taking of power has not been the fruit of politics; it has been the fruit of the sacrifice of hundreds and thousands of our peasants. There is no commitment other than that with the people and the Cuban nation. A man arrives to power without a commitment to anyone, except with the people, exclusively.

...

This time there will not be a Batista, because there will not be a need for a fourth of September,[7] which destroyed the discipline of the armed forces. What happened with Batista was that he installed indiscipline in the Army, because his policy consisted in flattering the political parties in order to diminish the authority of the officers.

We do not believe that all the problems are going to be resolved easily. We know that the road is full of obstacles, but we are men of faith, who always face the great challenges.

The people can be sure of one thing, and that is that we might be wrong on many occasions, but the one thing that no one ever will be able to say of us is that we rob, that we betray, that we make crooked deals.... And I know that the people will forgive us the errors and will not forgive shameless acts of ill will.

...

Never will we let ourselves be pulled by vanity or ambition. As our Apostle[8] said, "All the glory in the world fits in a grain of corn." There is no satisfaction nor reward greater than fulfilling one's duty, as we have been doing until today and as we will do always.

...

The rebels do not charge wages for the years that we have been struggling, and we feel proud of not charging payments for the services that we have lent to the Revolution. But it is possible that we will continue to fulfill our

---

7   Refers to the seizure of Columbia military base by sergeants on September 4, 1933, which led, after a short-lived progressive government independent of the USA, to a military dictatorship supported by the USA and headed by Fulgencio Batista.
8   José Martí. See glossary.

obligations without charging payment, because if there is no money, it does not matter, because there is will, and we do what is necessary.

...

They will be punished only as war criminals, because that is an inescapable duty with justice, and the people can be sure that we will fulfill that duty. When there is justice, there is not vengeance. In order to ensure that no one is attacked tomorrow, there must be justice today; there will be justice, but not vengeance or hate.

...

If Santo Domingo becomes an arsenal of the counterrevolution, if Santo Domingo becomes a base of conspiracies against the Cuban Revolution, if these gentlemen dedicate themselves to hatching conspiracies from there, it would be better that they soon leave Santo Domingo, because they will not be very safe there either.... The Dominicans have learned that it is possible to fight against tyranny and to overthrow it, and this example is precisely what dictators fear most; an encouraging example for America that has just been generated in our country.

All of the Americas are watching the course and the destiny of this Revolution. All of the Americas have their eyes on us, all accompany us with the greatest desires of triumph, and all will back us in our difficult moments. This happiness today not only is in Cuba, but in all of the Americas. As we have been happy when a dictator in Latin America falls, they also are happy today for Cubans.

...

I ought to warn the officials of the dictatorship, the representatives and the senators, not those that have not robbed, but those that have charged payments: they will have to return to the last cent what they have charged in these four years. Because they have charged illegally, and those senators and representatives will have to return to the Republic the money that they have charged. And if they do not return it, we will confiscate their properties, aside from what they have robbed, so nothing will remain of what they have robbed. That is the first law of the Revolution. It is not right to send to prison a man that has robbed a chicken or a peacock, while those that have robbed millions of pesos are enjoying life somewhere.

They should be careful. The thieves of today and yesterday should walk with care, because the revolutionary law can fall upon the shoulders of those that are guilty in the past and in the future, because the Revolution arrives to triumph with a commitment to absolutely no one except the people, who are the only ones to whom it owes its victory.

...

Temporarily the need for arms has ceased. The arms will be guarded where they will be within the reach of the men that will have the duty to defend our sovereignty and our rights.

But when are people are threatened, not only will 30,000 or 40,000 members of the Armed Forces fight, but 300,000, 400,000, or 500,000 Cubans, men and women, are able to fight. They will have the necessary arms, so that that all who want to engage in combat is armed, when the hour of defending our sovereignty arrives.

It has been demonstrated that in Cuba not only the men fight, but the women also. And the best proof is the "Mariana Grajales"[9] squad, which distinguished itself in numerous combats. And the women are soldiers as excellent as our best soldiers among the men.

I wanted to demonstrate that the women could be good soldiers. At the beginning, the idea provoked much resistance, because there were many prejudices, and there were men that said what while there were men with a shotgun, a rifle should not be given to a woman. And why not? .... We organized the units of women, and they demonstrated that women are able to fight. When in a people the men can fight and the women can fight, that people is invincible.

...

Today, on the taking of possession of the presidency of the Republic, Dr. Manuel Urrutia Lleó said that the Revolution was just... (INTERRUPTION) .... The entire country already is liberated territory. I will assume simply the function that he assigns me, and in his hands lies all the authority of the republic.

Our arms are inclined respectfully before the civil authority of the Republic of Cuba. I do not have to say that we hope that he will fulfill his duty, for the simple reason that we are sure that he will know to do so. I leave the Provisional President of the Republic of Cuba with the authority, as he now addresses the people.

---

9   See glossary.

To Speak the Truth Is the First Duty of All Revolutionaries

Compatriots:[1]

I know that speaking tonight here presents me with one of the most difficult obligations, perhaps, in this long process of struggle that was initiated in Santiago de Cuba on November 30, 1956.[2]

The people are listening, the revolutionary combatants are listening, and the soldiers of the Army are listening, whose destiny is in our hands.

I believe that this is a decisive moment in our history: the dictatorship has been overthrown. Happiness is immense. However, much remains to be done. We ought not deceive ourselves into believing that what lies ahead will be easy; perhaps all that lies ahead will be more difficult.

To speak the truth is the first duty of all revolutionaries. To deceive the people, to awaken false hopes, always brings the worst consequences, and I consider that the people should be alert against the excess of optimism.

How did the Rebel Army win the war? Speaking the truth. How did the dictatorship lose the war? Deceiving the soldiers.

...

A distance has been walked, perhaps a considerable step forward. Here we are in the capital; here we are in Columbia. The revolutionary forces appear victorious. The government is constituted, recognized by numerous countries of the world. It appears that peace has been attained. However, we ought not to be optimistic.

While the people laugh today, while the people are happy, we are worried. The more extraordinary the multitude that turned out to receive us, and the more extraordinary was the jubilation of the people, the greater was our preoccupation, because the greater was our responsibility before history and before the people of Cuba.

...

---

1 Selections from the speech delivered at his arrival to Havana in the Columbia military garrison, today known as Liberty School City, January 8, 1959. Stenographic version of the Office of the Prime Minister.
2 On that date, armed actions by the July 26 Movement were carried in that city, in support of the disembarking of the *Granma* planned for the same date, which actually occurred on December 2, 1956.

There are many kinds of revolutionaries. We have been hearing people speak of revolution for some time. Even on March 10,[3] it was said that a revolution had been made, and they invoked the word "revolution." Everything was revolutionary. The solders met here and spoke of "The Revolution of March 10." (LAUGHTER)

...

The first mention of revolutionary that we heard as a boy, we heard it said, "So-and-so was revolutionary, he was in a particular combat or a particular operation, or he placed bombs." A caste of revolutionaries was even created, revolutionaries who wanted to live off the revolution, who wanted to live on their being certified as revolutionaries, for having placed a bomb or two bombs. And it is possible that those that spoke more were those that had done less.

But it is certain that they turned to ministers to look for posts, to live as parasites, to charge a fee for what they had done in that moment, for a revolution that unfortunately did not arrive to be fulfilled. I consider that the present revolution is the first revolution that has greater possibilities for fulfilling itself, if we do not ruin it. ("No!")

...

The first thing that those of us who have done this Revolution have to ask ourselves is with what intentions did we do it. We have to ask:

if some of us were hiding an ambition, an eagerness for command, an ignoble intention;

if in each one of the combatants in this Revolution there as an idealism, or a pretense of idealism in pursuit of other ends;

if we did this Revolution thinking that once the dictatorship is overthrown we would enjoy the privileges of power;

if each one of us was going to live like a king, if each one of us was going to have a mansion, and life for us in the future would be a walk in the park, inasmuch as for that we had been revolutionaries and had overthrown the dictatorship;

if what we were thinking was to remove some ministers and to put others, if what we were thinking was merely to remove some men and replace them with others; or if in each one of us there was true unselfishness;

if in each one of us there was a true spirit of sacrifice;

if in each one of us there was the intention of giving all in exchange for nothing;

---

3   March 10, 1952, was the date of the *coup d'état* that launched the Batista dictatorship of 1952–1958.

and if at the outset we were disposed to sacrifice all to fulfill in a spirit of sacrifice the duty of sincere revolutionaries.

We must ask that question, because our destiny and the future destiny of Cuba and of the people can depend on our test of conscience.

...

It is of great interest to the people if we are going to do this Revolution well, or if we are going to incur the same errors of the previous revolution, and the one previous to that, and the ones previous to that. We are going to suffer consequences, because there is no error without consequences for the people. There is no political error that is not paid, sooner or later.

...

Today the people has the peace that they desired: a peace without dictatorship, a peace without crime, a peace without censorship, a peace without persecution.

...

I say and I swear before my compatriots that if any of my *compañeros*, or our movement, or I, were to be in any way an obstacle to the peace of Cuba, beginning right now we are at the disposal of the people, and the people can tell us what we have to do. I am a man that knows the meaning of sacrifice. I have shown it more than once in my life, and I have taught it to my *compañeros*. I have morality, and I feel myself with sufficient force and authority to speak in a moment such as this. ("*Viva* Fidel Castro!")

...

When the July 26 Movement was organized, even when we initiated this year, I considered that even though the sacrifices that we were making were very great, and even though the struggle was going to be very long, as it has been ... we comforted ourselves with one idea. It was evident that the July 26 Movement had poplar sympathy and the backing of the majority. It was evident that the July 26 Movement had the nearly unanimous support of Cuban youth.

...

I believe that we all ought to be from the first movement in a single revolutionary organization, be it another or ours. Because we were the same, those of us struggling in the Sierra Maestra, or those of us struggling in Escambray, or struggling in Pinar del Río; young men, and men with the same ideals. Why should there be half dozen revolutionary organizations?

Ours simply was the first. Ours simply was the one that fought the first battle at Moncada; that disembarked in the Granma on December 2; that struggled alone during more than a year against all the force of the tyranny; that when it did not have more than twelve men, maintained high the flag of the rebellion;

that taught the people that it could fight and it could win; and that destroyed all the false ideas over the Revolution in Cuba.

...

There is, besides, another question of fact: the July 26 Movement was the organization with the absolute majority. Is that not so? ("*Sí!*") How did the struggle end? I am going to say: the Rebel Army, that is the name of our army which was initiated in the Sierra Maestra. When the dictatorship fell, the Rebel Army had taken all of Oriente, all of Camagüey, part of Las Villas, all of Matanzas, La Cabaña, Columbia, the Police Headquarters, and Pinar del Río.

...

Does this mean that others had not struggled? No. Does this mean that the others do not have merits? No. Because we have all struggled, because the people have struggled. In Havana, there was no Sierra, but there are hundreds of dead, fallen *compañeros* assassinated while fulfilling their revolutionary duties. In Havana, there was no Sierra, but the general strike was a decisive factor that made the triumph of the Revolution complete.

Not only did the July 26 Movement design the guidelines for the war, but it also taught how to treat the enemy in war. This has been perhaps the first revolution in the world where a prisoner of war was never assassinated, where a wounded soldier was never abandoned, where no man was tortured. The Rebel Army designed this guideline.

...

Now the Republic, or the Revolution, enters a new phase. Would it be right that ambition or favoritism come here to place in danger the destiny of the Revolution? ("No!") What is it that interests the people, because it is the people that have the last word? ("Freedom! Freedom!") The people are interested, in the first place, in freedoms, in the rights that the dictatorship denied, and in peace.

...

It is necessary to speak in this form, in order that demagoguery, confusion, and division do not emerge, and that with the first sign of ambition, the people will recognize it.

...

How am I doing, Camilo?[4] ("*Viva* Camilo!")

...

All this I say to you, because I want to ask the people a question; I want to ask the people a question that interests me much, and interests the people much, for you to respond: Why are clandestine arms being stored in these

---

4 Camilo Cienfuegos. See glossary.

moments? Why are arms being hidden in different places in the capital? Why? And I say to you that there are elements from a certain revolutionary organization that are hiding arms, that are storing arms, and that are smuggling arms.

All the arms that the Rebel Army attained are in the barracks, such that they have not been touched by a single person. No one has carried them to his house, nor has anyone hidden them. They are in the barracks, under lock. The same in Pinar del Río, in La Cabaña, in Columbia, in Matanzas, in Santa Clara, in Camagüey, and in Oriente. No one has loaded trucks with arms in order to hide them anywhere, because those arms ought to be in the barracks.

...

Well, I want to inform you that two day ago, elements of a certain organization went to a barracks, it was the San Antonio barracks, barracks that are under the jurisdiction of *Comandante* Camilo Cienfuegos and under my jurisdiction, as Commander in Chief of all the forces, and the arms were collected there and taken away. Some 500 arms, six machine guns, and 80,000 bullets were taken.

Honestly, I tell you that a greater provocation could not have been committed. Because to do that to those who have experienced fighting here in the country for two year, to those that today are responsible for the peace of the country and want to do things well, it is a terrible thing and an unjustifiable provocation.

...

We have not stopped them or provoked them. We have left them in peace for that robbery of arms, an unjustified robbery, because here there is not dictatorship, and no one fears that we are going to become dictators. I am going to tell you why: one who does not have the support of the people and has to turn to force becomes a dictator, because he does not have the votes to aspire for office.

...

We never will need force, because we have the people, and besides, because the day that the people make a disagreeable face to us, nothing more than make a face, we are going away.

...

The President of the Republic has entrusted me with the most difficult task of all, the task of reorganizing the military institutions of the Republic, and he has assigned me to the charge of Commander in Chief of all the air, sea, and land armed forces of the nation.... That is a sacrifice for me. That charge for me is not a reason for pride nor vanity. It is for me a sacrifice. But I want the people to tell me that they believe that I ought to assume that function ("*Sí.*").

...

In addition, all revolutionary combatants that desire to belong to the regular armed forces of the Republic have the right to belong to the organization to which they belong, with their ranks.... The doors are open for all the revolutionary combatants that want to struggle and that want to do a task for the benefit of the country.

...

There no longer is an enemy facing us; it is no longer necessary to fight against anyone. If some day it becomes necessary to fight against a foreign enemy or against a movement that goes against the Revolution, they will not be fighting cats; they will fight an entire people.

The arms have to be in the barracks. No one has the right to raise private armies here. Perhaps those elements going by here with those suspicious maneuvers had found a pretext for doing that in the fact that my *compañeros* and I had been designated for a work that the President had assigned to us, and they have spoken of a political army. Political army? As I told you, we have all the people, and that is in truth our political army.

...

When they provoke us, none of us fears falling. Because when our patience has been exhausted, we look for more patience. And when our patience is exhausted again, we again search for more patience. That will be our norm.

...

This time I have omitted names, because I do not want to poison the atmosphere, because I do not want to increase tension. I simply want to warn the people of these dangers. It would be very sad if this revolution that has cost so much sacrifice—not that it is going to be frustrated, because this revolution will in no way be frustrated, because it is already known that with the people and with all that there is in favor of the people, there is not the least danger—but it certainly would be very sad if, after the example that has been given to the Americas, violence would return here.

The President of the Republic, with the right that corresponds to him—because he was chosen without conditions—has selected a majority of ministers from the July 26 Movement. He had his right, and on asking our collaboration, he received it fully. We assume responsibility with that Revolutionary Government.

...

What is important, or what needs to be said, is that I believe that the acts of the people in Havana today, the multitudinous mass concentrations of today, that mass of people kilometers long—because this has been astonishing, you saw it, and it will come out in the films and photographs—I believe, sincerely, that it has been excessive on the part of the people, because it is much more than we deserve ("No!").

In addition, I know that never again in our lives will there be such a mass concentration of people, except on one occasion—even though I am sure that there will be many mass gatherings—and that is the day that we die, when they have to take us to the tomb, on that day again will gather as many people as today, because we never will defraud our people![5]

---

5 This premonition was fulfilled at his death in 2016. The authors have wanted to emphasize it through italics.

We Are Revolutionaries Making a Revolution, Revolutionaries in Power!

Honorable Mr. President;[1]
   Ministers *compañeros*;
   Members of the Press:
Paradoxically, in the moments in which I receive this honor of being placed at the head of the Council of Ministers, I do not experience anything other than a profound preoccupation for the responsibility that has been placed on my shoulders, for the seriousness and the devotion that always I have place in the fulfillment of my duty.

...

Of the various tasks that I have been called upon to undertakes, in all of them I have acted on my own initiative. In this case, because it has been assigned to me, because I did not choose it, but you chose it for me. And only with a profound sense of the need to sacrifice for the country, true sacrifice and sincere sacrifice; because for us in the government, public office is not a position for enriching ourselves, a position for receiving honors, but a position for sacrificing ourselves.

...

The offices, as offices, are not important for me; the honors, as honors, are not important to me. Here, from this position, I continue being the same citizen that I have been always. As a citizen, I do not differentiate myself from any other citizen. I am equal to any other modest and humble Cuban, only that I am a Cuban with the same faculties as any other Cuban but to whom has been assigned a large and difficult task. Therefore, when I say that for me it is a sacrifice, I am speak very sincerely and I speak with seriousness.

I do not, however, fear the effort that I must realize; I do not fear for the difficulties that are found in the road. I am a man of faith, and I have always confronted obligations with resolve.

...

I reaffirm my respect for the limits of hierarchical authority, my absence of personal ambitions, my loyalty to principles, and my firm and deep democratic conviction.

...

---

1 Selections from a speech delivered at the taking of the oath of office as Prime Minister, in the Presidential Palace, February 16, 1959. Stenographic version of the Office of Prime Minister.

If from here I am able to serve, what interests me is to make the Revolution, what interests me is that the Revolution advances, what interests me is that the people do not wind up being defrauded, and they that receive from us all that they expect from us.

My only concern is that at the end of the day Cuba will have received from us all that it desires. And Cuba will have all that it desires from us, if the people help us, and if the people understand us.

...

I want to take advantage of this moment of the oath of office as Prime Minister to say to the workers and peasants that are present that we do not forget you; that the agrarian reform—the most expansive law, more all-encompassing than that of the Sierra Maestra,[2] that resolves the problem of peasants without land—is being drawn up and will be a reality within a few weeks.

...

There are many projects, and there is much work to be done. All the questions of importance to the country, all, absolutely all the questions of importance to the country, will be considered and will be resolved.

...

In relation to the public administration, our firm intention is to listen to the complaints that have been expressed, and to investigate the conduct and the work of each functionary. I am not in a hurry on this, because to substitute one official for another, one must look for a person that has all the qualities necessary for replacing the official with success, in order that a better job is done. But it is difficult to find officials in these times!....

Because there are those that are capable, but they do nothing, and if they are placed in a position, it could be thought that the *"bombines"*[3] are being favored. If we search for an official that has a revolutionary history but is not trained for the charge, then we run the risk that it will not be done well. The ideal would be to find a person with revolutionary merits and with capacities. Above all is the capacity, because the affairs of state have to be resolved with skill.

...

For us, an unquestionable principle is that a *Batistiano*, that is, a servant and collaborator of the dictatorship, cannot be in a position of trust. Such persons do not have revolutionary merits and do not have capacity, and I would call them *"bombines."* Naturally, because the state has to be administered by an

---

2 During the Revolutionary War, the Rebel Army emitted an agrarian reform law that was implemented in liberated territory.
3 Fidel defines the word below. The word fell out of use many years ago.

infinity of persons, one can have men that have not participated in the Revolution but have capacity.

...

There are also another series of questions. A great part of the officials of the state already were placed there after March 10. There were very few, really very few, citizens that did not accept a position in the government offered to them, in light of the conditions of high unemployment.

...

All who were candidates, as a result of the law against the electoral farce,[4] have lost for thirty years their right to exercise charges in the state, to vote, or to be elected. But there are an infinity of cases that do not fall into this category.

Those men already placed in the government have commitments, obligations, debts, and a strict standard of life. If they are displaced from their charges and lose the modest salary that they receive, a social problem would be created. Therefore, one must reconcile the two interests of the state: the interest of administration and the interest in reducing social problems.

The truth is that the economy of the country remains impoverished; the truth is that we have limited economic resources at this moment. It is not like before, when if they needed 100, 200, or 300 million pesos, immediately they could obtain them. We have to resolve the problems with what we collect. If we are collecting higher sums, it is because of the honesty of those that are collecting, and because of the collaboration of those sectors that, thinking that no one is going to rob the money now, pay taxes with pleasure, or at least, punctually.

...

The state must be made healthier; the state must be made more efficient; the state has to function better than any other non-public institution. Why does the word "public" have to be discredited? Why is it that public affairs, the public administration, always is referred to as the most deficient?

...

The state cannot make a profit. The men that serve the state have to be men of vocation in order that the administration of the State, which is of the people, in order that the state, that represents the interests of the people, functions better than any other type of institution.

---

4   Fidel refers to a law emitted in the Sierra Maestra during the revolutionary war, limiting the political rights of persons who had been candidates in sham elections during the Batista dictatorship.

Therefore, it is very necessary to restructure and reorganize the state. But of course, that has to take into account a series of social realities. It cannot be attained with simple good will.... But it has to be a firm intention to organize the state apparatus in a form truly efficient.

…

In this sense, we are going to propose an agreement with the Council of Ministers in order to bring tranquility to all. So that it will be known that when a change is made in charges of the state, the interest of the nation is being considered, only according to strict reasons of necessity, which never has been done in public administration.

…

For example, we, the rebel combatants, really have sacrificed in the first two months. The members of the Rebel Army did not receive a salary the previous month, and this month they are going to be paid, but less than what they ought to be paid. Has it been for lack of interest? No. The President of the Republic spoke with us on more than one occasion, speaking of the need to pay the combatants of the Rebel Army. These combatants, contrary to any other army in the world, even after they have triumphed, did not receive payments, while the soldiers that remained[5] were receiving payments.

I ought to confess that I have a great part of the blame for that, and it is because I saw that [Rebel] Army forming itself, I saw those men being formed in sacrifice and absolute unselfishness, and it pained me. I felt a certain nostalgia, thinking of that unselfishness, that purity, which was beginning to be lost from the moment in which, with the triumph just attained, they began to perceive a salary that they had never seen. However, I consider it necessary, and besides very just, that they receive a salary.

…

With this I want to say to you that it concerns me a great deal that the youth maintain its spirit of sacrifice, that the revolutionaries maintain their spirit of sacrifice; and that the bureaucratic appetites do not awaken among the elements of the Revolution, because it would weaken the Revolution.

…

Therefore, it is necessary that we who are governing make sacrifices, so that they see that we are leading a life truly of sacrifice and work. In order that the rest do not believe that is a cakewalk, in order that the others do not think that here we are living well, that we are enjoying life occupying such-and-such charge. That they know that it is very bitter, that they know that it is very hard,

---

5 Fidel refers to the soldiers of the regular army during the dictatorship that incorporated themselves into the rebel army.

that they know that there is much suffering. And that there is absolutely no envy of anyone who is occupying a charge, a charge that does not lead to profit and that does enable one to enrich himself.

And the first measure that is going to be proposed today in the Council of Minister is that we, the ministers, we are going to propose a reduction in salaries, beginning with the elimination of the secret expenses,[6] and that we earn what we need for the most basic things, because in the final analysis, when we were living clandestinely, we lived with anything.

Large cars, no; small cars! We are going to do this contrary to what state officials in the past did, in order that the people do not believe that to be a minister is a great and marvelous thing. Salaries? Modest salaries. Yes, naturally, a modest salary is necessary, in order that you do not have to walk, because you must transport yourself quickly; and in order that you do not go hungry and do not to act like a beggar. But modest salaries, because what matters is not what a minister earns. Those ministers that earned more were those that robbed. We are going to show that honesty is not a question of necessity, but a question of conviction.

...

Because we are not the ministers of Batista. We are not the leaders of the epoch of Batista. We are the same as the people.

The people ought not to say to us, "We ask." What the people ought to say to us is that "We are going to do," "We propose," "We are doing," because we are the same as the people. What happens is that many people are not aware of the change; they are living behind, they are living in the epochs of the past.

...

In essence, we seek the good will of all, even those interests that are adversely affected. We want to demonstrate to those whose interests are affected that it is not that we are adversely affecting their interests for the sake of doing so or out of hate, or because we want to hurt anyone, but because it is the right of the people, and we have the obligation to govern. Those who governed before us have organized things in a form that has left us with a million difficulties.

...

In taking any revolutionary measure, the Revolution burdens itself with many enemies. That is a consequence of having permitted things that ought not to have been permitted, and having run the country in a disorganized and

---

6 Secret expenses were additional payments that government officials historically received in Cuba, above their regular salaries.

anarchic manner. All is in the service of particular interests. Previously, when an avenue was constructed, it was not benefitting the people; it was benefitting the property holders of that zone, those that had a club; for the people, nothing. I do not vacillate in saying that the people have been the victim of every injustice.

...

I believe that the numbers runner has to disappear, as the drug dealer has to disappear. And the state has to provide a solution for those that find themselves in need to go to a high interest lender. These persons suck the salaries of the poor. Between pawnshops and sellers of furniture at long-term high interest, if the people earn sixty pesos, they have thirty, because they are being robbed.

...

The state sees the need to resolve the problem of housing, and therefore, we have developed a plan for the investment of one billion pesos in five years in the construction of housing. Which does not mean that capital will be invested only in housing, because we are thinking in investing at least two billion pesos in industry. We ought to clarify that this era, the revolutionary era, has been good for industrial investments, but bad for investments in land and for investments in home mortgages and apartment buildings for rentals, because that is passive capital, dead capital.

...

I estimate that in only two months, tens of thousands of men will be employed in construction, and that is going to mean a higher demand for articles of construction, which is going to mean more employment. And the more money that circulates, the more will be the demand for articles of consumption. All this has to be united to a campaign for the consumption of articles made in the country, in order to provide employment in the country, and in order to not drain our currency reserves.

...

We are disposed to provide all guarantees to national capital; we are disposed to provide all the protection that they ask, with only one condition: high salaries. It is the only condition that the Revolution puts on investments in new industries that ought to be developed. Now, they will have a domestic market very superior to what exists today. Because the agrarian reform that the revolution is developing will elevate five or six times the standard of living of the peasants, so that the market for industrial products will be five or six times greater. Joined with laws for the protection of national industry, this will mean an extraordinary increase in employment.

...

I believe that we will attain it. It is a dream, certainly, but Martí said that the idealistic dreams of today are the law of tomorrow. They called us dreamers when we initiated the struggle against Batista, and today we are making the revolutionary laws of the Republic. Moreover, even if we do not attain these objectives, to dream of them and to aspire for them is the first step in trying to attain them.

...

We propose to bring to an end as soon as possible the executions by firing squad, because we have to dedicate our energies to creative work. Constantly I am urging the war tribunals to speed up the work, that the trials be conducted, in order that at the beginning of March we will be able to see that a considerable number of criminals of war have been sanctioned as examples, and that the others will be condemned to years of forced work.

...

To execute is just. But to execute is not to make Revolution; to execute is to establish a fund for the Revolution, to execute is to do justice, to destroy the crime and to establish a precedent that remains very clear that the criminal has to pay for his crime; that he who murders a citizen has to pay for his crime. Above all, it will be a law for us and for future generations; because we execute the war criminal not in order to teach anything to the war criminals or to those that were before, but to teach ourselves and to teach future generations, in order that it will be strictly laid down and established.

But, what is the consequence of the campaign that was made against Cuba because of the first executions? Ah, to arouse and exacerbate the passions.... We ought to warn that crimes against the Revolution, crimes attempted against the lives of citizens in order to try to impose tyranny here again, for those, yes, the death penalty will remain permanent, as long as the Revolutionary Provisional Government lasts.

...

Today we are conducting the trial of Sosa Blanco. Some believed that we were going to be tolerant with Sosa Blanco. But we wanted to show in an irrefutable matter the substantial proof against him. There was even presented nothing less than a report by Mr. Cowley Gallegos—whose story, famous for his crimes, all the world knows—a secret report form Cowley Gallegos to the General Staff, informing of the crimes of Sosa Blanco. The report ought to be published in its entirety, in order that those who feel sorry for Sosa Blanco realize that even the criminal Cowley was horrified by the crimes of Sosa Blanco.[7]

---

[7] See Cowley Gallegos and Sosa Blanco in the glossary.

Of course, they are not going to overthrow the Revolution here. The Revolution could be overthrown if the Revolution is not made, if the Revolution does not fulfill its destiny, but as long as we are disposed to make it, the Revolution will not be overthrown, because it will have behind it all the people.... And so I see in Cuba an extraordinary process of everyone wanting to contribute to the triumph, because it is a reality, and because here everyone understands that we have to continue ahead. Because here everyone understands that the Revolution must be made, because if it is not made, it will fail. The failure of the Revolution would mean the abyss, civil war, a sea of blood, and in the end, the return of Batista, of Ventura, of Chaviano, of Masferrer, of Carratalá,[8] and of all that pack of criminals, because here there is not a happy medium.

We want at least six months to work completely, to dedicate ourselves entirely to this work, which is very difficult. If we do not do it, there is no one to do it; there is no one to do it, as we want to do it. Because to do it like those who came before, for that we do not do it, that is not needed. They left the work to us, and that helps us in it.

...

The people have to be very aware that the road is difficult, that the road is long, that the road is tiring, and that we have to sweat much struggling. And not only must we have that idea present, but we have to be always alert to not let enthusiasm die. Because this great work that the people of Cuba has imposed is not the work of a small-minded people, but of a great people, like ours.

---

8 See Batista, Ventura, Chaviano, Masferrer, and Carratalá in the glossary.

To Live on Our Knees, Why?

People of Cuba:[1]

We have gone a little distance, and it is convenient that we again plant our feet on the ground. One never knows what will be his most difficult appearance in a public tribunal. When I have considered some of them difficult, it did not take long for another to surpass it. And for me, none has been as difficult as that of today, when I find my ideas in discrepancy with those of the distinguished visitor, José Figueres.[2]

How can I express our discrepancy without lacking the elemental courtesy to which we owe our guest? It was difficult to speak to the people earlier today, because every revolution is in itself difficult and complex, and this visit is makes it even more so, when complex international problems are added to the internal complex problems of the country.

Without leaving the national sphere, our task is hard and difficult, because our Revolution by its nature has great problems, by virtue of it being a true revolution and not one more farce of the many that the Americas have seen; by virtue of it being a revolution and not a military uprising; by virtue of it being a root cure and not a simple pruning, where the old bad ones sprout again; and by virtue of it being a surgical operation, in which one must abandon the band aids for surgical cuts.

Therefore, against the Cuban Revolution are aroused the national reaction and international reaction, and against the Cuban Revolution are aroused all of the reactionary oligarchies of the continent. In addition, the campaigns of the press emanating from the trusts and monopolies of the large international news agencies have found echo in the reactionary press of America; and the cable agencies send the lies and calumnies that anyone writes in every corner of the continent.

...

I saw today that many fathers and many mothers were carrying their children on their shoulders. It was not only a demonstration of people, it was also a demonstration of feelings and of hope, the hope that a people harbors when they take their children to a patriotic march.

People carry their children on their shoulders only in the great moments in the history of the peoples; only in its finest hours, in its most luminous

---

1 Selections from speech delivered in the Presidential Palace, March 22, 1959. Stenographic version of the Office of the Prime Minister.
2 See glossary.

moments. And those children represent for everyone a symbol, because they will be the best fruits of what will be harvested by the sacrifices and the work that we all are carrying out today.

...

They will say to us that the future is uncertain. They said to us here that the future is uncertain, and in truth it is sad to think that those dreams related to the greatest hopes of the human species, that are the essence of the best emotions of the human species, that the paradise that we want to forge for our children, could be destroyed with atomic bombs.

In truth, it is painful and sad to think that all the houses that we have constructed with so many hopes could be destroyed with a single hydrogen bomb in a fatal second. In truth, it is sad to think that all the dreams of a people could be fatally destroyed by lack of understanding, by the conflicts of the world, because the day has arrived for the suicide of the species in an atomic world. In truth, it is sad. But why seed pessimism?

And much less, in the face of that, why seed conformity? Why say that in the face of that tragedy, what we have to do is join one of the bands? Why say that the whole of Latin America ought to join one of the bands?

Why not proclaim our right to live, although they kill us? Why not proclaim our right to live, although they destroy us? Why not say here the entire truth?

Why not say that there are military bases of one of those powers here [in Cuba and Latin America], whereas there [in the United States] the country is prepared to defend itself. There they have measures of civil defense, and there they have shelters in the face of the atomic attacks; and that we have here bases, but on the other hand, we do not have even a miserable hole to put ourselves in the event of a war? Why not say that while they play with the dangers of war, we are defenseless, we are here ready to be massacred without any hope?

Why not say these truths? Why not say besides that, having turned to the people of Cuba for support in all their wars, when the wars have ended, they took away the sugar quota[3] and have trampled on the people? Why not say that while it is solicited from us in the difficult days, in the time of peace we have suffered every injustice? Why not say that already we have endured war?

Why not say that in the name of that solidarity [with the "Free World"] they have dropped 500 pound bombs? Why not say that in the name of that solidarity they armed the dictatorship? When Costa Rica was invaded by Somoza's henchmen, the United States sent two or three P-51 planes. But here it was the

---

3 The sugar quota refers to commercial agreements between the United States and Cuba in which the USA agrees to buy a certain quantity of sugar.

opposite; they sent to Batista tanks and planes, in order to combat against the people.

Why not say that the aggressions that concern us at this moment do not come precisely from the other continent? Why not say that the aggressions that concern us come from the hands of mercenaries from the beaches of Florida or Santo Domingo?

...

What can destroy us? Living in humiliation, living on our knees, for what?

...

There is a reality, and it is that every day, very many people die. Some die of heart disease, others because an automobile ran over them, others from an epidemic, others of anything; or of hunger, as many people here have died. Because the greatest danger that we have had, more than danger, but the reality that we have had, is the number of children and the number of women, in the countryside above all, that have died for the lack of medicine and medical treatment or of food.

...

As we analyze it, we see that here the selfishness and the exploitation of the big trusts and monopoly interests have killed ten times more Cubans that the Batista dictatorship.

I have said that we all have to die of something. Fear of dying, why? If your illness has remedy, why be in a hurry? If it does not, why be in a hurry?

All things considered, we ought to continue ahead with our country, with our people, and with our own destiny; to continue forging our future, continue realizing our dream, and to defend that right with our lives.

This Law Initiates an Entirely New Stage in Our Economic Life and a Magnificent Future Awaits Our Country

We clearly feel the most conflicting sentiments in these moments.[1] I can affirm, after this tiring day of work, that our return to the Sierra Maestra would have been one of happiest moments of our life, on coming to decree the Agrarian Reform Law from the Sierra Maestra itself; if other sentiments would not have been on our mind and weighing upon us each minute, one could say in each second, in which all the memories of the Sierra Maestra are joined. Memories that are happy, on the one side; and sad, on the other, when one thinks of all the *compañeros* that fell here, many of whom are buried in the surrounding area; and when other present sorrows, of a kind not only emotional, affect one also. Because really this return is the culmination of a purpose that we conceived, and was brewing in our minds.

On arriving here, on speaking again to the people from this shelter—as it can be called—of *Radio Rebelde*, in the peak of one of the highest mountains of the Sierra—here still with its antiaircraft defenses that protected it, if not entirely, certainly in part—it is impossible to forget the sad memories of all those days in which the victory was but a hope and a fruit that, in order to attain it, one had to struggle much, and that, in the end, has been attained....

In transcendental circumstances like this, at times it is better to be the most simple as is possible. Really, the publication or the proclamation of the Agrarian Law will constitute one of the most transcendental events in the life of Cuba.

We understand that this Law initiates an entirely new stage in our economic life, and that a magnificent future awaits our country, if we all dedicate ourselves to work diligently.

It does not escape us that the Law is detrimental to particular interests. It does not escape us that the Law will produce a natural opposition that a revolutionary measure of this kind always produces. Of course, we are very conscious of its scope as well as the advantages that it offers for the country, but also recognizing that it adversely affects particular interests.

However, we desire to express here, as we have done in every one of these circumstances, that we do not make laws in order to adversely affect the interests of anyone, that we make laws for the benefit of the nation, even though

---

1 Selections of a speech delivered in La Plata, Sierra Maestra, May 17, 1959.

they can painfully damage some sector of the country; that we do not make laws out of hate or hostility toward anyone; that we do not feel hostility against any social sector; and that we understand perfectly that each one of us is in great part a consequence of the past, and that all of our interests and our acts, what we have done and what we are, what we receive and what we do, is in great part a consequence of the past.

...

We do not have the blame for what the nation has been before today; we do not have the blame for the lack of foresight; we do not have the blame for the miseries that the men and the generations that preceded us have sown in our country.

When these things are understood well, above all, when one goes to our countryside; when one comes across the huts; when one sees the spectacle of barefoot, rickety children, hungry, illiterate, and sick; when one sees the lives that they live, the houses that they inhabit. And in spite of all, how much nobility and how much goodness are harbored in the hearts of our men of the countryside! When one comes here and contemplates these things, that is when it is felt with more intensity than ever, the absolute conviction that the measures that we are taking are just, are necessary, and are beneficial to our country.

These measures offer to put an end to a situation that they left to us, and for which we are not responsible.

...

The data show, for example, that some 1.5% of property holders possess more than 46% of the national area in plantations, while 111,000 plantations of less than two *caballerías*[2] occupy less than 12% of the national area. Therefore, this law will not affect the immense majority of the owners of plantations. This law affects 1.5% of the property holders and, however, it will permit the Revolutionary Government to resolve the economic situation of more than 200,000 peasant families.

The interests of an insignificant part of the people are affected, but on the other hand, they will not be sacrificed in a total manner. Those affected conserve a considerable quantity of land, in order to be able to continue exploiting their plantations, in order to be able to continue maintaining more or less the same standard of living that they have had until today. While on the other hand, the problem of a very considerable part of our people is resolved, which is precisely the part most sacrificed, the poorest part, and the part that most

---

2 A *caballería* is a unit of measure for agrarian land surface, equivalent to 134,300 square meters—Translator's note.

would require the support and the solutions that the Revolutionary Government is able to offer. That part of the people is also the part that lacks income.

Two hundred thousand families means more than one million persons—according to the most conservative calculation. I am speaking of 200,000 families that are going to acquire lands, not counting the 150,000 families that possess land as sharecroppers, tenants, occupiers,[3] and contractors,[4] that is, in the distinct forms of possession that do not involve property ownership of the land. Until today, this has been a sector that has lived in perennial anxiety and in really uneconomical conditions.

What I mean to say in a straightforward manner is that, when the Agrarian Reform is carried out, approximately two million Cubans will increase considerably their incomes, which will strengthen the domestic market. And with the contribution to the domestic market, industrial development will be made possible, and with it, through agriculture and through industry, the economic problems of Cuba will be definitely resolved.

On the other hand, the property holders of those plantations affected by the Law with not have land taken without compensation. They will be compensated in government bonds, which certainly has security, that will mature in twenty years with an interest of 4.5%; bonds that will have a solid value, as a consequence of the strict administrative honesty that is being realized in Cuba, the increase of incomes, plus the increase of production, which will be carried out to a substantial degree in the coming years; an interest rate that will permit the holders of those bonds to negotiate them, changing them into funds that could be mobilized toward industry.

The Revolution cannot pay money in cash for the lands that it expropriates, inasmuch as the nation does not have at this moment resources to pay in cash for those expropriations. On the other hand, the nation will have those resources as the years pass, and it will have ample resources to pay that quantity and the interests in twenty years.

...

In addition, the Law is adapted to the principles of the Constitution of 1940. We expect that now—when many have been insisting on the precepts of the Constitution—it is not forgotten that the Agrarian Reform Law, the proscription of the large estate, is a mandate of our Constitution of 1940. But the parliament did not fulfill this mandate of the Constitution during the twelve years in

---

3 Peasants who informally occupied and cultivated land idle lands, without having legal title and without paying rent, generally living precariously on very small plots of land.

4 Labor organizers who rented land and organized work crews, generally acting as an intermediary with a landowning company.

which it was in force, from 1940 to 1952, because the Law was going to adversely affect particular interests, interests of course powerful, and by being powerful they caused much vacillation among our members of parliament.

A Revolution like this was necessary—a Revolution at the roots, like this; an honorable Revolution, like this; a difficult Revolution like this, a bloody Revolution, like this; in order to overcome all the obstacles opposed to the progress of our people and to the application of the measures most necessary in order to escape from the vicious circle and stagnation in which the economy of our country had fallen.

A Revolution like this was necessary for there to be agrarian reform. A measure that not only is advisable for our people, but is advisable also as the initial phase of bringing about development in all the countries of Latin America.

After this moment, Cuba will have with this measure the satisfaction of finding itself in first place among the Latin nations, for the tremendous scope and the possibilities that the law means for Cuba, and perhaps there never before has been a law that, before its application, had so much sympathy among the people.

...

It can be said without fear of doubt that some 98% of the people support the Agrarian Reform; that perhaps never has a measure counted with such unanimous support among the people; that perhaps never could it be said that a Law was the full expression of the absolute majority of the people, as is the case with the Agrarian Reform Law.

...

Given that this is so, given that its logic is irrefutable, if they who themselves are adversely affected today by the measure were to understand it, without being blinded by avarice and selfishness, to which no one has a right when it is made possible over the pain and suffering of others, if they understood this, they would also turn out to be beneficiaries.

On the other hand, no one that feels truly Cuban, no one that really feels stirring in them the spirit of patriotism, can avoid feeling pride for the country that through this measure will begin to recover its lands, will begin to recuperate those immense extensions of land that, for laxity, for abandonment, and for unscrupulousness by our past governments, had fallen into the hand of foreign companies, contradicting the ideals of the national heroes of our independence, contradicting the ideal of those Cubans who, in the first stage of our Republic, were profoundly concerned with the very harmful consequence that such circumstances were going to bring to the economy and to politics.

So the constitutional mandate authorizes the state to exhaust all necessary means to make it possible for the land to be returned again to Cuban hands, in compliance with this Law. Our country regains land, and it recovers it for our brothers, for our sons, that do not have work, that do not have land.

...

So with the Agrarian Reform, a work of extraordinary responsibility is initiated for us. We have the economic resources for it; we have the unanimity of the nation; we have the enthusiasm of our technicians, our university professors, and our agronomy and veterinary students; in all, we have the resources necessary for the Agrarian Reform.

This will work in firm steps, constructing on secure bases and with the criterion of doing absolutely everything without causing chaos in production, without paralyzing production, without improvising measures, but taking it step by step, which is the form of advancing most rapidly and with the greatest success.

...

Already there are various cooperatives organized, and various additional cooperatives organizing themselves in the lands recovered from the collaborators with the dictatorship.

...

Overall, we will create a technical organization, totally technical, with the participation of our most competent men for carrying forward this work. Granting not only lands, but farming equipment, technical assistance oriented to the economic cultivation to which those lands ought to be dedicated, scientific studies of the land, the most modern methods of cultivation and fertilization.

...

In this way, the measure of the Agrarian Reform ought to march parallel with all the other measures of the Revolution, in each one of which we immerse ourselves more every day. The benefits of each one are increasingly seen each day, not only in the plains but even in those isolated regions of the Sierra Maestra, where already large consumer cooperatives are established, and where already the credits are available beginning right now to advance credit to the peasants. And so, beginning in the Sierra Maestra, which was the place most destroyed by the war, which most suffered during the war, and is without doubt the poorest zone of the Cuban countryside.... One million pesos of credits will be dedicated immediately, which will have an interest rate of only 4% and payment terms of two years. This credit is merely the beginning.

...

The application of the measures will begin immediately. The surveyors will begin to work immediately, and they will begin to issue titles of property for all these lands of the state, in accordance with the law, as well as in those lands that are not state property but are within the limits comprehended by the Agrarian Reform Law.

So, in spite of the initial obstacles, in spite of the disadvantages that we had in assuming the responsibility of a government, including the reconstruction of the public administration with many inexperienced youth, the gains of the Revolution already are beginning to be displayed, and its fruits are beginning to be made evident.

We estimate that by the first of January of 1960, on completing the first anniversary, there will be many cooperatives organized and in full production; there will be many schools established; there will be many houses distributed; there will be many families that will have attained the direct benefits of our measures. That will then be the occasion for assessing what we are doing today and how we are progressing.

This does not mean that we are satisfied, or that we would not have been able to do more, or that we could not do more.

...

To speak, then, from this platform constitutes for us a reason for profound emotion, which joins with all the emotions that today we have received. So we leave again from this place with the infinite satisfaction of having fulfilled one promise more, and of having contributed to making possible the wellbeing of millions of compatriots who has been suffering, having been abandoned and forgotten; and who were those that in '68, in '95, and in this last liberating heroic deed[5] made the greatest sacrifices.

It was necessary to write, once and for all, on our unblemished, solitary star,[6] that formula of the Apostle,[7] that the country was of all and for all.

---

5   Fidel refers to the Cuban war of independence initiated in 1868, the Cuban war of independence initiated in 1895, and to the revolutionary war of December 2, 1956 to January 1, 1959.
6   Fidel refers to the single star on the Cuban flag.
7   José Martí (see glossary).

The Cuban People Is an Invincible People

Moderator: Nicolás Bravo, Assistant Director of CMQ News
Panelists:
Euclides Vásquez, Asst. Director of the newspaper *"Revolución"*;
Eduardo Héctor Alonso, Director of *Diario Nacional*;
Enrique Grau Esteban, staff of *Diario de la Marina*.

MR. ALBERTO IÑIGUEZ (HOST): Ladies and Gentleman:[1] As has been announced, present before the cameras and television and radio microphones is Dr. Fidel Castro Ruz, maximum leader of the Revolution, who will make an important pronouncement in relation to the present situation. At the petition of Doctor Fidel Castro himself, this appearance is made before the Panel of Journalists that we here have improvised. This panel is composed of Mr. Euclides Vázquez, Assistant Director of the newspaper *"Revolución"*; Mr. Eduardo Héctor Alonso, Director of *"Diario Nacional"*; Mr. Enrique Grau Esteban, of the staff of *"Diario de la Marina."* The Assistant Director del CMQ News, Sr. Nicolás Bravo, will act as moderator.

MR. NICOLÁS BRAVO (MODERATOR): The expectations reigning since the first hours of the morning have been such that, without further preamble, I am going to cede the word to Mr. Euclides Vázquez, who will formulate the first questions to our distinguished guest.

MR. EUCLIDES VÁZQUEZ: Dr. Fidel Castro: From the early hours of the morning, in which the newspaper *"Revolución"* and other organs of the television and radio news—and the newspaper "El Crisol"—divulged the news of your resignation to the country, and not only to the country, so that we can say that the continent is living in hours of great anticipation.

There has been much speculation concerning the reasons for your decision, which we all respect, including your desire to appear at the Conference of Foreign Ministers in Chile, your desire to dedicate yourself only and exclusively to the labor of the Agrarian Reform, and to more sensitive issues.... We understand that if these speculations were true, they would not have merited

---

1 Selections from the stenographic version of the appearance of the Maximum Leader of the Cuban Revolution on CMQ Television, July 17, 1959, in which he explained the reasons for his resignation as Prime Minister. Edited by the Delegation of Government of the National Capitol; 1959, "Year of the Liberation," Printing Section, National Capitol.

the extraordinary importance that they were given on the front page of *"Revolución."*

Therefore, we believe that we ought to initiate your appearance with some explanation of the fundamental reasons for your decision.

DR. FIDEL CASTRO RUZ: Of course, it is logical that if the motive for my decision had been any of the reasons that you enumerated, a step of this kind would not have been in any way necessary, for I understand well its implications.

In the first place, what more interests me—because there are things that are above all the others in the order of the values that interest the people—is that one ought not be worried at all for the destiny of the Revolution. I do not see any reason for the nation to concern itself with the personal destiny of men. I have always thought so and it seems to be that it is truly negative for the destiny of a nation to depend on particular individuals. Therefore, the first thing that I would like to express here is that I have absolute faith in the Revolution; that I have absolute faith in the destiny of Cuba, that is, that there ought not be uneasiness in the country with the respect to the destiny of this revolutionary process. This revolutionary process, which is the fruit of the sacrifices of the Cuban nation and in which the nation has placed so many hopes, is something so solid that nothing nor no one will be able to frustrate it.

I consider the Cuban people in these moments to be an invincible people; therefore, one must not be concerned with the destiny of the Revolution, because we all defend this Revolution, whatever be the place that corresponds to us in the struggle. Therefore, I want to say here that to resign a post does not mean renouncing the fulfillment of duty. Whatever be the position where we each find ourselves, from an important one to the most insignificant, we do not have in this life any reason to exist, and to be, other than to defend this work that we are doing. And what is more, I have not taken nor will I take a single step in my life that does not intend solely and exclusively to serve this cause, which with such loyalty and unselfishness we have defended.

That is to say, considerations of a personal nature do not concern me. Nor do passions, caprices, pride, or vanity concern me, nor any consideration that is not exclusively that of the interests of the country. When I was making the determination as to whether to resign, I was thinking only of that, and moreover, I never was thinking of resigning from the struggle.

I do not know if someone said that I was thinking of leaving the country. Someone who is disposed to die defending this cause in this country never will be able to leave this country, in the first place. So with this, I am saying all. I do not resign from, and I never will resign from, the Revolution.

...

The reason for the resignation is a reason that pertains to the internal dynamics of the Council of Ministers. Everyone knows very well that I am not a man accustomed to resigning, nor am I a man that likes to act in any manner other than with absolute clarity. I am the enemy of theatrics and dramatics.

I would add that for me to have to take this decision was something that I thought about and decided with as much resolve as when I have decided other important steps in my life. Beginning with the fact that I knew its transcendence, and since I am not one of those men that resign, the only thing that could lead to this resignation was that there was no alternative.

MR. NICOLÁS BRAVO: The people of Cuba do not understand why.

DR. FIDEL CASTRO RUZ: I am going to explain. Here nothing remains but to explain. I wanted to clarify certain basic questions first, above all, I wanted to say to the people that I am not a man who resigns, that I will never resign the struggle, because all of us have passed many hard tests, and no one ever saw us vacillate.

I have resigned a charge that I do not see as a prize or a privilege, that I see as nothing more than a place of work, a place where one has been fulfilling a duty; that I do not see as a place of honor, but a place of effort and work. Naturally, I would not have done it, if I had not seen the imperious need of doing so, for fundamental reasons that I want to clarify.

...

The resignation is the consequence of the impossibility continuing to exercise the charge under the present circumstances, given certain difficulties with the President of the Republic.

It is for me extremely delicate to express them, for various reasons. First, because he is the President of the Republic; and in the second place, because emotions are aroused, and I would like for the people to pay attention and to avoid any form of manifestation of hostility, any act that would belie the spirit of discipline that has characterized the people in this stage. Since the first of January, in all the public celebrations and demonstrations, the people of Cuba has demonstrated a very high civility, on the first of January above all; and in the subsequent days of our Revolution. I would like for the people to continue demonstrating it.

Therefore, the first petition that I want to make—and it is the only manner that I can speak with a little freedom—is to express the hope that the declarations that I am going to make be received by the people with absolute serenity. For me it is particularly delicate, and especially considering that emotions and passions can become evident. We Cubans all have a strong interest in resolving this crisis with the greatest and absolute serenity, equanimity, and order, because we cannot fall into errors.

All must support the public leaders of our country, all those that have been dealing with public opinion, the military chiefs, the union leaders, the students, and of all our institutions that during the day have been appealing to the people, asking them that they do not engage in strikes, asking them that they not organize demonstrations, asking them that they wait for my declarations tonight, and that undeniably has been an appropriate attitude on the part of all the leaders.

These things enhance the prestige of our people, above all when the American continent has its eyes on us at this moment. I consider that the first duty of all is to advise that equanimity and that sense of discipline that our public leaders have been instilling in the people during the entire day. That is what is most important.

I am going to turn to explain the heart of the matter. It would not be a conference; so if you like, you can interrupt me. I have spent all the afternoon thinking, I have spent many days thinking, reviewing papers, reading my speeches, in sum, organizing my ideas.

I did not come to give a speech. I always prefer to submit to the interrogation of public opinion through the journalist, therefore I did not come to pronounce a speech, although I will have to express some ideas here.

...

MR. EDUARDO HÉCTOR ALONSO (JOURNALIST): First, *compañero* Vázquez and I ask pardon for being before the cameras in this manner, but as already has been said, it is a question of an improvised panel. At the same time, we appreciate the demonstration of respect for and submission to the press, soliciting that we were here questioning, instead of pronouncing a speech.

It seems to me appropriate to ask Dr. Fidel Castro if the differences with the President of the Republic are of an ideological type or a functional type, that is, if they entail contradictions in revolutionary principles.

DR. FIDEL CASTRO RUZ: They are of a moral kind and a civic kind.

MR. EDUARDO HÉCTOR ALONSO: I would like that you explain.

DR. FIDEL CASTRO RUZ: Of a revolutionary kind, no. They are discrepancies of an ideological kind, because overall, we all have the duty of agreeing on the same road, and we have agreed up to now.

In addition, I ought to say that the differences are insurmountable, and that my reaction emerged from the occurrence of irreparable events, even more so now that I have taken this initiative, which is the only decision that I could take, if my duty is to protect the country from wrong, if I ought to protect the country from unnecessary and unjustifiable damage.

I would qualify the difference as of a moral order.

MR. EDUARDO HÉCTOR ALONSO: Would you explain, Doctor?

DR. FIDEL CASTRO RUZ: Yes. Everyone knows how my nomination to the office of Prime Minister occurred.

What is more, everyone knows that I have a special interest since this struggle was initiated in showing to the people of Cuba that I have no aspirations for public office. One idea I have made very clear is that men have to struggle for something more than positions, and they have to struggle for something more than for honors. And as I believe that firmly, it really is not difficult for me to resign a position, because positions do not interest me, and I never have concerned myself with questions of positions. My concern has always been the destiny of our country, that it be what it ought to be, and that someday our country would march on a road distinct from what it has marched until today.

I always struggled for an objective, not for an office or a position. Everyone knows that the idea of occupying an office in the government never even passed by my mind, neither the presidency of the Republic nor a minister. Everyone knows that I always was disposed to demonstrate to the incredulous or the suspicious that, while everyone is aspiring to the Presidency of the Republic, I was not ambitious. I always completely rejected the idea of personally occupying positions, occupying the presidency or the post of Prime Minister, or any other position in the government.

As a consequence, then, we tried to select a person for the Presidency of the Republic. We believe that there are many Cubans that could be President of the Republic. We have heard it repeated since school, that one must not believe in provincialism, that the exceptional virtues are not necessary, that only honesty is required, that only a little political tact is required, that only a clear sense of duty is required, and certain inflexible moral principles. Those moral principles ensure that a man never turns against his country, or turns against the interests of the people, turns against the interest of others. There is a fundamental principle that I believe, which is that the first principle that all public men and any revolutionary has to have is that the last interest is himself and the first above all are the interests of men, that before the interest in himself is interest in others.

MR. EDUARDO HÉCTOR ALONSO: Have those principles been contradicted?

DR. FIDEL CASTRO RUZ: Yes, and I am going to explain. I believe that many men possess the fundamental principles and the virtues necessary for being President of the Republic. And I believe that relations among men are conducive to particular situations, and therefore, the ideal men for positions of high authority are those with certain traits, a certain popularity, and other characteristics. They are not of the moral kind to which I have been referring, but of other characteristics that are necessary for holding a particular office, above all the high office of President of the Republic. And with reference to these characteristics, we chose among the existing personalities. We proposed Judge Manuel Urrutia Lleó for the Presidency of the Republic. We proposed him as a gesture, rooted in the trial of the Granma expeditionaries,[2] and for the references that in general existed toward his person.

...

Never was I able to conceive that between that person and us would emerge difficulties, because there was no reason for it. Believe me, we are men that exhaust all imaginable efforts to understand others, and in numerable cases, all the ministers, all the important officials of the state, all the important chiefs of the Revolutionary Armed Forces, know that I get along well with each and every one of them. They know that I always have gotten along well, not only with men of authority in the country, but also I always have gotten along well the last party member, with the soldier in the ranks, because I understand, and always I have understood his concerns, his character. I am not a man that provokes conflicts with others, because I have learned, perhaps by struggling with them, to understand others, and to conduct myself well with others.

Therefore, I had reasons for thinking that only under circumstances very adverse, with remote possibilities, could difficulties be produced. Not only that; I never had the idea on concluding the Revolution of seeing myself in need of occupying any public office. I believed sincerely that a group of men would be able to carry forward that task.

...

A month had transpired [since the triumph of the Revolution], and the Council of Minister had not been able to enact any measure of a fundamental social character. A month had gone by, which was beginning to provoke uncertainty, restlessness, and anxiety among the people. Time was being lost. We were running the risk that faith would be lost. Revolutionary laws had to be emitted, because in the Programs of the Revolution, in the Manifestos of the Revolution, in the meetings and in the speeches—like my speech, printed in a pamphlet, where I made my defense[3]—contained the fundamental principles and measures of the Revolution, that later began to be applied. But during a month, with grave damage to our prestige, not a single revolutionary measure had been produced. To the contrary, the measures that lead to the creation of

---

2 Fidel refers to Urrutia's vote in favor of absolving those accused of participating in the armed expedition that arrived in the yacht Granma, on the grounds that the Constitution of 1940 legitimates armed resistance, if the government were to deny individual rights.
3 Accused for his role in leading the attack on Moncada Barracks on July 26, 1953, Fidel made a detailed self-defense. His address to the court on October 16, which came to be known as *History Will Absolve Me*, was subsequently distributed clandestinely.

confidence in the people were far from being taken. One must awaken confidence in the people, because the people has been deceived many times; the people often has been forgotten. Believe me, we are still in a process of reparation and awakening of faith, which is greater with each passing day, which today is greater than three or four months ago. It is greater because the faith of the people has been fashioned and created with deeds, not with promises.

...

Revolutionary measures were not being taken, and the problems were becoming more complicated. In the country, the distribution of the plantations was occurring in an anarchic form, by peasants on their own account. The sugar cane harvest was at risk of not being carried out, with economic consequences that, simply, were going to be terrible, because the country must attain a level of foreign currency.

I have here a chart that I asked from the National Bank, some days ago, over the line of foreign currencies during the entire period from 1951 until today, in order that the people can see, in a graphic manner, in what difficult circumstances we were carrying forward the revolutionary work.

Someone had to intervene ensure that the sugar cane harvest be done. Invoking what? Invoking the patriotism of the workers, invoking the interests and the Cuban sentiment of the workers, invoking the interest for the Revolution of the workers, because it was the only form of resolving that problem.

...

So that, far from enacting revolutionary laws, during the first month a series of problems had been stimulated. Concerning this I would not want to speak, because all things considered I am here speaking and wanting to be as clear as possible. I would prefer that someday the ministers that participated in the cabinet during the first month of the Revolutionary Government speak of this. But permit me to finish my idea.

We were falling, then, into a very dangerous situation.

...

I saw it perfectly with the instinct of a public man, the minimum instinct of a public man, which, when one has some vocation for political problems, is carried with you.

...

I was very conscious that the Revolution was going to be more secure by not having one of its principal figures exposed to the great problems of the government, if its principal figure were to be wanted in the government. Because everyone knows that an infinity of governments arrive with popularity to the government, and in a few months, it does not have any popularity. That infinity of governments, that infinity of men that arrive to power and in a few months lack the prestige and lack authority, because the problems are difficult, very difficult, and when you occupy an governmental office, it is exposed.

...

So now I already was running a risk. It was better for the nation that in my position I would be held in reserve, and not a man on the front line, exposed to all the consequences of having to confront the enormous problems of Cuba in the middle of economic ruin, in the middle of a revolutionary process, exposing myself to being discredited. If right now the concern of the citizenry has been produced by the announcement of my resignation from the charge of Prime Minister, what would be then the situation of the citizenry if I were to be discredited in these moments, after six months of difficult government in which I would be able to make mistakes that anyone would make? Because I was not born in government, I was not born a statist; I was not born knowing all those problems. I have had to be guided exclusively by the attention, analysis, and concern that I have placed in this, and above all, I have given validity to the collaboration of the people.

...

QUESTION: I would like to ask the Prime Minister if that string of delays to which he alludes, in some cases enumerated, at the beginning of the revolutionary stage, constitutes an antecedent to the present crisis.

DR. FIDEL CASTRO RUZ: They are linked, because in the first place, there was no reason for me to become Prime Minister. There were a number of very competent *compañeros* there, who was able to have worked also, when I was substituted for the Prime Minister. For some reason they were not able to put forward those *compañeros*, but it is not I who could explain those causes. But when I was called, I was very conscious of it, and I was very conscious since we arrived in Havana that we had great problems ahead, as I said at that time, and I remember that I said so when we disembarked in Playa Colorada.[4]

...

If you would permit me to continue the explanation, following my exposition of things that everyone remembers, which are not things that I have made up. There began the period of five months in which all the Revolutionary Laws were approved and carried out. They could be enumerated one by one, but I believe that the proof lies with the people. The peoples do not react to purely metaphysical questions; the peoples react before reality, and simply put, an enormous effort was made in those five months, and we all made it. There has

---

4   The beach in eastern Cuba where the expeditionaries led by Fidel disembarked on December 2, 1956, to launch the revolutionary war.

been done all that could be done in those months, after that moment when the work began.

Who is able to judge the work that has been done? The people, because in those five months various problems have has been worked on, as everyone knows, and were resolved rapidly: the food problem, the problem of the old people's homes, the problem of the plantations, the problem of the sugar cane harvest.

I believe that I have spoken various times at the civic institutions, twice at the Lions Club, in nearly all the Federations of Industries, in the teacher's associations .... I have intervened in a great number of problems, not to complicate them, but to resolve them.

In all the projections I believe that we can feel satisfied, not for what we have attained, but for the effort made, because we could not have done more. That has been the work.

In addition, I undertook a trip of 25 days from Canada to Argentina, trying to strengthen the international relations of the country, in an effort of trying to counteract the campaigns.[5] Everyone should understand what a tour of a week in any country is, giving speeches, a tour of ten days in a country that does not speak one's own language, speaking and responding to five or six thousand journalists that questioned me. It is an effort, and speaking in universities in languages different from ours, and speaking for twenty-five days. It is an exhausting effort, and that has been my rest.

You see how many zones of agrarian development that have been promoted, from Guanacahabibes to Guanabacoa, passing by the Zapata's Swamp, the Isla de Pinos, northern Matanzas, the zone of Belice, the area of Niquero, and the zone of Camagüey. And the beef problem and the interventions in the large estates in that province; the thousands of tractors that already are working in all the rural areas of the country; the beaches now are public, and the plans of Public Works. Well, all that work has been done in the midst of attending all the meetings, all the mass meetings, all the interviews with the press, the meetings of the Councils of Ministers, the hours that I have spent on radio and television speaking to the people. Well, I have not had time to think about other things. What we have been doing is complying with duty.

...

I have been careful in every moment. I have placed special care in every moment with the little disposable free time, which is not much, except for minutes, trying to maintain the best relations with the President of the Republic,

---

5 The disinformation campaigns launched by governments seeking to discredit the Cuban Revolution.

for his condition as president. However, we many times observed in the Council of Ministers certain symptoms that would be able to cause difficulties.

MR. EDUARDO HÉCTOR ALONSO: Have these difficulties been intensified in recent days?

DR. FIDEL CASTRO RUZ: It is not that they have intensified; it is that they have nearly erupted.

Certain details of less importance are those that have brought out what was at the root of this problem. In the beginning, laws were immediately approved in the heart of the Council of Ministers and were approved by the President of the Republic, and they did not delay in appearing in the *Gaceta Oficial*.[6] Problems were caused when the appointments of the Presidency were brought to us, because I believed simply in the duty of investigating and knowing whom we were going to appoint, and in being very careful to ensure that the appointments were not the result of influence and friendships. Since everyone saw me as responsible for the government, I was not disposed to fall into the designation of persons that did not meet the requirements. It had to be done with the greatest delicacy, in order to not fall into the designation of a person that could be discredited as immoral.

...

He was not soliciting the appointments for approval, except for those that were not the most difficult.

The difficulties strictly speaking began forty or forty-five days ago, I do not remember exactly the day, at the root of the crisis of the Council of Ministers, of the change of the ministers. We were all surprised by a written request of the President, soliciting a leave of thirty day, at the same moment in which we were going to provoke a crisis in the Cabinet. When I arrived to the [Presidential] Palace with the problems and concerns of the changing of ministers and to choosing substitutes, I found a letter from the President soliciting a thirty-day leave.

How were we going to resolve that problem, when we have lived under a permanent international discrediting campaign and accusations of all kinds? How were we going to grant a leave to the President, if there is not a Vice-President, if there was not a substitute? If we had to explain the problem of conceding that license without there being a substitute, what were we going to do in the moment when we were going to change the ministers?

Well, everyone was extraordinarily concerned over that. What did we do? Well, we agreed to go to see the President, to speak to him, to explain to him, to ask him, to try to win his support, in order that he would withdraw that request

---

6   The official publication of the government of Cuba of the laws of the country.

for a leave that no one had anticipated, which created for us a tremendous problem when, all of a sudden, he want to renounce the Presidency without having a substitute. That is another thing, when those agreements were adopted in the beginning, I was not in the Council of Ministers.

...

But the first serious damage, resulting from an attitude that was increasingly more evidently hostile to the extreme, to the present extreme, occurred in those moments when all the laws were practically paralyzed. We now were arriving to the point that no law came out of the Council of Ministers, and none was able to pass to the *Gaceta Oficial*, because it needed the signature of the President.... The laws were being submitted for revision by the President of the Republic, creating a paralysis.

But in the final analysis, these things could have been tolerated and endured, except for one difficulty that in my understanding was not justified, and which was a setback for Cuban power. I refer to the law that would transfer the trials from the Military Jurisdiction to the Civil Jurisdiction, and that at the same time established new penalties for the counterrevolutionary crimes.

You [members of the press] that were with me during the trip through Latin America know well the concern that I had with respect to the question of the executions, that they not be excessive, that they would have a limit, a limit necessary for the rehabilitation of justice in our country.

MR. NICOLÁS BRAVO: You repeatedly expressed the view that those executions should be brought to an end as rapidly as possible.

DR. FIDEL CASTRO RUZ: The struggle was to overcome the practical obstacles that were provoked by the serious cases of war criminals, since I understood that the favorite arm of our enemies, in the first stage, was the executions, the Revolutionary Justice. In this second stage, it is communism. In this second stage, since there no longer is any of that, the accusation against us is that of communism. But in that entire first stage, a great campaign against Cuba was launched over the question of Revolutionary Justice. We already were bringing to an end the first stage when I toured the United States and Latin America. We already had plans for bringing the trials to an end, including the transferring of their jurisdiction from the military to the civil. Putting the executions to an end was an advanced step toward normalization. It was not easy to bring the people to the idea that justice has a limit, and we ought not to exceed that limit, because the people were really in an unfavorable mood toward those gentlemen responsible for those atrocities.

Public opinion was prepared. The Law was prepared. One had to make plans; one had to take measures with respect to the crimes against the Revolution, because one must defend the Revolution above all.

The citizenry was in agreement. More severe penalties for some crimes had to be established; for the counterrevolutionaries, the embezzlers, the bombs, the violent attacks, the landings in the country. But the intention was to utilize the opportunity to take those steps forward, to cease the executions and to transfer the crimes to civil jurisdiction, in order to normalize the country.

The establishment of "habeas corpus" was next, in order to legislate precisely over future crimes, which were to be tried in ordinary courts. It was a question of approving the Law, and one had to make a small modification in the Constitution. The modification in the Constitution was made, and later, we found that it appeared in a newspaper that the death penalty had been approved.

With the modification of the Constitution of the Republic, the President began to appear separately in the newspapers, because he approved the Constitutional Reform, in which the death penalty was established for certain types of crime. The Law that regulates that sanction is retained, while there is a a modification of the Constitution of the Republic establishing a death penalty in a vague manner, inasmuch as the laws of the Constitution establish the death penalty for this and for that, but it is supposed that it is regulated by Law, because it does not appear until a Correctional Judge applies the death penalty.

...

Complementary legislation was needed. It was approved [by the Council of Ministers] in conjunction with the Reform, and in the moment that we were expecting the reform.... At the same time, the end of the "habeas corpus" was approaching. Think what the delay in that Law implied for us. Suddenly all the Ordinary Tribunals were going to hear all the pending trials, with twenty-four hours to decide, or we would be obligated to open again trials suspended for not having the "habeas corpus," something completely negative.

...

That fact unfortunately coincides with an incident that also is well known. It coincides, unfortunately, and I think that it had to have contributed a great deal to create, to intensify, this crisis; and it is the problem of the house. The President, with outstanding debts from the pension that they had stopped paying to him in the last months of the dictatorship, plus his salary, had acquired a residence. After some time, two journalists—I believe in a newspaper that is published here in English—brought to light the matter of the house. Consequently, the President viewed as slanderous the form in which the report was written, and he brought a lawsuit with respect to the question of the house.

There was antecedent: on arriving to the charge of Prime Minister, the first measure that I proposed in the Council was the reduction of the salaries of the ministers. If we were asking the sugar workers to work, that they renounce all their demands and to make sacrifices; if we were asking everyone to wait, if we were asking for sacrifices, it seemed to me to make good political sense that we the ministers, that we ought to establish a salary of one thousand, five hundred pesos, approximately, which would reduce it by fifty percent.

The President of the Republic was earning exactly the same salary as the dictator Batista, that had been a salary excessively increased to the very respectable quantity of 100,000 pesos annually, and it had been a scandal when the dictator increase the salary to 100,000 pesos annually.

We did not ask to reduce the salary of the President of the Republic, but at the same time, it was a matter of basic political sense. If we were reducing salaries, the President of the Republic, in accordance with the spirit of sacrifice that was living the country and the political sense that the governors ought to have, of the political tact that the governors ought to have, he ought to reduce also, by at least 50%. Which still would have left him with the sum of 50,000 pesos every year.

We were not able to ask it of him. My understanding is that it is more than 100,000, between 10 and 12 thousand pesos monthly, between costs of representation and of different kinds. Although we reduced ours, we were not able to ask it of him, nor to reduce it, contributing to an additional error: he invests that money in the purchase of a residence, very early, at two or three months, investing in a residence. But that had not had greater importance.

The report emerges, coinciding with that report in which a reporter made a criticism of the President, that the President considered slanderous, a newspaper story on "The Revolution arrives to Zapata's Swamp." When I read the story, I was in a little house here [he shows the little house to the television viewers]. You will see, the little house that is .... And the story states, "Over floating barrels and with a completely metallic structure, Dr. Fidel Castro has constructed a small house in the middle ... [He continues reading]. Then, in the explanation here, "In this small hamlet ... [He continues reading].

What happens with this story? Well, in the first place, it is misleading. Although it is a very small house, the house is not mine. That house was constructed there for the workers of Zapata's Swamp, where Dutch technicians and the functionaries of the Ministry of Agriculture are going to carry out tasks; they are collecting trout and other fish, transplanting them to other lakes and other rivers. When I went to Zapata's Swamp, which is a solitary place, to rest one day, since also I slept there. Therefore, it was the house of Fidel.

We have not been able to go there for much time, since the time in which the incidents in Zapata's Swamp occurred.

But that report was not clear. That story in a certain sense would be able to give the impression that I manufactured a little recreation house, although it be of only one room, but affluent, as the citizens say, with the comforts of modern existence. There are some bunk beds there, where we fifteen or twenty persons were going to sleep. There is a stove, I think of gas, not of gas, but of liquid, that is, of bright light, and I believe that there is a fridge or something like that.

But in any event, that house is not mine. And my first reaction when I read that was of disgust, because I understood that one has to be careful, especially in discussing the problem of houses, to stay in a little house, although it be only one room. I did not make that house; I did not order that a house be made for me, large or small. I am very careful and sensitive with respect to the things that a revolutionary functionary ought to have.

So simply my first reaction was of disgust, ... and I protested in a letter that *compañero* Franqui viewed as a little inconsiderate toward him. That was the reason that I took it Tuesday in the evening, which is when this newspaper comes out, Tuesday the seventh, I agreed to withdraw it in order to avoid hurting the *compañeros* of the editorial staff and the director *compañero* of the newspaper. In the end, it was not published.

I then left for the central provinces. I remember exactly what trip I made, because I had worries.... I believe that I traveled to all the costal zones for the touristic centers, so I was not able to be here on Wednesday to present the letter, and I presented it on Thursday. I have the letter here, and tell me if some phrase could be interpreted as inconsiderate or offensive.

> "Havana, July 10, 1959
> "Mr. Carlos Franqui
> "Director of 'Revolution'
>
> "Esteemed compañero:
> In the issue of the newspaper 'Revolution' of last Tuesday, a report was published on the works in Zapata's Swamp, where there appears, among other things, a photo of a small house, with the caption: 'Over floating barrels and with a completely metallic structure, Dr. Fidel Castro has constructed a small house in the middle of the vastness of Treasure Lagoon. The neighbors of Zapata's Swamp know it as 'the house of Fidel,' since the Prime Minister utilizes it in his trips as a comfortable and tranquil abode.'

"I wish to declare that although that house is in the middle of the swamp and is as small and modest as anyone can possess, it is not mine, nor does it belong to me. It is a wood installation with floors of zinc or aluminum what was built in that completely inhospitable place for the works of drainage that are being carried out there.

"When I go to Zapata's Swamp, I take refuge in that shelter, like the engineers and technicians that are undertaking works and studies in that zone, a place that certainly I prefer for its solitude and isolation. But I cannot have a house, because my reduced salary as Prime Minister would not permit it. I have not earned sufficient salary in five months to buy that cabin in Zapata's Swamp.

"In the Sierra Maestra, there is also a house of guano, what the command headquarters were, which was constructed during the war, in which I lived for several months. There is where you and other compañeros worked with me for unforgettable hours, outlining the most important plans of the war, and writing the first revolutionary laws. Neither is that hut mine, nor is the 'Granma' nor any other property acquired for revolutionary or public ends. These objects will remain as symbols of this era of sacrifice and creation. They belong exclusively to the people and to history.

"I personally do not have anything, nor do I have interest in having anything. I only carry with me the self-sacrifice that has accompanied me in all tests and that I will never renounce.

"Fraternally,

"Dr. Fidel Castro"

Then, as this letter was coming out, there was a declaration of the President, saying that the Penal Law was approved, and that there did not exist discrepancies between the President of the Republic and me. I believe that this declaration was made the same Friday or Saturday, following the letter, and that was an unfortunate coincidence, because possibly the journalist did this story when he went with those of the Forum [on Agrarian Reform] to Zapata's Swamp, he brought it out there, and they put this case to me there, and I believed that it was my duty to deny it.

What other way did I have to clarify it? Why am I still worried that even a single citizen believes that I made a little house for myself? What more decent form do I have to clarify that? What blame do I have of the coincidence with a house in truth, of thirty or forty thousand pesos that had been bought, effectively with salary and not as a result of embezzlement or robbery? That was verging a little on the lack of tact, even a little immoral, as it were, to continue receiving exactly the same salary that received Mr. Fulgencio Batista for the presidency of the Republic.

But what blame do I have for that coincidence, which coincides with a state of bitterness, for who knows what reason? I only would like that it be kept in mind that one has to be concerned by these things in the middle of the problems of Cuba in the OAS [Organization of American States], with the attacks by Trujillo,[7] and in the middle of the treacheries of Díaz Lanz.[8]

In the middle of all these problems, to have to be attending to these things, because one has to attend to them. However, these things, in a form linked together, for errors that were not mine, were making the environment bitter, in such a manner that it produces a true state of hostility, antagonism, and enmity, gentlemen, between the President and me.

That, of course, was not important, because we have the duty to conceal all these problems. It does not even matter that the laws were held back. We were able to wait the ten days subsequent to approval by the Council of Ministers, at which time they become Law, if they are not expressly rejected. Or they can be returned to be approved by two thirds of the Council of Ministers. Naturally, it was a situation very disagreeable, to think that the laws were to be vetoed and that their remained no other recourse than to turn to that faculty; because that would be to create a state of tension.

To all this, other problems were added. We have the case of Dr. Díaz Roca, president of the Commercial Pension Fund, who was investigated and arrested by *compañero* Camilio Cienfuegos in consideration of the very numerous complaints against that functionary. The government was obligated to take the extreme measure of his arrest and his removal from office. Well, one of the papers to be signed by the Prime Minister was the proposal from the President of the Republic, designating again that functionary for another important post.

But in the end, that did not have importance. For that reason, it does not produce a crisis. The grave, very grave crisis, in the most difficult moment of the country, results from a style in which an official tries to blackmail us with the problem of communism. No official is permitted to do freely what he desires to do. Nepotism is not permitted, for we have sworn to not repeat the offenses of the past in our country; and to not permit that we be made victims of the most repugnant, must low, and most immoral of processes. Some want to put into practice a style in which, when someone is not permitted to do what

---

7 See glossary.
8 See glossary.

he has the desire to do, he plans to immediately to go to the outside world and accuse our Revolution of being communist.

...

Evidently, they want to put us in a position in which, when there is the least difficulty among us, they begin to prepare the conditions and the plan of Pedro Luis Díaz Lanz. It is really painful to have to express here, that the President of the Republic, in a rage of blindness, who knows from what passion, counseled by who knows whom, after the publication of this letter of Friday, July 10, begins to elaborate a plan that was exactly the plan of Mr. Pedro Luis Díaz Lanz.

This is an accusation that I am making. I am not making an official accusation. Rather, I am trying to explain precisely here in what tremendous difficulty we find ourselves in light of this fact.

I am saying the facts, and I not interpreting them. Sunday afternoon I received information from a functionary in the Presidential Palace of a conservation sustained with the President of the Republic, in which he was informed of facts that were really alarming.

With respect to the letter, he said that it was not first time that I had mistreated him, that it was the third time that I had mistreated him. The first was with respect to the casino games.... When there were made declarations by certain groups, certain leagues, concerning the Casino games, and I, speaking on television, said it was easy to express an opinion over those questions, when one had work, from some place where sustenance was assured without worry. But I was very far from thinking that the President of the Republic had noted that as an affront.

The second is a result of the license for which he asked. I had approached him in a laudatory manner, expressing the consideration that I had for him, and asking that he withdraw that license in order to avoid problems. He says that suddenly I had undergone a great change, perhaps because the Communist Party had put pressure on me.

And the third is that of Pedro Luis Díaz Lanz. That functionary of the Presidential Palace, who was accompanied by other *compañeros* of the Ministry, informed me of the exact words, which certainly were not the same as what Pedro Luis Díaz Lanz would say to Manuel Urrutia.

...

That day, Sunday evening, I was speaking in the Forum on Agrarian Reform until three in the morning. On leaving there, I had an appointment with the journalist Mathews,[9] and I was with him, conversing until 8:00 or 8:30 in the

---

9 See glossary.

evening. I lied down one or two hours, and when I awoke, the President was on television.

Those that are not in the "inside" would not be able to understand this like those of us that are. Concerning Pedro Díaz Lanz, the President said that he was a traitor, that if he had something to say, why did he not say it in Cuba, and why was he going away to say it outside the country? However, he did not defend the Revolution from the planning of Mr. Diaz Lanz. And what is more serious, in the moment when a discrepancy emerges, in the moment that this problem has emerged, in the moment that the problem of the Penal Law has emerged, all of which the Ministers were deeply concerned, that is the moment in which the President—in the middle of the campaign, of the bombing, and all the spectacle of defamations, of Mr. Díaz Lanz, of all the campaigns accusing the Revolutionary Government of being communists—that is the day in which the campaign of struggle against communism suspiciously is erected. Accordingly, as they begin to carry out the entire plan, Díaz Lanz leaves FAR (Revolutionary Armed Forces) and makes some declarations of this kind, suspiciously, because we never had spoken of that problem.

Already the ship, the launch, has been prepared, along with their ties with foreign agents; they make a second declaration, and they leave.

What is the situation of the Prime Minister of the Republic, before a fact like that? I view it as a situation of great import that I have not been able to prevent. Anyone who has been in circumstances like those has to understand the hard fact that something is going on, that approaching over our heads is the dagger of treason, that there is a plan conceived and hatched and in operation, of which the first steps are beginning.

...

Tell me if this not be really alarming for our people, disheartening for our people, that some morning through the international cables, we find ourselves in a volley of imputations, proceeding no less than from the President of the Republic.

...

A letter turned up allegedly in the pockets of the revolutionary Dominican Jiménez, a supposed letter of mine speaking of the problems of the Church and of wiping out the influence of the Church. When a letter is fabricated, when a letter is invented and is given as undeniable truth in Buenos Aires, when they are speaking of these things in the U.S. Senate, when all that coincides with other maneuvers and other campaigns, it is logical to suppose that they are even trying to mobilize the religious sentiment against a revolution that has not had the least friction, that has not had the least problem and the least difficulty with the religious institutions, a revolution that no one is able to have imputed the least act of hostility, disagreement, discussion, polemic, or struggle, with the Catholic Church, or with any church.

It is evident that this is being done outside the country and comes from the exterior. They have to be of concern to a Prime Minister who is very conscience of his obligations, very conscious of his duties and believes that he has fulfilled them fully. But also, coinciding with all that, it is said in a newspaper that the President of the Republic has spoken with energy and without precision .... [He reads].

So we can see that there is an effort here to depict the existence of two positions, to separate two positions: the position of the President and mine, trying to present me with a position of complicity or with a procommunist position in the country. Trying to present me so on the basis of what? In a declaration that emerges from a resentment, that emerges form who knows what reason of a personal kind?

Our suspicions were aroused beforehand, because of the moments in which there was a problem with the Prime Minister, and because a foreign Senate is carrying forward the most scandalous act of espionage against our country, of intervention in our internal affairs.

And all that coincides with the fact that another newspaper, which is a model of collaboration with the Revolution and with the country in these moments, publishes a headline saying, "Fidel is communist... says Díaz Lanz"

Can you to tell me, when were similar methods of publicity applied to a Prime Minister, to a leader in our country, as though it did not have importance to print such a headline; while the traitor Díaz Lanz publishes that letter, that Fidel is communist, and the newspaper vendors go shouting it in the street? Tell me if something similar was published on some occasion against some government official that had my responsibility; tell me if on some occasion they treated Mr. Batista in such form.

...

Tell me if, in order to resolve the problems of the country, I need prestige, I need that I am believed, that it is known that I always have spoken to the country with absolutely total frankness. Without this, it would be impossible for me or anyone to carry forward the overwhelming task that falls on the shoulders of a leader in a revolutionary process. Do you conceive that a Prime Minister has to be a victim with impunity of similar maneuvers, without being able to defend himself?

This would not have such extreme gravity, if it were known that there is indubitable testimony concerning what they are planning and that they are moving ahead with all the steps to carry forward with the most unjustifiable and the most incalculable of aggressions, that, to repeat, magnifies five times the case of Díaz Lanz.

What can the Prime Minister do in these conditions? The Prime Minister has defended his ideological position, the Prime Minister has spoken very clearly, as clear as anyone in Cuba has spoken in order to define his ideas, and I believe that no one has spoken more concerning these questions than the Prime Minister. They are written and recorded, and they are in the memory of the citizenry; no one has spoken with the clarity of the Prime Minister and has defined the position of the Cuban Revolution. I believe that it is indispensable, in order to make evident what all these maneuvers intend, that the definitions that the Prime Minister has made be repeated, of the revolutionary thought that is the sentiment of Cuba, because I do not do any other thing than interpret the sentiment of our people. We have given tests, and we want men with their own ideas and are not parrots that repeat foreign slogans; men that think for themselves. That we have been, and that I am, a man that thinks for himself and not as a tool or on the basis of a slogan, as I have seen in the Revolution. We want a man of judgment and of free ideas, as I would want all my compatriots to be, and these ideas must be expressed in order to ensure that the Revolution is on the right path. And all this runs contrary to the depiction of us by the large and malicious campaign. We do not know it this is done consciously or blindly, or it begins in conscience awareness and moves to conscious conspiracy. The worst blow that they could give to the Revolution is the coup that was developing.

...

Our Revolution is not red, it is olive green, which is the color of the uniform of the Rebel Army that left from the heart of the *Sierra Maestra*. To conclude, I am going to read parts of the speeches, in which we have defined the concepts of our Revolution on repeated occasions.

Here there is a declaration taken from the speech in the Civic Plaza in Havana, on May 8, which is a premonition of the problems that the Revolution presently is confronting, and it says:

> "I do not know if the defamation against our Revolution that it is communist or is influenced by communists is based only on the proposition that we do not persecute communists, and we do not execute communists.
>
> "I do not know in what form the ideas of the Revolution could be defined in order that it not be schemed against and not be defamed more than it is, and in order that they cease with the individual attacks against our Revolution.

...

> "We have tried to discuss our ideals, not with force but with reason and for the justice that it entails, because to do otherwise would be to accept the theory that some right ought to be suppressed. The most convenient for the Revolution would be to suppress the right of everyone, in order that only the men of the Revolutionary Government speak, but that would not be democratic.... All simply have the equal right to express opinions and to speak. Because we have that manner of thinking, because that is our political thought, one can egg on." [He continues reading].

...

Now well, can the people say to me, can the people reasonably say to us that we can refrain from denouncing these facts? Can the people reasonably say to me that the Prime Minister, without resigning, would be able to come here to make this declaration? Can the people say to me honestly that they believe that the correct procedure—after all this that is conspiring, after the anguish, of the campaign of defamation—would be an accusation that resulted in the removal from office of the President, through which I would be presenting myself, before the entire world, as a classic caudillo, removing and installing presidents of the Republic?. Can the people tell me if I had an option other than the procedure of resigning, in order to be able to express to the people these facts?

I was not able to patiently wait until these plans were carried out, nor to patiently wait for the conspiracy to unfold, because among my most sacred duties is that of defending this Revolution and defending my country from all dangers.

...

I was not able to fall into the error of giving the enemies of Cuba an opportunity to present the Prime Minister as a caudillo, as a dictator, and as a gentleman of the old school, who removes and installs presidents.

And as I understand that the holding of public office values nothing, inasmuch as my duty is not to be occupying or flaunting offices, when there remained to me no other way out other than to do what I have done, I arrived to the only solution; after many days of thought, and after no one found a solution and I saw the need of taking it personally, without consulting with the Council of Ministers—in that I expressed it only to some ministers—without consulting with the July 26 Movement, without consulting the Chiefs of the Armed Forces...

...

The attitude of the people has been spontaneous, in such manner that the task of all the *compañeros* has been to calm them during the day today. We are in a dilemma, from which we do not have a way out.

Hierarchically, we are under the President of the Republic. We were not able make these declarations without resigning office. The only thing that we were able to do is resign.

I trust in the power of our people, and in the destiny of our people.

I know that our [revolutionary] laws cannot be left behind.

I know that the no one can take away from the peasants their right to the land.

I know that rents are not going to increase.

I know that the beaches are not going to be closed again.

I know that the schools are not going to be closed again.

I know that nothing or no one will be able to take from our people their achievements. Because we have each and every Cuban to defend these gains, and I see the people of Cuba as too strong, too conscious, and too powerful, so that no one can turn the course of their destiny. Therefore, I am not worried.

I am resigning with the certainty that my resignation is the form in which I am lending service to the country. And with the certainly that I can leave from the situation to which they led me when they made me accept the charge of Prime Minister, where I arrived to that concern, and where they have been at the point of making me the victim of an unjustifiable trap. It is a question, simply, of preserving the prestige with which I am serving Cuba.

It is for this reason that I am resigning. And because, in addition, I do not want, whatever be the solution, that they can impute to me any personal ambitions and can give opportunity to the enemies of our Revolution to paint the Prime Minister, I repeat, as ambitious, as a caudillo, who capriciously has in his hands the destiny and the magistrates of the Republic.

MR. EDUARDO HÉCTOR ALONSO: Do you not believe, Dr. Fidel Castro, that at the head of each people that marches toward its destiny, there has to be the man that inspires the most confidence?

MR. EDUARDO HÉCTOR ALONSO: I am going to ask it in another form. Among the waves of rumors of these last hours, there is talk of those scruples of the chief of the Revolution—in this case, this title is better than that of Prime Minister—but I believe that above those scruples is the obligation of defending the Revolution, however much be your faith in the people.

DR. FIDEL CASTRO RUZ: And what am I doing, *compañero*, if it is not defending the Revolution?

Can you or someone tell me, or someone from the people tell me, if before this situation I had another alternative? I cannot resort to force; I cannot turn to the people, I have done all to the contrary.

I ignore in these instances what will be the decision of the President of the Republic.

I am satisfied with having come to warn the people of this situation. I am satisfied with alerting the people. I am satisfied with advising of the danger of treason. I cannot characterize it in another manner, because I consider that it is not an act of good faith, it is not an erroneous act; it is a premeditated act, it is an act of treason, of treason that did not arrive to be consummated.

MR. ENRIQUE GRAU ESTEBAN: Doctor, all of Cuba has declared today the firm position of not accepting your resignation. It seems to me that you do not have any other solution than that. I can assure you that if tomorrow you do not withdraw your resignation and Dr. Urrutia is removed from office, the nation will awake ... [inaudible].

DR. FIDEL CASTRO RUZ: You can be certain that the removal of the President from office will not come from me.

MR. ENRIQUE GRAU ESTEBAN: It is the desire of all Cuba...

DR. FIDEL CASTRO RUZ: I will defend the Revolution by all means, except by entering into a situation that is precisely what perhaps the enemies of this revolution are waiting.

In addition, I prefer to resign, because if the men who hold posts are characterized by ambition, I have to do all that is contrary to that.

The positions are not important to me. What I cannot allow—because it would be unjust—is that the Prime Minister of Cuba be presented as ambitious, as a gentleman that has hatched a maneuver to remove the president of the Republic, to install another, or to install himself.... I never would proceed in this form. And I have taken a step that has been one of the most bitter steps that I have taken in my life....

MR. EUCLIDES VÁZQUEZ: The Prime Minister, then, considers that the only possibility would be....

DR. FIDEL CASTRO RUZ: I consider anything possible. Among the things most serious that was going to happen was what the President of the Republic was plotting, concerning which the full Council of Ministers can give testimony. There is in the Council a group of very respectable men, without exception, and these men are imbued with a sense of duty, and they know and have worked with honesty. Beginning with Roa,[10] who is not a *compañero* of ours from the university, because he was a professor, and a man respected by all. But I put him as example, because he is not of the same revolutionary origin as us, he is of another generation. And all these respectable and serious men, unanimously, as men of state, back my attitude and my words, because they know that I would not be capable of fabricating such an account; the testimony of all the official of the state is unanimous in this situation.

---

10   See glossary.

Were we not able to defend the Revolution? I am saying that if the country is attacked, we are all going to be on the front line defending it; that if the Revolution is in danger, we are going to defend it, but with intelligence, not causing a defeat.

And so the decision of the President is pending.

Perhaps the Ministers meet to form a new government. Fifteen citizens that are in disposition to form a new government, or perhaps they be told to look for fifteen North American agents and install them as ministers here.

Such that the problem is that we are not able to turn to anything outside the Law or against the Law, to provoke an insubordination or insurrection of the people, if one uses force.

We have at our disposal an attribution that I do not believe convenient to use: to accuse the president of these actions, with the proof that there is, and to take him to trial. I do not believe that it would be intelligent to do that. It seems to me that he ought to be left at liberty to decide. If he wants to make declarations and speak concerning what he considers relevant, then he can do so; if the wants to make declarations for dissemination outside the country and for within the country, let him make them. This would not tend toward presenting him as a victim, which was a facet of the plan. Accordingly, the situation is that we have freed the country from a very grave danger.

QUESTION: What is your legal status after your resignation? Are you merely *Comandante* of the Rebel Army?

DR. FIDEL CASTRO RUZ: Well, the rank of *Comandante* has not been taken from me, and besides, I earned it in the Sierra Maestra.

QUESTION: With respect to the status of the Ministers?

DR. FIDEL CASTRO RUZ: I counseled them to not resign, and I asked them not to, because they wanted to resign, they wanted take a firm position in this situation. I asked them that they not resign, so as to not leave the state without representation, without the organ of power, which is precisely the Council of Ministers, the organism that has the constitutional faculty of designating the president, if the President were to resign. He says that I should ask for his resignation; I cannot, because that would incur what I cannot incur in any manner.

QUESTION: And how could he, with effectiveness, ask the Prime Minister to ask him for his resignation?

DR. FIDEL CASTRO RUZ: Well, he would have to obligate me to ask it of him.

QUESTION: What do you believe could pass tonight, or tomorrow, after your declarations, notwithstanding your exhortation for calm?

DR. FIDEL CASTRO RUZ: I am sure that the people will be calm, because the people know that we have to act in a dignified manner in all circumstances, without exaggerations nor excesses of any kind, and that the people have to trust in the public forces, and the public forces have instructions to avoid at all cost any type of excess.

In addition, I have not aroused hate. I have said what I had to say, and not for a trivial reason.

With respect to a legal proceeding of some form, who would lose? I have done something that frees me from those suspicions and puts the people on alert for struggle, so that at least we are exiting from this difficult situation, strengthening the Revolution and not weakening it, strengthening the Revolution and not weakening it. That is what we have done, and apart from that, I have a very legitimate interest, and it is an interest, not personal but national, of not being able to be presented as carrying forward with a maneuver to make the President of the Republic resign, and to put myself in his place. Therefore, I have taken the decision to simply resign, and I believe that with this explanation that I have given, the people understand the reasons that motivated it.

JOURNALIST: Following up your last affirmation that the people what is good for the country, do you believe that the Cubans are going to allow you to resign, considering how grave this would be?

DR. FIDEL CASTRO RUZ: Where is the gravity? Where is the damage to the Revolution? Because to resign is not to resign the Revolution. I am not resigning from the Revolution, and I am certain we will exhaust all necessary measures to avoid falling into traps, and that is my duty, and I am saying it now to guide the people.

I have the right to speak to the people, and that is what I am doing as a way of averting a difficult problem. The rest is imponderable, because one must be a fortune-teller to know that the President of the Republic will decide.

JOURNALIST: Then at this moment the future of the country depends on the decision of one person.

DR. FIDEL CASTRO RUZ: The future of the country is not in the hands of that person. What is in his hands is to act in one manner or another. The future of the country is in the hands of the country. No one should have doubts of that. The country itself will march united and as a single force. I am explaining to the people the situation.

JOURNALIST: Will you accept the will of the Cuban people?

DR. FIDEL CASTRO RUZ: It depends on what it be...

JOURNALIST: In the event that they express that you return to the government?

DR. FIDEL CASTRO RUZ: The people will have to consider one thing that is also of the utmost importance, and that is the impression of this situation, the manner in which the situation is going to be decided. If they want me to choose to appear as ambitious or as someone who has provoked this in order to resolve a power struggle in my favor....

JOURNALIST: You have been branded as communist but never as ambitious.

DR. FIDEL CASTRO RUZ: Why then can they brand me in one manner but not the other, when all the brandings have malicious intent?

...

MR. EDUARDO HÉCTOR ALONSO: In a moment of the interview, Dr. Castro referred to the difficult situation that was created when the President of the Republic took leave of forty-five days. I ask if the provision for that office is necessary in our constitutional mechanism.

DR. FIDEL CASTRO RUZ: It is not necessary, but the concentration of power in the office of the Prime Minister, without the office of the President of the Republic, would be too great a concentration of legal power, executive and legislative. It would be too great a concentration of power, if there were not the mechanism of the Presidency of the Republic, which is the office that certifies. That would be a problem.

That aside, it would be worthwhile to give to the orphanage the two million and something pesos that are spent on the Presidential Palace, because anyone who goes to the orphanage and sees those children in that situation understands that it would be better to give it those two and one half million. That salary in no form ought to continue; it is immoral.

MR. EDUARDO HÉCTOR ALONSO: It would be a good transfer of credit.

MODERATOR: Among the messages that I have been receiving since the program began, there is one that merits being read: "We request that you transmit to Dr. Fidel Castro the following message during his appearance tonight. The Civic Front of Martían Women fully support Dr. Fidel Castro, maximum and spontaneous leader of the Cuban Revolution, as we have been doing since the beginning of the revolutionary struggle. We exhort him to assume the First Magistrate of the Nation, as is demanding all the people of Cuba. Signed, Civic Front of Martían Women."

DR. FIDEL CASTRO RUZ: I thank you greatly for that support, but I ought to express my opinion. The Presidency of the Republic would be the same thing as being in a remote region of the country, like Punta del Este or Isla de Pinos, for one simple reason: I do not want to mortgage myself to that charge. I am not good for that charge. I believe that I am useful for what is unfolding, which is freer and more total, and more consistent with my character. I cannot go accompanied by motorcycles in the street; I need to walk even without escort.

But I would like that this problem and all this struggle be analyzed. In what economic state have we done this? And in what moment do these things pass? In moments in which personal attacks and assassinations are being planned. And I would like for you to tell me, if this campaign were to have success, where would it lead the country? In what situation would they leave the country, when here everyone is being accused of being communist, and they are carrying out these maneuvers? In what situation are they going to leave the country, with that confusion that they want to seed? Because in addition, such actions feed the enemy; note that after the action of Díaz Lanz, four mechanics went away. Imagine the agents here that are provoking desertion, and the battle that one must give against all those people!

Now, from the economic point of view, here are the graphs. There is a graphic that shows the data by month, and here is this year. The currency in '54, over 500 million pesos; and the currency in '59, when we took power, in the basement.

...

And look how they left the Republic, from 500 million, look how low, look how low, look how we found it, look at the graph of 500 million, and look here how low we found it. These are problems that are not problems without importance, that in this state of things, as the price [of our exports] is lower than ever, and the world production higher, and without for money to be given to us, we are doing it with our own resources. You will understand the effort that has been made.

This campaign against us cannot have justification, and the reason is that the people are so awake. It is clear that it does not have justification, and it is criminal that this would occur.

...

What I am interested in clarifying is that I am not resigning from the struggle. I am resigning an office, but I am not resigning the struggle. That is the one resignation that I never will make.

...

MR. NICOLÁS BRAVO: Doctor, if the July 26 Movement withdraws its backing of the government headed by Dr. Urrutia, as surely will happen, and he organizes his government, with whom would Dr. Urrutia govern?

DR. FIDEL CASTRO RUZ: I responded to that question a while ago. I do not know with whom. He has to know, perhaps with Attorney General Mario Hernández.

I have not made reference here to a series of problems, like for example the problem of the Judicial Power, where a cleansing[11] presided by him has been carried out, and that he continued regulating. Subsequently, it was considered that in some cases the question of personal interests had not been very clear. So it was a question of opening the purification again, provoking the uneasiness of the Judicial Power, as a result of rivalries of a personal type with a Judge who was a friend. Well, it was decided to do a general elimination, but then it turned out to be impossible for us to authorize that. We were trying to look for formulas, which included reminding everyone of the time when it was considered necessary to purify the Judicial Power. I went to the courts, and I met in the Supreme Court with all the Judges. I spoke to them, and I explained to them that it was a question of courtesy of one power of the state with another power. And after all that was done, the purification could not be done, because there was no formula that would be accepted other than one involving a general elimination against the Judicial Power. Well, we said that to do that was worse than to do nothing.

There were problems of distinct cases. For example, there was a registration of the country residence of Carlos Prío that was unnecessary and discourteous. We have given guarantees to those that support the Revolution. So you cannot, without consulting with anyone, and the Minister was not consulted, nor was the Prime Minister, with the political responsibility that he has. And they sent troops to register the residence of Carlos Prío. And you see the attitude that Prío has had, which has been an attitude in every moment correct when he left the country. He has defended us in New York, he defends us in Paris, everywhere. They did an unnecessary registration, an unjustified provocation that they ought not to have done. But the Attorney General of the Supreme Court was there.

...

And twenty problems of this type. It was not a unique problem, since the problems were constant, and one had to go immediately to rectify it. But none of that matters. I would have endured that for twenty years; it did not matter. The problem here, the grave problem that does not have solution, is the problem that has been explained here, beginning with the incident of the house.

Therefore, I say that it is a moral problem because I believe that no moral man would accede to a maneuver against us, in a difficult moment of the Revolution.

---

11   Involving the removal of corrupt judges from judicial office.

The turn to robbery is what pains me the most. It is robbery, in that here are utilized the campaign of *La Rosa Blanca*,[12] of Trujillo, and of seeking to obligate, going to treason. It is very serious, and one must put an end to it, because you cannot govern in such a form. I have laid out here that this constitutes treason on the part of those that are carrying out these actions, including Díaz Lanz and his group as well as a group of gangsters in the U.S. Senate that have been involved in the problem of Días Lanz.

...

MR. NICOLÁS BRAVO: I have a message that has just arrived that says the following: The Executive Committee of the Consortium of Cuban Institutions, after hearing the declarations of Dr. Fidel Castro, with the same responsibility with which on one occasion we asked for the resignation of the dictator Batista, solicits publicly the resignation of the President of the Republic, and believing ... (Applause) interpreting the feelings and the longings of the people of Cuba, demands of Dr. Fidel Castro that he assume fully the functions of the government, occupying the Presidency of the Republic. Signed, Executive Committee of the Consortium of Cuban Institutions.

DR. FIDEL CASTRO RUZ: Look that should not have applause. That shows... I am deeply grateful for that vote of confidence, but it is that.... Without a contrary attitude to that opinion, I believe honestly that that in no manner can be done. I would be very wrong if I were to do that. I believe that it would act contrary to the political intelligence that we all ought to have, and it would place me in a very difficult situation. Look, one must guarantee one thing to the people. The people does not have an interest in the position that one occupies: it has an interest in having its Revolution, its sovereignty, its liberty, and its destiny assured; and we are saying that, yes, all that is assured.

That is what interests the people. Who will ensure it? The people themselves ensure it, all the state officials ensure it, all the workers' leaders, all the revolutionary leaders, the Chiefs of the Armed Forces. Each soldier and each revolutionary combatant ensures it. One has the right to say so, because it is known. The Revolution is assured. The revolutionary laws are assured. The destiny of the people is assured. That is what is important. Is that not what is important? Do the people have confidence in what we are saying? Yes they do. The people can be calm, because that which is in their interests is assured.

What we now have done, what I have seen the need to do, is to act as in other moments in my life I have had to act, in a difficult form, many times. But I would be an incompetent and irresponsible person, if I were to permit the things that had been developing to continue forward. I had to defend myself,

---

12   See glossary.

although I would have had to sacrifice myself; not for the position, but from the genuine point of view of the work that I was doing. Because what one wants, is to work. Do you understand? What captivates our imagination and mind in this moment is what we are doing. Whereas during the war, the duty was to struggle, in peace it is to create. When one must return to fight and struggle, we will return to fight and to struggle.

...

MR. EDUARDO HÉCTOR ALONSO: Dr. Castro, do you believe that this crisis will be resolved with sufficient speed to not compromise the ceremony of July 26?

DR. FIDEL CASTRO RUZ: No one will compromise the ceremony of the 26th. The problem is that the people are going to the ceremony, because it is the 26th, to support the Agrarian Reform, to defend the sovereignty of the country against foreign interference in the internal affairs of Cuba and against the traitors. That is the call for the 26th.

In addition, it should be understood that at this moment we face an imponderable factor: the imponderable decisions of the President. The President can take many decisions: it is not known which he will take, if he remains, not wanting to resign; resigns; attempts to form a government; leaves the country or remains; seeks asylum; lives in the country. He is in a situation of knowing what he wants. He has taken a position morally treacherous; legally no, because he still has not done it, although he began to prepare the terrain. That in penal law is not a crime committed. Therefore, legally, he is within the law.

...

One must take into account a very important detail. It seems to me that President ought to be permitted to go to the Presidential Palace. It seems to me that he should be left in liberty to decide, and that in accordance with what he decides, the people can express themselves. Right? I understand well the backing that people want to give to the Revolution, that declaration of unity of thought, but I ought to warn and I ought to council the advisability that it be declared with full liberty for the President, in order to avoid that it seems like an overthrow of power. I believe that the declaration itself is the expression of the thought, and I am sure that the country is united.

The Ministers will be responsible for what I have said here. All the officials will be responsible for demonstrating it and assuring it. The Ministers share the daily work, and they know the inside of this question. They are honest men, moral men, virtuous men that react with justice. They are not the kind of men that would force the situation.

JOURNALIST: Do you know if there is an imminent meeting of the Council of Ministers?

DR. FIDEL CASTRO RUZ: My understanding is that the Council of Ministers are in the Presidential Palace. All the Ministers are in the Palace.

JOURNALIST: But is there an official meeting?

DR. FIDEL CASTRO RUZ: Well, they are there waiting on developments. I counseled them not to resign, because that would leave the state without legal authority.

QUESTION: Are there any moves within the national leadership of the July 26 Movement toward maintaining or withdrawing support of Dr. Urrutia?

DR. FIDEL CASTRO RUZ: I personally ought not to take steps, because that would involve my doing all, so therefore I am doing nothing. But I am sure that my perspective has the backing of the July 26 Movement. It is logical, because the developments that have occurred are very serious.

It is an incredible case, but nothing ought to surprise us here. We ought to be completely immune to surprises, since we went to bed one March 10 in Cuba thinking about elections, and we woke up with tanks in the street.

There was no solution to this problem other than my resignation. I am lending service to the country through a solution to this problem then strengthens the revolution. If have had not done this, one night he would have gone away to Miami to make a series of declarations, as did Pedro Luis Díaz Lanz. Imagine the consequences of that: the Council of Ministers would be obligated to ask his resignation. What would be the effect on the Revolution? So I had to stand before the people and explain, and with this the Revolution can leave the situation strengthened. He can now leave the country and make all the declarations that he was going to make, but no longer as a surprise attack on the Revolution, as he wanted; now he will have to confront the truth.

We do not need force. We need nothing more that microphones, to speak to the people and to say the truth.

...

There are forms of defending the Revolution, which would then justify any action against it. If we see that he is going to inflict harm on the Revolution, we have to defend it; but not with an approach defined in advance. We must hold back in our response, in order to avoid an institutional crisis of the Republic, because the President has the power to provoke a constitutional crisis. It can be resolved, because we are capable of resolving all, but we have to act in an intelligent manner, in order to not fall into the traps that they can set for the Revolution. Cuba has to go forward developing the capacity to confront its problems with intelligence, so that tomorrow they do not say that I have prepared a maneuver to remove the President from office. I have a strong interest, as the people and the world have an interest, in being exempt from such arguments.

...

JOURNALIST: Is the possibility of a foreign attack increasing, if it is true that it was prepared?

DR. FIDEL CASTRO RUZ: A foreign attack within a few hours would meet with resolute troops fighting against it. I am going to say one thing. The attacks have to be prepared, and if they precipitated an attack, they would arrive less prepared. Our troops in these moments are all in their barracks, the chiefs are in their posts, and everyone has exemplary discipline. With the least sign of enemy forces, in any zone of the country where they disembark, they immediately will have to confront everyone here. If that were to happen here, the people would have to be held back, because everyone would want to ask for a rifle. We would have to do what we did today, to say to the people that they wait, that they remain calm, that rifles are being brought to them, and they will have to wait their turn.

...

JOURNALIST: Doctor, you have expressed tonight that there are sufficient dignified and capable Cubans to occupy the presidency of the Republic. Would you like to mention one?

DR. FIDEL CASTRO RUZ: There are many.

JOURNALIST: I am interested in only one.

DR. FIDEL CASTRO RUZ: I do not want to mention anyone. I cannot satisfy you, because if I were to mention one of the many that there are, and not mention all the others....

JOURNALIST: Would you then like to mention various, or should I withdraw the question?

DR. FIDEL CASTRO RUZ: It is not a bad question. I am the one who cannot speak, because the Council of Ministers ought to resolve these things, and remember I do not want to insert myself in this problem. I do not want to be elector.

Now, I believe that there are many among the ministers themselves. There are *compañeros* among the present Ministers who are excellent persons who work with complete dedication. Definitely, the president ought to be one more among us all, he ought to be one more working, without an excess of formality and without a complex, as we say. We have to all work there as *compañeros*. The success is in working as a team, in which each plays his role. As I was saying when we spoke of the idea of eliminating the post of the presidency, it is not advisable to concentrate too much power. That is the issue.

MODERATOR: *Comandante*, with your permission, I interrupt to inform of news that has just been emitted from CMQ News moments ago. President Urrutia has asked us to send cameramen. I do not know what kind of declaration he is going to make.

DR. FIDEL CASTRO RUZ: I believe that he has the right to reply. He should reply if he has arguments in response; if not, pass later the cameras for my...

MR. NICOLÁS BRAVO: *Comandante*, President Urrutia is going to make declarations, but off camera. It will take three hours or more, and by remote control.

DR. FIDEL CASTRO RUZ: If he is going to make declarations off camera, why does he want the cameras? It seems to me that the Ministers ought to declare also, informing what they know concerning this problem.

MR. NICOLÁS BRAVO: *Comandante*, we are going to install the remote control in the Palace.

DR. FIDEL CASTRO RUZ: I am finishing soon.

MR. NICOLÁS BRAVO: In order to give the President the opportunity to express his perspective and express some decision publicly. I suggest, if it is not too much to suggest, that we recess, and that once that the cameras are installed there and after the President of the Republic has finished, we continue our program.

DR. FIDEL CASTRO RUZ: The Ministers ought to speak. We can do that, but ensuring that it does not fall into a spectacle.

I am interested in hearing what he has to day with respect to what concerns the country, and I am at your disposition to respond immediately, if need be, and also to the Ministers. I ask that the Ministers be consulted, so that this does not become a personal conflict. The Ministers ought to be consulted, and the Ministers that are meeting in the Palace should be informed that the cameras are there, in order that they can express their opinions. We have to avoid that a spectacle be produced; any reply should be made, but not in the context of a spectacle.

...

MR. NICOLÁS BRAVO: *Comandante*, I suggest that you permit me to interrupt, with the news that just arrived in my hands. I am informed, through the Minister of Defense, that the President of the Republic has just presented his resignation.[13]

---

13 Urrutia initially was firm in maintaining that he would not resign; he had requested that television cameras be installed in the Presidential Palace, with the intention of responding to Fidel. Inasmuch as it would have taken three hours to install the television equipment, it was agreed that the President would make his declaration by radio remote control. The Minister of National Defense, Augusto Martínez Sanchez, sent a note to Fidel, asking him what he should do. Fidel sent him a note saying, "As long as the President occupies the office, one must respect his dispositions." However, *Comandante* Gilberto Cervantes Núñez and Lincoln Llaguno, brother-in-law of Urrutia, both of whom had maintained constant contact with the President, ultimately persuaded him that he had no choice but to resign. Martínez Sanchez sent a note to Raul Castro, informing him that

DR. FIDEL CASTRO RUZ: I believe that the people have been able to follow the events of this crisis as possibly never has occurred in any country.

MR. NICOLÁS BRAVO: We are making history.

DR. FIDEL CASTRO RUZ: I believe that this is an historic event, of that there is not the least bit of doubt. We all have an interest that our acts can be judged in the future, with complete honesty. For the first time, the people have the importance that they have today. Speaking with the people is the vehicle through which they can be informed. All the country is interested in the problems being faced and in informing themselves with respect to these questions.

No one can compel the President of the Republic to take a perspective. At this moment, we do not know what decision he will make and what plans he has; it is not known what perspective he is going to take. He remains at full liberty. I believe that it is correct for us to leave him in full liberty to plan. If he wants to remain, or if the wants to leave the country; he is at full liberty to decide over his future.

MR. NICOLÁS BRAVO: Without any pressure.

DR. FIDEL CASTRO RUZ: Without pressure of any kind. I have been saying to the people since I arrived here that I had serious matters to explain, and that the only thing that I asked was equanimity and discipline, and that there would not be demonstrations or acts of hostility, because that is dynamite for the state of spirit of the people. If I do not specifically appeal to the people to maintain calm, they will speak of us of in other countries, and they will speak of the comportment of the people.

MR. NICOLÁS BRAVO: Through what process will the promotion to the position occur?

DR. FIDEL CASTRO RUZ: The Council of Ministers will decide over the promotion to the position of Prime Minister.

MR. NICOLÁS BRAVO: The Council of Ministers will decide? And if you were called again, can we have from you an indication of your good will?

DR. FIDEL CASTRO RUZ: Would it not be better to convince everyone that the best result of the crisis is that which does not guide me to the post of Prime Minister, given the decision that I had to take?

MR. EDUARDO HÉCTOR ALONSO: Do you not believe that it would be difficult to convince the people? Do you have confidence in your persuasive power?

---

the President had resigned, and asking for security protection for the President, which Raúl was able to provide. Raúl passed this information to the moderator.

DR. FIDEL CASTRO RUZ: Trust in the power and in the faith that sustains it. You have to remember that I have spirit, too. It is not only cold reason that is involved in these considerations. I have to be in a state of spirit, because I have had to take a dangerous step; dangerous no, shocking.

MR. EDUARDO HÉCTOR ALONSO: And do you not feel compensated with the attitude of the people?

DR. FIDEL CASTRO RUZ: I responded earlier, to an identical question, that I would have preferred that none of this had occurred, because it would have been much better for us if this problem had not occurred.

Now this is subject to interpretation. All the civic institutions, all the sectors of the country, were marching forward, in their finest moment. The country has been filled with glory on the international level, with the role played by its representative to the OAS,[14] and with the comportment of the people, which led to a rectification of the attitude of the Senate of the United States on the part of the Executive of that country. All these things bring glory to our country.

Everyone has reason to be tranquil, except for us; at times, we are those that have to be suffering these things, which are not known and are not going to be published.

I consider that it was very serious that neither *mi compañeros* nor anyone in the Council of Ministers were finding a solution. Then, with the arrival of Raúl Roa, and after a series of considerations, I arrived to the conclusion that there did not remain for me any other road, because it was not even known at that moment if they were able to cause a situation. All the reports and conversations revealed an advance in the plan, always in the same direction as that of Díaz Lanz; an inconceivable thing, incredible, but true. Imagine what it would have been for us to have to take measures of criminal sanctions to confront an act of that kind, and what consequences it would have.

Criminal sanctions are not advisable. We have to move forward. We cannot waste the opportunity that we have now in our country.

Rather than force, I have used political instinct, tact, and a strategy to confront a difficult problem. For any other government, it would be easy. For Batista, it was easy to solve a problem like this. He sent a tank to resolve the problem. But for us it is not so easy. It is especially not easy when we are taking our first steps, and the banner of extreme anti-communist declarations is put against us. When they are accusing us with anti-communism in the United States, to do nothing would not be an adequate response.

---

14 Organization of American States.

There is a news cable in which it is said that the problem was the danger of communist infiltration, which is unacceptable, because it presents a completely false situation, by creating a division between two points of view. But here there is no more than one point of view, and it is that which is in accord with the principles of our Revolution and with the sentiments of our people.

And all the rest is to add fuel to the fire of intervention, aggression, and counterrevolution. That is one thing clear. Everyone knows it. The people are intelligent. Look at the reaction of the people.

As I was coming here in the automobile, I listened on the radio to the questions that the people were asking. They did not know what had caused the problem. The people were totally uninformed, lacking in information. However, they had faith. There were a little sad and a little uncertain, and therefore, the first thing that I said to the peasants, all the people, everyone, was that everything is assured, because the Agrarian Reform continues, everything goes ahead.

...

JOURNALIST: Would you council that they meet this same night in order to resolve the national crisis?

DR. FIDEL CASTRO RUZ: Yes, I believe that they should meet and resolve this situation. The sooner that we come out of this tension, the better. The best thing about this situation is that it makes the Revolution stronger tomorrow than yesterday.

JOURNALIST: Are you making the prediction that the Revolution will become stronger with this episode?

DR. FIDEL CASTRO RUZ: Yes, the episode has strengthened the Revolution, because problems have been removed, and more unity has been created. It has removed threats; all the Ministers were conscious of the fact that we did not know what day something was going to happen. We knew that there was complete uncertainty on the part of all the Ministers. So there is more harmony and more savings, including, in my view, the two million pesos that are spent on the budget of the Presidential Palace. The Palace ought to be an office where the President and the Ministers stay one day, if there is need. The Palace should not even have been used as a meeting of the Council of Ministers. We converted the Bureau of Investigations[15] into a park, and similarly, it would have been preferable to convert the Palace at least into a museum. We changed the name of the Columbia military camp, and we are converting it into a School

---

15   See glossary.

Center.[16] We are dismantling La Cabaña.[17] I said from the beginning, when I arrived in Havana, that I did not like the Palace at all. On that day when I arrived in front of the Palace, I said that I did not like the Palace at all, and I imagine that everyone disliked it a little, because everybody passed by that Palace in previous years when it was a hideout for criminals.[18]

...

[The program closed with the singing of the National Anthem and the anthem of the July 26 Movement by Dr. Castro and those in attendance in the studio].

---

16   It was called "Liberty" School City, a name that is maintained today.
17   See glossary. The San Carlos de la Cabaña Fortress was used by Batista as a military prison and was converted by the Revolutionary government into a military academy and later into a museum and cultural center.
18   The Presidential Palace was abandoned as the seat of the Revolutionary government; the Palace later became the Museum of the Revolution.

In Cuba, There Is a Democracy Where the People Discuss Their Problems Directly

Distinguished revolutionary leaders of Latin America that do us the honor of visiting us;[1]

Heroic peasants of Cuba;

All compatriots:

On this day, so full of memories for all of us, it is difficult to not feel overwhelmed by the most profound of emotions....

In speaking at this moment, the first question, the first idea that comes to mind is to ask myself why such a large weight of gratitude weighs over me, a citizen equal to all of you, for the excessively generous demonstration of affection and devotion that you have given....

I was asking myself as well why that demonstration of extraordinary jubilation when it was announced that I was complying with the will of the people, when it was demanded of me to return to the post of Prime Minister. It cannot be because of the modest work that I have carried out up to now. The only logical explanations for that jubilee is that the people know very well that I am not interested in holding office, and the people know very well that I am not prepared to sacrifice an inch of the interests of the nation, that I am not prepared to sacrifice an inch of my sense of the duty and unselfishness that always have driven me in this struggle, not for the post of Prime Minister nor for all the offices of Prime Minister in the world combined.

...

To those that in the name of democracy slander us, hypocritically invoking the word, we are able to say: Democracy is this! Democracy is complying with the will of the people. Democracy is, as Lincoln said, government of the people, by the people, and for the people.

...

No government for the landholders, as there had been before today, nor government of the large interests, as there had been before today, but government of the people, by the people, and for the peasants, above all. For the peasants above all, because no one can deny that the peasants constituted that part of

---

[1] Selections from the speech delivered at the peasant mass meeting held on July 26, 1959, in which Fidel accepts the popular demand to return to the post of Prime Minister. Stenographic version of the Office of the Prime Minister.

our people most forgotten and suffering. Government of the people, by the people, and for the humble above all, because the humble constituted the great majority of our people and the part most forgotten and suffering of our people.

And for those that do not understand and do not want to understand, that is the secret of the tremendous force of the Cuban Revolution. That force does not come from having overthrown the bloody dictatorship that was oppressing us, because the dictatorship could be overthrown and the conditions that made that dictatorship possible could be maintained in the country. The dictatorship could be overthrown in order to continue with politics as usual.

...

But it was not so. The dictatorship was overthrown in order to make a revolution. The dictatorship was overthrown not only to free the people from crime, murder, torture, and oppression, but also to free the people from poverty, as criminal and as cruel as the overthrown dictatorship.

...

That is, for our detractors and in the eyes of our enemies, the crime that we have committed: to turn our eyes toward the always forgotten, to turn our eyes to those who needed us, to turn our eyes to those that really needed here a revolution that would free them from so much evil and so much suffering.

And how have we done it? The Revolution did not take power through a *coup d'état*, because the *coups d'état* nearly never, or never, turn out to be revolutions. We did not take power by means of fraud or political maneuvering. We have deprived absolutely no one of the right to express opinions, the right to write freely, and the right to express oneself freely....

It the people were not with our Revolution, if the people had wanted to go in a different direction, we would not again be Prime Minister of the Revolutionary Government. The decision remained in the hands of the people. The people could have said that I not return, as it was able to say and did say that I return. So I have not complied with the will of one man or a group of men; I have complied with the will of the people.

Let our enemies say and write what they want; let the enemy interests of our Revolution say and write what they want. The most important thing that matters to us is what our people think, and what our people think will be what the brother peoples of America will think, when beyond all the paid campaigns, the step to the truth is opened.

...

So we return again to the work that we have been doing for some months; we return again to our task of bringing forward the revolutionary laws; we return to our struggle without rest to make the aspirations of our people a reality....

That faith permitted us to have the security to say that if they continue with the campaigns against the revolutionary justice, we were going to unite a million Cubans in front of the Presidential Palace, and a million Cubans gathered in front of the Presidential Palace.

That faith enabled us to say that, if they continued the campaigns against the agrarian reform, saying that the peasants did not want it, we were going to unite a half million peasants with their machetes in the capital of the Republic.

...

When we act in such manner, we know that were are making use of another sacred right of the peoples, which is the right to sovereignty. We know that we are exercising that right to our sovereignty, and that no one has to the right to interfere in the sovereignty of a people, that no one has the right to oversee the acts that a people with an overwhelming majority is carrying out....

We Cubans proclaim that we are not enemies of any people, that we are not the enemies of the citizens of any country, provided that they respect the laws of our country, provided they respect the sentiments of our country, provided that they want to be our friends. If they extend their hand to us, we extend our hand; if they open their arms, we open our arms.

...

I am sure that if—like the illustrious visitors of other countries here today—the citizens of any other country of the world, those in which they have tried to inculcate all types of prejudices and lies against our revolution, would have been able to be present this week in the capital of the Republic, they would be here seeing what is our Revolution, which breaks all records in human generosity, human fraternization, and breaks all records of unity and integration....

We, unfortunately, are not able to arrange for the divulgence of our truths through the media of communication that inform the world. We are not even able to count on the impartiality of those media of information. We are not the owners of those agencies that are in charge of spreading unimaginable slanders against Cuba.... We are not able even to count with the impartiality of these organs; we must be victims of all those slanders.

...

How wrong are those that believe that they can return here to seek to reestablish their privileges, their businesses, their buildings, they plantations, and their bank accounts. The criminals that so cowardly fled on January 1 now are serving as instruments of the enemies of our country, now are in conspiracy with the worst enemies of Cuba, with the presumed intention of returning to our country. They are wrong; they will never again have those businesses.

...

The agrarian reform continues! The agrarian reform continues! And it not only continues, but it is even better. Because now we have 20 million pesos more in the budget, 20 million that we have recuperated from the bank accounts of the embezzlers, 20 million pesos that they left in flight, 20 million that blood suckers extracted from the economy of our people, and from the resources of our people. And the agrarian reform today has received from this mass meeting 20 million pesos more for the peasants.

...

They also are far from being right if they believe that assassinating leaders is going to assassinate the Revolution. I only want to say to the people that they also are brutes when they believe that by assassinating leaders of the Revolution, they are going to destroy the Revolution. Because our country has a reserve of men, and our country has a reserve of leaders!

...

No man is or will be indispensable. The only thing indispensable here—I say it because I feel it—is the people. If the Revolution did not have the people, it would be lost. The people is what is important, and the people is what the Revolution has! In addition, it is consoling to think, it is consoling to think that they can kill a man, but they cannot kill a people, just as a man can be a traitor, but a people cannot be traitor.

...

Today we are meeting in the capital; today we are gathering here in the capital. The slogan for this 26 of July was a half million peasants to the capital. The slogan for next year's July 26 will be a half million citizens to the Sierra Maestra, half millions citizens to share with the peasants.

...

In thinking about this moment of exceptional emotion, arising from the awakening of freedom, the awakening of faith and hope... never have we felt so proud of our flag, our flag of the single star, as when we saw it today flying in the wind, bathed by the rays of the sun at dusk. We felt that infinite jubilation, that was the dream of so many men that struggled without seeing it fulfilled: the jubilation of feeling in this generation all the emotion and all the dreams of several generations. On seeing it fly, on seeing it so spotless, and on seeing it so beautiful, and on seeing it so honored, the symbol of the country and all that is related to that sentiment that causes men to die when the hour of dying to defend it arrives; on seeing it today, on seeing the high seat of honor in which we have placed our flag, I felt so happy that I saw in that moment the reward for all the sacrifices that we have made and all the sacrifices that we will have to make in the future.

The Entire Nation Stands without Fear

Workers;[1]
Peasants;
Students;
All Cubans:

You and we have much to speak. In this great mass meeting of today, there are important questions to treat. It is not only, or it ought not to be only, a moment of enthusiasm; it ought to be, above all, a moment of reflection, because the peoples have to look for the causes of their problems.

It is not enough to know what; it is necessary that the people know why. We are satisfied with the support of the people; we are satisfied with their extraordinary enthusiasm. But above all, we desire that the people reflect; we desire that the people think; because the people ought to have an explanation of the problems that arise. The people ought to know the reasons behind things.

I do not come to declare; I come to reason with the people. I do not come to make a speech; I come to converse with the people.... Because if the battle arises, there will be battles! If they attack us, they will find us all as a single army! ["*Sí!*"]

...

But it is important to know the reasons behind things. Why do they attack us? Why do we have to meet here again? Why are there traitors? Why do they want the Revolution to fail? What is the Revolution accused of? Why do they make certain accusations? What ends are they pursuing? How ought the people confront those maneuvers and those intentions? How is victory attained? What measures have been taken? What measures are going to be taken? What measures are we disposed to take in order to defend the Revolution?

Before proceeding, I want to read first some news: "UPI, *3:38 p.m.—Officials of the customs services in Miami are investigating the news that six or seven airplanes are in flight, from the region of Miami toward Havana, in order to drop counterrevolutionary flyers over the mass meeting in support of Castro....*"

...

---

1 Selections from the speech delivered before the people congregated at the Presidential Palace to reaffirm their support for the Revolutionary Government and as protest against the cowardly aggression perpetuated against the peaceful people of Habana by airplanes proceeding from foreign territory, October 26, 1959. Stenographic versions of the Office of the Prime Minister.

At the same time, already here on the platform, we received the following communication proceeding from the Headquarters of the Regiment of the Rebel Army in the province of Pinar del Río. It informs that *"a small aircraft has flown by the city, dropping some home-made explosives and also a firebomb in the Niagara sugarcane factory, and it burned a house between the post office and the living quarters. It was at 6:30 p.m.; and also they dropped propaganda leaflets."*

...

That is to say that the Miami authorities themselves admit that six or seven planes left from that region toward Cuba, and that they do not yet know the outcome of the flights.

...

But, why do they attack us? Why do the criminals have such audacity? Why do the North American authorities have such tolerance? Why? Already we explained it on one occasion, in a moment like this, when all the people assembled to defend the country against the campaign of slanders.

First, there were the campaigns of slander, and we saw the need to assemble all the people in order to deny those campaigns of slander. And on that occasion, I said that they were preparing the terrain for a later assault against us; and that those campaigns were due to the intention of preparing the road for other later actions.

...

And I ask myself, what would occur, what would the people of the United States say if small aircraft, or planes, proceeding from Canada or any other nearby country, devoted themselves to dropping firebombs and shrapnel on North American factories and houses?

...

Another question that we have to address is: Why do they carry out the bombings? What ends to they seek? Are they thinking that they are going to throw the people into terror? But why submerge the people in terror? One must ask, what objectives are they pursuing, and with what end do they seek to submerge the people in terror?

It cannot be any other purpose than that of intimidating the people. That is to say, they are threatening the Cuban people, on the one hand, with economic strangulation, removing the sugar quota; and on the other hand, they are submitting the people to terror; in order that, harassed on the one side by economic problems and on the other side by terror, the Cuban people will renounce its magnificent revolutionary process, renounce its aspiration to plant justice in our soil.

...

What has the Revolutionary Government done? The only thing of which they can accuse the Revolutionary Government is having made revolutionary laws; the only thing of which they can accuse the Revolutionary Government is having taken revolutionary measures.

...

We are going to discuss publicly, we are going to respond once again to the slander and the detractors of the Revolution, in order that they speak honestly again, in order that they be unmasked, in order that they admit that the accusation that they make against us, that we are communists, is made exclusively by those who do not have the courage to say that they are against the revolutionary laws. And so, inasmuch as they have nothing to say of the Revolutionary Government, inasmuch as they have nothing of which to accuse the Revolutionary Government, they turn to the provoking of fear and to hackneyed pretext of the specter [of communism] that they have been seeing for fifty years.

...

But it is that one thing occurs; it is that one thing occurs: if we plant rice, we prejudice foreign interests;

if we produce fat, we prejudice foreign interests;

if we produce cotton, we prejudice foreign interest;

if we reduce the electricity rates, we prejudice foreign interests;

if we reduce telephone rates, we prejudice foreign interests;

if we enact an agrarian reform, we prejudice foreign interests;

if we enact a law over petroleum, as soon is to be decreed, we prejudice foreign interests

if we enact a law on mining, as soon is to be decreed, we prejudice foreign interests;

if we establish a merchant marine, we prejudice foreign interests;

if we want to find new markets for our county, we prejudice foreign interests;

if we want that there is bought from us at least as much as we buy, we prejudice foreign interests.

That is the explanation. We have made revolutionary laws that prejudice national and foreign privileges, and it is for this that they attack us, it is for this that they call us communists, it is for this that they accuse us, preparing all possible pretexts for an assault against our country.

...

To speak clearly, I say that not only those that drop bombs are to blame, but also those who instigate them from here....

The attack is against the Revolution, the attack is against the revolutionary measures. Those are the causes, and that is the reason for the accusations against us.

But inasmuch as the Revolution is not something of mine, but is of the people, and we here do not do anything but interpret the sentiments of the people, the need of defending the Revolution is explained; the duty of defending the Revolution is explained, and it is the people that have the word!

And here, before all our compatriots in assembly, I am going to express and I am going to consult the people concerning the reestablishment of the revolutionary tribunals. I want that each citizen express his desire, I want that each citizen decide concerning this question, and that those that in agreement that the revolutionary tribunals be reestablished, raise your hand. (THE MULTITUDE, WITH HANDS HIGH, EXCLAIM: "To the wall!"[2]).

Since it is necessary, since it is necessary to defend the country from aggression, since it is necessary to defend the country in the face of air attacks from foreign lands, since it is necessary to defend the country from treason, tomorrow the Council of Ministers will meet to discuss and to decree the law that would reestablish again, for the time that is necessary, the revolutionary tribunals....

From today, we proclaim that we do not fear anything or anyone, that we do not fear the measures that are plotted against us, nor do we fear taking the measure that we have to take to combat those that want to destroy us! ...

Today the whole nation, standing, fears no obstacle. The entire revolutionary nation, standing, fears nothing or no one.

...

If we cannot buy airplanes, we will fight them on land, when the hour for fighting on land arrives.

If they continue with the launching of bombs, we will the construct underground shelters and tunnels that are necessary. That the people be ready for war; that the peasants and workers begin training immediately, also the students; that the war tribunals, the revolutionary tribunals remain constituted; that the pilots downed here know that the firing squad inevitably waits for them; that we will defend the country fighting in all the terrains that are necessary; and that if they do not sell us planes in England, we will buy them where they sell them to us; and that is there is not money for combat planes, the people will buy the combat planes. And right here, right here, *compañero*

---

2 Meaning, "put them up against the wall and shoot them."—Translator's note.

Almeida,[3] I deliver to you the check of the President of the Republic and the Prime Minister, as a contribution toward the purchase of planes... ("Fidel! Fidel!")

(FIDEL READS A NOTE THAT IS BROUGHT TO HIM): "Fidel, they launched a grenade in the newspaper 'Revolution'; there are wounded; news from Franqui" [Director of the newspaper] (To the wall! To the wall!).

And we take an oath of the people, of you and we, that either Cuba triumphs or we all will die! More than ever, we make ours the words of our National Anthem, "Run to the combat, Cubans, so that the country sees you with pride; do not fear a glorious death; to die for the country is to live!"

---

3   See glossary.

The Working Class and the Cuban Revolution

Delegates:[1]

I was invited tonight to the closing ceremony of the workers' congress. When the hour approached in which we had to attend this closing ceremony, news somewhat disheartening arrived to us, that the program of activities had fallen behind, and that an atmosphere of tension reigned in the Congress. "That is bad," said all the *compañeros* that had spoken to me. They told me that I ought to not come to the Congress; they told me that I was not able to come to the Congress in the conditions in which it was found, that I was not able to be running risks.

...

You, in a gesture of solidarity, have stood and applauded when I spoke of risks. It is possible that no one is referring to risks of a physical kind. Moreover, one must not think about those risks, since, all things considered, no Cuban ought to be worrying about those risks at this hour.

They were referring to risks of a moral type; they were referring to risks of an assembly thrown into confusion; they were referring to a real risk: the risk of a disgraceful spectacle that you are producing here tonight.

I have not come here, *compañeros*, to make demagoguery. I believe that it would be unworthy of the greater or lesser confidence that the people of Cuban can have in us, if I were a man capable of coming here or anywhere to make demagoguery.

...

It is said that there are groups against groups—I am not going to analyze the dimensions of the groups—, and that there were shouts, that on occasions there were even insults, that irresponsible voices—that cannot be revolutionary voices and can only be echo of counterrevolutionary voices, proceeding perhaps from the chorus of criminals of war and of the gangs that escaped in flight their crimes against Cuba,—shouts even against the ministers of the Revolutionary Government, and there was not lacking even the insinuation that shouts had been made against the Prime Minister.

Of course, there is only one attitude that I could have. *Compañeros*, I say to you: hierarchies are not important to me, government posts are not important

---

1 Selections from a speech delivered at the closing ceremony of the Tenth Congress of the Confederation of Cuban Workers (CTC for its initials in Spanish), held in the CTC theater, November 21, 1959. Stenographic version from the Office of the Prime Minister.

to me, my personal situation is not important to me. The only thing important to me is the Revolution! Any personal reverse does not matter. Why would my person be important, if I cannot even be useful to help the Revolution?

...

It was difficult to accept the idea that there would be a difficult situation in attending a congress of workers, for whom has been done all that we have done. All things considered, it is not a question of a meeting of landholders, it is not a question of a meeting of the association of large cattle ranchers. It is a question of a meeting of workers, of workers, yes! Why will we not be able to discuss with the workers? In what circumstance will be not be able to speak with the workers?

...

It is necessary to remember those sad days without hope in which, for the second time, a tyrant planted his claws in the soil of our country, which he maintained in his hands unbeaten for eleven years. And the workers, what were they able to do? Is it that perhaps an organized working class in impotent? What were the workers able to do?

You will remember well those "leaders," that were leaders of the party of government; you will remember well those leaders, that we call governmental leaders; and you will remember well, each one of you, what the immense majority of those leaders had done within twenty-four hours of the criminal *coup d'état*. They had passed shamefully, with weapons and knowledge, with unions and federations, to the ranks of the oppressor! If I am lying, if I am saying something that is not consistent with the truth, if this information is historically false, I want you to say so ("No!").

That is to say, the working class was betrayed miserably; it is to say, the working class was not able to develop a resistance to the reactionary *coup d'état*.

And not only that, but that group, representatives of those in command, were strengthened, in shameful and indecent conspiracy with the tyranny, and it kept the working class crushed for seven years.

...

It is necessary, then, that we remember those day in which there did not even exist the date of July 26.... It is necessary that we remember that date, because that date cannot be remembered except with a deep devotion and respect for the men that died that day.

...

If there was a majority bound also to that name [of July 26], how can it be explained, what sense is there in the fear for the presence of the Prime Minister in the workers' congress, where the connections to that name formed the majority? Why such fear? Why such fear? ... Could it possibly be that in the name of the 26 of July there could be a blow to the prestige of the founder of that movement and the Prime Minister of the Revolutionary Government?

...

If we have not changed, if we are exactly the same, if we are the same of the 26 of July and the second of December, of the Moncada attack and the "Granma" disembarking, of the Sierra Maestra and of the revolutionary laws, if we have not changed, we have the right to speak in the name of the 26 of July!

...

Therefore, therefore I came. And if coming here could be damaging to the Revolution, it would be because the Revolution would be in a very bad situation, this people would be in a very bad situation, and this working class would be in a very bad situation. Simply put, one would have to arrive to the conclusion that we are not capable, nor do we have sufficient drive, nor do we have sufficient spirit—the people of Cuba—to make this Revolution.

...

The mere fact, *compañeros*, that the principal leaders of the workers have had concern about the presence of the Prime Minister in the heart of the congress is itself nearly a reason for shame. Because the day that the Prime Minister of the Revolutionary Government, in the middle of a revolutionary stage, in the difficult moments of the Revolution, when its enemies are increasingly more daring, when the maneuvers against the Revolution are increasingly more intense ... that he has to run moral risks to attend a Congress, it is because the hour has arrived to be thinking that the moment needs a Eusebio Mujal.[2] How paradoxical it seems, how paradoxical it seems! But there is scarcely distance between the historic stages of maximum action and maximum reaction, and you will have heard it said many times that the extremes touch. So that it could occur that when the Revolution approaches the moment of extreme revolutionary force, the moment of extreme counterrevolutionary force also is approaching.

...

It is necessary to know, and to remember, and to recognize—those that had not had time to think about it—that a revolution is a very serious and momentous process in the life of the peoples, and that one does not play with a revolutionary process; that great errors cannot be committed in a revolutionary process; that one cannot bat an eye in a revolutionary process, because those that blink lose.

...

---

2 See glossary.

I believe that you are the same delegates to whom I spoke with three days ago, I believe that you are the same persons, I believe that you cannot be different from three days ago.... However, what strange thing has occurred?

...

What a strange thing—if you were the same as that solemn night—what a strange thing has happened that, on entering here today, it seemed like something of a madhouse? There was even a moment in which I believed that I was not going to be able to continue speaking, because I heard shouts from here and shouts from there, and I had the impression that you were playing with the revolution in your hands.

...

I cannot feel but true sadness when I see that the working class is nullifying its capacity to defend itself and to defend the Revolution.

Because this that I see here tonight, the spectacle of this night here, is not the image of a working class to which rifles can be delivered; because if the rifles were given to those on one side, those that shout on the other side would be at their mercy; and if those on the other side received the rifles, those of the opposite side would be at their mercy. And if the rifles were delivered to the two that shout, they would kill each other.

...

In view of the future scenario of a war of that kind, considering that reality, it would be appropriate here to say the same: it is preferable that it be taken to another, rather than taking it whole to the working class, thereby dividing the working class into pieces.[3]

...

That is to say, here there are no mysteries; here there are no mysteries of any kind. There is great clarity in our position on this point. We said that we understood what was advisable to the workers; we said that the situation that was presented to the Revolution would require virtually organizing the workers as an army. I said, in addition, that the fact that the workers were organizing and preparing themselves inspired terror in the reaction. I said it clearly, because I said something that cannot be doubted: the working class wants to constitute itself as an army in order to defend the Revolution.

...

I spoke very clearly. I said that all had to be unified, that differences had to be resolved harmoniously; that it had to be a model congress, that it had to be

---

3   Fidel makes reference to the Bible. When Solomon faces the decision of delivering a child to two mothers that claim him, he decides that the creature be cut in half, in order that each one receive part. So the true mother renounces the claim in order to save her son.

a model congress! I spoke clearly. Someone tell me if my expressing of these things is incorrect ("No"!).

...

Tell me if I spoke of harmony, of harmonic solution to the differences, saying that if the enemy is uniting—because one has to be blind to not see that the enemy is uniting—we have to unite.

As a tactical and strategic sense of the revolution, in a moment is which the areas of action are defined, in which we are confronting a reactionary enemy that is unifying, the enemies of the working class, the enemies of the peasants, the enemies of the people; is it not correct to express that we ought to unify?

Is it that we are not united here? Is it that, when you came to the Congress, there had not been unity, and you had not been integrated into an organization? That is to say, here there is a unification of workers. Why? In order to approve measures that are good. And if a measure is good for the workers, do all approve it? It is assumed that all consent when a measure is good.

...

What is important is that there are truly revolutionary leaders; what is important is that there are not leaders who in difficult moments do like those leaders of that other CTC, who, in twenty-four hours, joined the ranks of the enemy.

...

Later, you can form a leadership of a group; that is not important. But that they be true revolutionaries!

...

That is the central question, that is the fundamental question. And I believed that it was worth coming here in order to say simply that we have to shake, we have to shake....

Some spoke of melons.[4] I remember one thing, *compañeros*, I remember that I saw that same word in the newspaper of Masferrer, and it had all the flavor of the followers of Masferrer and Mujal and the members of *La Rosa Blanca*,[5] *compañeros*, the unmistakable symptom of those winds, those little winds that still are floating here in this dense atmosphere, *compañeros*.

I said that one must not only shake the tree, but even kill the roots. In referring to such a shake-up, you can be assured, *compañeros*, that the Revolutionary

---

4 The melon fruit is green on the outside and red on the inside. Thus the word was used by the enemies of the revolution, alleging that the members of the July 26 Movement of Fidel wore green uniforms, but they were secretly red, that is, they expressed support for the positions pronounced by the Movement, but in reality they were communists.—Translator's note.

5 See Masferrer, Mujal, and Rosa Blanca in the glossary.

Government, even in a situation of minorities, would not be opposed if you said to us tomorrow that, by majority, a group of exceptional people, some very exceptional, had attained the removal an executive of a counterrevolutionary CTC.

Because, everything considered, we are in a struggle against a counterrevolution, and against the counterrevolution we are going to struggle, whether those of the counterrevolution be many or few, and whether we be many or few, *compañeros*. In addition, *compañeros*, we know what it is to struggle when we are few, because those times in which we were few are still fresh. But they were good times!

So it is good to declare these concepts, in order that there does not come by here some blackmailer that intends to make the Revolution tremble and to make the Revolution vacillate. But he will do neither, because beyond are the masses. And we will say to them these words and all the words that are necessary. Insofar as it is necessary to go to each and every one of the factories and unions of Cuba with the truth in hand, we will go, *compañeros*....

One must be conscious of the political role of class, and that it does not occur that the working class end up as it has in the past. And here it would be appropriate to say: Remember the Tenth of March![6] Remember the Tenth of March! Remember the Ninth of April![7] It is necessary to remember, in order that success does not go to our head, and to have consciousness of how weak we were and how powerless we were in order to do something for the country!

...

I say to you honestly, in accordance with the tasks that we all have, in accordance with our duties, that a working class in such conditions as we saw it this night, in a kind of rage and insanity that was breathing in this congress, is a powerless class, a class that cannot be provided with arms, a class that cannot collaborate with the Revolution.

...

And I am very aware of how happy and festive would be the houses of the reactionaries, if they were able to annul the working class, that is to say, if they attained so much as to even weaken it, if they obligated the Revolution to struggle union by union to reconquer revolutionary leadership. Because even though the working class could be betrayed, it could not be definitively annulled.

...

---

6   Refers to the March 10, 1952 Batista *coup d'état*.
7   Refers to the general strike convoked by the July 26 Movement on April 9, 1958, which failed.

So we are speaking with complete awareness of the realities. And among the realities is that in these hours the reaction can present the workers' congress as a dagger thrust into the heart of the Cuban Revolution ("Never!").

To conclude, then, there is something tow which we ought to be in agreement, and I believe that we are nearly all in agreement, and it is that one must sweep away from the breast of the working class the last vestiges of mujalism. One must shake it from its roots!

The problem is not the problem as the reaction wanted to present it. Rather, the issue is that one must choose a leadership, if necessary go and look among the most unknown men, but that they be true revolutionaries!

...

That is to say, if you want that the Revolution, the Revolutionary Government has confidence in the organization of workers, the sweeping has to be complete.

Yes, I believe that we are all completely in agreement ("Agreed"). Is it not toward there that we ought to direct our effort? ("*Sí*"). So why distract it in accordance with the interests of the enemies of the Revolution, and not in sweeping? A broom is what we need to brandish here. We all choose a broom. Let the broom be the symbol of this congress, in order to clean up the mess!

Will some have to sacrifice positions or plans? Well, let them sacrifice them! Who here has said to anyone that he values something more than the Republic?

...

I believe that that *compañero*—he that you designate—ought to act with practical sense, the spirit of forming groups, to listen, that is to say, you have to choose those *compañeros* that are satisfied with the things expressed here.

...

I believe that the responsibility of the person that you select here, be it the *compañero* David Salvador or whoever it be, is considerably large.

...

What I propose is the policy of total eradication, as an agreement of the Congress, of the last vestiges of mujalism and of immorality in the working class; as an agreement that it is the mandate of this assembly and will be the task of the executive that is nominated. The fulfillment of the mandate of shaking to the roots is an order of the Congress to the executive that, by nomination of a *compañero*, is indicated.

...

Those that are in agreement that it be *compañero* David Salvador (THEY RAISE THEIR HANDS).

I would like that it be verified if the agreement is unanimous or is by majority.

Compañeros: There is a proposal for a vote of confidence in David Salvador. One moment, *compañeros*. All be seated.

Those that are in agreement with the vote of confidence raise your hand, lifting the blue card (THE COMPAÑEROS LIFT THEIR HANDS).

Those that are against the vote of confidence (NO ONE LIFTS THEIR HANDS).

It is unanimous, *compañeros*, the vote of confidence! (APPLAUSE)

...

Be certain that the mandate must be fulfilled. The mandate of the congress is what is important here. The policy accepted, the line adopted by the congress, is the total eradication. A scalpel in hand, a scalpel! And that is a mandate, that is a mandate for which *compañero* David Salvador has a very great responsibility before the working class and before the Revolution.

...

And remember this, remember that which history teaches us: that these revolutionary processes do not have a happy medium, that either they triumph fully or they are defeated. History teaches us that it goes from extreme revolution to extreme reaction.

And of course, be assured that we will not be counted among the defeated. They will be able to number us among the dead, but never among the defeated!

With this, *compañeros*, I believe to have fulfilled the duty that I imposed on myself. I thank you all for the attention and the respect with which you have received me.

I make this recognition, because I came here, and the prestige of the Revolution was not damaged, nor was their damage to the moral prestige of the Prime Minister. Once more—in front of pessimists, even pessimist *compañeros*—I have had the opportunity to demonstrate that faith in the peoples, above all faith in the humble men of the people, never is betrayed.

Thank you very much.

We Have Kept Our Promises to the People

...

And finally, let us conclude with this problem of the ideological aspect.[1] I believe that we in the Revolutionary Government, simply put, have not done anything other than to comply with what we promised to the people.

"*Say where we are going.*" The Revolution said where it was going, long before we arrived to the beach of Belice.[2]

I believe that I do not need more than fifteen minutes, at the most twenty, to finish: Our conduct, our stance, our approach as we have acted; if we have been some deceitful liars to the people, or if we have been men that always said the truth. On this matter, I only want to explain in this trial the political aspect of our Revolution, our line.

Here is the first that I wrote after March 10; we were beginning to say what we thought three days after March 10.

Revolution no: theft.... Patriots no: tyrants, usurpers, reactionaries, adventurers thirsty for hate and power. It was not a putsch against President Prío; it was a putsch against the people. Although there was not stability, the people were responsible for deciding in a civilized form, to choose who would govern, by will and not by force. No one denies that the money would run in favor of a candidate imposed, but that would not alter the result, any more than it did in 1944, when the funds of the Public Treasury were wasted in support of the candidate imposed by Batista. It would be completely false, absurd, ridiculous, and infantile for Prío to attempt a coup d'état. Chaos was being suffered, but it has been suffered for many years, waiting for the constitutional opportunity to justify wrongs. And you, Batista, who fled cowardly for four years and did useless political maneuvering another three, appear now with your belated, disruptive, and poisonous remedy, tearing to shreds the Constitution, when only two months remained to arrive at the objective through legitimate means. All alleged by you is a lie and cynical justification; it is vanity rather than patriotic decorum, ambition rather that ideals, and appetite rather than citizen nobility.

Again the boots, again Columbia [military headquarters] dictating laws, again the tanks roaring menacingly in our streets, again brute force prevailing

---

1 Selection from the testimony of the Prime Minister of the Revolutionary Government Fidel Castro, in the trial against the ex-*comandante* Huber Matos [see glossary], in Liberty City, December 14, 1959. Taken from: *And the light was made*, Federation of Cuban Workers (CTC), Liberty City, December 14, 1959 [in Spanish].
2 The place where 82 men disembarked from the *Granma* on December 2, 1956, to initiate the revolutionary war, located in the region of Manzanilla in the former province of Oriente.

over human reason. We were accustomed to living within the Constitution; we went twelve years without great setbacks, in spite of errors and ramblings. Better conditions of civic living are only attained through long effort. You, Batista, have just demolished in a few hours that noble ambition of the people of Cuba.

As much bad as Prío did in three years, you were doing before. Your coup, then, is unjustifiable. It is not based on any serious moral reasoning, nor in social doctrine, nor on policy of any kind. Its only reason for being is force; its only justification, the lie. Your majority is in the Army, never in the people; your votes come from rifles, never consciousness, with which you can win a military coup, but never a fair election.

Your assault to power lacks principles. Laugh if you want, but power is legitimated through principles. Principles are more powerful than cannons in the long run, because principles form and nourish the peoples. With principles, the people are nurtured in the task; for principles, they die.

Do not call a revolution that outrage, that disruptive and inopportune coup, that dagger that just has been thrust in the back of the Republic! Trujillo has been the first to recognize your government; he knows who his friends are in the clique of tyrants that flog America. That says better than anything the reactionary, militarist, and criminal character of your theft.

No one even remotely believes in the governmental success of your old and corrupt clique, in which there is too much thirst for power, and the constraints on power are very limited, when there is no longer neither Constitution nor law, but only the will of the tyrant and his henchmen. I know beforehand that your guarantee for life will be torture and castor oil.[3] Your henchmen will kill, and you will consent with tranquility even when you do want to, because all must be paid to them! The despots are masters of the people they oppress, and slaves of the forces through which they sustain the oppression!

In your favor now will rain lying and demagogic propaganda, proclaiming the good and the bad, and over your opponents will rain vile slander; as others did, and it was worth nothing in the minds of the people. But the truth that illuminates the destiny of Cuba and guides the steps of our people in this difficult hour, that truth that you will not permit to be said, everyone will know. It will run from mouth to mouth in each man or woman, although no one would say it publicly nor write it in the press; and all will believe it, and the seeds of heroic rebellion will be sown in every heart! It is the compass that there is in each conscience!

I do not know what is the insane pleasure of the oppressors in putting the cruel whip on the human back. There is tyranny again, but there will be again Mella,

---

3 Refers to a torturing technique of injecting castor oil in large doses.

Trejos, and Guiteras.[4] *There is oppression in the country, but some day there will again be freedom! I invite Cubans of courage: it is the hour of sacrifice and struggle. If your life is lost, nothing is lost! 'To live in chains is to live submerged in dishonor and insult; to die for the country is to live!'*[5]

Such we began our struggle, three days after the tenth of March of 1952, calling the people. The rest is lengthy. There are many documents, but since already it has been spoken of what is defined, to where we are going, and how we are going, and this was defined much time ago, I ought to cite some things from "Manifesto number one of the July 26 [Movement] to the people of Cuba"[6]— some paragraphs only, concerning economic and social problems.

To those that accuse the Revolution of disrupting the economy of the country, we respond: for the peasant without land, the economy does not exist; for the millions of Cubans without work, the economy does not exist; for the railroad workers, dockworkers, sugar workers, henequen[7] *workers, textile workers, bus drivers, and so many other sectors for which Batista has reduced salaries mercilessly, the economy does not exist. It will only exist for all of them through an avenging revolution that will distribute the land, will mobilize the immense wealth of the country, and will liberate the social conditions, putting privilege and exploitation to an end.*

Is there any possibility that such a miracle could be expected of the candidates to be Representatives in the partial elections that are announced? Or is it a question perhaps of an economy for the Senators that earn 5,000 pesos per month, for the millionaire generals, for the foreign trusts that exploit the public services, for the large landholders, for the tribe of parasites that prosper and enrich themselves at the cost of the state and the people? Welcome, then, to the Revolution that disrupts the economy for the few who enjoy from it abundant bread! In the end, man does not live by bread alone.

And another question for those that speak of the economy? Is not Batista committing the credit of a country for thirty years, is the public debt not surpassing 800 million pesos, is their not a deficit of more than 100 million, is he not pawning the currency reserves of the nation to the foreign banks, looking for money like a desperate person? Can one play in such manner with the destiny of a country? Did someone authorize him to undertake these crazy credit adventures; did he consult the people in some way? Finally, how many millions do persons very linked

---

4   See Mella, Trejos, and Guiteras in the glossary.
5   In the final two lines, Fidel quotes from the Cuban national anthem, which was adopted as the national hymn on November 5, 1900 by the Cuban Constitutional Assembly. The manifesto of March 13 was published in *El Acusador* on August 16, 1952.
6   Emitted in the name of the Revolutionary Movement of July 26 on August 8, 1955.
7   Henequen fiber is used to make sacks.

to Batista transfer periodically to North American banks? More than ever, we have to be concerned, because we and the coming generations will have to pay the terrible consequences of that corrupt and unrestrained policy.

We are paying more: the persecution against our country is increasingly greater, the campaigns, even to deprive us of tourism, the campaigns are made daily. Right here: *Canadian Pacific will join the tourist boycott against Cuba:*

NEW YORK.—*The Canadian Pacific Steamship announced that it is studying the suspension of its stopovers in Havana of its travel tours, in view of the unfavorable reaction of the passengers to the political events of that Republic. L.S. Thompson, tour manager, said that the company previously intended to send its ships of 25,000 tons, 'Express of the Plane,' and 'Express of Kingland,' to Havana during the tourist season. Eight tourist companies—'Home Line,' 'North German,' 'Lloyd,' 'Holland American,' 'Hamburgo American,' 'Clipper Line,' 'Cunard Tourist American,' and 'Grace Line'—have eliminated Havana from their itineraries.*

They have eliminated Havana from their itineraries; when Havana is the city most calm, when there do not appear cadavers of assassinated youths, when there is no crime, when there are no tortures, when a people is living for the first time in a pageant of true peace, of respect, and of hope; so a tourist boycott against Cuba, which they did not do against the bloody tyranny, because the bloody tyranny defended those big interests.

And so in the review *Bohemia*, in an article entitled, 'Confronting all,'[8] because here there no longer remains any other remedy than to say 'Confronting all,' in order to be able to bring the Revolution forward, I wrote:

> *Without a cent I left from Cuba, determined to realize what others had not achieved with millions of pesos. I turned to the people, I visited the Cuban emigration, I launched a manifesto to the country soliciting aid, and I placed myself to begging for the country, raising cent by cent what was necessary to win its freedom.* This is not written now, this was written when I was in exile.

[He continues reading from the Bohemia article]. I said publicly in Palm Garden of New York: 'The Cuban people desire something more than a simple change of command. Cuba longs for a radical change in all the fields of public and social life. One must give to the people something more than liberty and democracy in abstract terms; one must provide a decent standard of living to each Cuban. The state cannot be disinterested in the fate of any of its citizens that have been born and reared in the country. There is no greater tragedy than that of a man capable of and

---

8   The article was published on January 8, 1956. On *Bohemia*, see glossary.

willing to work who goes hungry, along with his family, for the lack of employment. The state is unavoidably obliged to provide work for him, or to maintain him while he does not find it. None of the formulas that today are discussed contemplate that situation, as if the serious problem of Cuba consists in the form of satisfying the ambitions of a few politicians displaced from power or desiring to arrive to power.'

I said publicly in the Flagler theatre: 'We will unite our compatriots behind the idea of full dignity for the people of Cuba, of justice for the hungry and the forgotten, and of punishment for the powerful men that are to blame.'

And I finished that article: *In Cuba, there has been no justice. They send to jail an unfortunate who robs a chicken, while the great embezzlers enjoy impunity. It is simply an unspeakable crime. When has a judge condemned a powerful man? When was an owner of a sugarcane factory stopped for detention? When was a rural guardsmen[9] brought to prison? Could it be that they are untainted, that they are saints? Or is it that in our social regulation, justice is a great lie applied to the measure of its convenience to the established interests?*

The fear of justice is what has led the embezzlers and the tyranny to agreement. The embezzlers, stunned by the shouts of revolution that resound with growing force, like church bells that call evil men to the Last Judgement, in all the multitudinous mass meetings, have attended to the prudent words of Ichaso[10] in his Political Cavalcade of the Bohemia *of December 4, 1955: 'Fidel Castro has turned out to be a rival too dangerous for certain leaders of the opposition, who during these three and one-half years have not managed to take a suitable stance before the Cuban situation. Those chiefs know it very well. They feel already evicted by the volume that the Revolutionary Movement 26 of July is attaining in the anti-Marxist battle. The logical reaction of the politicians before this evident fact ought to be to confront the revolutionary action of* fidelismo *with a determined political action.'*

The embezzlers have listened to the cordial calling that the Batistian councilman of Havana, Pedro Alomá Keesel, has made in a governmental organ on December 14: 'Without exception, we politicians have much interest in stopping the insurrectional plans of Fidel Castro. If we are asleep at the switch and persist in closing the political roads, we will be opening to Fidel Castro the revolutionary

---

9   Prior to 1959, the Rural Guard was the military body charged with maintaining order in the rural zones.
10 See glossary.

way. I would like to see who, of the opposition and of the government, is going to save us, if fidelismo arrives to triumph in Cuba.'

They know that I left from Cuba without a cent, however, they fear that we would make the revolution; they recognize, therefore, that we can count on the people. The nation is at the moment of witnessing the great betrayal of the politicians. We know that for those who take a dignified stand, the struggle will be hard. But the number of enemies that we have in front of us does not intimidate us; we will defend our ideals before all.

Young is he who feels within himself the force of his own destiny; who knows how to think against the resistance of the opposition, and at the same time, is able to endure against the established interests. The opposition, with its political maneuvering, is in full decadence, and it is discredited. First, they demanded a neutral government and general elections; then they concentrated in asking only for general elections in 1956; now they no longer speak of any year. They will end removing the last fig leaf and accepting any arrangement with the dictator. They have not been discussing principles, only the details of raiding the budget of the unfortunate Republic.

And here we return to the economic and social problems: *The peasants, tired of speeches and promises of agrarian reform and the distribution of the land, know that they can expect nothing of the politicians.*

A million and a half Cubans are without work, because of the incompetence, lack of foresight, and greed of the bad governments. They know that they can expect nothing of the politicians.

Thousands of sick persons are without beds and medicines. They know that they can expect nothing of the politicians, who ask for a vote in exchange for a favor, and whose business lies in the fact that there always are many needs, enabling them to buy consciences at a low price.

The hundreds of families that live in huts and multiple family dwelling units; or pay exorbitant rents; in which workers earn starvation wages; whose children do not have clothes or shoes for school. The citizen who pays for the most expensive electricity of any country in the world, or who solicited a telephone ten years ago that has not yet been installed. How much they have had to suffer the horrors of a miserable existence. They know that they can expect nothing of the politicians.

The people know of the hundreds of millions stolen by the foreign trusts; and the hundreds of millions that the embezzlers have robbed; and the privileges enjoyed by thousands of parasites without providing services, nor producing anything for the society; and the leakages of all kinds through gambling, vice, clandestine commerce, etc. They know that Cuba could be one of the most prosperous and rich countries of America, without émigrés, nor unemployed, nor hungry persons, nor the sick without beds, nor illiterates, nor beggars. The people expect nothing of the political parties, organizations of godmothers and godfathers that pull strings in order to make representatives, senators, and mayors.

Of the Revolution, an organization of combatants united in a great patriotic ideal, the people expect all, and they will have it.

December 25, 1955.

And here, the points that we were indicating in this Manifesto:[11]

First: Proscription of the large estate, distribution of the land among peasant families, nonseizable and untransferable concession of the property to all existing small tenant farmers, contractors, sharecroppers, and precarious agricultural workers; government economic and technical aid; reduction of taxes. Two: Recognition of all the gains of the workers' movement, eliminated by the dictatorship. Three: Immediate industrialization of the country, by means of a vast plan outlined and implemented by the state, which ought to mobilize resolutely all the human and economic resources of the nation, in a supreme effort to free the country from the moral and material prostration in which it finds itself. It cannot be imagined the existence of hunger in a country so privileged by nature, where all the warehouses ought to be full of products, and all the hands working laboriously.

In addition: Reduction of all rents, to the true benefit of the two million, two hundred thousand persons that pay a third of their income in rent; construction by the state of decent housing in order to give shelter to the four hundred thousand families crowded together in filthy multiple family dwellings and huts; providing of electricity to two million, eight hundred thousand persons of our rural and marginal urban populations that lack it; and initiation of a policy that intends to convert each renter into a property holder of the apartment or house that he inhabits, over the base of a long term mortgage. Nationalization of public services. Construction of ten children's cities for the housing and integral education of two hundred thousand children of workers and peasants, who at present are not able to feed and clothe them. And already the Rebel Army is constructing that first city. *Expansion of culture; preliminary reform of all the teaching methods, to the last corner of the country, so that every Cuban will have the possibility of developing his mental and physical aptitudes in the environment of a decent life. General reform of the fiscal system. Reorganization of public administration. Establishment of educational and legal measures necessary for putting an end to all vestiges of racial or sex discrimination, which lamentably in exist social and economic life. Social security and government unemployment insurance. Restructuring of the Judicial Power and abolition of the Emergency Tribunals. Confiscation*

---

11   Fidel again reads from the "Manifesto No. 1 of the 26 of July Movement to the People of Cuba," emitted by the Revolutionary Movement of 26 of July on August 8, 1955.

of all the property of the embezzlers, in order that the Republic recover the hundreds of millions that have been taken with impunity, which can be invested in the realization of some of these initiatives.

That is to say, this Revolution is not doing anything but complying with the program that was promised, when many, perhaps nearly all, believed that we were no more than a few naïve dreamers.

The 26 of July confronts the 10 of March! With these words, this article began its conclusion, ending with the following words:[12]

> For the Chibacista[13] masses, the 26 of July Movement is not something distinct from the Orthodox Party; it is the Orthodox Party without a leadership of landowners, without large sugar estate owners, without financial speculators, without industrial and commercial magnates, without lawyers of the big interests, without provincial chiefs of any kind. The best of the Orthodox Party is combatting next to us in this beautiful struggle. We will afford to Eduardo Chibás the only homage worthy of his life and his holocaust: the freedom of his people, which those who have done nothing more than shed crocodile tears over his tomb never will be able to offer.
>
> The 26 of July Movement is the revolutionary organization of the humble, by the humble, and for the humble....
>
> The 26 of July Movement is the hope of redemption for the Cuban working class, to which the political cliques can offer nothing. It is the hope of land for the peasants that live as pariahs in the country that their grandparents liberated. It is hope of return for the émigrés that had to leave their native land, because they were not able to work or live in it. It the hope of land for the hungry and of justice for the forgotten.
>
> The 26 of July Movement makes its own the cause of all those that have fallen in this struggle since the tenth of March of 1952, and it proclaims serenely before the nation, to its wives, to its sons and daughters, to its fathers and mothers, and its brothers and sisters, that the Revolution will never compromise with murderers.
>
> The 26 of July Movement is the fervent call to close ranks, extended with open arms, to all the revolutionaries of Cuba, without the small minded party and other differences that have been divisive in the past.

---

12   Fidel reads from the article, "The 26 of July Movement," of March 19, 1956.
13   The followers of Eduardo Chibás, the leader of the Orthodox Party of the Cuban People. See glossary.

> The 26 of July Movement is the wholesome and avenging future of the country; it is the word given before the people; it is the promise that will be fulfilled—March 19, 1956.

Who spoke more clearly to the people? Who spoke more clearly? We said that we would come in '56, and we even said the day that we were coming, when everyone was expecting that we would be left discredited.

If in the period...—this was November 19, 1956. A month and something remained to see if we would comply. They were pursuing us. And I simply bring this up here as a demonstration that we were always acting honorably, that not only was there the promise for '56, but also here we said:

> If in the period of two weeks after the publication of this interview, if there is no national solution, the 26 of July Movement will be at liberty to initiate at any moment a revolutionary struggle, as the only saving formula. We ratify fully the promise of 1956, but even in that circumstance, we declare that if in the midst of the struggle Trujillist[14] elements invade Cuba, we are disposed to make a truce and to return to our nannies against the enemies of the country.

That is to say, *If in the period of two weeks after the publication of this interview, if there is no national solution, the 26 of July Movement will be at liberty to initiate at any moment a revolutionary struggle, as the only saving formula.*

That was on November 19, and on December 2, that is, thirteen days later, two days before the completion of the two weeks, we arrived in Cuba. I believe that we have been men that have spoken clearly, and perhaps, if some still have doubts, here is the transcript of *History will absolve me*.[15] I am going to read only the socio-economic aspect, where it is demonstrated that the promise has been fulfilled, that our Revolution said much time ago, much time ago, where we were going and how we were going:

I said that social factors established our possibility of success, because we had the certainty of counting on the people. When we speak of the people, we do not mean the comfortable and conservative sectors of the nation, those who welcome any regime of oppression, any dictatorship, any despotism, prostrating themselves before the master of the moment until they grind their foreheads into the ground.

---

14   Refers to Rafael Leónidas Trujillo, dictator of the Dominican Republic. See glossary.
15   The document known as "History will absolve me" was Fidel's address of self-defense to the court on October 16, 1953, during the trial for his leadership of the attack on Moncada military garrison on July 26, 1953.

We understand the people, when we are speaking of struggle, as the vast unredeemed masses, to whom all make promises and who are deceived and betrayed by all; who yearn for a better, more dignified and more just nation; who are moved by ancestral aspirations of justice, having suffered injustice and mockery generation after generation; and who long for significant and sound transformations in all aspects of life, and who, to attain them, are ready to give even the very last breath of their lives, when they believe in something or in someone, and above all when they believe sufficiently in themselves. The first condition of the sincerity and good faith of a proposal is to do precisely what no one is doing, that is to say, to speak with complete clarity and without fear. The demagogues and the professional politicians work the miracle of being good in everything and on good terms with all, necessarily deceiving everyone in everything. The revolutionaries have to proclaim their ideas valiantly, define their principles, and express their intentions, so that no one is deceived, neither friends nor enemies.

We are calling the people to struggle:

the six hundred thousand Cubans who are without work and desiring to earn their bread honorable, without have to emigrate form their country in search of sustenance;

the five hundred thousand workers of the countryside who inhabit miserable huts, who work four months of the year and pass the rest of the year hungry, sharing poverty with their children; who do not have an inch of land to sow, and whose existence would move more to compassion, if there were not so many hearts of stone;

the four hundred thousand industrial workers and day laborers, whose pensions have been completely embezzled, whose gains are being eliminated, whose housing consists in infernal multiple family dwellings, whose salaries pass from the hands of the employer to those of the merchant, whose future is the layoff and the dismissal, whose life is perennial work and whose rest is the tomb;

the one hundred thousand sharecroppers, who live and die working land that is not theirs, always contemplating sadly, like Moses, the promised land, in order to die without arriving to possess it; who have to pay a share of their products for the plot of land, like feudal serfs; who cannot love the land, nor improve it, nor make it more attractive by planting a cedar tree or an orange tree, because that would ignore the day that a bailiff will come with the rural guard to tell them that they have to leave;

the thirty thousand teachers and professors, so self-denying, sacrificing, and necessary to the better future for subsequent generations, and so badly treated and paid;

the twenty thousand small merchants, overwhelmed by debt, ruined by the crisis, and plagued by graft imposed by corrupt government officials;

the ten thousand young professionals—doctors, engineers, lawyers, veterinarians, educators, dentists, pharmacists, journalists, artists, sculptors, etc.,—who leave from the classrooms with their degrees, desiring to struggle and full of hope, only to find themselves in a dead end street, with all doors closed, deaf to their appeals and pleas.

That is the people, which suffers every misfortune, and which therefore is capable of fighting will total courage! To that people, whose roads are paved with deceptions and false promises, we are going to say: 'We are not going to give to you, but here you now can struggle with all your force in order that freedom and happiness by yours!'

We did not say..., never did we way that the people were the bullies, landowners, middlemen, real estate owners, or the plague of parasites that have kept our people submerged in ruin and hunger. I said what we meant by people, and if they did not know it, if they did not understand it o did not want to hear, I am not to blame.

[Fidel continues reading from a later point in *History will absolve me*]: *All these revolutionary laws and others would be inspired by strict compliance with two essential articles of our Constitution, one of which mandates that the large estate be proscribed and, with respect to the effects of its elimination, the Law would assert the maximum extension of land that each person or entity can possess for each type of agricultural exploitation, adopting measures that lay the basis for reverting the land to Cubans; and the other categorically orders the state to employ all the means at its disposal to provide work to all those that lack it and to ensure a decent life to every manual or intellectual worker. None of revolutionary laws, therefore, could be discredited as unconstitutional.*

The problem of the land, the problem of industrialization, the problem of housing, the problem of unemployment, the problem of education, and the problem of the health of the people: there I have there expressed concretely six points, whose resolution would have directed resolutely our efforts, together with the attainment of public liberties and political democracy.

Perhaps this exposition looks cold and theoretical, if one does not know the appalling tragedy in which this country is living with respect to these six areas, combined with the most humiliating political oppression.

Some 85% of Cuban small farmers are paying rent and live under the perennial threat of eviction from their plots. More than half of the most productive lands are in foreign hands. In Oriente, the widest province, the lands of the United Fruit Company and the West Indian unite the north coast with the south coast. There are two hundred thousand peasant families that do not have a meter of land to plant viands for their hungry children, and on the other hand, there remain without cultivation, in the hands of powerful interests, nearly three hundred thousand caballerias[16] *of productive lands. If Cuba is basically an agricultural country, if a majority of its population is peasant, if the city depends on the country, if the countryside forged the independence of the nation, if the nobility and prosperity of our country depend on a healthy and vigorous peasantry that loves and knows how to cultivate the land and on a state that protects and advises the peasant, how is it possible for this state of affairs to continue?*

Except for a few food, wood, and textile industries, Cuba continues being a factory that produces raw materials.... Everyone is in agreement that the need to industrialize the country is urgent; that it needs metallurgical industries, paper industries, chemical industries; that it must improve animal breeding, cultivation, the technology and elaboration of our food industries, in order to hold out against the ruinous competition from European cheese, condensed milk, liquor, and oil industries and the North American canned food industries; that tourism could be an enormous source of wealth; but the possessors of capital demand that the workers suffer a terrible ordeal, the state does nothing, and industrialization waits forever.

As serious, or worse, is the tragedy of housing. There are in Cuba two hundred thousand huts; four hundred thousand families of the countryside and the city live housed in shacks and multiple family dwelling units, without the most elementary conditions of hygiene and health; two hundred thousand persons of our urban population pay rents that absorb between a fifth and a third of their incomes; and two million, eight hundred thousand of our rural and marginal urban population lack electricity. Here the same thing happens: if the state proposes to reduce the rents, the owners threaten to paralyze all construction; if the state does not become involved, the owners construct in moments when they perceive a high level of rent, but later, they do not lay down a single foundation stone more, even though the rest of the population lives exposed to the elements. The electric monopoly does the same: it extends the lines to the point that it perceives a satisfactory profit, and from there it is not important to them that persons live in darkness for the rest of their lives. The state does nothing, and the people continue without houses and without light.

Our system of education is entirely consistent with the above. In a countryside in which the peasant is not owner of the land, why do they want agricultural schools? In a city in which there are not industries, why do they want technical or industrial schools? Everything is within the same absurd logic: there is neither the one thing, nor the other. In any small country in Europe, there are more than two hundred technical and industrial arts schools; in Cuba, no more than six youths

---

16   A caballeria is a unit of measure for agrarian land surface, equivalent to 134,300 square meters—Translator's note.

earn diplomas, with nowhere to be employed. In the countryside, less than half the children of school age attend—barefoot, half naked, and malnourished—small public schools; and often, the teacher has to purchase with her own salary the necessary study materials. Is this how a great country can be made?

Ninety percent of the children of the countryside are devoured by parasites that pass from the earth through the toe nails of the bare feet. The society is moved by news of a kidnapping or murder of a child, but it remains criminally indifferent to the mass murder that is committed with so many thousands and thousands of children that die every year for lack of resources. And when a father works four months of the year, with what can he buy clothes and medicines for his children? Rickets will spread, and at the age of thirty, they will not have a healthy tooth in the mouth, they will have heard ten million speeches, and in the end, they will die of poverty and disappointment. Access to hospitals, always jam-packed, only is possible through the recommendation of a political magnate that will demand of the unfortunate his vote and that of all his family, in order to ensure that Cuba will always continue being the same or worse.

When you try an accused for robbery, your honorable judges, you do not ask how much time has he been without work, how many children does he have, or how many days of the week does he eat. You do not worry at all about the social conditions of the environment in which he lives; you send him to jail without further thought. The rich that burn warehouses and stores to collect form insurance policies do not go to jail, because they have plenty of money to pay for lawyers and to bribe judges. You send to jail an unfortunate that robs for money, but none of the hundreds of thieves that have robbed the state ever slept even a single night behind bars: you dine with them at the end of the year in some aristocratic place, and they have your respect. In Cuba, when a state official becomes a millionaire overnight and enters into the company of the rich, he can be received with the same words of that affluent character of Balzac, Taillefer, when he toasted a youth who had just inherited an immense fortune: 'Gentlemen, let us drink to the power of gold! Mr. Valentín, a millionaire six times over, has just ascended to the throne. He can do all, he is above all, as happens with all the rich. From now on, equality before the law, allocated under the Constitution, will be a myth for him; he will not be submitted to the laws, but the laws will be submitted to him. For the millionaires, courts and sanctions do not exist.'

The future of the nation and the solution to its problems cannot continue to depend on the selfish interests of a dozen financiers and on the cold profit calculations that ten or twelve magnates draw up in their air conditioned offices. The country can no longer continue being on its knees imploring for miracles from a few golden calves that, like that of the Old Testament demolished by the anger of the prophet, do not make miracles in any form. The problems of the Republic can *be solved only if we decide to struggle for it with the same energy, honesty, and patriotism that our liberators devoted to create it. And it is not with statesmen of the style of Carlos Saladrigas,*[17] *whose statesmanship consists in leaving everything as it is, and passing life mumbling nonsense about "total free enterprise," "guarantees to investment capital," and the "law of supply and demand," as if they will resolve the problems. In a mansion on Fifth Avenue,*[18] *these ministers can chat blithely until there no longer remains even the dust of the bones of those that today demand urgent solutions. And in the present world, no social problem is resolved by spontaneous generation.*

A revolutionary government, with the backing of the people and the respect of the nation after ridding the institutions of corrupt and venal officials, would proceed immediately to industrialize the country, mobilizing all the inactive capital, one thousand and five hundred million, that passes presently through the National Bank and the Bank of Agricultural and Industrial Development; and undertaking the momentous task of study, management, planning, and implementation, by technicians and men of total competence, completely different from the scheming of the politicians.

A revolutionary government, after setting up as the owners of their plots one hundred thousand small farmers that presently pay rent, would proceed to finish once and for all with the problem of the land, first, establishing, as the constitution orders, a maximum extension of land for each type of agricultural enterprise and acquiring the excess by means of expropriation, restoring the usurped lands to the state, draining marshes and swamp lands, planting enormous nurseries and reserving zones for reforestation; secondly, distributing the remaining available land among peasant families, with preference to the most largest, promoting agricultural cooperative for the common utilization of high-cost equipment, refrigerators, and the same technical, professional management in cultivation and animal breeding, facilitating, finally, resources, equipment, protection, and knowledge useful to the peasantry.

A revolutionary government would resolve the problem of housing, reducing rents resolutely by fifty percent, exempting from any tax the houses inhabited by the owners themselves, demolishing the infernal multiple family dwellings and constructing in their place modern multiple story buildings, and financing the

---

17 See glossary.
18 Fifth Avenue is a principal boulevard in the Miramar section of Havana, which in 1953 was lined with mansions and expensive houses. After the triumph of the Revolution, the fleeing Cuban bourgeoisie abandoned most of the mansions, and they were converted into buildings for public uses, such as office buildings, embassies, and schools.

construction of housing in the entire island on a scale never seen, under the criterion that, if the ideal in the countryside is that each family possess its own plot, the ideal in the city is that each family live in its own house or apartment. There are sufficient stones and plenty of hands in order to provide decent housing for every Cuban family. But if we continue waiting for the miracles of the golden calf, a thousand years will pass, and the problem will be the same.

With these three initiatives and reforms, the problem of unemployment automatically would disappear and prevention and the struggle against disease would be a much easier task.

Finally, a revolutionary government would proceed to the integral reform of our education, placing it in tune with the above initiatives, in order to prepare appropriately the generations that are called to live in a more happy country. The words of the Apostle are not forgotten: 'In Latin America, a very grave error is being committed: among peoples that live nearly completely from the products of the country, education is exclusively for urban life, and it does not prepare for the peasant life.' 'The happiest people is that which has better educated its sons, in the instruction of thought and in the management of feelings.' 'An educated people always will be strong and free.'

Cuba would be able to accommodate very well a population three times greater; there is no reason, then, that poverty exists among its present inhabitants. Markets ought to be packed with products; pantries of the houses ought to be full; all hands ought to be producing industriously. No, that is not inconceivable. What is inconceivable is that men go to bed hungry while there remains an inch of land not seeded; what is inconceivable is that there are children that die without medical assistance; what is inconceivable is that thirty percent of our peasants do not know how to sign their names, and ninety-nine percent do not know the history of Cuba; what is inconceivable is that the majority of the families of our countryside are living in conditions worse than the Indians that Columbus found on discovering the most beautiful land that human eyes had seen.

To those that call me a dreamer, I say to them as did Martí: 'The true man does not look to the side that is living better, but to the side that is fulfilling duty. And that is the only practical man, whose dream of today will be the law of tomorrow, because he that has placed his eyes on the depths and has seen the peoples enraged, in flames and bloodstained, in the trough of the centuries, knows that the future, without a single exception, is of the side of duty.'

He who speaks is not the dreamer of yesterday, but the Prime Minister of the Revolutionary Government, which has fulfilled all its promises. When was a revolution more clear than this one? When has a revolution in the world complied more exactly than this one?

That is my response, gentlemen of the Court, in order that the Court judge.

Concerning my feelings with respect to those that take the wrong road, I say that I am sorry; at a personal level, without hate, without resentment, what the Court decides does not matter, the Court can condemn them or it can absolve them. If it absolves them, it is not important: HISTORY WILL CONDEMN THEM!

PART 2

1960: Year of Agrarian Reform

∴

Introduction to 1960: "Year of Agrarian Reform"

During the course of 1960, the national liberation character of the revolutionary process was deepened through anti-capitalist measures, without which the revolution would have fallen, like so many others in Latin America and the underdeveloped world.

Fidel Castro was the leader, the rebel, the person armed with high ideals of social justice, who led through the adverse circumstances of the international arena and the conditions confronting Cuban society and the revolutionary process itself. He went beyond the limits imposed by the prevailing conditions with a commitment to break definitively with bourgeois neocolonial ties and dependency on the United States and its Atlantic allies. During the course of the year, imperialist aggression intensified and this created a context for a profound transformation of social relations, institutions and the Cuban people. This transformation became central to the gains of the Revolution.

It was the year of the Agrarian Reform, and on the basis of its application, economic activities were carried out that transformed the entire agrarian structure of the country. Indeed, the National Institute of Agrarian Reform, along with the Rebel Army, constituted the new matrix of revolutionary institutionality as the previous state structure was being transformed daily in order to conform to the new reality and the social needs of the population.

The masses erupted with tremendous force. They were the motor of the process of transformation and the agents of its defense in the face of the multiple dangers that threatened it. Thousands of new leaders and directors emerged from the population, assuming responsibilities in the economy, defense, and across all spheres of social life.

In assuming the difficult role of leadership over the revolutionary process, Fidel was instrumental in a variety of ways. Of primordial importance was the education of the masses through the power of his words, his reasoning, and his explanations concerning the central role of imperialism and its Latin American allies—groups in the Organization of American States (OAS)—who were striving to overthrow the Revolution. His speeches aimed to transform the mentalities inherited from the past, so that the Cuban people could arrive to the realization that a new world was being created through their relentless class struggle.

In this general context, the following actions marked the unfolding of the year:

- Land was being redistributed to thousands of peasants. At the same time, People's Farms were being established on state lands; cooperatives composed of agricultural workers in the immense sugar producing sector of the economy were being formed; a network of People's Stores was created that offered food and general consumer products as well as farm tools to the rural population at subsidized prices. These measures all implied a radical transformation of the countryside and of the quality of life of the peasants and rural workers.
- Large industrial and service companies, both national and foreign, became the property of the nation. This included various branches of production, including sugar, tobacco, textile, chemical, metallurgical, transport, aviation, petroleum, and mining enterprises, as well as the marine port installations.
- Large scale implementation of educational reform began. Ten thousand primary school classrooms were created, as military barracks were converted into schools, and the construction of large educational centers was initiated. The reform of the universities also began.
- The foreign policy of the Cuban Revolution acquired new dimensions as Cuba identified with the national liberation movements all across the globe. Diplomatic relations with numerous African and Asian countries were established. Cuba also reestablished relations with the Soviet Union and the Eastern socialist countries while it also recognized the People's Republic of China as the legitimate representative of the Chinese people.
- Fidel Castro brought the voice of Cuba to the United Nations, denouncing the policy of aggression of U.S. imperialism.
- Various state institutions were eliminated, with their remaining useful functions assumed by other institutions. In many instances, the changing reality was well ahead of the institutional processes.
- The policy of the United States, aimed at destroying the Revolution, entered a new phase. On March 17, 1960, the National Security Council of the United States approved two documents to this end, namely, *The Program of Covert Activities against Castro* and *The Program of Economic Pressure against the Castro Regime*.[1] These documents contemplated military measures, propaganda, the creation of a counterrevolutionary opposition, and activities designed to create difficulties in the economy and to degrade the standard of living of the Cuban people. The opening salvos of economic war against Cuba included the cancelation of previous agreements for the purchase of

---

1 The documents in Spanish are entitled *Programa de Acción Encubierta contra Castro* and *El Programa de Presiones Económicas contra el Régimen de Castro.*

sugar[2] and political maneuvers designed to deprive Cuba of petroleum imports.
- The revolutionary and counterrevolutionary camps continued to polarize throughout the year. In the revolutionary camp, there was a process of coordination on the part of the three revolutionary political organizations: the July 26 Movement, the March 13 Revolutionary Directorate, and the Popular Socialist Party (the first Communist Party of Cuba). At the same time, various mass organizations emerged, such as the Committees for the Defense of the Revolution (CDRs) and the Federation of Cuban Women (FMC). The youth movement was unified into the Association of Young Rebels while the worker's movement were renovated, removing Mujalist[3] elements from positions of power in the labor unions. And the University Student Federation (FEU) continued to mobilize its base in service of revolutionary tasks.
- The program contained in *History Will Absolve Me* was fulfilled as the goals of the *Declaration of Havana*, namely, the elimination of the capitalist exploitation, were embraced.

The need to defend the revolutionary process demanded that priority be given to elevating the nation's defensive capacity. Thousands of citizens began to learn military techniques and the popular militias constituted the principal area in which revolutionaries were integrated into national defense, independent of their occupation or social class. Homemakers, workers, students, employees, intellectuals, former guerrillas in the Sierra Maestra, and participants in the clandestine resistance in the cities[4] all joined together in training and preparation for combat. All were now considered part of one mass category: *revolutionaries*. The leadership of the Revolution, headed by Fidel, and with them the people of Cuba, took on the risks implied by being the first free territory of the Americas.

---

2 During the neocolonial republic, there were commercial agreements between the United States and Cuba in which the USA agrees to buy a certain quantity of sugar.
3 See the Introduction to the Year 1959 as well as Eusebio Mujal in the glossary.
4 See "clandestine resistance" in the glossary.

The Revolution Converts Barracks into Schools

Students, workers, employees, military personnel, and the people in general:[1]

...

It is good to remember what occurred during the past year. The first months were lost. The state was completely disorganized. We had to look for men, above all to know how to distinguish between someone loyal, truly loyal, and someone who was a fraud, carrying within himself the virus of betrayal of the Revolution and the country.

There has not been a year of revolutionary government, but only a few months of revolutionary government. But this coming year of 1960 is going to be an entire year of revolutionary government, because the government has more experience and the people have more experience.

...

We all now feel like we did at the end of the first year of the war. We had the opportunity to learn much during the course of that first year, and so it has been with respect to the first year of the Revolutionary Government. We have had to work much, it has been a difficult work, but we have the satisfaction of seeing that the work of the Revolution has advanced. This is not only seen here; it is seen above all in those places where our people most needed the Revolution; it is seen above all in the countryside; and it was observed above all during the Christmas season in all the towns in the interior of the Republic, where there was an unrestrained happiness, without exception, as if someone had given an order, which no one gave, but which the people gave to themselves, of expressing in all the corners of Cuba their unrestrained and extraordinary happiness.

...

We know where we are going; and we know the fruits of the work of our Revolution. The counterrevolutionaries also ought to know where they are going and what will be the bitter fruits of their work in the counterrevolution. We know what the prize is of honest men; we know what the result is of their doing good. They ought to know, without the least doubt, what will be the result of those who choose to do evil.

Today it seems to me that our flag waves freer and more beautiful than ever. This morning has been a truly happy morning.

---

1 Selections from the speech delivered during the ceremony that turned over the Fifth District Police Station to the Ministry of Education, January 11, 1960. Department of Stenographic Versions of the Revolutionary Government.

Another center of torture and crime was demolished and converted into a park: the Bureau of Investigations.[2] This sinister police station of the dictatorship, which was witness to the worst horrors of the tyranny, will be converted into a school.[3] Some of those horrors were worse than others, or all were equally horrifying, but this building won fame, because it was the hideout of one of the worst gang of murderers that the history of the peoples has ever known.

In truth, many desired to put the bulldozers to it and destroy it, but all things considered, the building is constructed, and we have to make use of it, for something that is diametrically opposed to the use that it had before. We are going to remove those portholes, we are going to remove those towers and sentry boxes, and we are going to convert it into a school center. The bulldozers could destroy it, but I believe that a school center destroys it even more.

Thus, it will be a symbol of our Revolution, which converts into schools and places of study those buildings that yesterday were centers of crime.

This means, above all, one thing, which is that at the same time that we destroy the past, we have to build the future. We would deceive ourselves if we were not to understand that the future has to be constructed. We would deceive ourselves if we were to not understand that the task is long. We would deceive ourselves if we were not to understand our difficulties and our limitations.

We would deceive ourselves, because the reality is that we only have what they left us. They left us with hundreds of thousands of illiterate persons and we have before us the task of educating them. They left us with a large shortage of technicians and educated men, and we have that lack and that shortage of men necessary for the work that our country has to carry out.

That is to say, we have nothing other than what they left us, and with the little that we have, we have to build our country of the future.

How different will be the task of the men that govern our country in future years! How different this Cuban generation will be in ten years! How many thousands and thousands of technicians, how many thousands and tens of thousands of qualified men!

...

There will no longer be a single illiterate person in our country. Our school cities, our universities, all of the centers of education that we are creating today will have brought their first fruits. And thus for each task there will be a competent person, for each task there will be a responsible person, for each task there will be a qualified person. Because what is crucial in each work

---

2 See glossary.
3 Refers to the Fifth Police Station. See glossary.

undertaken by the government, from the most important to the most modest task, is in being able to count on a competent person to lead each task and each work. When there is a competent person, everything goes well; then there is not a competent person, everything goes badly.

We do not have what the past did not leave. They did not prepare the future generations in past times, and we find today a generation that is full of patriotic love, full of courage, disposed to carry out any task, but it is a generation emerged from the past. And with the few that we have, in the economic sphere as in the technical sphere, we have to carry out the great task of the future.

...

The Future of Our Country Necessarily Has to Be a Future of Men of Science and Thought

Distinguished members of the Academy of Science;[1]
 Compañeros speleologists;
 Ladies and gentlemen:
 ...

We have to convert our young people, we have to awaken them, and hopefully, in future years the Speleological Society will grow, and our scientific institutions will grow, and legions of Cubans will join them. Today the circle of researchers is still limited because conditions have made the road to knowledge difficult.

The future of our country necessarily has to be a future of men of science; it has to be a future of men of thought. This is precisely what we are especially seeding; opportunities for greater knowledge and intelligence, since a very considerable part of our people did not have access to culture nor science, the majority of our people. It was a luxury for which they were not able to even hope for, because they did not have the opportunity. Thus, with half of our population being rural, only five percent of the children of peasants arrived even to the fifth grade.

How much intelligence was wasted by that omission! How much intelligence was lost! Intelligence that today will be incorporated in the life of the country; intelligence that today will be incorporated into culture and science. For that, we are converting fortresses into schools; for that, we are constructing school cities; for that, we are filling the island with teachers, in order that the country in the future will have accomplished men of knowledge, researchers, and scientists.

You, who have been the pioneers, will see that in some not too distant day, the first fruits of the seeds that today we are planting will begin to be harvested, in order that the university stops being a place where only a part of our people have access, in order that all of our people have access to the university. Therefore, we consider that the best system is that which provides opportunity to go to the university, not for the privileged but on the basis of intelligence.

And so we are thinking of organizing the small schools in the countryside, we are thinking of organizing rural centers of secondary education, and we are

---

[1] Final paragraphs of a speech delivered in an event of the Speleologist Society of Cuba, in the Academy of Sciences, January 15, 1960.

thinking of organizing school cities, so that the most intelligent children, the most intelligent of each school, will have the opportunity to arrive to the universities, and will have the opportunity to climb to the place most outstanding of our culture.

Therefore, what we hope of you is that you will help us. What we hope of you is that you continue working, because Cuba greatly needs you. Cuba greatly needs men of thought, above all men of clear thought, not only men that have accumulated knowledge, but also men that place their knowledge on the side of the good, of the just, for the country. Because we live in a moment in which the role of knowledge is of exceptional importance, because only intelligence can guide the people through moments of great transformations and in the moments in which the enterprises are being undertaken by our people.

Among men of thought, we must fight the battle; among men of thought, we must form the legion that will provide the resources of their intelligence to the Revolution in this hour. Because there are men that have accumulated knowledge, but they do not employ it except in benefit of their own interests, they do not employ it except for selfish ends, and we need men of thought that employ it for the good of others.

Overall, you have had privileges, provided by nature or by conditions, and that has permitted you to acquire insights that can serve you for understanding our problems better, to see things more clearly. Because I have learned clearly that the problems of our country are so evident that anyone who does not understand them does not want to; anyone who does not see them does not want to see them.

Here really there are not men that are mistaken. Among men of thought, there are not men that are wrong. Illiterates can be wrong, although today they are seeing more than ever. Those that did not have the opportunity to go to school can be wrong, but today even the peasant that does not know how to read or write knows the problems of the Revolution; he knows what his interests are and he knows on what side he ought to put himself. In moments like this, the man of thought that positions himself against the revolution is not wrong; rather, he is a conscious enemy of justice, a conscious enemy of the interests of the people; a conscious enemy of his country. He could not be merely mistaken.

Men that have acquired a certain degree of culture understand the political, economic, and social problems of our people, and if they position themselves against the Revolution, they do not do it in error, but because they have the option of placing themselves with the people or with the interests of the privileged minority; they have the option of placing them with the people and the interests of the people, or with their personal interests, selfishly choosing the road of their interests or the road of the interests of the privileged minority.

Therefore, we need men and women of thought that are opposed to those that give in; opposed to the deserters of the truth; opposed to those that wrote letters to the Service of Military Intelligence,[2] informing on their *compañeros* to the repressive government bodies; opposed to those that are traitors to thought; opposed to those that in this hour are aligned with the side of evil and on the side of their interests. We need those that would do what Núñez Jiménez[3] and the other good members of the Speleological Society did, who persevered, who resisted, who maintained themselves linked to the truth, in order to have the infinite satisfaction of this refreshing moment, this encouraging moment, this emotional moment. We need those who would act they did, as though in this minute all the bitterness and past sufferings were just beginning.

That example ought to teach us what we are living in this hour, and that in this hour also we will have deserters, as we will have loyal men, but with the knowledge that the men that persevere, the men that resist, the men that defend a just cause and know how to carry forward that cause, will be victorious.

In addition, we are beginning today. Tomorrow, after an assessment like what you did today, tomorrow, after a longer assessment, the loyal men, the men that survive—because tomorrow, like yesterday, perhaps also we will have to lament losses—tomorrow the loyal men and women will again meet; tomorrow the men of thought that position themselves on the side of dignity and on the side of truth will again meet to make an assessment, and again like today, Núñez Jiménez and other *compañeros* will again make history, because of one thing we can be sure, and it is that we are beginning; and of another thing we can be sure, and it is that we will arrive to the goal.

---

2   See glossary.
3   See glossary.

The Choice Is *Patria o Muerte*

Compañeros and *compañeras:*[1]
There are moments that are very important in the life of the peoples. There are moments that are extraordinary, and such as this tragic and painful moment that we are living on this day.

...

We have attained the triumph of the people after seven years of bloody struggle and immense sacrifice. In those times, any citizen could be tortured, any citizen could be murdered in the streets of the cities or in the countryside; a most atrocious tyranny was reigning in our country. In addition, there was nothing to prevent the arrival from the United States of ships loaded with bombs and ships loaded with shrapnel, which on the other hand were not exploding in the port of Havana.

...

They are combatting a just revolutionary regime, a human revolutionary regime, a regime that has tried so much to defend the interests of the people, the interests of our suffering and exploited people—exploited by the monopolies, exploited by the large landowners, exploited by the privileged—, a regime that has freed the people from all those injustices, a regime of the majority of the country, a humane regime.

Before, they were supporting a criminal and inhumane regime, a regime of the monopolies and of the privileged. Democracy goes to the aid of the criminals, and it aids the exploiters!

Democracy is this that we have, where man has value, and always will have more value than money! Because for money, we will never shed a drop of human blood; for money, for selfish interests, we will never sacrifice a drop of human blood.

This is not an isolated event. Who is surprised by the explosion of a ship with workers on board? Who is surprised by a sabotage that costs the blood of workers? Who is surprised, when scarcely a month ago—if it has even been a month—a North American plane, proceeding from North American territory with a North American pilot and with a North American bomb—tried to

---

1   Selections from the speech pronounced during the funeral of the victims of the explosion of the ship *"La Coubre,"* March 5, 1960. Stenographic version of the Offices of the Prime Minister—Authors' note. "Patria o Muerte" means "Country or Death" or "Homeland or Death." Because of its common use as a slogan in Cuba, it is expressed in the original Spanish in this book. See Translator's Note.—Translator's note.

attack a center where there were more than 200 people at work. On that occasion, I said: "What would have been today the pain of our people and what would have been today the tragedy of our people, if instead of those two corpses of mercenaries, we would have had to bury some dozens of workers?" As though those words had been something of a premonition, today we arrive in mass demonstration to bury several dozens of workers and rebel soldiers.

Is it surprising that the criminal perpetrators of that sabotage were not worried about the number of victims that they were going to leave, or about the men that they were going to murder? Is it surprising, if no more than a month ago, they were going to drop a hundred pound bomb in the middle of an operating factory, in the midst of more than 200 workers? When that event occurred, with the proofs in hand, we serenely spoke to the people and explained what had occurred. We exhibited the proofs, and we even said to them that they should send their technicians, in order that they could see that all that we had said was rigorously accurate. A month has passed, and they still have not arrested anyone in the United States, nor have they expelled any war criminal from the United States, nor have they found any culpable person, nor have they troubled anyone. On the contrary, a few days after the small planes returned, hardly a week had passed, when they bombarded the locality when the Prime Minister of the Revolutionary Government resides. If all this has happened, is it surprising?

Is it surprising that they would explode a ship full of workers, if they were going to explode a bomb over a sugar factory, if they were not worried about bombing a zone where there were children, dropping in that region bombs of one hundred pounds. Is it surprising, if yesterday there was published in the review *Bohemia* the photographs of their air fleet, calmly at rest in North American airports, without anyone bothering it? Is it surprising, if yesterday we received the news that José Eleuterio Pedraza[2] is in Washington?

Is it surprising, if these things have been occurring? But on this occasion, the blow has been hard, and it has been bloody.

Is it surprising, when a series of acts shows the collection of powerful interests that are grouped against our Revolution? When scarcely some days ago, they released a great quantity of corn as a substitute for Cuban honey in the fabrication of alcohol? When a few days ago, they withdrew the inspectors that observe the cultivation of fruits and vegetables that we export to that country? When, as everyone knows, they want to subordinate the sovereignty of our country, through the means of not buying our sugar? That is to say, in these

---

2   See glossary.

days they are going to present to the Congress a law that would grant to the President of the republic the right, at any moment, to eliminate the sugar quota, to reduce it, or to not buy anything, if he makes such a determination.

And what does that indicate? It indicates that our country has a very weak economic structure. But why does our country have a weak economic structure? Because foreign masters gave that structure to our economy, an economy of agricultural monoculture, an economy of the large estate, an economy of an underdeveloped country, a weak economy, a consequence of the policy of the foreign masters of our economy for fifty years.

And now, benefitting from that dependency from which we want to free ourselves, taking advantage of that situation from which we are trying to become independent—that is what our economic independence means—benefitting from that dependency, they want to adopt methods that intend to crush our rights and to subdue our sovereignty.

This means that, if we make laws here, if we adopt measures that benefit our people, they assume the right to starve our people. That is, utilizing the economic advantage that they enjoy as a consequence of the monoculture, the large estate, and the underdevelopment that continue here, they are trying to restrict the rights of our people to act in an independent and sovereign manner, with the threat of killing us from hunger.

What does that imply, if not an economic Platt Amendment?[3] What does that denote, if not a warning that, if we take measures against the large estates, measures against the monopolies, measures for the benefit of our people, they will take reprisals against us? Since we are a small country, with a weak economy, if we make an effort to attain a strong economy, to attain our own economy, they threaten to kill us with starvation.

What is that, if not an attempt to infringe upon the sovereignty of a country, an attempt to restrict the independence of a country? What is that, if not a government assuming the right to decide over the future of another country, using measures of reprisal?

The measures that we are taking are against the monopolies, are against monopoly interests, and not against the North American people. Furthermore, the measures that they are taking are not measures for defending the North American people; they are measures of reprisal against the Cuban people.

And that, naturally, needs to be proclaimed by a Revolutionary Government. A government of the people is needed to proclaim it; a government

---

3 See glossary.

without fear is needed to proclaim it, without fear of the threats or the reprisals, without fear of the military maneuvers.

And we, a Revolutionary Government, can ask: Why military maneuvers in the Caribbean? For what purpose are the maneuvers involving beach landings against positions occupied by guerrillas? For what purpose are the maneuvers of troops transported in planes in offensive operations?

Because, what we have understood is that the problems of the world are discussed in the summits, as they are called. We have understood that the problems of the world are problems of guided missiles, of advanced science and technology. But we have not heard it said that the problems of the world are problems of guerrillas, nor have we heard it said that the problems of the world are problems here in the Caribbean, and that there are difficulties of an international character in the Caribbean.

...

When we see maneuvers of Marine Infantry, beach landings against guerillas, we ask ourselves for what and why. Are they thinking of landing—I ask myself—, or are they intending to intimidate? Do they want to frighten us? Do they want to make clear that at any moment we could be invaded, since there are spokespersons who speak of possibilities, and among the possibilities of which they speak are landings here?

Who has said that anyone could effect a landing here? Who said that here a landing could be carried out with tranquility? Among the probabilities, it is good to mention it on a day like today, because in truth we Cubans already are too strong in patriotism and public spiritedness for them to make use of those insinuations against us. Therefore, among the possibilities of which they speak, permit me to say that we are simply amazed when they speak, with such tranquility, of sending the Marines here. As if we count for nothing, as if in the case of that eventuality Cubans would do nothing, as if we Cubans would not resist any landing here, any troop that intends to subdue our people!

It is good that it be said, that we say it once and for all here today, in these moments when we come to place in their tombs a considerable number of soldiers, workers, and citizens..., when we come in sorrowful pilgrimage to bring their remains to the tombs, tranquilly, serenely, as we are fulfilling a painful duty, and we know how to fulfill it.... Because we Cubans have learned to look at death serenely and without being perturbed, because we Cubans have acquired a true sense of life, that considers life undignified when it is not lived with freedom, when it is not lived with self-respect, when it is not lived with justice, when it is not lived for something, and for something great, as are living Cubans in this moment. Here in this ceremony, among these dead, resulting from who knows what murdering hands, we say once and for all that we do not fear any troops landing in this country, ... that we will not delay a second in taking our rifles and in occupying our posts, without batting an eye and without vacillating, before any foreign troops that land in this country.

And it is good that we say it as those who in truth are decided to do what is promised, without displays of emotion. And in the event that anyone doubted it, yesterday it was demonstrated forever to the most pessimist.

Anyone who observed the people yesterday, anyone who had seen that episode at the same time marvelous and terrible:

- anyone who had seen how the multitudes advanced toward the fire, how the soldiers, workers, police, sailors, firemen, and militias advanced; how they advanced toward that place of danger, how they advanced toward that place of death, with composure;
- anyone who had seen what Cubans did yesterday; whoever had seen the soldiers and the people advancing toward the danger in order to rescue the wounded, in order to rescue the victims in a burning ship, in a zone that was burning, when it was not known how many explosions were going to occur;
- anyone who had known of those waves of Cubans, swept up by the explosions, who died not in the first explosion but in the second, anyone who would have seen the comportment of the people as they conducted themselves yesterday;
- anyone had seen the people direct the traffic; anyone had seen the people establish order;
- anyone had seen the people advance toward that explosion that left behind a cloud, one reminiscent of a mushroom cloud of a nuclear explosion; anyone who had seen the people advance toward that mushroom cloud with knowing what it was—
- can be sure that our people is a people in the condition of defending itself, it is a people capable of advancing against the mushroom clouds of the nuclear bombs.

...

And that occurred yesterday. It is not a fantasy; it is a reality that all the people witnessed. It is a reality, in which we have had to pay with dozens of courageous lives, of men that fell when they were going to save the lives of their *compañeros*, who gave their lives calmly and coolly in order to save the lives of those that were imprisoned in the twisted iron of that ship, or among the rubble of the buildings; of firemen that advanced without agitation to extinguish fires in buildings full of explosives. Anyone who saw scenes like those of yesterday, anyone who observed a people so dignified and so virile and so generous and so honest like our people, has to know that it is a people that will defend itself against any aggression.

...

Moreover, if that unfortunately would occur, above all unfortunate for those that engage in aggression against us, we once again would have not an option other than that with which we initiated the revolutionary struggle, that of liberty or death. Only now, liberty means something more still: liberty means country. *Our only option would be **Patria o Muerte**.*[4]

...

They also are wrong when they believe that they are going to defeat us through economic reprisals. And here it would be appropriate to say that it is better to go hungry in liberty than to live in opulence enslaved; that it is better to be poor but to be free, even though it costs a great deal, and even though the road of the development of our resources would be long—someday we also will have attained this goal—, but it is better to be poor but free than to be rich but enslaved. Especially here in Cuba, because we were slaves and poor, but now at least we are poor but free, and someday, we will be free and also rich.

So we cannot be bought with economic opportunism, especially since here no one ever saw economic advantages; here what everyone saw was poverty, injustice, exploitation.

...

Cuba, our people, has done nothing other than to struggle against wrongs, it has done no other thing than to make an effort to overcome those wrongs, we have done no other thing than to claim what is ours; we have done no other thing than to defend ourselves and what is ours.

...

We have come to the end of one of the saddest days, but also one of the most unwavering and most symbolic for our country.

...

But it is true that it is painful. And here we are fulfilling this painful duty, and we will fulfill it as many times as is necessary. We will fulfill it one day as a procession, and the following day as a funeral, if it be necessary. We know how to fulfill it, because behind those that fall others come, behind those that fall others come standing tall.

...

What an impressive sight it is, that of a people standing tall. What a marvelous and impressive sight it is, that of a people standing tall. What a sight like

---

4 Italics added.

this of today, to see marching together those that some years ago, it would have seemed like a dream to see them marching as they were marching today.

...

Therefore, I saw today our country stronger than ever; I saw today our Revolution more solid and invincible than ever, our people more valiant and heroic than ever. Today it was as if in that blood, the blood of soldiers and workers, the blood of Cuban workers and French workers.... French workers fulfilling their duty also died transporting that merchandise that would serve to defend our sovereignty, and for which we have not forgotten them in their hour of helping us, in their hour of aiding the families of Cubans that fell. We have not forgotten those workers of France that fell in that mindlessly destructive act carried out by murderous hands, by enemies of the workers here and in any part of the world; who in that event of yesterday united with ours the blood of France, from where emerged those shouts of liberty in the first great revolution of the modern history of humanity. They united the blood of French workers with the blood of Cuban workers.

...

And so, on saying goodbye to the fallen of today, to those soldiers and workers, I do not have any other idea, in saying goodbye, except the idea that symbolizes this struggle and that symbolized what is today our people: Rest together in peace! Together workers and soldiers, together in your tombs, as together you struggled, as together you died, and as together we are prepared to die.

And on saying goodbye, at the threshold of the cemetery, a promise, not only the promise of today but also the promise of yesterday and of always: Cuba will not be intimidated; Cube will not retreat; the Revolution will not be stopped; the Revolution will not retreat; the Revolution will continue forward victoriously, the Revolution will continue unswerving in its march!

And that is our promise to those that have died, because to die for the country is to live. We will carry the *compañeros* always in our memory as something of ours; not in the memory in the heart of a man, or of men, but the only memory that never can be erased: the memory in the heart of a people.

Democracy Is This

Distinguished visitors of Latin America and the entire world that join us today;[1]
Workers;
Peasants;
Students;
Professionals;
Militias of the country;
Youth patrols;
All Cubans:
On other occasions, we have met in great assemblies, sometimes to defend our country against slander, sometimes to commemorate a patriotic anniversary, and sometime to protest an aggression. But in no previous moment has the people met in greater number nor in a celebration so meaningful as this of today, in which the International Day of the Workers, and therefore the day of Cuban workers is commemorated. But it is, in addition, the day of Cuban peasants, of all those that produce, the day of the humble of our people.

It is the day not only of those that work with their hands and with their intelligence producing goods and services for the country, but also the day of those on whose shoulders rest, in this decisive hour of the country, the defense of the country and the defense of the Revolution. It is also the day of the rebel soldier, of the heroic combatants of the revolutionary army; and it is also the day of all the members of the Revolutionary Armed Forces, the day of the members of the revolutionary militias, because the soldiers of the Rebel Army also are peasants and workers.

Therefore, today is the day of all revolutionaries, of all revolutionaries united, because upon this unity is based and will always be based the success and the force of our Revolution.

...

Only a few months ago there was not a single workers or peasant militia organized. The order to organize the militias was issued in the month of October, precisely October 26, as a result of the mass protest against the air incursion that cost more than forty victims among our citizens.

Six months ago, we did not have a single workers' militia; six months ago, the workers did not know how to manage arms; six months ago, the workers

---

1 Selections from a speech delivered on the commemoration of the International Workers' Day (May Day), in Civic Plaza, May 1, 1960. Department of Stenographic Versions of the Revolutionary Government.

did not know how to march; six months ago, there was not a single militia company to defend the Revolution in case of aggression. And in six months, not only have the militias been organized, but they have been trained.

...

Cuba is a country eminently peaceful and civil. In Cuba, we detest military marches, uniforms, and arms; because for us they were always symbols of oppression and of mistreatment, symbols of privileges, and symbols of abuses.

The arms and the uniforms have been disagreeable for us. And yet, in six months we have organized and trained more than 1,000 companies of workers, student, and peasant militias! In only six months, a formidable organization, which parades here today, has been developed! That shows what the Cuban people is capable of doing.

...

We have had to learn many things; and we have learned everything, without exception. Today, for example, when the organized units of the people were passing in an interminable number for six consecutive hours; when we have had the opportunity to see the tremendous force of the people; when we have had the opportunity to see the invincible force of the people, we ask ourselves: Is this people of today the same people of yesterday?

If we were so strong within ourselves, if there was in the breast of our people such force, how was so much abuse and so much exploitation against our workers possible? How was it possible for there to be so much abuse against our people, so much pillage, so much robbery, and so much plundering of our people? If we had so much force, how was so much crime possible? How was it possible that a handful of men, a gang of mercenaries, and a plague of political maneuvering could maintain and direct at its whim, for half a century, the destiny of a country?

Ah! In the breast of our people an extraordinary energy and an extraordinary force existed, but we did not know it, or we had stopped meeting and organizing. Therefore, the privileged and more educated minority were able, with the aid of foreign interests, to do what they had done to our people, with a tremendous force enclosed in its breast.

And this has been the great lesson of this day. Because never before have we Cubans had the opportunity to see our own force, as we have today; never before were the Cuban people able to have full awareness of its own force, as we have today. That interminable river of columns has been necessary, parading for seven hours, in order that our people would have a concrete idea of its own force.

...

What was a parade of the First of May before? Today, the workers have not brought a single demand, whereas before the workers were hardly able to carry the host of posters that they brought on their shoulders on the First of May.

...

What else could the worker do? The worker knew that what he did not do for himself, no one would do it for him; the worker knew that what he did not work to attain for himself, no one would attain for him.

...

They made up a democracy for you, a rare and strange democracy in which you, who are the majority, count for nothing; in which you, peasant and worker, who produce the great part of the wealth, and who together with the intellectual workers, produce the totality of the wealth; you who produce all, would not even have the opportunity of learning, in some cases, how to write your name.

They made for you a strange democracy, a rare democracy in which you, who are the majority, do not even exist politically within the society.

They spoke to you of the rights of the citizen, and those rights included: that your child would be able to die of hunger before the apathetic look of the government; that your child would remain without learning a single letter; that you yourself would have to sell your work at the price that they wanted to pay you for it, if someone were interested in buying it.

They spoke to you of rights that never existed for you. Your children did not have assured the right of a school; your children did not have assured the right to a doctor; your children did not have assured the right to a piece of bread; and you yourself did not have assured the right to work.

They made up a democracy for you in which you, who are the majority, would count for nothing. And so, in spite of your tremendous force, in spite of your sacrifices, in spite of the fact that you were working for others within that national life, you, in spite of being the majority, do not govern, and you count for nothing.

And they called that democracy!

Democracy is that in which the majority governs,

democracy is that in which the majority counts,

democracy is that in which the interests of the majority are defended;

democracy is that which guarantees the citizen, not only the right to think freely, but also the right to know how to think, the right to know how to write what is thought, and the right to know how to read what is thought and what others think; the right to bread, the right to work, the right to culture, and the right to count within the society.

Democracy, therefore, is this, this democracy of the Cuban Revolution! (PROGLONGED APPLAUSE)

Democracy is this, in which you, the peasant, count, and you receive the land that we have recovered from usurious foreign hands that exploited it!

Democracy is this, in which you, agricultural sugar worker, receive 80,000 *caballerías*[2] of land in order that you do not have to live along dirt roads in sugar plantations!

Democracy is this, in which you, worker, have your right to work assured, without which they can throw you to the street to go hungry!

Democracy is this, in which you, student from a poor family, have the opportunity to earn a university title, if you are intelligent, although you are not rich!

Democracy is this, in which you, child of a worker, or child of a peasant, or child of any humble family, have a teacher and have a school where you will be able to educate yourself!

Democracy is this, in which you, elderly person, will have assured your sustenance when you no longer can attain it through your own efforts!

Democracy is this, in which you, black Cuban, have the right to work without anyone taking it away for stupid prejudices!

Democracy is this where you, woman, obtain full equality with all the other citizens, and you even have to right to take up arms to defend your country, together with the men!

Democracy is this, in which a government converts fortresses into schools, and in which it wants to build a house for each family, in order that each family has a roof over its head!

Democracy is this, which wants a doctor to attend to each sick person!

Democracy is this, which does not recruit a peasant in order to make him a soldier, to corrupt him, and to convert him into an enemy of the worker and of his own peasant brother, but converts the soldier, not into a defender of privileges, but into a defender of the rights of his brothers, the peasants, and the workers!

Democracy is this, which does not divide the people into sectors among the humble, some confronting others!

Democracy is this, in which a government searches for the force of the people, and unites it! Democracy is this, which makes the people strong, because it unites it.

---

2 A *caballeria* is unit of measure for agrarian land surface, equivalent to 134,300 square meters—Translator's note.

Democracy is this, which delivers a rifle to peasants, delivers a rifle to workers, delivers a rifle to students, delivers a rifle to women, delivers a rifle to blacks, delivers a rifle to the poor, and delivers a rifle to any citizen that is prepared to defend a just cause.

Democracy is this, in which the rights of the majority not only count, but it delivers arms to that majority! And only a government really democratic, where the majority governs, can do that! A pseudo-democracy never would be able to do that.

We would like to know what would happen if blacks in the South of the United States, who so often have been lynched, were delivered, each one of them, a rifle. What an exploiting oligarchy never would be able to do, what a military caste that oppresses and plunders the people never would be able to do, what a government of the minority never would be able to do is to deliver a rifle to each peasant, to deliver a rifle to each worker, to deliver a rifle to each student, to deliver a rifle to each humble citizen, to deliver a rifle to each one of those who compose the majority of the people.

And that does not mean that the rights of the others do not count. The rights of the others count to the same degree that the interests of the majority count, in the same scope as the rights of the majority; but the rights of the majority ought to prevail over the privileges of the minority.

That real democracy, that indisputable democracy, that sincere and honest democracy, is the democracy that exists in our country since the first of January of 1959.

That democracy has been expressed in this form; it has been expressed directly, in the intimate union and identification of the government and the people; in this direct agreement; in this making and struggling for the good of the great majority of the country, and in the interests of the great majority of the country.

We have exercised that direct democracy, then, with more purity, a thousand times more purity, than that false democracy where all the means of corruption and fraud are used, in order to distort the true will of the people.

And that democracy has prevailed in this direct form, because we are in a revolutionary process. Tomorrow, it will be as the people want; tomorrow it will be as the needs of our people, the aspirations of are people, and the interests of our people demand.

Today it is a direct relation between the government and the people. When the revolutionary process has advanced sufficiently, and the people will understand—and with the people the Revolutionary Government also will understand—we are going to make new procedures. Once the principal tasks and the principle goals of the Revolution, among them, as we have seen today, in the first place, the defense of the Revolution and the defense of the country. Then the people and the government will adopt the procedures that the circumstances of a consolidated and victorious Revolution demand of you and of us.

Here no one is occupying public office for reasons of ambition or pleasure. Here we only are complying with our duty; here we all are in the same position and disposition of sacrifice; here we all are in the same disposition of work; here we all have the same intention, which is the intention of serving a cause.

Our enemies, our detractors, ask for elections....

(PROLONGED EXCLAMATIONS OF: "Elections for what? Elections for what? We already voted for Fidel! We already voted for Fidel!").

A Latin American government leader has declared recently that there ought to be admitted to the Organization of American States only those government leaders that were the product of an electoral process, as if a true revolution like that of Cuba, could arrive to power behind the backs of the people; as if a true revolution like that of Cuba could arrive to power against the will of the people; as if the only democratic process for taking power is the electoral process, so frequently prostituted, distorting the will and the interests of the people, and bringing to power in many cases the most inept and the most clever, not the most competent and the most honest.

As if after so many fraudulent elections, as if after so much treacherous and false politics, as if after so much corruption, it would be possible to get the people to believe that the only democratic process for a people is an electoral process; and not, on the other hand, that democratic process through which a people, not with a pencil, but with its blood and with the lives of 20,000 compatriots, struggling with arms against a professional and well-armed army, trained and equipped by a powerful foreign state, broke the chains. It broke the chains that enslaved it, it broke with the privileges, it broke with the injustices, it broke with the abuse and the crime forever in our country, and it initiated a true democratic state of progress, of liberty, and justice.

...

The revolutionary process is not merely the stage of the revolutionary war. The war was the stage of rebellion; afterwards came the stage of the Revolution. Before, the war was the consequence of the rebellion of our people; now, the Revolution is the consequence of the creative spirit of our people.

And what in these moments is the principal task that we Cubans have ahead? What is the response to that question? What is it that each Cuban today ought to know? And why is that now our fundamental task? And what are the reasons for which our country is threatened with aggression?

What has the Revolution done, if it not be for the good of its people? What has the Revolution done, if it not be for justice? What has the Revolution done, if it not be to defend the interests of the great majority of our country, of the most humble classes of our country, who constitute the immense majority. And who not only constitute the majority—and they have therefore an evident right to be included in the destiny of the country—but they constitute, in addition to being the majority, the sector of the country most in need. They constitute, besides being the majority, the most suffering sector of the country; they constitute, besides being the majority, the most exploited sector of the country.

...

Why were they not concerned with our people before? Why were they not concerned with our people when there were hundreds of thousands of families living in miserable huts here? Why were they not concerned with our people when everyone was in poverty, when the peasants lived along dirt roads in plantations, seeding cassava, tubers, and sweet potatoes?

Why were they not concerned with Cuba, the affairs of Cuba, nor questions of Cuba when in our country dawn broke with murdered youths in the streets, when the police stations and the prisons were centers of torture, when the peasants were murdered *en masse*, when there was so much injustice and so much abuse here? Why did it not merit even a single line in any of the newspapers that today attack our Revolution? Why?

...

And now, the murderers of yesterday are received in the Senate of the United States in order to "report" on things in Cuba!

But even stranger things are occurring, which brings us to the reality that we have ahead. Without there having existed the least problem or difficulty, the President of Guatemala sent for his ambassador, and without their having occurred the least incident, broke diplomatic relations with Cuba and declared that in the Sierra Maestra—in the Sierra Maestra, from where have come those soldiers that today paraded here—troops are being prepared to invade Guatemala.

It was an accusation so unfounded, it was an accusation so absurd, that it would have lacked a logical explanation for us or for anyone, if it were not for the news that we received that the North American Department of State was preparing an aggression against Cuba through the Government of Guatemala.

...

The enemies of our Revolution know that they have not advanced in their aim of organizing a fifth column in Cuba; the enemies of the Revolution know that the Revolution is stronger every day; they know that the Revolution is more organized with each passing day; they know that they will not be able to defeat the tremendous social and revolutionary forces that support the Revolution. They know this very well, they know that they cannot organize a counterrevolution here, because they know that they do not have a place to begin, nor do they know how to begin nor with whom to begin. So they want to destroy the Revolution through a maneuver of an international kind.

What a coincidence, that the withdrawal of the Guatemalan ambassador in Cuba and the declarations of the President of Guatemala has occurred exactly the same week in which the ten thousand *caballerías* of land of the United Fruit Company passed to the hands of the National Institute of Agrarian Reform in order to distribute them to the peasants. What a coincidence! What a coincidence!

And what a coincidence that it has come from nothing less than Guatemala, where the United Fruit Company is the all-powerful institution; that it has come from Guatemala, where the United Fruit Company organized and inspired the aggression against the democratic government of that country![3]

...

A few weeks after the explosion of the ship bringing arms, certain newspapers were citing sources well informed concerning the government of the United States, revealing that pirate ships opposed to the Cuban Revolution were determined to attack ships that bring arms to our country.

...

That is to say, they want to reduce us to a state of total powerlessness, as the dangers and the threats grow.

...

That is the reality of our Revolution. Why? Why do they want to punish our Revolution? They want to punish the example; they want to destroy the example.... They want to destroy the Cuban Revolution in order that the example of the Cuban Revolution will not be copied by the sister peoples of Latin America.

...

And there is something more, most important of all. We are all immersed in a great task. The Revolutionary Government and the people are immersed in

---

3   Fidel refers to the 1954 invasion of Guatemala by a non-governmental military force financed by the United Fruit Company, trained and equipped by the United States, directed by Guatemalan Colonel Castillo de Armas, with the organization and tactical support of the U.S. Department of State, under Secretary of State John Foster Dulles, and the CIA. The invasion overthrew the government of Jacobo Arbenz Guzmán, which had appropriated unused land of the United Fruit Company, constituting 8% of the land that it owned in the country, compensating the owners with government bonds, in order to distribute the land to 100,000 peasant families.

great deeds. What we want is to see these deeds resulting someday in a new reality....

What man does not want to see his dreams converted into reality someday, his ideals converted into reality? And if in all of us burns the desire for the wellbeing and happiness of our people, to the extent that we want that it one day be a reality, we cannot possibly be the invaders. Those who want to see a great work attained, those who struggle for a great work, cannot be the invaders. The invaders can only be those who do not want us to carry out that work.

...

And if we have to face sacrifices that are necessary, we will do it with pleasure, because that will be the greatness of this generation of Cubans, and that is what it means to say *"Patria o Muerte."* (EXCLAMATIONS OF *"Patria o Muerte!"*).

To shatter the country one must first take our lives away. We are prepared to have our country and to leave a dignified country to future generations. That brief phrase of ours is the expression of our determination as a people; in that phrase we say all, and we are saying all that we have to say. That is our determined stance.

Therefore, we are going to speak clearly. We have the duty before us to warn, to warn those lunatics that go around looking for pretexts for armed aggression against our country, that we are not going to give them those pretexts, and that, in addition, we warn the world against any pretext hatched to justify an aggression against Cuba.

...

It is not possible to speak more clearly. In order that nothing remains to be said, to add solely, for Cubans, that we ought to be always alert, that we do not know for how many years we will have to be alert; that is the price that we have to pay for this work: Always be on the alert against any aggression, surprising or expected....

If the Prime Minister is absent (EXCLAMATIONS OF: "No! No!)—in any moment, ... if the Prime Minister is absent—I mean, if the enemies of the Revolution carry out an aggression—the only realistic option and the only objective is to know what one must do, and to know that you immediately have a substitute for the Prime Minister, and you are going to name him. Already in that mass rally, I proposed Raúl for Prime Minister, if the Prime Minister is absent (PROLONGED OVATION).

And if both are absent, the President of the Republic will meet with the Council of Ministers and designate another Prime Minister. Here one must be prepared for all the contingencies.

When a people takes on a task like that which the Cuban people has undertaken; when a people, small as in the case of Cuba, has powerful adversaries like Cuba has today, all the contingencies have to be foreseen. And that people ought to know what it has to do. And what is has to do, above all, is to know that never can that people be divided before an enemy action; the reaction of the people always has to be to close ranks!

...

So then, the only thing that remains to me, on this First of May, is to reaffirm that determination, that determination of all to continue fulfilling our duty, in our posts, and to ask everyone to do the same. To express our faith in the future of our country, our faith in the solidarity of the brother peoples of the Continent, for which we are struggling, because they will learn from our experience, they will learn from the good decisions that we make, and they will learn from the errors that we make.

...

To those of brother peoples of America [who are here], go to tell them what Cuba is. Go to refute the lies that are written against this generous and noble land. Go to tell them that this people is not here because it follows a leader, that this people is here for very profound reasons, that this people is here because in the life of the Revolutionary Government, we have known how to comply with our duty to the people, and the people are loyal to those who are loyal to them, and the people have faith in those that have faith in them.

Go to say to the brother peoples that here there is a Spartan people, and of us they will be able to say what was written in the gravestone on the way to Thermopolis: "Go to say to the world that here lie 300 Spartans that preferred to die before surrendering."

That is what the Americas expect of us; that is what the world expects of us. We will know how to repay the sympathy and the solidarity that we have received.

We all swear, soldiers of the Rebel Army, militias, peasants, workers, students, youth; we hoist our Cuban flag; we lift are rifles; we lift our machetes, in order to swear that we will comply with our slogan of *Patria o Muerte*!

The Slogan for the People Is: *Venceremos*!

Compañeras and *compañeros*:[1]

...

Love of country is a spiritual raw material that produces much more energy that uranium or hydrogen. This is forgotten by those that despise the peoples, those that detest the feelings of the people.

What a shame that they forget these truths, since they would be able to save themselves from many bad things, to avoid wrongs not only to the victimized country but also for the victimizing country. If they are crazy enough to commit aggression against us, there is not the least doubt that they will be defeated, and no one knows the consequences of that defeat for the aggressors.

...

Of course, each measure that they take always will have our countermeasure! And so, in response to each economic aggression, we take one revolutionary measure more. Perhaps we will be even on the day that Cuban becomes the full owner of all that there is in Cuba.

Therefore, we have nothing to fear. Facing the struggle with decisiveness and optimism, because we never have been more right, and never have we had more certain prospects for success. We never have had a greater opportunity.

The Revolution has had problems with them, but everyone knows why. It has not been because we are neighbors; it has been a question of economic interests.

The Revolution would not have had problems with them, if our lands had not been foreign owned, if they had not been in foreign hands;

the Revolution would not have had problems, if our public services had not been in foreign hands;

the Revolution would not have had problems, if the economy of the country had not been in foreign hands.

Because foreign hands possessed our resources and our economy, the Revolution has had problems with the "neighbor of the North," which it would not have had, if those interests had not interceded.

---

1 Selections from a speech delivered in the closing ceremony of the First Revolutionary Congress of the National Federation of Barbershop and Hair Salon Workers, held in the theater of the Federation of Cuban Workers, June 7, 1960. Stenographic version of the office of the Prime Minister—Authors' note. "*Venceremos*" could be translated as "we will win" or "we will overcome." Because of its common use as a slogan in Cuba, the Spanish is used in this book. See Translator's Note.—Translator's note.

The Revolution did not have another road to choose because if the Revolution would have submitted before those interests, it would not have been a Revolution. The Revolution has had problems, because our riches were in foreign hands. And the problems, absolutely all, have had that origin. What I am saying is not new for Cubans; all Cubans know it. All Cubans know that any Revolution that affects North American interests will have problems.

Cuba, then, is not to blame. The Revolution is not to blame. At fault are those voracious hands that had put their claws on our riches!

Therefore, we are able to look to the future with courage and with faith. They are not rich in talent, really. We have nothing to fear from the many mistakes that they are committing. Just as they have been mistaken in all their steps with respect to Cuba, no one has the last doubt that they will continue being wrong, and that they will continue to go against the fortitude of our people, and they will continue failing. In reality it would be better, for them and for Cuba, if they were to reconsider, because if they continue the error of taking the disastrous road of aggression, it would be bad for Cuba, but it would be worse for them! (APPLAUSE)

In the long run, we will be victors. In the long run, we will be victors in any circumstance, whether it be in front of the economic aggression or in front of the military aggression! ... In the long run, we will be victors. And with our victory, it could be that the brother peoples of Latin America also will awaken.

And these peoples, sooner or later, will follow the road of Cuba. The admiration that they feel for our people is not in vain, because our people will not let them down. Cuba will not lose its resolve; Cuba will rise to the occasion.

In any circumstance, although they are trying to put us in a *cordon sanitaire*, the struggle of Cuba will aid the liberation of the peoples of Latin America. Winning economically before the economic aggressions, and winning militarily before the military aggressions, the example of Cuba will be the example that the fraternal peoples of Latin America will follow, sooner or later.

In any event, the Cuban Revolution—as we said on the First of May—is a reality in the history of the world, one of those realities that weigh heavily on those not resigned to them. It will be a reality that will not be able to be erased. We are today the first trench of America....

The humble masses of all the peoples of this continent look to Cuba. Full of hope, they do not vacilate in affirming—without any vacillation—that Cuba is their example, that their triumph depends on the triumph of Cuba.

And that is the role we Cubans are playing in the first trench of America. And we will know how to defend that trench! The enemies of our nationalities and our brother peoples of Latin America will never take that trench!

That trench will be maintained, firm and invincible, because we are in it, those of us that have the privilege of being in that trench will not lose it. Those of us that have the privilege of playing this role that Cuba is playing in the history of this continent will rise to the occasion, with the certainly that we will be victorious, that our people will be victorious. Cost what it may, our people will be victorious.

Because its sons have decided to defend it, because its sons have the courage, the patriotism, and the unity that are needed in an hour such as this; because its sons have said, "*Patria o Muerte!*"

And they have said, "*Patria o Muerte!*" because that is the slogan of each Cuban. For each one of us individually, the slogan is "*Patria o Muerte!*," but for the people, that in the long run will come out victoriously, the slogan is, "*Venceremos!*"

Latin America Does Not Have the Right to Make a Revolution

Compañeros delegates of the youth of Latin America and from all the countries of the world that visit us;[1]
Workers' leaders of the Americas;
People of Cuba:
For us this meeting of representatives of the youth of the peoples of Latin America, from all over the continent, inasmuch as the bad thing about America is not the people of the United States, but the system implanted on the North American people and on the Latin American people by Yankee imperialism....

This ceremony of today, this event of these days, this meeting of representatives of the youth of our continent, has to be extraordinarily emotional for all of us.

...

We are say that there is a new revolutionary scene in this continent, and in saying this, we are not denying the efforts that other peoples have made to free themselves. It would be more correct to say that it is the second revolution of America, or to be more exact, the second liberating revolution of America. The first was against the Spanish colonial yoke, and this second and latest against the Yankee colonial yoke.

...

The revolutions were not authorized in the Americas. The only revolutions authorized in America were the revolutions "made in the United States!" That is, the *coups d'état* that here were called "revolutions," or even the revolutionary movements where the North American government was disposed to permit it.

The exploited workers, for social and economic reasons, are revolutionaries; the hungry and landless peasant is also, necessarily, revolutionary; the young man, by temperament, is revolutionary; all the exploited people and every exploited social class are, by nature, revolutionaries. The exploited peoples and the exploited social classes have to be, necessarily, revolutionaries. The germ of the revolution was in the social and economic reality of the Americas.

---

1 Selections from a speech delivered during the closing ceremony of the First Congress of Latin American Youth, August 6, 1960, in which the nationalization of U.S. companies was announced. Stenographic version of the Office of the Prime Minister.

However, what right do our peoples have to make revolutions? None, because the right to make a revolution, that is, the right to break chains, is an immemorial right of men; the right to destroy injustice, the right to abolish exploitation, is an immemorial right of men. That right was impeded not only by the repressive forces that, within the borders of each one of our countries, impede the most minimum manifestation of inconformity, rebellion, and protests. The right to make revolution was impeded not only by the military castes, the professional armies, the repressive political police. It was impeded not only by the monopolistic control of arms and force. It also was impeded through the spiritual means of the peoples, through their press, their universities, their centers of education, and the national and international media of information....

We defeated here the professional mercenary army that was in the service of international and national privileges. Here we overcame the monopoly that those interests have over the media of communication.

Everyone knows that the ideas of rebellion and of justice that inspired the Cuban Revolution were not written in the newspapers, nor were they explained in the radio and television stations. Everyone knows that the ideas that generated the Cuban Revolution were not inspired in the textbooks of our history, because to the shame of those that contributed to that criminal submission to foreign interests, our history books taught to our youths and our children that we owe our liberty to the empire that had snatched it from us.

...

Everyone knows that the Revolution did not emerge from the peasant organizations, because the peasant organizations were absolutely impeded in our country. Everyone knows that the Revolution did not emerge from the workers' organizations, because the workers' organizations, in their eagerness ("Fidel!") to control all.... (FIDEL CASTRO LOSES MOMENTARILY HIS VOICE; EXCLAMATIONS OF "Take care of yourself!" "Take care of yourself!" "Rest!" "Rest!").

I have recovered my voice, I have recovered (EXCLAMATIONS OF "Rest!"). Don't make noise, and let me, I have recovered my voice; let's go, work with me and do not make noise.... (THE EXCLAMATIONS CONTINUE: "Rest!" CHANTING "Raúl, Raúl, Raúl!")

Announcer: Fidel wants to continue talking. Fidel does not want to leave, because he feels well, only a little loss of voice.

Comandante Raúl Castro: Beloved *compañeros* (APPLAUSE).

It is not by mere chance that this occurs in what has to be a historic moment for Cuba and for Our America. That is the truth! It is not a question of fate, or of an ominous prediction; it is, simply, a small reversal without importance, because a voice has gone away for a moment, but here it is, and here it will be! (PROLONGED APPLAUSE AND EXCLAMATIONS OF "Fidel!")

...

(RAÚL SHOWS A DOCUMENT. APPLAUSE AND EXCLAMATIONS OF "Fidel, Fidel, Fidel!"). It could have been avoided, if the beloved and admired *compañero* Fidel would have dedicated time to taking care of himself (EXCLAMATIONS OF: "Take care of yourself; take care of yourself!")

At this moment, he feels badly and we feel badly, because the important declarations that he was making, to inform the people and Our America of the fruits that we have attained, is an honor that is appropriate only for him! Therefore, we are not going to take much time, nor are we going to delay much more, we know that you are anxious to know the objective of this meeting.... Fidel has to rest now, and he will recuperate, because it is nothing serious, as he has assured us.

We will read these revolutionary laws that we have here today.... And we swear that when he is recovered, when he is again able to direct his people, as always he has done, magnificently and brilliantly, with historic and profound exposition, and not only of Cuba. Because today here he will not speak of Cuba, but of all lf our Latin America. Therefore, we swear, Cuban brothers, to make preparations for the largest demonstration that our country has ever seen.

Republic of Cuba, Executive Power. Resolution. (In each "Whereas," you will be able to observe that everything is explained).

Whereas: Law No 851, of July 6, 1960, published in the Gaceta Oficial *of the Republic on July 7, authorized the nationalization of assets and companies that are the property of natural or legal persons of the United States of America, through the compulsory purchase of properties and companies, by means of resolutions by the appropriate authorities, when they consider it advisable for the defense of the national interest* ("Cuba *Sí,* Yankees No!" "Fidel!" "Fidel, give it to the Yankees hard!" "What does he have, that the Americans can't with him!").

We are going to make a little effort: He, speaking in a low voice; and you, maintaining silence, for five minutes only. Meanwhile, let us sing the National Anthem, led by Almeida. (THE NATIONAL ANTHEM IS SUNG, FOLLOWING WHICH FIDEL CASTRO CONTINUES TO SPEAK).

Comandante Fidel Castro: *Whereas: the basis for said Law is the attitude, by the Government and Legislature of the United States of America, of constant aggression, with political ends, against the fundamental interests of the Cuban economy, as was made evident by the amendment to the Sugar Law by the Congress of said country; through which exceptional powers were conceded to the President of said country to reduce the participation in its sugar market of Cuban sugar producers, as a weapon of political action against Cuba.*

Whereas: The President of the United States of America, making use of the mentioned exceptional powers, and in an obvious attitude of economic and political aggression against our country, has proceeded to reduce the participation in the North American market of the Cuban sugar producers, with the undeniable purpose of aggression against Cuba and against its development and revolutionary process.

Whereas: this fact constitutes a reiteration of the continued conduct of the government of the United States of America, which has sought to prevent the exercise by our people of its sovereignty and its integral development, in accordance with the despicable interests of the North American monopolies that have created obstacles to the growth of our economy, and which has sought to prevent the affirmation of our political freedom.

Whereas: In view of such facts, those with appropriate authority, conscious of their high historic responsibility, and in legitimate defense of the national economy, have the obligation to take necessary measures to counteract the damage caused by the aggressions to which our nation has been subjected.

Whereas: In conformity with our constitutional and legal order, in the exercise of our sovereignty, understanding that it would be practical to exercise the power conferred by Law No. 851 of July 6, 1960 before the consummation of the aggressive measures referred to above, that is, to proceed to the expropriation by the State of assets and companies that are the property of legal persons that are nationals of the United States of North America, as a decision justified by the necessity of the nation to compensate for the damage caused to its economy and to affirm its economic independence.

Whereas: The Cuban Electricity Company and the Cuban Telephone Company have constituted a typical example of the extortionist and exploiting monopolies that have sucked dry the economy of the nation and evaded the interests of the people for many years.

Whereas: The Sugar Companies seized the best lands of our country under the protection of the Platt Amendment, a despicable clause curtailing the national economy, which facilitated the invasion of the country by the imperialist capital of its insatiable and unscrupulous foreign masters, which have extracted many times the value of what they invested.

Whereas: The petroleum companies continuously swindled the economy of the nation, charging monopoly prices, which meant for many years the substantial expenditure of funds, and a desire to perpetuate privileges in defiance of the laws of the nation; and they hatched a criminal plan of boycott against our country, obligating the Revolutionary Government to intervene.

Whereas: It is the duty of the peoples of Latin America to be inclined toward the recuperation of its national riches, taking them away from the control of the monopolies and foreign interests that impede the progress of the peoples, promote political interference, and infringe upon the sovereignty of the underdeveloped peoples of America.

Whereas: The Cuban Revolution will not be stopped until the total and final liberation of the country;

Whereas: Cuba is a shining and stimulating example for the fraternal peoples of America and all the underdeveloped peoples of the world, in its struggle to free itself from the brutal claws of imperialism.

Whereas: In making use of the powers vested in us, in accordance with what is stipulated in Law No. 851, of July 6, 1960,

WE RESOLVE:

FIRST: It Is decreed the nationalization, by means of compulsory purchase, and the consequent adjudication in favor of the full control of the Cuban state, of all the assets and companies located in the national territory, and the rights and shares resulting from the operations of said assets and companies, which are the property of legal persons that are nationals of the United States of North America, or operating companies in which nationals of said country have predominant interest, that are related to the following:

1. Compañía Cubana de Electricidad;
2. Compañía Cubana de Teléfonos;
3. Esso Standard Oil, S.A., División de Cuba;
4. Texas Company West Indian;
5. Sinclair Cuba Oil Company, S.A.;
6. Central Cunagua, S.A.;
7. Compañía Azucarera Atlántica del Golfo, S.A.;
8. Compañía Central Altagracia, S.A.;
9. Miranda Sugar Estates;
10. Compañía Cubana, S.A.;
11. The Cuban American Sugar Mill;
12. Cuban Trading Company;
13. The New Tuinicú Sugar Company;
14. The Francisco Sugar Company;
15. Compañía Azucarera Céspedes;
16. Manatí Sugar Company;
17. Punta Alegre Sugar Sales Company;
18. Baraguá Industrial Corporation of New York;
19. Florida Industrial Corporation of New York;
20. Macareño Industrial Corporation of New York;
21. General Sugar States;
22. Compañía Azucarera Vertientes Camagüey de Cuba;

23. *Guantánamo Sugar Company...* (EXCLAMATIONS OF "It is no longer!"
24. *United Fruit Company* ("It is no longer!")
25. (THE EX-PRESIDENT OF GUATEMALA, JACOBO ARBENZ, COMES TO THE PLATFORM AND IS EMBRACED BY COMANDANTE FIDEL CASTRO)[2]
26. *Compañía Azucarera Soledad S.A.* ("It is no longer!")
27. *Central Ermita, S.A."* ("It is no longer!")

That is, all the enterprises of the electric company, all the enterprises of the telephone company, all the assets, of course, and enterprises of Texaco, of Esso ("It is no longer!"), Sinclair ("It is no longer!"), and in addition, the thirty-six sugar cane factories that the United States had in Cuba ("It is no longer!," "It is no longer!").

Therefore—softly, softly, because they cannot hear—*the Cuban state is declared substituted in place of the legal persons related to the above, with respect to the assets, rights, and shares mentioned, as well as the active and passive members of the capital of the referred enterprises*, et cetera, et cetera, et cetera.

Signed: Dr. Osvaldo Dorticós,[3] *President of the Republic.* And he that is speaking to you, the Prime Minister of the Revolutionary Government.

As you know, in accordance with the Law of July 6, 1960 of defense of the national economy and the sovereignty of the country, those assets will be compensated.

They are going to be compensated. How? With bonds that mature in a term of 50 years, at 2% interest, with a fund....

With what are we going to pay? Very well: with a fund that will be established with a fourth part of the value of the sugar that they buy from us above three million tons, that is, that when they buy from us sugar above three million, or three million and one-half, or four million, for example, what is above three million, with a quarter of what surpasses three million, provided that the price be 5.40 dollars per *quintal*,[4] with a quarter of the value. Do you understand well? ("*Sí!*"). With a fourth part of the value of what they buy from us of sugar above three million, provided that the price be $5.4 dollars per *quintal*, or more. Such that the bonds will be paid with that fund, in fifty years. There is a period of fifty years to pay it.

This is the Law, a resolution adopted in accordance with the Law, approved by the Council of Ministers and authorized by the President of the Republic

---

2   See footnote 17.
3   See glossary.
4   A *quintal* is a unit of measure, commonly used in Cuba, equivalent to 100 pounds—Translator's note.

and the Prime Minister, in order to adopt these measures in defense of our economy. No, no, no, I am not going to lose my voice....

...

They always had our sugar, sugar that was ours, but the dividends of which they themselves took through the companies that were the owners of the principal sugar cane factories, and in addition they paid a price lower than the world market during the war years, when they did not have anywhere to buy sugar, and our workers were sacrificed, our agricultural producers were sacrificed, in order that they would have sugar, a lot of sugar, the prices of which, in the end, they set.

They eliminated a million tons from our quota, when the sugar already was produced, with the obvious intention of starving us into surrender, and of twisting the destiny of our country by means of economic aggression. And we clearly warned them that the aggressions against Cuba and the quotas that they eliminate would be paid [by nationalizations], sugar cane factory by sugar can factory, and property by property.

However, a detail was lacking, a detail—oh!, still some things remain. We will be discussing in due course, *coup* by *coup*; in due time, *coup* by *coup*!

...

Unequivocal proof, because, how can you have democracy where there are no people? How can you have democracy where the people do not participate, where the people do not act, where the people do not count?

...

The Revolution has called many people together in a few hours. This, however, is not our largest demonstration; we have not mobilized the city, and we have not mobilized the towns in the interior of the country. Here we see the blue shirts, which are our workers' militias; and here we see the green shirts of our peasant women militias.

The Revolution is able to gather many more people than this, and not only in the capital. The Revolution gathered them in the middle of the countryside, in the Sierra Maestra, because revolution is democracy above all, revolution is the people in action and struggle. Democracy is not in the forms. The hypocrites pay false respect to the forms; the false values are anchored in the forms. The true and profound values are held in action, and they take root in the action and in the essence.

...

They are anchored in the form, while we are anchored in action and to the essence. Action constantly informs our reasoning.

I had been interrupted when I was at the point of explaining that the official organizations of the workers [in the time of Batista], in their desire to control all, they had controlled all, by means of the gun and corruption. At that time, the instruments of the workers' struggle, in the middle of a regime of exploitation, were controlled by the servants of those interests and privileges.

Therefore we, taking the people of Havana as a representation and as an expression, in their sentiments, of the sentiments of the nation, we want to ask the people a question....

The people here, in front of us, we want also to consult with you, in order that the people also participate directly in this measure and that, therefore, raise your hands those that subscribe to this determination of the Revolutionary Government (THE PEOPLE IN FULL RAISE THEIR HANDS) (PROLONGED APPLAUSE AND EXCLAMATIONS OF "Already we voted! Already we voted!").

We are going to speak of the militias for a little bit. Who says that the militias do not have arms? What do you want, that I say now where they are? All of your arms are deposited, in points where in a very short time they will all be in your hands.

I want you to know that they are tested, lubricated, with ammunition and bayonet, absolutely everything. Already I have said that the militias were not going to march more without arms, because we now have the arms.

Now, you know that those with responsibilities spent a month in the Sierra Maestra and now they will undergo a course of intensive training. You all are to undergo an intensive training course, in order that you can organize true battalions with maximum efficiency. Because it is not enough to have the arms, you have to know how to use them better and more effectively, in order that he that collides with us here will know what he is up against. There are arms for everyone, and they are such high-quality arms that when you see them, you are going to be astonished.

The Revolutionary Government was not carried to power by money from some bank, or some monopoly, of some political machinery. The Revolution arrived to power because it is consecrated with a backing, which is not the backing that involves going to a ballot box to vote once every four years. The Revolution arrived to power with that true backing that the peoples give, when they give all that they have; because they give their sons, they give their husbands, they give their brothers, they give their loved one, and they give their blood to attain something.

And with blood, with sacrifice, without so much as an airplane, without so much as a tank, without Garand rifles, without millions from some trust, without political machineries, without newspapers to promote the cause, without networks of press, without UPI nor AP. The Revolution arrived to power with the blood and sweat of the people, and its functionaries are the most legitimate representatives of that people. And it is maintained in power in spite of the trusts, the political machineries, the newspapers, and the press.

...

They have created among us a fatalist mentality that makes each citizen think that without them the world is sunk, that against them no one would be able to govern. Because among many other arms, that arm of fatalism is worth much, superstition is worth much, and those traditional lies are worth much. They have made our people believe also in a geographic fatalism, which is not the same as fatalism; it was in any event a fatalism, but not the same fatalism.

And in spite of all that, in spite of the influence that they have here, our people have broken the chains, our people maintain its attitude and its line. What does that mean? That our power is a thousand time more legitimate than the power that they uphold, and that we here do not represent the high-interest lender, nor the estate owner, nor the monopolist, nor the banker; we here represent the victims and those exploited and extorted by all those interests.

...

Therefore, it is good that the people have voted here also, and of course, the Revolutionary Government is doing nothing other than interpreting the will of the people, of the people! ...

And the delegates of the youth congress with us also have voted, because they also have the right to vote here.

Because the problem of Cuba is not only the problem of Cuba. The problem of Cuba is today the problem of all of Latin America, but not only of Latin America. The problem of Cuba is the problem of the blacks in the South of the United States; the problem of Cuba is the problem of the "wetbacks" that work in the frontier zone with Mexico; the problem of Cuba is the problem of the progressive intellectual of the United States, it is the problem of the North American worker, of the North American farmer, and also of the North American people.

...

Especially noteworthy, one of the largest sugar cane factories was the property of the United Fruit Company. From now on, that factory will have the name of Guatemala, in homage to the Guatemalan people, cowardly riddled with bullets by the airplanes of the United Fruit Company, in homage to the people of Guatemala, in homage to the Guatemalans that died murdered or shot by the mercenary hordes of Castillo de Armas that is, the hordes of Foster Dulles, armed by United Fruit and the State Department.[5]

---

5 See footnote 15.

Revolution means the destruction of privilege, the disappearance of exploitation, the creation of a just society where men receive the fruit of their efforts, where the nations receive the fruit of their natural riches, and where men live from their work. Those that live without working are only those that cannot work, are too old, or are too young to produce.

...

And what do the Yankees want? Do they want that we defy the OAS? Well, if so, it makes clear that they are saying what we say: that they have the OAS as an instrument for impeding revolutions in America.

...

We ought to express here that the next meeting of the OAS is nothing other than a Yankee maneuver against Cuba, and we ought to express here that what Yankee imperialism is proposing in the meeting of OAS is a trap against Cuba.

...

Can it be imagined that, in the middle of an aggression against our country—an aggression that directly violates the agreements of that Organization of American States, an organization that violates continental law—, in the middle of an aggression against Cuba, the government of the United States convokes the OAS in order to discuss the problems of Cuba; in the same moment in which it shares among the other governments of Latin America the quota that they took from Cuba?

...

What do they believe? Do they believe that Cuba is going to remain silent? No, the empire and the foreign ministers of America ought to be prepared to hear the voice of Cuba! Cuba will go to the OAS to express its positions; they will decide what they consider advisable.

...

Cuba is going to the OAS to denounce, Cuba is going to the OAS to denounce the aggression against its economy!

But Cuba is not going to denounce the aggression against only its economy. Cuba is going to the OAS to denounce the aggressions that have been perpetuated against the economy of the peoples of Latin America....

What does it matter that they condemn us? What does it matter that Washington maneuvers? What does it matter that the headlines support them? And after that, what?

...

The Cuban Revolution, which was born without the permission of Washington—as Washington knows—, which was born without the permission of the OAS—as the OAS knows—, will continue on, in spite of Washington and in spite of the OAS. It will continue on, because we are determined that it will continue on. It will continue on because we the sons of Cuba are prepared to die so that the country can continue living!

And it will continue living, it will continue living, because we have the solidarity of the workers, the students, the youth, the intellectuals, and the peasants of America! And it will continue living, because we have the solidarity of all the exploited peoples of the world! And it will continue living, because we have the solidarity of all the liberated peoples of the world!

...

In addition, to the shock of Washington and the Pentagon, Cuba does not considered itself tied to the United States by any commitment, if it is desired! ... Let it be known that Cuba does not feel tied to the United States for any military commitment; Cuba, attacked by the United States, does not consider itself tied to the United States for any military pact.

...

That means that to be a friend of Cuba is to be a crusader for a just cause, it is to be a crusader for a redeeming cause, it is to be an apostle of justice, and apostle of the truth....

You [young people of Latin America] should know that, when you are persecuted, here in Cuba there are millions of brotherly arms that are waiting for you; you should know that Cuba is your country, and that here in Cuba the homes of the sons of our people are also your homes. And that when, within the frontiers of your country, the henchmen in the service of the exploiting empire want to deprive you of your country, you have a country here (APPLAUSE), although the duty of all is to struggle, there or here. America is only one: a field of struggle for freedom, a field of struggle for dignity and for justice. Here or there, we all will have to say "*Patria o Muerte!*" Here or there, we all will say in the long run, "*venceremos,*" and we will be victorious.

Women, the Decisive Factor in the Revolution

Compañeras of the Federation of Cuban Women:[1]

In this hall many meetings have been held. This is the theater of the workers, and here we have had many events in this Revolution of the workers and the peasants.

But, in spite of the enthusiasm that always has reigned in all the occasions in which the workers have met, rarely has the atmosphere been filled with so much optimism, so much happiness, so much combative spirit. Today something that has been observed in all the public meetings is being demonstrated, and that is the extraordinary revolutionary spirit of Cuban women.

The Revolution has, without doubt, a very strong backing of the women's sector of our population. Therefore, from the first moments, the active participation of Cuban women was observed in a series of activities. It was nothing new for our country.

Our country can feel fortunate with respect to many things, but among them, the most important of all, is the magnificent people that it possesses. Here not only the men struggle; here, like the men, the women struggle.

And it is not new. History tells us of the great women in our struggles for independence, and one of them is they symbol of all: Mariana Grajales, who said to her smallest child, "Grow up quickly, so that you too can go to fight for your country!" And in the present historic stage of our people, there are many events that will remain recorded always, in which Cuban women played a leading role....

All the mothers that saw their sons fall, murdered or in combat, have been heroic mothers. And also worthy of recognition are those mothers that saw their sons drawn to crime by the despicable tyranny, because they also have had to suffer the consequences of the horrible past.

...

Therefore, it is good to remember; therefore, it is good to organize; therefore, it is good to unite; therefore, it is good to prepare yourself to struggle. Therefore, this step that Cuban women are taking today is one victory more for our people, one force more of our people.

---

1 Selections from a speech delivered in the ceremony uniting all the revolutionary women's organizations, creating the Federation of Cuban Women. Held in the theater of the Federation of Cuban Workers, August 23, 1960. The Federation of Cuban Women is a mass organization; 84% of Cuban women aged 14 or older are members. Department of Stenographic Versions of the Revolutionary Government.

This unification of all the women's sectors of the Revolution is constituting a force, an enthusiastic force, a numerous force, an important force, and a decisive force for our Revolution.

...

Therefore it has been a happy coincidence; it has been a happy and significant coincidence that in the precise moment of intrigue against our country, in which the powerful empire mobilizes all its millions and all its influence in order to maneuver against our country, enclosing our country and justifying aggressions against our country there in the breast of the OAS, today, precisely today, this Federation of Cuban Women has been constituted, as a dignified response, as an eloquent response, in which we, for our part here, in the first place, very tranquil; in the second place, very sure; in the third place, very clear; and in the fourth place, very united ("Unity! Unity!")

...

The "yes, sir" has been ended forever in our country, which has learned to say "no," and is showing the other peoples of America.

...

We are friends of those that would be our friends. We proclaim the aspiration of humanity for justice and peace. We exchange our products with those that are disposed to exchange their products with us.

Cuba no longer is, and will never be again, an appendage to your economy.

Cuba no longer is, and will never be again, a country that votes in the United Nations for what you indicate, but for what our dignity and our sovereignty indicate.

We will be friends of the Soviets and of the Popular Republic of China, because they have shown themselves to be our friends, while you attack us and want to destroy us; and because they do not come here speaking in the insolent language of your representatives, who are accustomed to giving orders.

...

Every mother wants her children to be able to study. Every mother wants that, if her child has the vocation, he would be able to study in the university. Before only a group of families with resources could go to the university; rarely for the humble families was there opportunity. Mothers want that tomorrow their sons and daughters will not work for the benefit of others, but will work for the benefit of themselves and their country.

...

If we have to fall, we will all fall, struggling for the good. If we have to fall, we will all fall, but struggling for freedom. If we have to fall, we will all fall, struggling against abuse and against crime. If we have to fall, we will all fall, but struggling for our country, for our dignity, and for the happiness of our people.

...

Today, women are gathered and they are constituting this Federation of Cuban Women, united in that word: *cubanas*,[2] and united in that flag that they carry in their hands. And they have been united in order to work, for working and struggling; they have been united for all the tasks that the Revolution brings to us; they have been united to help the country in any circumstance. If tomorrow the task is combat, they will lend their effort; if today the task is work, they will lend their effort.

There are many things that must be done, and many things that you can do. Now, the primary task is to organize, to gather all the *cubanas* that want to work for their country. Those thousands and thousands of women, tens of thousands of women, hundreds of thousands of women that want to do something. There is much to do, there is much to be done by the people, and there is much to be done by women.

Right now, already the women's youth brigades are organizing. And already the first institutions are being organized to teach and prepare all those young women that are neither in school nor have work.

And in addition, one must study all the problems of Cuban women. One must study the problems of women that have to work and do not have a place to leave their children. Right now, day care is insufficient. It cannot be expected that the municipal government or the state do it all, because the municipal governments and the state have limited resources, and they need them to satisfy urgent needs. On the other hand, by organizing the young women, organizing those tens of thousands of young women that are not going to school nor have work, and who can be victims of all the vices, we will have the human personnel that we can prepare, and we will be able to organize all the day care[3] that the working mothers of Cuba need. That is a task.

And there is another great task, a task that is the order of the day: to aid the peasant families, to aid the peasant women of the cooperatives. One must teach them, one must prepare them. There can be established institutions to educate those families, to teach them to carry out numerous works. There are the cooperatives, which constituted a nucleus where an important work can be developed.

---

2 Literally, female Cubans, or Cuban women and girls, which cannot be expressed in a single word in English.—Translator's note.
3 The day care centers that were organized were later given the name Children's Circles.

Women are participating actively in the tasks of the Revolution. Of the 1,412 voluntary teachers that went to the Sierra Maestra, approximately 50% are women.

Women are actively carrying out tasks, and organized, women can contribute greatly to make the last vestiges of discrimination disappear.

...

Women can be useful in every sense. Women can use arms, and women can engage in combat. So instead of a certain number of combatants, taking into account the women combatants, we will have double the number of combatants.

Only one must organize and prepare them. And also to constitute their combat units, Women's Combat Units, in order that the women do not think that they are being relegated only to other tasks. They ought to be given the opportunity in all areas, and they ought to be prepared for all the tasks. They ought to be, above all, the great reserve in the armed struggle; they ought to be those that substitute for the male combatants, when they fall, if we have to fight.

...

That there not be a single place in Cuba where the Federation of Cuban Women is not constituted; that there is not a single revolutionary woman that is not joined to the Federation of Cuban Women. And you will see how the Revolution will be able to count on one force more, on a new organized force, on a tremendous revolutionary and social force.

Hence, today, on the same day that there [in the OAS] they argue, we celebrate with jubilation this historic and promising day of the establishment of the Federation of Cuban Women.

And now, to work, to organize, and to put into action the creative spirit, the enthusiasm of the Cuban woman, in order that the Cuban woman, in this revolutionary stage will make the last vestige of discrimination disappear; and in order that the Cuban woman, for her virtues and her merits, will have the place that she deserves in the history of the country.

Declaration of Havana

Joined[1] to the image and the memory of José Martí, in Cuba, a free territory of America, the people, using the inalienable powers that arise from the effective exercise of the sovereignty expressed in the direct, universal, and public suffrage, have constituted the National General Assembly.

In our own name, and recognizing the feelings of the peoples of Our America, the National General Assembly of the People of Cuba:

1) Condemns in every respect the so-called "Declaration of San José of Costa Rica," a document dictated by North American imperialism, and an attack on the national self-determination, the sovereignty, and the dignity of the brother peoples of the continent.

2) The National General Assembly of the People of Cuba strongly condemns the open and criminal intervention of more than a century that North American imperialism has practiced against all the peoples of Latin America. More than once, they have invaded the soil of the peoples, in Mexico, Nicaragua, Haiti, Santo Domingo, or Cuba, which have lost, before the greed of the Yankee imperialists, extensive and rich zones like Texas; vital strategic centers like the Panama Canal; entire countries like Puerto Rico, converted into occupied territory. In addition, the peoples have suffered humiliating treatment by the U.S. Marines, both against our women and daughters and against the highest symbols of the histories of our countries, such as the statue of José Martí.

Those interventions were reinforced by military superiority, unequal treaties, and malicious submission by the traitors that governed our countries. During the course of more than one hundred years, they have converted Our America—the American that Bolívar, Hidalgo, Juárez, San Martín, O'Higgins, Sucre[2] and Martí wanted free—into a zone of exploitation, the backyard of the Yankee

---

1 Taken from Aeroviz, the official organ of the National Air Federation, Havana, October, 1960. This document was presented by Fidel to a mass meeting of one million persons at the Civic Plaza (today the Plaza of the Revolution). It began to be called the First Declaration of Havana in February, 1962, when a second declaration was made. As is seen in the conclusion of his September 26, 1960 address to the General Assembly of the United Nations (included in this book) and his October 13, 1960 television address (also included), Fidel considered that the 1960 First Declaration of Havana formulated the basic principles that would guide a new stage in the Cuban Revolution.

2 All were patriots that headed the struggles for independence from Spain at the beginning of the nineteenth century: Bolívar in the present territories of Venezuela, Colombia, Ecuador, and Bolivia; Hidalgo and Juárez in Mexico; San Martín in Argentina; and O'Higgins in Chile.

political and financial empire; and into a reserve of votes in international organizations, in which the Latin American countries have appeared as a line of tied donkeys of "the rough and brutal North that despises us."[3]

The National General Assembly of the People declares that the acceptance of that continuous and historically irrefutable intervention, by the rulers that officially assume the representation of the countries of Latin America, betrays the independence ideals of their peoples, erases their sovereignty, and impedes true solidarity among our countries, which obligates this assembly to repudiate it in the name of the people of Cuba and with a voice that takes in the hope and the determination of the Latin American peoples and the liberating emphasis of the immortal national heroes of Our America.

3) The National General Assembly of the People also rejects the attempt to preserve the Monroe Doctrine, utilized until now, as José Martí foresaw, "in order to extend the domination of America" of the voracious imperialists, in order the better inject the poison, as also was denounced by José Martí, "the poison of the loans, the canals, the railroads." Therefore, facing up to the hypocritical Pan-Americanism that is nothing more than the predominance of the Yankee monopolies over the interests of our peoples and Yankee use of the governments prostrated before Washington, the Assembly of the People of Cuba proclaims the liberating Latin Americanism pulsated in José Martí and Benito Juárez. And, in extending friendship toward the North American people—the people of the lynched blacks, the persecuted intellectuals, the workers forced to accept the direction of gangsters—it reaffirms its will to march "with all the world and not with a part of it."

4) The General Assembly of the People declares that the unsolicited aid offered by the Soviet Union to Cuba, in the event that our country were attacked by imperialist military forces, could never be considered as an act of interference, but would constitute an evident act of solidarity. It honors the government of the Soviet Union that offers it as much as the cowardly and criminal aggressions against Cuba dishonor the government of the United States. Therefore, the General Assembly of the People declares before America and before the world that it accepts and is grateful for the support of the rockets of the Soviet Union, if its territory were invaded by the military forces of the United States.

5) The National General Assembly of the People of Cuba categorically denies that there has existed any intention on the part of the Soviet Union

---

3 The three quotations in the Declaration are in the original document, without citing the source.

or the Chinse Popular Republic to "utilize the economic, political, and social position of Cuba... to break continental unity and to place in danger the unity of the hemisphere." From the first until the last shot, from the first to the last of the twenty thousand martyrs that it cost the struggle to overthrow the tyranny and to capture revolutionary power, from the first to the last act of the Revolution, the people of Cuba have acted on its own absolute and free determination. Therefore, the Soviet Union and the Chinese Popular Republic can scarcely be blamed for the existence of a revolution that is, precisely, the response of Cuba to the crimes and injustices established by imperialism in America.

On the other hand, the National General Assembly of the People of Cuba understands that the policy of isolation and hostility toward the Soviet Union and the Chinese Popular Republic, advocated by the government of the United States and imposed by it on the governments of Latin America; the aggressive and militarist conduct of the North American government; and its systematic denial of the entrance of the Chinese Popular Republic in the United Nations, in spite of the fact that said government represents nearly the totality of nearly six hundred million inhabitants; do indeed place in danger the peace and security of the hemisphere and the world.

Therefore, the National General Assembly of the People of Cuba ratifies the policy of friendship with all the peoples of the world, and it reaffirms its objective of establishing diplomatic relations, including with all the socialist countries. And from this moment, in the exercise of its sovereignty and free will, expresses to the Peoples Republic of China that it agrees to establish diplomatic relations between our two countries, and that, therefore, the relations that up to today Cuba has maintained with the puppet regime in Formosa, which is sustained by the ships of the Yankee Seventh Fleet, are terminated.

6) The General Assembly of the People reaffirms, and it is certain of doing so as an expression of a common judgment of the peoples of Latin America, that democracy is not compatible with financial oligarchy, with the existence of discrimination against blacks and the outrages of the Ku Klux Klan, and with the persecution that removed scientists like Oppenheimer[4] from their positions; that prevented the world from listening to

---

4 J. Robert Oppenheimer (1904–1967) was the director during World War II of the Manhattan Project, which developed the atomic bombs dropped on Hiroshima and Nagasaki. Following the war, he was Chairman of the General Advisory Council of the newly created Atomic Energy Commission. In 1954, because of his associations with members of the Communist Party, Oppenheimer's security clearance was removed, which resulted in a loss of influence–Translator's note.

the marvelous voice of Paul Robeson,[5] prisoner in his own country; that took the Rosenbergs[6] to death, before the protests and the horror of the entire world, and in spite of the appeals of the governments of various countries and of Pope Pius XII himself.

The Cuban People's National General Assembly expresses the Cuban conviction that democracy cannot consist only in the exercise of an electoral vote that nearly always is fictitious and is manipulated by the large estate owners and the professional politicians, without the right of the citizens to decide their own destiny, as this Cuban People's General Assembly is now doing. Democracy, in addition, will only exist when the peoples are truly free to choose, when the humble are not reduced—by hunger, social inequality, illiteracy, and legal systems—to the most ominous powerlessness.

Therefore, the Cuban People's National General Assembly:

Condemns the large estate, source of misery for the peasant and a backward and inhumane system of agricultural production;

condemns the starvation wages and the dreadful exploitation of human work by illegitimate and privileged interests;

condemns illiteracy, the lack of teachers, schools, doctors, and hospitals, the lack of protection of the aged that prevails in the countries of America;

condemns the discrimination against Blacks and Indian people;

condemns the inequality and the exploitation of the woman;

condemns the military and political oligarchies that maintain our peoples in poverty, impede their democratic development and the full exercise of their sovereignty;

condemns the concession of natural resources of our countries to the foreign monopolies as a submissive policy that betrays the interests of the peoples;

---

5 Paul Robeson (1898–1976) was an internationally known singer and actor who performed regularly in England as well as the United States. He was involved with various progressive and leftist causes, and he supported the Soviet Union. Because of his outspoken criticism of the United States, his passport was revoked from 1950 to 1958, preventing him from performing outside the USA—Translator's note.

6 Julius Rosenberg (1918–1953) and Ethel Rosenberg (1915–1953) were tried and convicted of spying for the Soviet Union and providing top-secret information; they were executed on June 19, 1953. Following their sentencing, an international campaign for clemency sought to stop the execution, with many prominent intellectuals, scientists, and artists of the world participating. At the time, many in the international Left believed the case to be a political frame-up, driven by Cold War paranoia—Translator's note.

condemns the governments that do not listen to the sentiments of their peoples in order to comply with the mandates of Washington;

condemns the systematic deceit of the peoples by agencies of dissemination that respond to the interest of the oligarchies and to the policy of oppressive imperialism;

condemns the monopoly of the news by Yankee agencies, instruments of the North American trusts and agents of Washington;

condemns the repressive laws that prevent workers, peasants, students, and intellectuals, the great majority in each country, from organizing and struggling for their social and patriotic demands;

condemns the monopolies and the imperialist companies that systematically plunder our resources, exploit our workers and peasants, bleed and keep backward our economies, and force the politics of Latin America to submit to their designs and interests.

"The Cuban People's National General Assembly condemns, in sum, the exploitation of man by man, and the exploitation of the underdeveloped countries by imperialist finance capital.

"Therefore, the Cuban People' s National General Assembly proclaims before the people of the Americas:

the right of peasants to the land;
the right of workers to the fruit of their labor;
the right of children to education;
the right of the sick to medical attention and hospital care;
the right of the youth to work;
the right of students to free, experiential and scientific education;
the right of Blacks and Indians to 'the full dignity of man';
the right of women to civil, social, and political equality;
the right of the elderly to a secure old age;
the right of the intellectuals, artists, and scientists to struggle, with their works, for a better world;
the right of states to the nationalization of the imperialist monopolies, thereby rescuing national wealth and resources;
the right of nations to their full sovereignty;
the right of the peoples to convert their military fortresses into schools, and to arm their workers, their peasants, their students, their intellectuals, Black and Indian peoples, women, young people, old people, and all the oppressed and exploited, in order that they can defend, by themselves, their rights and their destinies.

7) The Cuban People's National General Assembly proposes:
The duty of workers, peasants, students, intellectuals, Blacks, Indians, youth, women, the elderly, to struggle for their economic, political, and social demands;

the duty of the oppressed and exploited nations to struggle for their liberation;

the duty of each people to solidarity with all the oppressed, colonized, exploited, and attacked peoples of the world, regardless of where they are and the geographical distance from them. All the peoples of the world are brothers!

8) The Cuban People's National General Assembly reaffirms its faith that Latin America will march soon, united and victorious, free of the ties that convert their economies into wealth transferred to North American imperialism, and that impede them from hearing their own voice in meetings where tamed foreign ministers sing the shameful chorus to the despotic master. It ratifies, therefore, its determination to work for that common Latin American destiny that will permit our countries a true solidarity, deeply rooted in the free will of each of one of them and in the common aspirations of all of them. In the struggle for that liberated Latin America, in opposition to the obedient voice of those that usurp their official representation, the genuine voice of the peoples now emerges, with invincible power, a voice that takes its first steps in the entrails of the coal and tin mines, in the factories and sugar cane processing plants, in the sheathed lands where the lower class, the mestizos, gauchos, and Indians, inheritors of the legacy of Zapata and Sandino, take up arms for their liberty; a voice that is resounds in its poets, its novelists, its students, its women and its children, and its elderly that are unable to sleep.

To that fraternal voice, the Cuban People's National General Assembly responds:

PRESENT!

Cuba will not fail. Cuba is here today to ratify, before Latin America, before the world, as a historic commitment to its unwavering choice: *Patria o Muerte*!

9) The Cuban People's National General resolves that this declaration shall be known as The "Declaration of Havana."

Havana, Cuba, Free Territory of America, September 2, 1960

Speech in the General Assembly of the United Nations

Mr. President;[1]
   Distinguished delegates:
Although we are known for speaking extensively, do not worry. We are going to do what is possible to be brief and to express what we understand to be our duty to express here. We also are going to speak slowly, to assist the interpreters.

Some will think that we are very disgusted with the treatment that the Cuban delegation has received. It is not so. We understand perfectly well the reasons for what occurred. Therefore, we are not irritated, and no one ought to be worried that Cuba will cease placing its grain of sand in the effort to ensure that the world understands. Therefore, we are going to speak frankly.

...

The speakers who have preceded us have expressed their concerns with respect to the problems that interest the entire world. Those problems interest us, but, in addition, in the case of Cuba, a special circumstance exists. Cuba is in this moment a concern for the world. Various delegates have rightly expressed here that among the different problems that presently exist in the world is the problem of Cuba.

In addition to the problems that today concern the world, Cuba has problems that are of concern to her, that are concerns for our people.

It is spoken of the universal desire for peace, that it is the desire of all the peoples, and therefore, it is the desire also of our people. But that peace that the world desires to preserve is a peace that we Cubans have not expected for some time. The dangers that other peoples of the world can consider more or less remote are for us very near. It has not been easy to come her to express in this assembly the problems of Cuba. It has not been easy for us to arrive here.

I do not know if we of the Cuban delegation are privileged. Are we the representatives of some kind of worse government for the world? Are we, the representatives of the Cuban delegation, deserving of the mistreatment that we have received? And why precisely our delegation?

Cuba has sent many delegations to the United Nations. Cuba has been represented by various persons, and however, exceptional measures now have

---

1   Selections from a speech delivered to the General Assembly of the United Nations, New York, September 26, 1960. Stenographic version of the Office of the Prime Minister.

been applied to us: confinement to the island of Manhattan; instructions to all the hotels that they not rent us rooms; hostility; and, under the pretext of security, isolation.

Perhaps none of you, distinguished delegates; who arrive not as individuals representing no one, but as representatives of your respective countries; which each one of you represent in your arrival to this city of New York, referring each one of you to the things that are of concern; perhaps none of you have had to suffer the personally humiliating and physically humiliating treatment that the President of the Cuban delegation has had to suffer.

...

Humiliating treatment, attempts at extortion, eviction from the hotel where we were staying. And when we changed to another hotel, we did all that was possible to avoid difficulties, refraining completely from leaving the hotel, not going anywhere other than this hall of the United Nations, the few times that we have attended, and we accepted an invitation to a reception in the embassy of the Soviet government. However, that was not enough for them to leave us in peace.

There was here, in this country, a large Cuban immigration. More than 100,000 Cubans have moved to this country from their own land, where they would have desired to stay forever, and where they desire to return, as those that were obligated for social and economic reasons to abandon their country always desire to return. Those Cuban immigrants dedicated themselves to work, and they respected and respect the laws. As is natural, they had feelings for their country, and they had feelings for the Revolution.

They never had problems. But one day another type of visitor began to arrive to this country: criminals of war began to arrive, and individuals that had murdered, in some cases, hundreds of our compatriots, began to arrive. Here they quickly found themselves encouraged by publicity and encouraged by the authorities, and this encouragement was reflected in their conduct, which was the source of frequent incidents with the Cuban population that for many years had been working honestly in this country.

...

When we were obligated to abandon one of the hotels of this city, we headed toward the headquarters of the United Nations, while other steps were being taken. A hotel gave us lodging, a humble hotel of this city, a hotel of the Blacks of Harlem. This response arrived while we were conversing with the Secretary General. However, a functionary of the Department of State did all that was possible to impede our lodging in that hotel. At that moment, like magic, there began to appear hotels in New York. Hotels that had denied lodging to the Cuban delegation previously, now were offering to provide lodging for us, even without charge. But we, out of elementary reciprocity, accepted the hotel in Harlem. We understood that we had the right to expect that we would be left in peace, but no, we were not left in peace.

Once in Harlem, in view of the fact that they were not able to impede our stay in that place, they began the defamation campaigns. They began to spread throughout the world the news that the Cuban delegation had lodged in a brothel. For some gentlemen, a humble hotel of the neighborhood of Harlem, of the Blacks of the United States, has to be a brothel. And in addition, they have been trying to paint with infamy the Cuban delegation, without respect even for the *compañeras* that belong to or work with our delegation.

...

The problem of Cuba. Perhaps some of you have been informed, perhaps some not. Everything depends on the sources of information, but, without doubt, for the world, the problem of Cuba has emerged during the course of the last two years. It is a new problem.

The world has not had much reason to know that Cuba existed. For many, it was something like an appendage to the United States. Even for many citizens of this country, Cuba was a colony of the United States. On the map, it was not; on the map, we appeared with a color distinct from the color of the United States. But in reality, it was a colony.

And how did our country become a colony of the United States? It was not precisely for its origins. Those that colonized Cuba were not the same men that colonized the United States. Cuba has ethnic and cultural roots very different, and those roots were consolidated for centuries. Cuba was the last country of America to liberate itself from the Spanish colonial government, from the Spanish colonial yoke, with apologies to his Excellency the representative of the Spanish government. And because it was the last, it had to struggle especially hard.

...

Cubans struggled alone for thirty years, for their independence. Thirty years that laid the foundation of our love for freedom and for the independence of our country.

But Cuba was a fruit—according to the opinion of a President of the United States at the beginning of the past century, John Adams, it was like an apple of the Spanish tree, waiting, called to fall as soon as it matures, into the hands of the United States. And the Spanish power had worn itself out in our country. Spain no longer had the men nor the economic resources to maintain the war in Cuba; Spain was defeated.

The apple was apparently mature and the government of the United States stretched out its hands.

One apple did not fall; various apples fell into its hands. Puerto Rico fell, the heroic Puerto Rico that had initiated its struggle for independence together with Cubans. The Philippine Islands fell, and various other possessions fell.

However, the most expedient form for dominating our country was not the same, because our country has sustained a tremendous struggle, which had the support of world opinion. The most expedient form of domination had to be different.

...

After two years of military occupation of country, the unexpected emerged. In the same moment in which the people of Cuba, through a Constitutional Assembly, were drafting the Constitution of the Republic,[2] a new law emerged in the Congress of the United States, a law proposed by Senator Platt, a sad memory for Cuba.

In said law, it was established that the Constitutional Assembly of Cuba ought to have an appendix, by virtue of which it was conceded to the government of the United States the right to intervene in the political problems of Cuba, and in addition, the right to lease certain spaces in its territory for naval bases or coaling stations.

That is to say, by means of a law emanating from the legislative authority of a foreign country, the Constitution of our country had to contain that disposition, inasmuch as it was very clearly indicated to the delegates of our Constitutional Assembly that if they had not approved the amendment, the forces of occupation would not have been withdrawn.

...

So began the new colonization of our country, the acquisition of the best agricultural lands by North American companies; concessions of its natural resources, its mines; concessions of the public services, for the exploitation of the public services; commercial concessions; concessions of every kind, that together with the constitutional right—constitutional right to force—of intervening in our country, they converted our country from a Spanish colony into a North American colony.

The colonies do not speak, the colonies are not known in the world until they have the opportunity to express themselves. Therefore, our colony was not known to the world, and the problems of our colony were not known to the world.... Let no one be deceived. We become fools when we allow ourselves to be deceived. Let no one be deceived; there was no independent republic; there was a colony, where he who gave orders was the ambassador of the United States.

---

2   Constitution of 1901.

Again, the Cuban nation had to recourse to struggle to gain its independence. It attained it after seven years of bloody tyranny. Tyrannized by whom? Tyrannized by those whom in our country were nothing more than the instruments for the economic domination of our country.

...

The military group that tyrannized our country was supported by the most reactionary sectors of the nation and it was supported above all by the foreign economic interests that dominated the economy of our country. Everyone knows, and we understand that even the government of the United States itself recognizes, everyone knows that this was the type of government preferred by the monopolies. Why? Because with force all the demands of the people can be repressed; with force, the strikes for better conditions of life can be repressed; with force the peasant movements to possess land can be repressed; with force, the most aspiring faces of the nation can be repressed.

...

What did the Revolution find on arriving to power in Cuba? What marvels did the Revolution find on arriving to power in Cuba. It found, in the first place, that 600,000 Cubans with aptitude for work did not have employment....

Three million persons of a total population of a little more than 6 million did not enjoy electric lights nor the benefits and comforts of electricity; 3,500,000 persons of a total population of a little more than six million lived in shacks, huts, and slums, without the minimum conditions of habitability.

In the cities, housing rents absorbed up to a third part of the family income. The electric service as well as the housing rents were among the most expensive of the world.

Thirty-seven and one half percent of our population was illiterate, did not know how to read nor write; seventy percent of our rural child population did not have teachers; two percent of our population was suffering from tuberculosis, that is, 100,000 of a total population of a little more than six million.

Ninety-five percent of our rural child population was suffering from parasites. The infant mortality rate was very high; the standard of living was very low.

Eighty-five percent of small agriculturalists paid rent for the possession of their lands, which reached 30% of their crude incomes; while one and one-half percent of the total of property owners controlled 46% of the total area of the nation.

The ratios of the number of hospital beds for a determined number of inhabitants was ludicrous, when compared with the countries in which there is moderate attention to medical care.

The public services, electric companies, and telephone companies were the property of North American monopolies. A great part of the banking sector, a great part of the commerce of importation, the majority of the sugar production, the petroleum refineries, the best lands of Cuba, and most important industries in all the sectors, were the properties of the North American companies.

The balance of payments in the last ten years, from 1950 to 1960, has been favorable to the United States with respect to Cuba, in the amount of one billion dollars. This without counting the millions and hundreds of millions of dollar stolen from the public treasury by corrupt governments of the tyranny, which were deposited in the banks of the United States and in European banks.

A billion dollars in ten years. A poor and underdeveloped country in the Caribbean, which has 600,000 unemployed, contributing to the economic development of the most highly industrialized country in the world.

...

What alternative was there for the Revolutionary Government? To betray the people? ...

What has the Revolutionary Government done? What is the crime committed by the Revolutionary Government, for which we received the treatment that we have received here, for which we have enemies as powerful as we have, as has been shown here?

Did problems with the government of the United States emerge from the first moment? No!

Is it that we, on arriving to power, had the objective of looking for international problems? No!

No revolutionary government that arrives to power wants international problems. What it wants is to devote its efforts to resolving its own problems; what it wants is to carry forward its program, like any government wants that truly is interested in the progress of its country.

The first situation that we considered as an unfriendly act by the United States was the fact that it opened its doors to every gang of criminals that had left our country stained with blood. Men that had murdered hundreds of defenseless peasants, who did not cease in torturing prisoners for many years, who killed left and right, were received here with open arms. That surprised us.

Why that unfriendly act by the authorities of the United States toward Cuba? Why that act of hostility? ... The Batista regime was maintained in power with the aid of the government of the United States. The Batista regime was maintained in power with the aid of tanks, airplanes, and arms supplied by the government of the United Sates. The Batista regime was maintained in power thanks to the employment of an army whose officers were instructed by a military mission of the government of the United States. We hope that no official of the government of the United States will deny this truth.

...

I have here a document (he shows it). Do not be surprised by its condition; it is a worn document. It is an old military agreement, by virtue of which the Batista tyranny had received generous aid from the government of the United States. Especially important is Article 2 of this agreement.

"The government of the Republic of Cuba commits to making effective use of the aid that it receives from the government of the United States of America in accordance with the present agreement, with the objective of carrying out the defense plans accepted by both governments, in accordance with which the two governments will take part in important missions for the defense of the Western Hemisphere; and, unless previously the consent of the government of the United States of America is obtained"—I repeat—*"unless previously the consent of the government of the United States is obtained, the aid will not be devoted to ends other than those for which it was given."*

The aid was devoted to combatting Cuban revolutionaries; it later had the consent of the government of the United States.

…

The Revolutionary Government begins to take the first steps. The first is to reduce the housing rents that families were paying by 50%, a very just measure, since, as we said previously, there were families that were paying up to a third part of their incomes.... It did not create a problem with the monopolies. Some North American companies had large buildings, but they were relatively few.

Later came another law, which annulled the concessions that the tyrannical government of Fulgencio Batista had given to the telephone company, a North American monopoly. Under the protection of the defenselessness of the people, they had obtained profitable concessions. The Revolutionary Government annuls those concessions and restores the prices of the telephone services to the level that they had been previously. The first conflict with the North American monopolies begins.

The third measure was the reduction of the electricity rates, which were the highest in the world. The second conflict with the North American monopolies emerges. Now we were beginning to appear like communists; now they were beginning to smear us in red, because, simply, we had collided with the interests of the North American monopolies.

But then comes the third law, a necessary law, an inevitable law, inevitable for our country, and inevitable, sooner or later, for all the peoples of the world, or at least for all the peoples of the world that have not yet done it: the Agrarian Reform Law.

It is clear that, in theory, everyone is in agreement with agrarian reform. No one dares deny it. No one that is not an ignorant person dares to deny that agrarian reform is, in the underdeveloped countries of the world, an essential condition for economic development....

And we took that step: we really did an agrarian reform. Was it radical? Was it a radical agrarian reform? Was it very radical? It was not a very radical agrarian reform. We did an agrarian reform adjusted to the needs of our development, adjusted to our possibilities for agricultural development.

...

Well, there emerged the first true difficulty. The same also had occurred in the neighboring Republic of Guatemala. When an agrarian reform was carried out in Guatemala, problems in Guatemala emerged....

Immediately, the problem of the payment was provoked. It began to rain notes from the US Department of State.

They never asked us about our problems. Never, not even for commiseration or for the large part of the responsibility that they had in it, did they ask us how many were dying of hunger in our country, how many were suffering from tuberculosis, how many persons were without work. No. An expression of solidarity with respect to our needs? Never.

All the conversations with representatives of the government of the United States were based on the telephone company, the electric company, and the problem of the land of the North American companies.

How were we going to pay? Of course, the first question that they had to ask was with what are we going to pay, not how, but with what.

...

What did the North American Department of States express to us concerning their aspirations with respect to their affected interests? Three things: prompt payment..., "prompt, efficient, and just payment." Do you understand that language? "Prompt, efficient, and just payment." That means, "Pay right now, in dollars, and what we ask for our plantations."

We were not yet 150% communists. We were looking a little more of a shade of red. We did not confiscate the lands. We simply proposed that we would pay in twenty years, in the only manner that we were able to pay: in bonds, which would have matured in twenty years, earning 4.5% interest, amortized annually.

...

We carried out the agrarian reform. Surely, for a representative of Holland, for example, or of any country in Europe, our limits placed on the size of the plantations would be nearly astonishing. They would astonish for their extensive size. The maximum limit that our agrarian reform law established was some 400 hectares. In Europe, 400 hectares constitutes a true large estate. In Cuba, there were North American monopolist companies that had up to nearly 200,000 hectares. That's two hundred thousand hectares, if someone believes that they have not heard well. In Cuba, an agrarian reform that reduced the maximum limit to 400 hectares was an inadmissible law to those monopolists.

But in our country not only the lands were the property of the North American monopolies. The principal mines also were the property of those monopolies. Cuba produces, for example, a lot of nickel, and all the nicked was exploited by North American interests. Under the tyranny of Batista, a North American Company, Moa Bay, had obtained a concession so profitable that in only five years—listen well—in only five years it was going to recover an investment of 120 million dollars. Some 120 million dollars of investment, recovered in five years.

...

So the Revolutionary Government has enacted a mining law, requiring those monopolies to pay a tax of 25% on the exportation of those minerals.

...

The attitude of the Revolutionary Government had been too bold. It had collided with the interests of the international electric trust, it had collided with the interests of the international telephone trust, it had collided with the interests of the international mining trusts, it had collided with the interests of the United Fruit Company, and it had collided, in effect, with the most powerful interests of the United States, which, as you know, are closely associated among themselves.

And that was more than what the government of the United States, that is, the representatives of the monopolies of the United States, were able to tolerate.

And so began a new stage of harassment of our Revolution. I pose this question to anyone who objectively analyzes the facts, anyone who is disposed to think with honesty, not to think in accordance with what the UPI or the AP says, but to think with intelligence, to draw conclusions from your own reasoning and to see things without prejudices, with sincerity and with honesty: Were the things that the Revolutionary Government had done enough to justify the decreeing the destruction of the Cuban Revolution? No.

...

That is to say, when the North American press and the international agencies informed the world that Cuba was a red government, a red danger 90 miles from the United States, a government dominated by communists, the Revolutionary Government had not even had an opportunity to establish diplomatic and commercial relations with the Soviet Union.

...

Aware of the dependency of our economy on its market, the government of the United States initiates a series of warnings that it would snatch from us our sugar quota, and in parallel, other activities took place in the United States, the activities of the counterrevolutionaries. The airplanes were coming and going. They were not tests.... Pirate airplanes were continually flying over our territory, dropping firebombs.

...

What is certain is that at least in this peaceful hemisphere, we were a country that, without being at war with anyone, we had to endure the incessant harassment of pirate airplanes. And were those airplanes able to enter and leave with impunity the territory of the United States?

...

What was one of the arguments that the enemies of the agrarian reform put forward? They said that the agrarian reform would being chaos to agricultural production, and production would diminish considerably, that the government of the United States was concerned that Cuba would not be able to fulfill its commitments to supply the North American market.

The first argument, then, is that the agrarian reform was the ruin of the country. (It would good for at least the new delegations here present to familiarize themselves with some of these arguments, because perhaps someday they will have to respond to similar arguments). It did not have such a result. If the agrarian reform had been the ruin of the country, if agricultural production had descended, then the North American government would not have had need to carry forward its economic aggression.

...

Cuba has not been ruined; they had to try to ruin it.... We wanted to increase our exports. That is what all countries want; it could be a universal law.

...

We wanted to sell our products, and we went in search of new markets. We agreed to a commercial accord with the Soviet Union, by virtue of which we sold a million tons of sugar, and we bought a certain quantity of Soviet articles and products.

...

When the sugar stocks began to diminish, to the benefit of our economy, we then received a blow: at the request of the President of the United States, the Congress approved a law that gave the president or the executive branch the power to reduce the importation of sugar from Cuba, to the level that he deemed appropriate.

...

Such a measure was expressly prohibited by regional international law. Economic aggression, as all the delegates here from Latin America know, is expressly condemned by regional international law.

However, the government of the United States violates that law; it brandishes the economic weapon; it takes from us our sugar quota, nearly one million tons. That was that; they were able to do it.

What defense remained to Cuba, confronted with that reality? To turn to the UN, to come to the UN to denounce the political aggressions and the economic aggressions, to denounce the air incursions of pirate airplanes; and to denounce the economic aggression, as well as the constant interference of the government of the United States in the politics of our country and the subversive campaigns that are being carried out against the Revolutionary Government of Cuba.

We turn to the UN. The UN has the authority to involve itself in these questions. The UN is, within the hierarchy of the international organizations, the highest authority. The UN has authority, even above that of OAS.

The UN is familiar with the issue. It has asked the OAS for an investigation; and the OAS is meeting. Very well. What was to be expected? That the OAS protect the attacked country; that the OAS would be able to condemn the political aggressions against Cuba; and above all, that the OAS would be able to condemn the economic aggression against our country. That was what was to be expected.

On the other hand, what came out of Costa Rica? Oh, the outcome there in Costa Rica was a miracle of ingenious production. In Costa Rica, the United States is not condemned, or more accurately, the government the United States—permit me to avoid any confusion concerning our sentiments with respect to the people of the United States. The government of the United States was not condemned for the sixty incursions by pirate airplanes; it was not condemned for the economic aggression and for many other aggressions. No.

They condemned the Soviet Union. What an extraordinary thing! There was no aggression by the Soviet Union against us; no Soviet airplane had flown over our territory. However, in Costa Rica they condemned the Soviet Union for interference. The Soviet Union had limited itself to saying that, in the event of a military aggression against our country, Soviet artillerymen, speaking figuratively, would be able to support the attacked country.

...

It is enough to note for the record how our country remained without defense, and something more: the interest that the question not be brought to the United Nations, perhaps because it is considered that it would be easier to obtain a technical majority in the OAS. That view is not very understandable, for we have seen that here, in the UN, technical majorities have functioned many times.

...

Nearly 500 million dollars were recovered from the politicians that had enriched themselves during the tyranny. Nearly 500 million dollars, in property and currency, is the total value of what was recuperated from the corrupt politicians that had been plundering our country for seven years.

The appropriate investment of that wealth and those resource permits the Revolutionary Government, in addition to developing a plan for industrialization and for the increase of our agriculture, to construct housing, construct schools, and bring our teachers to the most remote corners of our country and to provide medical assistance, that is to say, to carry forward a program of social development.

And precisely now, as you know, in the meeting in Bogotá, again the government of the United States proposed a plan. A plan for economic development? No. It proposes a plan for social development. What is understood by that? Well, it too is a plan for making houses, a plan for making schools, a plan for making roads. Does that, by chance, resolve the problem?

How can you have a solution to social problems without a plan for economic development? Are they trying to fool the peoples of Latin America? How are the families that inhabit those houses going to live, if the houses are in fact built? What shoes and clothes are the children going to wear, and what food are they going to eat? Is it perhaps that they do not know that families that do not have clothes nor shoes for the children do not send them to school?

With what resources are they going to pay the teachers? With what resources are they going to pay the doctors: With what resources are they going to pay for medicines? Would they like a good remedy for saving medicines? Increase the nutrition of the people; what is paid to improve the nutrition of the people will be saved in hospitals.

So, confronting the tremendous reality of underdevelopment, the government of the United States comes out now with a plan for social development. Of course, now they are concerned with the problems of Latin America. Until now, they were not at all concerned. What a coincidence that now they are concerning themselves with these problems! They possibly will say that the fact that the concern emerged after the Cuban Revolution is pure coincidence.

...

Although we are not included in that aid, it does not concern us. We do not become angry by such things. We are resolving, beginning a good while ago, those same problems of the schools, the housing, and so on.

...

But what is occurring? Why does the government of the United States not want to speak of development? Very simply, because the government of the United States does not want to fight with the monopolies, and the monopolies demand natural resources and markets for the investment of its capital. There is here a great contradiction, and therefore there is not going to be a true solution to the problem. There is not going to be a program of public investment in the development of the underdeveloped countries.

It is good that it is said here with total clarity, because in the end, we, the underdeveloped countries, we are here the majority. Even if some ignore it, we in the end are witnesses to what is happening in the underdeveloped countries.

...

The government of Cuba always has been disposed to discuss problems with the government of the United States, but the government of the United Sates has not wanted to discuss its problems with Cuba, and it will have its reasons for not wanting to discuss the problems with Cuba.

Right here is the note sent by the Revolutionary Government of Cuba to the government of the United States, January 27, 1960. It says:

> The differences of opinion between both governments that are subject to diplomatic negotiation can be resolved, effectively, by means of such negotiations. The government of Cuba is at the best disposition to discuss without reserve and with absolute amplitude all these differences, and it declares expressly that it understands that there do not exist obstacles of any kind that impede the realization of such negotiations through any of the means and instruments traditionally adequate to this end.
>
> On the basis of mutual respect and reciprocal benefit with the government and the people of the United States, the government of Cuba desires to maintain and to increase economic and diplomatic relations, and it understands that, on this basis, the traditional friendship between the Cuban and North American peoples is indestructible.

On February 22 of that same year:

> *In accordance with its objective of resuming by diplomatic channels negotiations already initiated over pending affairs between Cuba and the United States of North America, the Revolutionary Government of Cuba has decided to name a commission with attributions to this effect, in order to begin its process in Washington on the date agreed by both parties.*
>
> *The Revolutionary Government of Cuba wishes to clarify, however, that the resumption and later development of said negotiations necessarily have to be conditioned on the government or Congress of your country not*

adopting any measure of a unilateral character that would prejudice the results of the above mentioned negotiations or that could occasion damage to the Cuban economy or people.

Clearly, the adhesion of the government of your Excellency to this point of view would not only contribute to the improvement of relations between our respective countries, but also would reaffirm the spirit of fraternal friendship that has tied and that binds our peoples.

It would permit, in addition, that both governments would be able to examine in a calm atmosphere and with the most ample examination the questions that have affected the traditional relations between Cuba and the United States of North America.

What was the response of the government of the United States?

The government of the United States cannot accept the conditions for negotiation expressed in the note of your Excellency, to the effect that that there ought not be taken measures of a unilateral character by the government of the United States that could affect the Cuban economy and its people, be it through the legislative or executive branches. As President Eisenhower expressed on January 26, the government of the United States, in the exercise of its own sovereignty, must remain free to take the steps that is considers necessary, aware of its international obligations to defend the legitimate rights and interests of its people.

That is to say, the government of the United States does not condescend to discuss with a small country like Cuba its differences in their relations.

What hope does the people of Cuba have in the solution of these problems?

Well, all the facts that we have been able to observe conspire against the solution of these problems. It is good that the United Nations consider this seriously, because the government of Cuba and the people of Cuba are very concerned with the aggressive direction of the government of the United States in relation to Cuba, and it is good that we are well informed.

In the first place, the government of the United States considers that it has the right to promote subversion in our country. The government of the United States is promoting the organization of subversive movements against the Revolutionary Government of Cuba, and we denounce it here in this General Assembly. We denounce, concretely, for example, that in a Caribbean Island, in a territory that belongs to Honduras and known as the Swan Islands, the government of the United States has taken military possession. There are U.S. Marines there, in spite of it being Honduran territory. And there, in violation of international laws, stripping a brother people of a piece of its territory, violating the international radio agreements, it has established a powerful radio transmitter, which it has placed in the hands of war criminals and subversive groups that stay in this country. And there, in addition, they are conducting training and exercises oriented to subversion and armed landings on our island.

...

But there is today a situation more alarming for our people. It is known that, by virtue of the Platt Amendment, imposed by force on our people, the government of the United States assumed the right to establish naval bases in our territory. A right imposed by force and maintained by force.

A naval base in the territory of any country is reason for just concern. First, we are concerned that a country that maintains an aggressive and warlike policy is in the possession of a base in the heart of our island, which puts our island at risk with respect to the dangers of any international conflict, of any atomic conflict, without our having anything to do with the problem. Because we have absolutely nothing to do with the problems of the government of the United States and with the crises that the government of the United States provokes. However, there is a base there in the heart of our island, which entails for us a danger in the event of any bellicose contingency.

But is that the only danger? No, there is yet another danger that concerns us more, since it is more likely. The Government of the United States has repeatedly expressed its concern that the imperialist government of the United States would stage an attack against that base, buried in our national territory, as a pretext to try to justify an attack against our country!

I repeat. The Revolutionary Government of Cuba is greatly concerned, and I state it here, that the imperialist government of the United States will take a self-inflicted aggression as a pretext to justify an attack against our country! And this concern of ours is growing, due to the increasing aggressiveness and the increasingly alarming symptoms.

Here, for example, is a UPI cable that arrived to our country, which reads as follows:

> *Admiral Harley Burke, chief of naval operations of the United States, says that if Cuba intends to occupy the Guantanamo Naval Base, we will fight back. In an interview in the magazine US News and World Report—pardon any deficiency in the pronouncing these words—Burke was asked if the Navy was concerned by the situation that prevailed in Cuba under the regime of Castro.*
>
> *'Yes, the Navy is concerned not for our base in Guantanamo, but for the entire Cuban situation,' Burke responded. The Admiral added that all the North American military forces are concerned. 'Is it due to the strategic position of Cuba in the Caribbean?,' Burke was asked.*
>
> *'Not particularly,' he expressed. 'It is a question of a country whose people were normally friendly with the United States, who like our people and*

whom also we like. In spite of this, there has been present an individual with a small group of hardened communists that are determined to change everything. Castro has taught hatred of the United States and has done much to ruin his country.'

Burke declared that we would react quickly if Castro were to take some decision against the base in Guantanamo. 'If it involved taking the place by force, we will fight back,' he added. In response to the question if the threat made by Khrushchev that Soviet rockets would support Cuba had caused him to think twice about such a decision, the Admiral said, 'No, because he will not launch their rockets; he knows very well that he will be destroyed if he were to do it.'

He means that Russia will be destroyed.

...

You see how they make a calculation, a calculation that is very dangerous, because this gentleman essentially calculates that in the event of an attack against us, we are going to be alone. It is simply a calculation of Mr. Burke, but we imagine that Mr. Burke is mistaken. We imagine that Mr. Burke, in spite of being an admiral, is mistaken. (Voices are heard from the Soviet delegation, from Khrushchev himself, and applause).

Admiral Burke, then, is playing irresponsibly with the fate of the world. Admiral Burke and all those of the aggressive militarist group are playing with the fate of the world. They really do not consider it worthwhile to concern themselves with the fate of each one of us. But we understand, the representatives of the different countries of the world, that we have the duty to be concerned with the fate of the world, and we have the duty to condemn all those that play irresponsibly with the fate of the world.

...

And that is not all. Yesterday there appeared here another news cable from UPI, containing declarations of a North American senator, I believe that his name is pronounced Stail Bridge [Styles Bridges], a member, according to my understanding, of the military committee of the Senate of the United States, who said today:

The United States ought to prepare at all cost its Guantanamo Naval Base in Cuba. We must go as far as is necessary to defend that gigantic installation of the United States. We have naval forces there, we have marines; and if we were attacked, I certainly would defend it, because I believe that it is the most important base in the Caribbean region.

This member of the Senate Armed Forces Committee does not completely discard the use of atomic weapons in the event of an attack against the base.

What does this mean? This means that not only are they creating hysteria, not only are they systematically preparing the environment, but they even threaten us with the use of atomic weapons. And really, among many other things that occur to us, one of them is to ask this Mr. Bridge if it does not give him shame to threaten with atomic arms a small country like that of Cuba (PROLONGED APPLAUSE).

...

Therefore we ought to declare here, in the first place, that this idle talk concerning attacks has a foundation in creating hysteria and preparing the conditions for aggression against our country. We never have spoken, we never have said a single word that implies the idea of any type of attack against the Guantanamo Naval Base.

Because we are interested, more than anyone else, in not giving to imperialism pretexts for aggression against us, and we declare so here categorically. But we also declare that, since the moment in which that base was converted into a threat for the security and tranquility of our country, and a threat for our people, the Revolutionary Government is considering very seriously to solicit, within the canons of international law, the withdrawal of those naval and military forces of the government of the United States from that portion of the national territory. And the imperialist government of the United States will have no option but to withdraw its forces, because how will it be able to justify before the world a right to install an atomic base, or a base that poses a danger for our people, on a piece of our national territory, on an island that unmistakably is territory where the Cuban people have settled?

How will it be able to justify before the world some right to maintain sovereignty over a piece of our national territory? How will it be able to present itself before the world, in order to justify that arbitrariness? Inasmuch as it will not be able to justify before the world such a right, when our government solicits it, within the canons of international law, the government of the United States will have to comply with that law.

But it is necessary that this Assembly be very well informed concerning the problems of Cuba, because we have to be very alert against deception and confusion. We have to explain very clearly all these problems, because the security and the destiny of our country depends on doing so. And therefore, we ask that the record show very clearly these words, especially taking into account that there appears to be little possibility for improving the opinion or the erroneous interpretation of the politicians of this country [the United States] with respect to the problems of Cuba.

Here, for example, are declarations of Mr. Kennedy that will astonish anyone. Concerning Cuba he says: *We ought to use all the force of* OAS *to prevent*

Castro from interfering with other Latin America governments, and to return freedom to Cuba. They are going to return freedom to Cuba!

We ought to lay down our intention of not permitting the Soviet Union to convert Cuba into its base in the Caribbean, and to apply the Monroe Doctrine. More than halfway through the twentieth century, this [presidential] candidate speaking of the Monroe Doctrine!

We ought to ensure that Prime Minister Castro understands that we propose to defend our right to the Guantanamo Naval Base. The third to speak of the problem, the third!

We ought to let the Cuban people know that we sympathize with their legitimate economic aspirations.... And why did they not sympathize before? *...that we know of their love for freedom, and that we will never be satisfied until democracy returns to Cuba...* What democracy? The democracy made for the imperialist monopolies of the government of the United States?

The forces that are struggling for freedom in exile—lend attention, so that then you understand why there are planes that fly from North American territory toward Cuba; lend attention to what this gentleman says—*and in the mountains of Cuba ought to be aided and supported; communism ought to be kept confined and should not be permitted to expand to other countries of Latin America.*

...

The problem of Cuba is no more than an example of the problem of Latin America. How long will Latin America be waiting for its development? Well, according to the criteria of the monopolies, it will have to wait forever.

...

The problems of Latin America are like the problems of the rest of the world, of Africa and Asia. The world is distributed among the monopolies. Those same monopolies that we see in Latin America, we also see in the Middle East. There, in Iran, in Iraq, in Saudi Arabia, the petroleum is in the hands of the monopolistic companies that financial interests of the United States, England, Holland, and France control. It is the same that happens, for example, in the Philippines. It is the same that happens in Africa. In essence, in any corner of the earth.

The world is divided among the monopolistic interests. Who would dare to deny that historic truth? And the monopolistic interests do not want the development of the peoples. What they want is to exploit the natural resources of the peoples and to exploit the peoples. And the sooner that they recuperate the invested capital, the better.

...

In the speech of Premier Khrushchev, there is an affirmation that powerfully calls for our attention, for its value. It was when he said that "the Soviet Union did not have colonies; it did not have investments in any country."

Oh! How tremendous would be our world, our world today threatened with cataclysms, if the delegates of all the nations would be able to say equally, "Our country does not have any colony; it does not have any investment in any foreign country?"

Let us turn to this question. This is the crux of the matter, and furthermore, it is the key to peace and war, the key to the arms race and to disarmament. Wars, since the beginning of humanity, have emerged fundamentally for one reason: the desire of some to rob others of their wealth. If the philosophy of looting were to disappear, the philosophy of war would disappear! If the colonies were to disappear, if the exploitation of the countries by monopolies were to disappear, then humanity would have reached a true state of progress.

...

There is something that really alarmed us considerably in the speech of the President of the United States, when he said:

In the zones in development, we ought to try to promote peaceful change, as well as to help bring about social and economic progress. In order to do this, in order to achieve this change, the international community ought to be able to be present in necessary cases, through the sending of observers or forces of the United Nations.

...

We wish to state here that the Cuban delegation does not agree with such an emergency force until all the peoples of the world can feel assured that the emergency force will not be put in the service of colonialism and imperialism; especially when any of our countries might, at any moment, become the victim of the use of such a force against the right of ours peoples.

There are several problems concerning which the different delegations already have spoken. Simply for considerations of time, we want to leave for the record only our opinion concerning the problem of the Congo.

From our anti-colonialist position, in opposition to the exploitation of the underdeveloped countries, we condemn the form in which the invention of the UN forces in the Congo was carried out. Those forces were not in action there against the interventionist forces, which was the reason they had been sent. Time was allowed, thus promoting the first opposition. When further time was allowed, the opportunity was created for the second opposition. Finally, while they occupied there the radio stations and the air fields, the opportunity was given for the emergence of the third man, as are called those saviors that emerge in such circumstances. We know this only too well, because in 1934 in our country also, one of these saviors emerged, whose name was Fulgencio Batista. In the Congo, his name is Mobutu....

That is to say, the hand of the colonialist interests has been clear and evident in the Congo, and therefore our opinion is that it has been badly done, that it has favored the colonialist interests. All of the facts indicate that the people of the Congo and the right in the Congo are on the side of the only leader who remained there defending the interests of his country, and that leader is Lumumba.

...

With respect to the problem of Algeria, we must say that we are one hundred percent on the side of the right of the people of Algeria for their independence. In addition, it is absurd how many ridiculous things are given artificial life by creative particular interests; it is ridiculous to pretend that Algeria is part of the French nation. Other countries also have pretended it, in order to maintain their colonies in other times. It is called "integralism," and historically, it failed.

Let us analyze the question in reverse, if Algeria were the metropolis, and it declared that a piece of Europe forms an integral part of its territory. That is simply very farfetched, and it lacks common sense. Algeria, gentlemen, pertains to Africa, as France pertains to Europe.

Beginning several years ago, however, that African people is fighting a heroic struggle against the metropolis. Perhaps while we are discussing here calmly, shrapnel and bombs of the French army are falling on Algerian hamlets and villages.

...

We are, then, on the side of the Algerian people, as we are on the side of the peoples under the submission of the colonial governments that remain in Africa, and on the side of discriminated blacks of the Union of South Africa. And we are on the side of the peoples that desire to be free, not only politically, but also free economically, because it is very easy to place a flag, a shield, an anthem, and a color on the map. There is a truth that we all ought to know as fundamental, and it is that there is no political independence if there is not economic independence; that political independence is a lie, if there is not economic independence. Therefore, we support the aspiration of being free politically and economically, and not only to have a flag, a shield, and representation in the UN.

We want to express here another right, a right that has been proclaimed by our people in mass assembly in recent days: the right of the underdeveloped countries to nationalize without compensation the natural resources and the investments of the monopolies in their respective countries. That is to say, we advocate the nationalization of the natural resources and the foreign investments in the underdeveloped countries.[3] If the highly industrialized countries also desire to do it, we are not opposed.

...

There also is the proposal of the President of the delegation from Ghana, which we desire to support. The proposal is that African territory be free of military bases, and therefore free of nuclear arms; that is to say, a proposal to free Africa from the dangers of an atomic war. Something similar already has been done with respect to Antarctica.

Why, as the road toward disarmament advances, are we not also advancing on the road to the liberation of certain areas of the earth from the danger of nuclear war?

If Africa is to be reborn, that Africa that today we are learning to know, ... that Africa that is being raised with leaders like Nkrumah and Sekou Touré, or that Africa of the Arabic world of Nasser, that true Africa, the oppressed continent, the exploited continent, the continent from where millions of slaves emerged, that Africa that has so much pain in its history, with that Africa we have a duty: to preserve it from the danger of destruction.... (PROLONGED APPLAUSE). We fervently support this proposal.

Concerning the question of disarmament, concern the question of disarmament, we fully support the Soviet proposal. We view it as a correct, precise, well-defined, and clear proposal.

We have read carefully the speech delivered here by President Eisenhower. He does not speak, really, of disarmament, nor of the development of the underdeveloped countries, nor of the problem of the colonies.

...

The history of the world has taught tragically that the arms races always have led to war; but, however, never before has war meant a catastrophe so great for humanity as is it does in this moment, and therefore, never has the responsibility been greater.

The Soviet delegation already has addressed this problem that concerns humanity so much—a problem that relates to the existence of humanity—presenting a total, complete, and ample proposal....

Why do they desire that the General Assembly not discuss the problem of disarmament? Why does the delegation from the United States not want to

---

3 It was not until 1974 that the United Nations approved the Charter of the Economic Rights and Duties of States, in which appears the concept of an "appropriate" compensation in accordance with the right of the state to nationalize.

discuss this problem among all of us? Is it that we do not have a perspective? Is it that we ought not talk about this problem? Is it that a commission has to meet? Why not make it more democratic?

That is to say, let the General Assembly, all the delegates, discuss here the problem of disarmament, and let everyone put their cards on the table, in order that it be known who want and who do not want disarmament, who want and who do not want to be playing at war, and who betray that aspiration of humanity. Because humanity never out to be brought to catastrophe by selfish and illegitimate interests! ...

It ought to be discussed before the great assembly of the entire world, because in the event of a war, not only will those responsible be exterminated. Hundreds of millions of innocent persons, who do not have the least culpability, will be exterminated. And therefore we, who meet here as representatives of the world—or a part of the world, because the world is not complete here yet, and it will not be until the People's Republic of China is here—ought to take measures.

...

Now, what are the difficulties facing disarmament? Who are those that are interested in being armed? ... It is the colonialists who are the enemies of disarmament. One must struggle in the terrain of the public opinion of the world, instilling disarmament, just as one must instill in the public opinion of the world the right of the peoples to their political and economic liberation.

...

War is a business. One must expose those that engage is war-related commerce, those that enrich themselves with war. One must open the eyes of the world, showing who are those that engage in a commerce that plays with the destiny of humanity, those that trade in the danger of war, above all in time in which war can be so horrifying that no hope would remain for freeing and for saving the world.

...

One point remains that, according to what we have read in some newspapers, was going to be one of the points of the Cuban delegation, as is logical, the problem of the People's Republic of China.

Other delegations have already addressed this point. We want to express here that it is really a denial of the reason for being of the United Nations and of the essence of the United Nations that the problem has not even been discussed here. Why? Because it is the will of the government of the United States. Why is the Assembly of the United Nations going to renounce its right to discuss this problem?

In recent years, numerous countries have entered the United Nations. It is a denial of historical reality and of life itself to oppose discussion in the UN of the right of the People's Republic of China, that is, the right of 99% of the inhabitants of a country of more than 600 million inhabitants, to be represented here.

It is simply absurd and ridiculous, that this problem is not even discussed. For how long are we going to continue with this sad performance of not even discussing this problem, when here are present, for example, the representatives of Franco in Spain.

...

China represents one-fourth of the world. What government is the true representation of that people, of that people that is the largest of the world? Simply, the government of the People's Republic of China. Another regime is maintained there by the Seventh Fleet of the United States which intervened in the middle of a civil war.

...

One must teach world opinion, including, therefore, North American opinion, to understand problems from another angle, from the angle of others. We underdeveloped peoples should not be presented as aggressors; revolutionaries should not be presented as aggressors, as enemies of the North American people. We cannot be enemies of the North American people, because we have seen North Americans like Carleton Beals[4] or Waldo Frank,[5] illustrious and distinguished intellectuals like them, departing with tears thinking of the errors that were committed, and of the lack of hospitality toward us.

In conclusion, we consider out duty to bring to the attention of this Assembly the essential part of the Declaration of Havana. The Declaration of Havana was the response of the people of Cuba to the Charter of Costa Rica. Not 10, nor 100, nor 100,000 Cubans assembled; more than a million Cubans assembled.

---

4 Carleton Beals (1893–1979) was a journalist, writer, and political activist with an interest in Latin American revolutions, especially in Mexico and Cuba. He supported the Fair Play for Cuba Committee—Translator's note.

5 Waldo Frank (1889–1967) was a well-known novelist and literary critic, specializing in Spanish and Latin American literature. He was an activist who opposed the military draft during World War I and who supported textile workers in the U.S. South. In 1935, he was elected Chairmen of the League of American Writers, which was organized by the Communist Party, USA; but he broke with the Party in 1937, as a result of its treatment of the exiled Russian revolutionary Leon Trotsky. Following a visit to Cuba in 1959, he published a sympathetic account of the Cuban Revolution, and he was Chairman of the Fair Play for Cuba Committee—Translator's note.

Anyone who doubts it can go to count them in the next mass meeting or general assembly that we have in Cuba, with the certainty that they are going to see a spectacular event of a fervent people and a conscious people, which you rarely have had an opportunity to see, because it only is seen when the peoples are passionately defending their most sacred interests.

In that assembly of response to the Charter of Costa Rica, in consultation with the people and by acclamation of the people, these principles were proclaimed as the principles of the Cuban Revolution.[6] Anyone who wants to know that is the line of the Revolutionary Government of Cuba, well, this is our line!

---

6 Fidel refers to the Declaration of Havana, which is included in this edition.

We Are Going to Establish a System of Collective Revolutionary Watch

Compañeras and *compañeros*:[1]

...

One had to have lived ten days in the heart of the imperialist monster to know that the monopolies and the mass media are united. As we are enemies of the monopolies, and as we have clashed with all the most powerful monopolies of the empire, the news agencies combat us, unanimously, with very few honorable exceptions. And they do not combat us with reasons, because reasons are precisely what they lack.

They combat is with lies, with falsehoods of all kinds, with every kind of fabrication. It reminds us our naïve days, when we believed here the comic strips that the imperialist agencies of information made, the magazines of the monopolies, the newspapers of the monopolies, the cartoons of the monopolies, the movies of the monopolies, the slogans of the monopolies, the tall stories of the monopolies, the gossip of the monopolies, the holdups of the monopolies, the plundering of the monopolies, the robberies of the monopolies, the crimes of the monopolies, the shamelessness of the monopolies, the insults of the monopolies, the humiliations of the monopolies (EXCLAMATIONS OF "Fidel, give it to the Yankees hard!"). Because we were naïve, they got us to believe that the holdup was good, that robbery was noble, that exploitation was just, and the lie was true and the truth was a lie.

And all that false propaganda is the propaganda that rains incessantly on the North America people; like us before, it tries to deceive and confuse incessantly.

All is motivated by the thirst for profit, by material interests, by money. They are going to pay inch by inch for the propaganda, and this explains the outcome.

...

We saw shame [for the conduct of the U.S. government and the press], we saw honor, we saw hospitality, we saw chivalry, we saw decency in the humble Blacks of Harlem.

---

1 Selections of a speech delivered upon his arrival from the United Nations, at a rally in front of the Presidential Palace, September 28, 1960. Department of the stenographic versions of the Revolutionary Government.

(THE EXPLOSION OF A BOMB IS HEARD). A bomb? Leave ... ! (EXCLAMATIONS OF "Put them against the wall and shoot them! Put them against the wall and shoot them! *Venceremos*! *Venceremos*!) (THEY SING THE NATIONAL ANTHEM AND EXCLAIM: "*Viva* Cuba! *Viva* the Revolution!")

Everyone already knows who paid for that small bomb. They are the little bombs of imperialism.

...

They believe .... Of course, tomorrow they are going to charge His Honor. They will say to him, "Note well, in the same moment that they were speaking of imperialism, the bomb sounded." (EXCLAMATIONS OF "Put them against the wall and shoot them! Put them against the wall and shoot them!)

Did they catch him? Is there some news? There is no news verified. But, how naïve they are! They accomplished nothing when they dropped bombs of 500 pounds and up to 1000 pounds that say "Made in USA"; they attained nothing not even when they dropped bombs of hundreds of pounds of napalm. In spite of their airplanes, their canons, and their bombs, the soldiers of Batista were not able to take the Sierra Maestra, nor were they able to escape the sieges, and they had to surrender. How are they going to advance now behind those little bombs? (EXCLAMATIONS OF "Put them against the wall and shoot them! Put them against the wall and shoot them!)

It is part and parcel of the powerlessness and the cowardice. How are they going to come here to affect the people with little bombs, if the people is here in a plan of resistance, no longer the little bombs (EXCLAMATIONS OF "*Venceremos*! *Venceremos*!"), the people have a plan of resistance to what they throw or what falls, even if they were atom bombs, gentlemen!

How naïve they are! When for each little bomb for which the imperialists pay, we construct 500 houses!

For each little bomb that they can place in a year, we form three times more cooperatives!

For each little bomb for which the imperialists pay, we nationalize a Yankee sugar cane factory!

For each little bomb for which the imperialists pay, we nationalize a Yankee bank!

For each little bomb for which the imperialists pay, we refine hundreds of thousands of barrels of petroleum!

For each little bomb for which the imperialists pay, we construct a factory to give employment to our country!

For each little bomb for which the imperialists pay, we create 100 schools in our countryside!

For each little bomb for which the imperialists pay, we convert a military barracks into a school!

For each little bomb for which the imperialists pay, we enact a revolutionary law!

For each little bomb for which the imperialists pay, we provide arms for at least a thousand members of the militias!

Compañero Osmany gives us a good idea, because we are dedicating that little bomb to the Regiment of Santa Clara, converting what remains of it in a month into a school city.

We are going to say also to *compañero* Llanusa that the little bomb be dedicated to a new workers' social circle.

These naïve persons appear in truth to believe that if the U.S. Marines come, they will immediately be able to relax and enjoy coffee here.

We are going to establish a system of collective watchfulness. We are going to establish a system of collective revolutionary watch!

We are going to see how the lackeys of imperialism can move about here, because we live in the entire city. There is not a building or an apartment of the city, nor a block in the city, that is not well represented here.

We are going to introduce, against the campaigns of aggression of imperialism, a system of revolutionary collective watch. Everyone knows who lives in the block, what those that live in the block do and what relations they had with the tyranny; and to what they are dedicated, with whom they meet; and in what activities they are involved.

Because if they believe that they are going to be able to confront the people, they are going to have a tremendous disappointment. Because we are establishing a revolutionary watch committee in each block … in order that the people keep an eye, in order that the people observe. They will find that when the mass of the people is organized, no imperialist, no lackey of the imperialists, no one that has sold out to the imperialists, no instrument of the imperialists can move about.

…

They are playing with the people, and they do not yet know who the people is; they are playing with the people, and they do not yet know the tremendous revolutionary force that there is in the people.

New steps must be taken in the organization of the militias. We must attend to the formation, immediately, of the militia battalions, zone by zone, in all the regions of Cuba; selecting each man for each arm; and giving structure to the entire great mass of militia members, in order that as soon as possible our units of combat are well organized and trained.

…

One of our impressions during this trip, an important one, is the level of hate that imperialism feels toward our revolutionary people; the degree of hysteria against the Cuban Revolution to which imperialism has arrived; the degree of disheartenment to which imperialism has arrived with respect to the Cuban Revolution.

You already have seen it: confronting the accusations of Cuba, they still are thinking how to respond, because in reality they have no basis from which to respond.

It is, however, important that we all are very conscious of the struggle that our Revolution is carrying forward; it is necessary that we all know perfectly well that it is a long struggle, long and hard.

It is important that we realize that our Revolution has confronted the most powerful empire in the world. Of all the colonialist and imperialist countries, Yankee imperialism is the most powerful, in economic resources, in diplomatic influence, and in military resources. It is, in addition, an imperialism that is not, like English imperialism, more mature and experienced; it is an arrogant imperialism, blinded by its power.

It is a barbarous imperialism, and many of its leaders are barbarian; they are barbarous men that can stand alongside those cave dwellers of the earliest times of humanity. Many of their leaders, many of their chiefs, are like "animals." It is, without any doubt, the imperialism most aggressive, most militaristic, and most dimwitted.

And we are here on the front line: a small country, of limited economic resources, facing it, fighting a dignified, determined, firm, and heroic struggle for its liberation, for its sovereignty, for its destiny.

One must be very conscious of the fact that our country is confronting the empire most ferocious of contemporary times, and in addition, one must realize that imperialism will not tire in its effort of trying to destroy the Revolution, of trying to create obstacles in our road, of trying to impede the progress and development of our country.

One must be constantly aware that this imperialism hates us with the hatred of the masters against the slaves that are rebelling. We are for them like slaves that have rebelled, and we have rebelled well! There is no hatred more ferocious than the hatred of the master against the rebelliousness of the slave; and to that is added a situation in which they see their interests in danger, not only their interests here, but their interests everywhere.

The Moncada Program Has Been Carried Out

Today a stage has been fulfilled.[1] In twenty months, the Revolutionary Government has completed the Moncada Progrma, and in many aspects has surpassed it.

We had a series of ideas at that time. These ideas today are clearer and more precise. The problems that we saw then from a distance, we see today with more clarity and more certainty, because we have more experience, and because, in addition, the facts have shown that the dreams of yesterday can become reality.

Therefore Martí said on an occasion when they called him a dreamer that "the true man does not look to the side that was living better, but to the side that was fulfilling duty, and that was the only practical man, whose dream today would be the laws of the future."

Our dreams of yesterday have become the laws of today, and insofar as we have been able to improve some of those ideas, better still. As in this Law of Urban Reform, that came out well developed, the ideas being developed as we proceeded, and over all, the objective was fulfilled.

In our country, governments often offered programs, but they never were fulfilled. Perhaps for that reason many did not believe us, and they did not listen to us when we launched a modest program. Without pretentions of being perfect in conception and in the proposed solutions, we proposed our clear program, and it is written in different documents. On one occasion, we said that the Revolution was the Revolution of the humble, by the humble, and for the humble. In other manifestos, we spoke even of all the measures that the Revolution is applying, including those school cities.

Today we are able to declare with satisfaction that that program has been fulfilled. Many did not believe in the program, and therefore many people are astonished, but they have no reason to be astonished, because we had not made any commitment of accommodation to the large estate owners, nor to the great exploiters, nor to the monopolists, not to the foreign interests that plundered the economy of our country. Nor did we make a commitment to tolerate privileges. robbery, political maneuvering, or corruption.

---

1 Selections from a television appearance of October 13, 1960. "The Moncada Program" refers to the revolutionary program outlined by Fidel on October 16, 1953 in his self-defense during the trial for his leadership of the attack on Moncada military barracks. Fidel's address to the court was subsequently distributed clandestinely, and it became known as "History Will Absolve Me."

We made a commitment to put an end to all the blights, to struggle for that, joined with the people. And we have not betrayed the people, we have not betrayed those who have died for the Revolution, who are the only ones with whom we had commitments. Our commitment with the people and the commitments to the Revolution have been fulfilled.

Here, for example, today I was reviewing the discourse pronounced to the Civic Institutions, on that occasion in which we spoke of the fact that they had married us to the lie, they had taught us to live with it, and therefore it seemed to us that the world was collapsing when we heard a truth.

On that speech we spoke, two months after the triumph of the Revolution, with such clarity that it is worthwhile to read again those words, because we were analyzing all the problems in the areas of education, the economy, agriculture, housing, which today are resolved. They applauded, and here are the words with the applause.

We treated all the themes, and is it not possible to reread, but the representatives of the middle and professional classes were meeting there. We spoke with the clarity with which always we have spoken, but above all, we spoke with the same clarity as when we initiated the revolutionary struggle, when we spoke of the people. When we spoke of the six hundred thousand Cubans without work, of the five hundred thousand workers of the countryside that lived in huts, that did not have land, of the industrial workers, of the small agriculturalists, of the teachers, overall, of the sectors that needed the Revolution. We said:

> That is the people, which suffers all the misfortunes, and is, therefore, capable of fighting with all courage. To that people, whose anguished road is paved with deceptions and false promises, we were not going to say, 'we are going to give you,' but, 'here you have, struggle now with all your force in order that freedom and happiness be yours.'

And that was exactly what we did.
...
And we can repeat to the peasants and to the people: here you have your land; here you have your schools and your hospitals; here you have fortresses converted into schools; here you have the factories that were foreign monopolies; here you have your Electricity Company and Telephone Company; here you have your refinery. Whereas before you had nothing. If today you have, today you have all that we have given you, today you have something for which to struggle.

That is to say, we have not made promises, but we have changed the realities, giving the people reason to struggle and to defend what they have. And we believed in that; we believed that when the people were given, the people would respond, and the people would defend what it had achieved.

We spoke on that occasion of the law that would concede nonseizable and untransferable ownership of the land to all the small contractors, subcontractors, tenants, sharecroppers, and occupiers, who worked on parcels of five or six *caballerías* of land. We said that we were going to deliver free title to them, as we have done.

We presented the confiscation of the property of the embezzlers; we spoke of the Agrarian Reform, and of the Integral Reform of Education, of the nationalization of the electric trust and the telephone trust, of the problem of the land, of the problem of industrialization. And here there is a paragraph that said:

The problem of the land, the problem of industrialization, the problem of housing, the problem of unemployment, the problem of education, and the problem of the health of the people: there I have expressed concretely six points, whose resolution would have directed resolutely our efforts.

Then we said that, *Perhaps this exposition looks cold and theoretical, if one does not know the reality.* And we said, *Some 85% of Cuban small farmers are paying rent and live under the perennial threat of eviction from their plots. More than half of the most productive lands are in foreign hands. In Oriente, the widest province, the lands of the United Fruit Company and the West Indian unite the north coast with the south coast. There are two hundred thousand peasant families that do not have a meter of land to plant viands for their hungry children, and on the other hand, there remain without cultivation enormous quantities of land.*

We spoke of the problem of housing: *There are in Cuba two hundred thousand huts. Four hundred thousand families of the countryside and the city live housed in shacks and multiple family dwelling units, without the most elementary conditions of hygiene and health. Two hundred thousand persons of our urban population pay rents that absorb between a fifth and a third of their incomes. And two million, eight hundred thousand of our rural and marginal urban population lack electricity.*

Here the same thing happens: if the state proposes to reduce the rents, the owners threaten to paralyze all construction; if the state does not become involved, the owners construct in moments when they perceive a high level of rent, but later, they do not lay down a single foundation stone more, even though the rest of the population lives exposed to the elements.

We spoke of the problem of education, and above all, we said the following:

> *The future of the nation and the solution to its problems cannot continue to depend on the egoistic interests of a dozen financiers and on the cold profit calculations that ten or twelve magnates draw up in their air conditioned offices. The country can no longer continue being on its knees imploring for miracles from a few golden calves that, like that of the Old Testament, do not make miracles in any form.*
>
> *The problems of the Republic can be solved only if we decide to struggle for it with the same energy, honesty, and patriotism that our liberators devoted to create it. And it is not with statesmen of the style of Carlos Saladrigas, whose statesmanship consists in leaving everything as it is, and passing life mumbling nonsense about "total free enterprise," "guarantees to investment capital," and the "law of supply and demand," as if they will resolve the problems.*
>
> *In a mansion on Fifth Avenue, these ministers can chat blithely until there no longer remains even the dust of the bones of those that today demand urgent solutions.*
>
> *A revolutionary government after cleansing the institutions, would proceed to industrialize the country.*
>
> *And in the present world, we said, no social problem is resolved by spontaneous generation. A revolutionary government, with the backing of the people and the respect of the nation after ridding the institutions of corrupt and venal officials, would proceed immediately to industrialize the country, mobilizing all the resources of the Nation, and undertaking the momentous task of study, management, planning, and implementation, by technicians and men of total competence.*
>
> *A revolutionary government, after setting up as the owners of their plots one hundred thousand small farmers that presently pay rent, would proceed to finish once and for all with the problem of the land. First, establishing, as the constitution orders, a maximum extension of land for each type of agricultural enterprise and acquiring the excess by means of expropriation, restoring the usurped lands to the state. Draining marshes and swamp lands; planting enormous nurseries and reserving zones for reforestation; distributing the remaining available land among peasant families, with preference to the most largest; promoting agricultural cooperatives for the common utilization of refrigerated equipment; and the same technical, professional management in cultivation and animal breeding, facilitating,*

finally, resources, equipment, protection, and knowledge useful to the peasantry.

A revolutionary government would resolve the problem of housing, reducing rents resolutely by fifty percent, exempting from taxes the houses inhabited by the owners themselves, demolishing the infernal multiple family dwellings and constructing in their place modern multiple story buildings, and financing the construction of housing in the entire island on a scale never seen. Guided by the criterion that, if the ideal in the countryside is that each family possess its own plot, the ideal in the city is that each family live in its own house or apartment. There are sufficient stones and plenty of hands in order to provide decent housing for every Cuban family.

Finally, a revolutionary government would proceed to the integral reform of our education, placing it in tune with the above initiatives, in order to prepare appropriately the generations that are called to live in a more happy country.

This program not only has been fulfilled, it has been further developed, and it has been exceeded. At that time, we did not have any idea of the Youth Brigades of Revolutionary Work, which today are a reality; or of the Voluntary Teachers, which today also is a reality in the entire countryside of Cuba.

We spoke then of converting the Columbia city into a great school city, and so it has been, as Columbia Military Base has been converted into "Freedom" School City, with lodging for two thousand poor university students, and with classrooms for more than ten thousand pupils. But not only has the Military Camp of Columbia been converted; all the Military Regiments of the Republic have been converted, and a large number of military barracks in all the island.

There is housing for four thousand university scholarship recipients. Two university cities are being constructed, and a third will be built; ten thousand classrooms have been created by the Revolution; twenty-five thousand houses have been constructed; fifty villages already are being completed through the island; the public beaches. Many of the things that at that time did not cross the mind of any of that group of revolutionaries are at present a reality in our country.

So the Program has been carried out. And not only has the program been carried out, but there were additions to the program. In every area where it was possible to improve, improvements have been made, adjusted to the realities of our country. We are able to have the satisfaction that we are able to present ourselves before the people with a promise entirely fulfilled.

This document[2] guided the conduct of the Revolution in the first stage. Those that are called the "disillusioned" or "disappointed," we do not explain why.... Well, better said, yes, we do explain why. It is because they did not believe in what we were saying, because they believed that the Revolution was going to mediate; that the men of the Revolution were going to be corrupt; they believed that this was no more than words.

When the words were converted into reality, then they called themselves "disillusioned." It is true, they were fooled, because they believed that the army of the established interests never would be destroyed; and therefore they are disillusioned. They believed that there never would be a people armed, and as there is a people armed, they are disillusioned. They believed that no Revolution would be able to resist imperialism, and therefore they are disillusioned. Therefore, those scoundrels call the leaders of the Revolution traitors; they call traitors those who have complied with what they placed before the people, those that have fulfilled their commitment to the people.

That document [*History Will Absolve Me*] was the fundamental document of the Revolution.

The Revolution today has a new document, the document that the people in the National General Assembly approved: the Declaration of Havana. The Declaration of Havana was not a program of a group of men, but a synthesis of the aspirations of a people. Principles were expressed in that document, in which the rights and duties of the human being and of the peoples were proclaimed.

To this Declaration we can add one right more: the right of each family to decent housing. The Declaration proclaims: *The right of peasants to the land; the right of workers to the fruit of their labor; the right of children to education; the right of the sick to medical attention and hospital care; the right of the youth to work; the right of students to free, experiential and scientific education; the right of blacks and Indians to the full dignity of man; the right of the woman to civil, social, and political equality; the right of the elderly to a secure old age; the right of the intellectuals, artists, and scientists to struggle, with their works, for a better world; the right of States to the nationalization of the imperialist monopolies, thereby rescuing national wealth and resources; the right of the countries to free commerce with all the peoples of the world; the right of nations to their full sovereignty; the right of the peoples to convert their military fortresses into schools, and to arm their workers, their peasants, their students, their intellectuals,*

---

2   The document known as "History Will Absolve Me," the printed version of the declaration of self-defense to the court made by Fidel on October 16, 1953.

the black, the Indian, the woman, the young person, the old person, and all the oppressed and exploited, in order that they can defend, by themselves, their rights and their destinies. One right more we have created: the right of each family to decent housing.

In this way, the ideal of our Revolution has been amplified and developed, making concrete these rights, making concrete these duties, and condemning what we condemned:

> *The Cuban People's National General Assembly condemns, in sum, the exploitation of man by man, and the exploitation of the underdeveloped countries by imperialist finance capital.*
>
> *The National General Assembly of the People of Cuba:*
> *Condemns the large estate, source of misery for the peasant and a backward and inhumane system of agricultural production;*
>
> *condemns the starvation wages and the dreadful exploitation of human work by illegitimate and privileged interests;*
>
> *condemns illiteracy, the lack of teachers, schools, doctors, and hospitals, the lack of protection of the aged that prevails in the countries of America;*
>
> *condemns the discrimination against Blacks and Indians;*
>
> *condemns the inequality and the exploitation women;*
>
> *condemns the military and political oligarchies that maintain our peoples in poverty, impede their democratic development and the full exercise of their sovereignty;*
>
> *condemns the concession of natural resources of our countries to the foreign monopolies, as a submissive policy that betrays the interests of the peoples;*
>
> *condemns the governments that do not listen to the sentiments of their peoples in order to comply with the mandates of Washington;*
>
> *condemns the systematic deceit of the peoples by agencies of dissemination that respond to the interest of the oligarchies and to the policy of oppressive imperialism;*
>
> *condemns the monopoly of the news by Yankee agencies, instruments of the North American trusts and agents of Washington;*
>
> *condemns the repressive laws that prevent workers, peasants, students, and intellectuals, the great majority in each country, from organizing and struggling for their social and patriotic demands;*
>
> *condemns the monopolies and the imperialist companies that systematically plunder our resources, exploit our workers and peasants, bleed and keep backward our economies, and force the politics of Latin America to submit to their designs and interests.*

This is today the program of the Revolution for the new stage of long work that we have ahead, of many years, for us and for those that come after us; a great work in the areas of industrialization, of the development of our economy, of education, programs for the full literacy of the people, in improving the conditions of housing, the conditions of health in our country. And in addition, a role to play in the world.

It is not going to be an easy task. Remember always what we once read in the Bible, that many were called and few are chosen. Many were called or appeared at the beginning of the Revolution, and very few selected.

At the present time, the imperialist enemy is undertaking a campaign to leave us without technicians. Traitors and persons who feel resentment are joining that campaign, including traitors that occupied posts in the Revolutionary Government. For example, the engineer Manual Ray, who today is one of the ringleaders of the counterrevolution, and who has not had qualms in linking himself to groups that place bombs, or to the America Embassy in its campaign to take away engineers, offering them fabulous salaries in the United States, in Puerto Rico. It is a campaign to deprive us of technicians in the refineries and a campaign to deprive us of doctors. This is not unknown to imperialism, inasmuch as in its own country it denied medical assistance to a Cuban shot by henchmen with total impunity. The campaign wants to deprive our people of doctors, to leave the people without doctors, offering high salaries for doctors to relocate to another country; and there are doctors so miserable and so traitorous that they have responded to that call. There are engineers so miserable, so cowardly, and so traitorous that they have responded to the call; and there are technicians so miserable, so cowardly, and traitorous that they have responded to that call.

...

Those technicians that left our country deserve at least that we deny to them the right to ever again return to our country. We are not going to prohibit their departure. Let them leave, those that want to leave; we do not want anyone here by force. But we are going to penalize them with the loss of the right to vote and of Cuban citizenship, those technicians that were fulfilling functions in the government, or in nationalized companies, or in organisms of the state, who abandoned their country in order to work in the service of imperialist interests in another country.

Not all left, of course; many remained. All the doctors will not leave. Although it is true that often we lacked technicians in the Sierra Maestra, many doctors arrived to the Sierra Maestra.

...

There can be great changes in the world, in one form or another. And the traitors could arrive one day to the moment in which they do not have any place to go.

But the people ought to know of all of these weapons that are being used against the Revolution. Therefore, we ought to make haste in creating technicians, because not satisfied with all the despicable acts that they have carried out against our country and all the aggressions that they have committed against our country, they now are using all their resources and all their fortune to leave the country without technicians.

...

This is another problem that we are going to confront, and that we will confront, as we have confronted all the aggressions and all the maneuvers.

I believe that, basically, all has been said. Those that want to have fear, from now on, it is because they want to, or because they have some lack, or some complicity. All those that want to work and to struggle have the opportunity.

The Moncada program has been completed. We are entering into a new stage. The methods are different. Our principles are today synthesized in the Declaration of Havana, and the task that we have ahead is the task that will occupy our time and our energy, ours and that of those who come after us.

...

On few occasions has a group of men had the satisfaction that we have had of presenting, before our people, a program fulfilled.

MODERATOR: In the name of Fidel, the Independent Front of Free Broadcasters, I give thanks to Dr. Fidel Castro for his important appearance tonight, and to the *compañeros* on the panel. Good night, ladies and gentlemen of the television audience. Until next Thursday.

PART 3

1961: Year of Education

Introduction to 1961: "Year of Education"

The year of 1961 was proclaimed as the "Year of Education," placing emphasis on the goal established by the Revolution to overcome illiteracy. Major events of the year included the mass literacy campaign, the declaration of the socialist character of the Revolution, and the first great defeat of U.S. imperialism in Latin America.

In an address before the UN General Assembly, Fidel Castro committed the Revolution to the eradication of illiteracy during the year of 1961. This goal was achieved through an enormous popular mobilization, and especially significant were the "Conrado Benítez" Brigades composed of young people and adolescents who brought reading and writing to every corner of the country.

The great task of forging a nation-wide literacy campaign was carried out in the context of redoubled imperialist aggressiveness, displayed in various forms. *Outside the country*, a mercenary force was organized and trained for a military action against the Revolution. *Within the country*, counterrevolutionary factions were organized to carry out sabotage and other destabilizing activities, including the organization of armed gangs, principally in the mountainous zone in the center of the country. This was combined with a *disinformation campaign* with respect to the Revolution and its transformations, utilizing the transnational news agencies and the oligarchy-owned newspapers of the continent. At the same time, an attempt was made to isolate Cuba from the peoples of Latin America, using the Organization of American States (OAS) and the most reactionary incumbent governments of the region. In all these terrains, the Revolution waged a tough struggle through the combative participation of the people, which increased in the face of each aggression.

On April 15, as a prelude to the mercenary invasion, B-26 combat planes, painted with insignias of the Cuban Air Force, bombed three airports in Cuba, with the objective of destroying on the ground the few combat planes that the country possessed. During the mass funeral for the victims of the deceitful bombardment of the Cuban airports, Fidel proclaimed the socialist character of the Revolution.

Although the three mentioned events were the most significant of 1961, other important events marked the year, making it one of the defining years of the Revolution. Included among them were:
– A massive military preparation of the population was maintained in anticipation of a direct attack by the United States. In a short time, the people

mastered modern military techniques and thousands of experienced chiefs, officers, and combatants emerged.
- Educational work was extended to the entire society. Classrooms were created in workplaces and courses were taught to thousands of peasant men and women. Teachers were trained for the different levels of education.
- Large-scale voluntary work was initiated with enthusiastic participation in the sugar cane harvest, which was dubbed the First Sugarcane Harvest of the People.
- The restructuring of the state apparatus advanced as new agencies were created, while others were reorganized.
- The worker's movement actively participated in all the tasks of the Revolution, with the support of the Confederation of Cuban Workers and its member unions that promoted socialist norms and values.
- The process of unification of the revolutionary forces moved forward and after the victory at Playa Girón,[1] the Integrated Revolutionary Organizations (ORI) were formed through the union of the 26 of July Movement, the March 13 Revolutionary Directory, and the Popular Socialist Party.
- The massive study of Marxism-Leninism began in the Schools of Revolutionary Instruction, under the direction of the ORI.
- In the international arena, Cuba utilized the United Nations as a platform for the denunciation of imperialist aggression; it confronted the maneuvers of the United States in OAS; and it reaffirmed its Third World perspective.

Of course, this brief review cannot reveal all the extraordinary complexity of the year of 1961 nor the activities developed by Fidel Castro, that resulted in the conditions for publicly proclaiming the socialist character of the Revolution and for defeating the imperialist armed aggression on the beaches of Playa Girón.

With respect to Playa Girón, we consider it helpful to expand our commentary on the defeated imperialist project. A well-equipped, trained, and logistically advised military force was prepared outside of Cuba. Its mission was to occupy a piece of Cuban territory, from which a U.S.-created provisional government would be proclaimed. In order to attain this objective, a precarious unity among the representatives of the various counterrevolutionary factions

---

1 Playa Girón, which perhaps could be translated as Giron Beach, is a town along Bahía de Cochinos, generally translated into English as the Bay of Pigs. In the United States, the custom is to refer to both the place and battle that took place there as the Bay of Pigs; in Cuba, however, the locale and the battle always are rendered as Playa Girón. In translating Cuban texts, references have been left as Playa Girón, in accordance with the Cuban custom.—Translator's note.

was fashioned, creating a fictitious Cuban Revolutionary Council, responsible for representing a supposedly "free Cuba."

The operation included canons, tanks, and air support. It chose an ideal location for a conventional confrontation with its limited objective. The plan was to occupy a geographic zone of the country, where there could swiftly be built a landing strip and constructions, and which was separated from firm land by a swamp, with only three ways of access by highway, over which parachutists were to be landed in order to impede the passing of the Cuban forces.

The Cuban foreign minister at the United Nations, with evidence of the plan, denounced the preparations for the military aggression. In the days during which the invasion was unfolding, he confronted and exposed the fallacies of the U.S. spokesperson.

The operation was ultimately defeated in less than seventy-two hours. On April 23, in the television program "The Popular University," Fidel Castro explained the development of the battle of Playa Girón, and he showed evidence of the participation of the United States in the planning, organization, and execution of the mercenary invasion. So resounding was the defeat that on April 24, President Kennedy admitted responsibility of the part of the U.S. administration for the debacle. On the following day, April 25, he made the blockade official, stipulating what he called an embargo on all merchandise bound for Cuba.

A detailed analysis of the operation of imperialist aggression shows that, from a technical point of view, it was flawless. But it did not count on a people in Revolution, with a political leadership headed by Fidel that with creativity, courage, and decisiveness proved well positioned to shatter the imperialist intentions of the invaders.

With the objective of destabilizing the country, counterrevolutionary gangs were also organized in the mountainous zones of Cuba, supplied with arms and provisions from the United States. These and other counterrevolutionary organizations carried out terrorist acts and acts of sabotage that affected commercial centers and industries. Such activities were supplemented with acts of piracy by gunboats that attacked economic objectives and, at opportune moments, the population. Furthermore, light aircraft launched incendiary bombs over sugar plantations.

In the face of this comprehensive campaign of aggression, the militias and the Rebel Army prove in a short time to have attained mastery over modern military techniques. The organs of security of the Revolution, with the support of the people, were able to neutralize the counterrevolutionary activities and the banditry that it confronted, impeding them from establishing a base of internal support. For example, the Cuban operation known as the Cleansing of Escambray, developed at the beginning of the year, managed to eliminate a dangerous counter-revolutionary nucleus prepared by the Central Intelligence Agency in support of the military aggression.

There also were psychological operations developed through various methods of subversive propaganda. The Radio Swan[2] and "Operation Peter Pan"[3] operations are examples. The educating efforts of Fidel and other leaders of the Revolution confronted and neutralized these ideological campaigns.

There also were developed acts of economic sabotage waged against Cuba, imposing an embargo on merchandise bound for Cuba by means of specific procedures even before it was made official.

The speeches of Fidel Castro labored to explain the meaning of the Revolution, declaring the socialist character of the Revolution, and analyzed the class composition of the forces that were confronted at Playa Girón. Together, they constitute important documents for understanding this historic period of the Cuban Revolution.

Among the methods utilized by the counterrevolution was the indiscriminate assassination of those that supported or fulfilled tasks of the Revolution. Victims of this policy include a young Black teacher, Conrado Benítez, and an adolescent who was a teacher in the literacy campaign, Manuel Ascunce. Such acts, combined with indiscriminate terrorist actions, made it necessary for the Revolution to impose the death penalty for violent crimes against the counterrevolution. Other radical measures were taken by the Revolution, such as the limitation of the "diplomatic" personnel of the U.S. embassy in Havana (more than 200) to the same number of personnel as the Cuban Embassy in Washington (eleven). The speech of May 1 is an extensive piece, but it is decisive for understanding these revolutionary decisions.

The year of 1961 was a year of hard tests in the terrain of defense, inasmuch as after Playa Girón, imperialism intensified its aggressions. But it would not attain its objective. The Revolution persevered and continued moving forward.

---

2 See glossary.
3 See glossary.

The Revolution Is a Struggle to the Death between the Future and the Past

...

In the first place, a revolution does not occur without cause.[1] Those that believe that we are the cause of the Revolution are wrong. Paradoxically, those who are the causes of the revolution are those that do not want the Revolution.

There would not have been a Revolution if there had not been so much injustice among our people. We ought to start from this base: the blame for the revolution in our country belongs to the great abuses to which our people have been subjected for many years; it belongs to the exploitation to which our country is submitted, and always has been submitted. Anyone can understand that, without these circumstances, a revolution in our country would not have taken place.

...

What is a revolution? Is it, by any chance, a peaceful and tranquil process? It is a bed of roses?

Revolution is the most complicated and convulsive of all historic events. This is an infallible law of all revolution that history teaches. No true revolution can ever avoid being an extraordinarily convulsive process. If it is not so, it is not a revolution.

When the foundations of a society are shaken, only a revolution is capable of shaking them. Only a revolution is capable of shaking the foundations and the pillars upon which a social order is erected. If the foundations are not shaken, a revolution has not taken place, because a revolution is like destroying an old building in order to build a new one, and the new building is not constructed on the foundations of the old building. A revolutionary process has to destroy in order to build.

That is what we have been doing for two years: destroying the foundation of that old building. Therefore, those that identify with the old building, the building of their privileges and extraordinary advantages at others' expense, which has been destroyed by the Revolution, look with sadness and discouragement at the demolition that we are accomplishing.

...

---

[1] Selections of a speech delivered at a march in the Civic Plaza, January 2, 1961. Department of stenographic versions of Revolutionary Government.

After two years, when the enemies of the Revolution have gone from words to deeds, the facts reveal, with increasing clarity, a conflict between these two criteria, these two forces: between the forces of the past and the forces of the future, between those attached to yesterday and those attached to tomorrow; between those that wanted the continuation of a system and of an existence that was locked into the most inconceivable injustices, and those of us that are determined to make for our people a new world.

The collision between the old world and the new world was inevitable, and as that collision becomes more intense, it is necessary to clarify, to make clear our ideas to the people, not only to help the people to understand, but also to clarify our ideas to the enemies of the people.

...

The Revolution is not always understood, even by those that receive benefits from it. It is possible that even some of the beneficiaries of the Revolution are not capable of understanding that they are benefitting.

Some are genuine sons of the past, products of the past. This privileged minority has received an education, has held political power, has monopolized the media of culture and the dissemination of ideas, and has tried to mold the thought of the people to its way. This minority influences a greater or lesser part of the people.

...

The privileged minority and the great interests affected by the Revolution have made an extraordinary effort to get the beneficiaries of the Revolution, the men and women liberated by the Revolution, to conspire against the Revolution, so that the people liberated by the Revolution turn against their Revolution. This is an invariable tactic of the dominant classes when they are displaced from power.

...

However, it is much easier to deceive the foreign peoples, and it is much easier to deceive the sister peoples of our continent, than our own people, because we are witnesses to the events. But for the great masses of America, a good part of the news that is received is through agencies that are deeply rooted enemies of our Revolution.

...

If we want to understand things as they must occur, we have to remember that no revolution is free of slander, and there are circumstances that are so inexorably repeated that is virtually impossible for us to hope to be free of them. The distortion of the truth, the worst misrepresentations and the worst aggressions, have been the first results of all the great revolutions in the history of humanity.

If we want to measure the merit of our Revolution and the value of our Revolution, it would be enough to observe the hate against it felt by the great reactionary interests of the world; it would be enough to observe the hate against it felt by the worst and the greatest exploiter of modern imperialism; it would be enough to observe the hatred against it felt by the most reactionary press of the world, and the tremendous campaign of misrepresentations that began to be directed against it from the first day; in order to understand, to the satisfaction of our people, that our Revolution also will pass to history as a great revolution.

...

However, as there is no greater lesson than events, it is necessary that events teach us, it is necessary that the events themselves lead the people, the great mass of the people, to a greater understanding of what a revolution is. And above all, that a revolution is not a bed of roses; that a revolution is a struggle to the death between the future and the past; and that the nature itself of every revolutionary process makes any other alternative impossible. The collision of interests is too intensified in a revolution for it to occur in any other manner.

...

Both forces have their objectives and their tactics; both forces know the resources on which they depend. Every counterrevolution is a force; and there is no revolution that does not generate a force against it. The revolution itself generates the forces that combat it.

The counterrevolution relies on parasites and social dregs. That army of elements, at time numerous, that lived by prospering on decay; that numerous army of men that also were satellite parasites, small parasites that revolve around large parasites, and that in our country we know them as henchmen, informers, demagogues, loafers, men who live off vice, gambling, drug trafficking, smuggling, white slavery, and crime. Counterrevolutions depend on all social lumpen, the cowards, the vice lords, the wretched, and the parasites, because they support the powerful in the defense of their privileges, by killing and oppressing the people.

In our country, however, a very special, addtional circumstance has occurred, because the most powerful support of the counterrevolution, its principal support, was not that lumpen of the wretched, of parasites, exploiters, murderers, vice lords, and cowards. The most powerful support of the counterrevolution was a force that is felt in all the world, a force very powerful; so powerful, that it creates conflicts in all continents of the world; so powerful, that it interferes in the problems of a great part of the nations of the world; so powerful, that it aspires to decide destinies, and in many cases, the destinies of peoples.

The fundamental support of the counterrevolution in Cuba has come to be, necessarily, the support of the great foreign monopolies, that is, the support of the great imperialist forces. That force is powerful, very powerful. Across the Americas, how many governments can say "no"? How many politicians can say "no"? That force is so powerful that few, very few, politicians can do so and the number of governments that can say "no" are truly exceptions. That force is so powerful that the majority of public men, and the immense majority of the governments of this continent and of the other continents, always have to say "yes." And our people said to the powerful, to the powerful to whom many said "yes," our people said "no"! (Proclamations of "Cuba *sí*, Yankees no!").

...

The powerful empire decided on the destruction of the Cuban Revolution; the Cuban Revolution unavoidably had to clash with the powerful empire. Is there anyone in this world so naïve to believe that an agrarian reform could be carried out, depriving the large imperialist companies of land, without colliding with imperialism? Is there anyone in the world so naïve to believe that the public services could be nationalized without colliding with imperialism? Is there anyone so naïve to believe that any country can aspire to have an independent economy and an independent political life without clashing with imperialism?

...

So the counterrevolutionary force found its support in imperialism, and the struggle of the Cuban Revolution ceased being a struggle within the national context; it became a struggle between the interests of the nation and the interests of imperialism. And this fulfills a law of all revolutions: the defeated reactionaries in a country always look for support in foreign reactionary forces. There is in the world solidarity among the forces of reaction, and always, in all revolutions, the reactionary class has tried to return to domination of the country with the support of international reactionaries. But in this case, it came across the struggle of David and Goliath: the struggle of a small people against an imperialist giant whose long arms reach the peoples in all the continents of the world.

...

Imperialism became the head of the counterrevolution, and in this moment, we find ourselves involved in a struggle in which the counterrevolution has the full support of that powerful empire. Perhaps that is the great merit of our Revolution; perhaps that is the great merit that history will recognize in our revolution; that it did not confront a small enemy, but a very powerful enemy, and that powerful enemy has been responsible for agitating the counterrevolution here. And the counterrevolutionaries have been stirred up; the counterrevolutionaries have been agitated.

...

Without imperialist support, what capacity would the enemies of the Revolution have? The enemies of the Revolution would not dare even to raise their voice; the enemies of the Revolution would not dare to challenge the great mass of the people; the enemies of the Revolution were trembling before the people, trembling before the great majority of the people. However, imperialism released them from that fear; imperialism gave them hope; imperialism gave them support and resources. But above all, it gave them the belief that someday they would be able to control that great mass. It made them think that no matter how great the popular support for the Revolution, sooner or later, the Revolution would be destroyed by imperialism, and then, they the counterrevolutionaries would walk over the shattered hopes and ideals of our people.

...

From a past in which life was shameful, from a past in which life was without hope, the Revolution has taken the nation to a moment in which it feels like a great honor to be a son of this nation. (EXCLAMATIONS OF: "Cuba *sí*, Yankees no!)

The Revolution has awakened the moral consciousness of the people. The Revolution has awakened human solidarity among the men and women of our people. The Revolution has abolished egoism, and it has converted generosity into the principal virtues of each citizen. The Revolution has gathered the best of the nation; the Revolution has swept; the Revolution has purified; the Revolution has cleaned; the Revolution has redeemed.

But the counterrevolutionaries were not able to accept it. The counterrevolutionaries, aided by their imperialist masters and entirely in the service of imperialism, paid by the disgraceful gold of that imperialism, insist on degrading the country, insist on returning the country to its prior corruption and filth.

And they place bombs... (EXCLAMATIONS OF: "firing squad, firing squad!") that killed innocent children. They inflict wounds, without concern for whether they be men or women, attempting to destroy the resources of the people.

...

But today, against whom do they place the bombs? Against the scrupulous and honest men that govern the country? Against what do they place the bombs? Against military barracks that we have converted into schools? Against what do they place the bombs? Against the teachers that we have sent to our peasants? Against what do they place the bombs? Against the doctors that we have sent to every corner of the country? Against what do they place the bombs? Against the lands that we have delivered to the peasants? Against the houses that we have given to the people? Against what do they place the bombs? Against the two hundred thousand new jobs that the Revolution has created for the people?

...

The cowards, encouraged by imperialism, have been filled with false nerve that leads them to the belief that the shameful, protected by the powerful, can triumph. The cowards have been filled with false nerve, as a result of the fact that the revolution has been generous and extraordinarily human. The shameful have been filled with false nerve, once they knew of the interest of the Revolution in avoiding rigorous measures, in avoiding extreme measures. The counterrevolutionaries have been filled with false bravado. They know that no security agent is going to beat them or torture them. They know that that is an unmovable principle of the Revolution. The Revolution at one point closed the revolutionary trials and suspended the executions, and later reestablished the revolutionary trials;[2] but it has been very generous and very benign with the counterrevolutionaries and traitors. As a result, the counterrevolutionaries walk with brazen.

Placing bombs and committing acts of sabotage has become a lucrative business, without risk. If they are not discovered, they receive the lavish funds that the American embassy pays here for terrorism (EXCLAMATIONS OF: "Out!"). If they are not discovered, there is a swarm of CIA, FBI, and Pentagon agents that have been operating here with impunity ("Out!"), and these agents are those that have equipped the terrorists with the most modern instruments of destruction; they are those who have supplied the terrorists with high-powered explosives; they are those that have supplied the terrorists with highly-effective chemical substances; they are those that have supplied the terrorists with all means of destruction and sabotage; they are those that have supplied the terrorists with bases there, in the territory of the United States, in order that their airplanes are harassing constantly our countryside and our cities; they are those that have given protection there to the criminals; they are those that have murdered soldiers here and have gone into hiding there; they are those that hijack airplanes, even at the cost of the life of the passengers; they are those that constantly have sent arms to various places in Cuba in order

---

2 See glossary.

to try to promote insurrections; and they are, above all, those that have given encouragement to the miserable *gusanos*.[3]

...

The Revolution has had much patience; the Revolution has allowed a plague of intelligence security agents, disguised as diplomatic functionaries of the American Embassy, that have been here conspiring and promoting terrorism.

But the Revolutionary Government has decided that within 48 hours, the Embassy of the United States will not have here not one functionary more than what we have... (THEY INTERRUPT HIM WITH A PROLONGED OVATION)... Permit me... Permit me... Permit me... Permit me to finish the idea. Our form of expression has served in this case to discover a desire of the people. We were not going to say all the functionaries, but not one functionary more than what we have in the United States, which is eleven. These gentlemen have here more than 300 functionaries, of which 80% are spies... (EXCLAMATIONS OF: "Gone with them!")... If they want to all go... ("Gone with them!") If they all want to go, then they can go. Gone with them! ("Cuba, *sí*; Yankees, no!").

While on the one hand they have been pressuring the governments of the Latin American peoples to break relations with us, they, through their diplomatic representation, have introduced here a true army of agents-conspirators and promoters of terrorism.

And they have arrived to such disrespect for the interests of the people, that in recent days, when we were looking for houses in order to establish a teaching center for voluntary teachers, we discovered that three functionaries of the Embassy lived in the houses of a con artist gentleman, who had gone to the United States and had left them the houses. These three gentlemen from the Embassy, in spite of the Urban Reform,[4] like scoundrels, did not even want to pay rent.

...

Therefore, the Revolutionary Government adopts the position expressed here. We do not break with them, but if they want to go, then let them go.

A revolution is a struggle to the death between the people who want to march ahead and the counterrevolutionaries who want to go back to corruption. As we have expressed, with the Revolution there is no alternative: either the counterrevolution annihilates the Revolution, or the Revolution annihilates the counterrevolution. Either the counterrevolutionaries annihilate the revolutionaries, or the revolutionaries annihilate the counterrevolutionaries.

---

3   *Gusano*, which literally means "worm," was a common designation in Cuba for a person of Cuban nationality who acts against the Revolution.
4   The Urban Reform of 1960, among other measures, reduced housing rents.

On the upcoming day of the fourth, the Council of Ministers will meet to agree on a law very severely punishing with the death penalty, not only the terrorists, but the ringleaders of the terrorists. Punishing severely, not only the placing of bombs, but the possession of explosives of any kind. Punishing with the death penalty those that have explosives and inflammable substances used for sabotage. Punishing with the death penalty any act of terrorism against the Revolution, and any act of terrorism against national resources. And applying the penalty through a summary procedure, so that in 72 hours after having committed an act of terrorism or sabotage, the terrorist or saboteur would be sanctioned by the revolutionary tribunals.

We know how to liquidate the terrorists; we know who the terrorists are. We know who supports the terrorists, the interests that here are allied with the terrorists. We know that the terrorists are hiding in the houses of the privileged gentlemen or of those that are adversely affected by the Revolution. We know that the terrorists are hiding in the houses of the rich. We know which social class supports terrorism, and which social class protects terrorism. We know how to liquidate terrorism, not liquidating only the terrorists, but also annihilating all of the privileges and economic interests of those who support the terrorists.

If we have to occupy one by one the houses of the privileged that help the terrorists, we will occupy them, and we will establish school centers there, or we will bring there to live the residents of the neighborhoods of indigents that still remain in the capital!

...

Therefore, this year will be a year of struggle, a year of hard battle, but this year we are going to liquidate the counterrevolutionaries! (EXCLAMATIONS OF: "*Venceremos, Venceremos!*").

...

By here marched but a small part of the forces on which the nation counts to defend itself, but you were witnesses to the gallantry, the fighting spirit, and the enthusiasm of those men and women. We ought to say here that these men have been deprived for months of their spare time, and on occasion they have been deprived of the warmth of the home in order to take courses for various months, at times without seeing the family, in order to train in the use of these arms. The men that operate anti-tank artillery are all members of workers' militias, with twenty to thirty years of age; the men that operate heavy mortar are members of workers' militias, with less than twenty-five years of age; the men that operate anti-air weapons are young men with an average age of seventeen years; the men that operate bazookas are youth brigades that have scaled Pico Turquino five times, and they have passed very hard tests. Men of the people, men of humble extraction, who marched today, before the illustrious visitors that accompany us, the pride of the nation!

Joined with the destiny of our country, the destiny of the world and the destiny of humanity will be at stake. Humanity will continue ahead, of that there is no doubt; man will overcome evil, and humanity will overcome all injustices.

...

Let us hope that those men that in some manner influence the decisions of the United States will have the minimum of common sense that humanity possesses; humanity wants peace and does not want war.

...

The destiny of the world is at stake in these moments. An aggression against our country would find a tenacious and prolonged resistance; it would be an aggression against the world. That they would leave us alone! (APPLAUSE). Because we know that we are not alone, because we know, we are sure, that an imperialist aggression against Cuba would bring its own destruction. However, we do not want that they commit suicide at our cost.

...

Therefore, today as we march to our houses, or to our posts, we ought to carry the sentiment that we are living in a transcendental moment of the history of our country and the history of the world; and we carry with us the conviction that our slogan, *Patria o Muerte!*, is not only a slogan in the name of the country, but also in the name of humanity.

What the Imperialists Cannot Forgive

Compañeros of the Rebel Army and the Revolutionary National Militias and all Cubans:[1]

This is the second time that we meet on this same corner. The first was on the occasion of that act of sabotage that took the lives of nearly a hundred workers and soldiers.[2]

…

Since the beginning of the Revolutionary Government, the highest priority of the enemies of the Revolution was to impede our people from arming itself.

The first steps of our enemies were aimed at keeping our people unarmed. With the failure of the political pressures that had been undertaken in order to prevent us from obtaining arms, and with the failure of the first diplomatic steps, they turned to sabotage. They turned to the use of violence in order to prevent those arms from arriving in our hands, in order to make the acquisition of those arms more difficult, and in the end, to attain the cooperation of the government from which the arms originated in the suppression of sales to our country.

…

We were just beginning, however, and for many persons in this country, and even outside the country, it was difficult to believe that the government of the United States would be capable of carrying out such a thing; it was difficult to believe that the leaders of a country would be capable of carrying out in practice such an operation.

…

We did not yet know well our enemies, nor did we know well their methods. We did not yet know what the Central Intelligence Agency of the government of the United States was. We had not yet had opportunity to see for ourselves on a daily basis their criminal activities against our people and our Revolution.

It was not merely an isolated fact. Our country had already suffered a series of aggressions. Already our country had endured a series of incursions by

---

1 Selections from a speech delivered at 23rd and 12th Street, in front of Colón cemetery, during the funeral rites of the victims of the bombings at distinct places in the Republic, on April 16, 1961. Department of stenographic versions of the Office of the Prime Minister. [*In the speech, Fidel declares the socialist character of the Revolution. The authors*]…

2 Fidel refers to the funeral rites for the victims of the terrorist attack on the ship "*La Coubre*," March 4, 1960. The authors.

pirate airplanes that one day dropped propaganda, on another day burned our sugar cane, and on another day dropped a bomb on one of our sugar factories.

...

However, the flights did not stop. The air incursions continued for a long time, and on one occasion one of those incursions cost our country a high number of victims. However, those facts did not have the character of a military attack. They were acts of harassment by pirate airplanes, which one day burned sugar cane, another day dropped grenades, on another day dropped propaganda, and in the end, made our country the victim of a systematic harassment, and tried on occasion to inflict economic damage; but never in a manner that indicated a military type of attack.

...

In recent days, weeks ago, a pirate ship penetrated our port of Santiago de Cuba, shelled a refinery located there, and at the same time produced casualties among the soldiers and sailors that were stationed as the entrance of the bay.

Everyone knows that an operation of this kind, with ships of that nature, could not be carried out except by ships supplied by the US somewhere in the Caribbean zone. This fact puts our country in a special situation, compelling us to live, in the middle of the twentieth century, as the peoples and villages on this continent were obligated in the sixteenth and seventeenth centuries, as the cities and peoples were forced to live in the epoch of the pirates and the buccaneers.

No people of America has experienced this type of struggle, neither excursions by pirate airplanes and pirate ships, nor international sabotage organized by powerful organisms that have very powerful economic and technical resources at their disposal. Our country has become perhaps the only country in the world whose peoples and cities could be harassed by pirate airplanes and whose ports could be attacked by pirate ships. To the best of our knowledge, except in situations of war between two countries or of civil war, there never has existed a case of a country subjected to this type of attack by pirate airplanes and ships, involving a systematic campaign of destruction, like that being carried out by that secret body of the government of the United States against the lives and wealth of Cubans.

But with all that, none of these facts indicates an aggression of a typically military character, as does the case of yesterday. It is not a question of a flight of a pirate airplane; it is not a question of an incursion by a pirate ship. It is a question of nothing less than a simultaneous attack on three different cities of the country, at the same hour, at daybreak. It is a question of an operation in accordance with the rules of a military operation.

Three simultaneous attacks at daybreak, at the same hour, in the City of Havana, in *San Antonio de los Baños*, and in Santiago de Cuba, three points distinct from each other, carried out by air bombers of the type B-26, with the dropping of bombs of highly destructive power, with the launching of rockets, and with machine gun fire over three distinct points of the national territory. It is a question of an operation with all the characteristics and all the rules of a military operation.

It was, in addition, a surprise attack. It was an attack similar to those types of attacks that the destructive governments of Nazism and fascism were accustomed to carrying out in assaulting nations....

When the imperialist government of Japan wanted to enter that war, it made no declaration of war and issued no previous warning. At daybreak on a Sunday, if I remember correctly, on December 7 or 8, 1941, Japanese airplanes and ships attacked in a surprising form the naval base of Pearl Harbor, destroying nearly all the ships and planes of the naval forces of the United States in the Pacific.

...

The people of the United States mobilized in reaction to that aggression, and the people of the United States do not want to forget ever that treacherous and cowardly form in which its ships and planes were attacked at daybreak in the month of December of 1941. And that event remained a symbol of treachery. That event has endured in the history of the United States as an event that means crime, baseness, and cowardice.

Pearl Harbor symbolizes treachery for the United States; Pearl Harbor reminds the people of the United States of baseness, cowardice, and crime. Pearl Harbor was an event that the history and opinion of the United States has anathematized as an undignified event, a treacherous event, and a cowardly event.

We do not intend by this to make comparisons, because when the Japanese fought against the North Americans, it was a fight between two imperialist countries. It was a fight between two capitalist countries. It was a fight between two exploiting governments. It was a fight between two colonialist governments. It was a fight between two governments that were attempting to dominate the markets, the raw materials, and the economy of a considerable part of the world.

...

We are not a country that exploits other peoples. We are not a county that has taken control, nor are we struggling to take control, of the natural resources of other peoples. We are not a country that is trying to impose labor on the workers of other peoples for our benefit.

We are entirely to the contrary: a country that is struggling so that its workers do not have to work for a North American millionaire caste; we constitute a country that is struggling to rescue our natural resources, and we have rescued our natural resources from the hands of the North American millionaire caste.

We are not a country with a system in which a majority of the people, a majority of the workers, of the masses of workers and peasants, are working for an exploiting and privileged minority of millionaires. We do not constitute a country with a system in which the great masses of the population are discriminated against and passed over, as are the Black masses in the United States. We do not constitute a country with a system in which a minority of the people live parasitically, at the cost of the work and sweat of the majority of the people.

We, with our Revolution, not only are eradicating the exploitation of one nation by another nation, but also the exploitation of some men by other men! Yes!

We have declared in an historic general assembly that the exploitation of man by man is condemned. We have condemned the exploitation of man by man, and we are eradicating in our country the exploitation of man by man! (Fidel! Fidel!)

...

The fight between the United States and Cuba is a fight over different principles, that is, it is a fight between those that lack any human principle and those that have raised the banner of the defense of human principles ("*Venceremos!*")

... The crime of yesterday, however, was a crime of the imperialist exploiter against a people that wants to free itself from exploitation, against a people that wants to establish justice. It was a crime of the exploiters of man against those that want to abolish the exploitation of man! (APPLAUSE AND EXCLAMATIONS OF: "*Venceremos!*").

If the attack on Pearl Harbor was considered by the people of the United States as a crime and a treacherous and cowardly act, our people have the right to consider the imperialist attack of yesterday as a fact twice as criminal, twice as cunning, twice as treacherous, and a thousand times more cowardly! ("Cuba *sí*, Yankees No!").

And if the people of the United States considered it within their rights to pass judgment on the government that prepared and perpetuated that surprise attack in the Pacific as a government of low and despicable persons, our people have the right to qualify as a thousand times more vile and miserable the government that prepared that attack against our country!

If the people of the United States had the right to designate as cowardly that surprise attack, that is, that attack by a powerful country against another powerful country, by a country that has many ships and airplanes against another country that has many ships and airplanes, we have the right to describe as a thousand times more cowardly that attack by a country that has many ships and airplanes against a country that has very few ships and airplanes! ("*Venceremos!*").

All the same, when the Japanese attacked Pearl Harbor, they faced up to their historic responsibility with respect to the event. When the Japanese attacked Pearl Harbor, they did not try to hide that they were the organizers and executors of that attack; they faced up to the historic consequences and the moral consequences of their action.

In this case however, the powerful and rich country prepares the cowardly and surprise aggression against the small country, a country that does not have the military means to respond to the aggression, although it does have the means to resist until the last drop of blood!... ("*Patria o Muerte!*").

You can be sure that the imperialist government of the United Sates acts in this manner with us because we are not a powerful country. You can be sure that it acts in this way with us because it knows that we are not able to respond to those criminal and cowardly acts that they carry out against us in the manner that they deserve. You can be sure that if we were a militarily powerful country, the imperialist government of the United States would never dare to perpetuate such acts against us.

...

Through these moments, we learn so many things of which other peoples do not have consciousness. As a result of these moments, we are one of the peoples that has learned the most, in less time, in the history of the world. The events of yesterday are going to teach us; the painful events of yesterday are going to illustrate, and they are going to show us, perhaps with more clarity than any other event that has occurred up to now, what imperialism is.

...

Will it be shown that the imperialists truly represent something so evil? Will it be demonstrated that there is too much passion in all the accusations that are made? Will it be shown that all the things that we have heard said about North American imperialism are a product of sectarianism? Will all the things that are said about North American imperialism be proven true, or will they be shown to be impudent? Will the North American imperialists show themselves to be evil, bloodthirsty, despicable, and cowardly? Or will the things that are said about the North American imperialists be shown to be exaggeration or a product of sectarianism or an excess of passion?

...

How difficult it was to know what was happening in the world when our country did not have any news other than North American news? How many deceptions did they cultivate in us, and of how many lies were we made victim?

... Yesterday, as everyone knows, air bombers proceeding from outside the country penetrated the national territory at exactly 6:00 in the morning. Divided into three groups, they attacked three points in the national territory. In each one of those points, our people defended themselves heroically; in each one of those points, the courageous blood of the defenders was shed (APPLAUSE). In each of those points, there were thousands, and when there were not thousands, hundreds and hundreds, of witness to what happened.

It was, in addition, an event that was expected; it was something that was expected every day. It was the logical culmination of the burning of the sugar cane fields, of hundreds of violations of our air space, of the pirate air raids, of the pirate attacks on our refineries by craft that penetrated at daybreak. It was a consequence of what everyone knows; it was a consequence of the plans of aggression that are conceived by the United States in complicity with lackey governments of Central America. It was the consequence of air bases of which all the people and the entire world know, because even their own newspapers and the North American news agencies have published it. Their own agencies and newspapers wore themselves out speaking of the mercenary armies that they organize, of the air fields that they have prepared, of the airplanes that the government of the United States had given them, of the Yankee instructors, of the air bases established in Guatemalan territory. All the people of Cuba know this; the entire world knows it.

The attack occurred yesterday in the presence of thousands and thousands of people. And what do you think the Yankee rulers have said in the face of this incredible fact? Because it not like the explosion of *La Coubre*, which was carried out as a cunning and hidden act of sabotage. It is a question of a simultaneous attack on three points in the national territory, with shrapnel, bombs, rockets, and warplanes that everyone saw. It is a question of a public fact, an expected fact, a fact that, prior to its being carried, the world knew it.

I am going to explain it to the people, in order that a historic record will be left, in order that our people will learn once and for always, and in order that the peoples of America will learn, that part that can learn, although it be only a ray of light of the truth. I am going to teach how the imperialists proceed.

...

Yesterday, they not only attacked our land, in a prepared cunning and criminal attack, as everyone knows, with Yankee planes, with Yankee bombs, with

Yankee arms, and with mercenaries paid by the Yankee Central Intelligence Agency. They not only did that, and not only destroyed national assets, and they not only destroyed the lives of youths, many of whom were under the age of twenty. But in addition, in addition, the government of the United States yesterday tried to swindle the world. The government of the United States yesterday tried to swindle the world in the most cynical and shameful manner that has ever been conceived.

And here are the proofs, here are the proofs of how imperialism acts, of all the operating mechanics of imperialism, of how imperialism not only commits crimes against the world, but also swindles the world. But it swindles the world not only robbing its petroleum, its minerals, the fruit of the labor of its peoples, but also it swindles the world morally, inflicting on the world the lies and the most truculent things that anyone could imagine.

And here are the proofs. We are going to read before our people what imperialism said to the world. We are going to show what the world knew yesterday; what they said to the world, and what perhaps they have made to believe tens and tens of millions of human beings. What thousands and thousands of newspapers published yesterday, what thousands and thousands of radio and televisions stations broadcast yesterday, concerning what happened in Cuba, of which the world knew, or a great part of the world, a considerable part of the world, through the Yankee agencies of United Press International:

Miami, April 15. UPI. *Cuban pilots, who escaped from the air force of Fidel Castro, landed in Florida with World War II bombers after having flown from Cuban military installations, in order to avenge the treason of a coward among them. One of the B-26 bombers of the Cuban air force landed at the Miami International Airport, riddled by the fire of anti-aircraft artillery and machine guns, with only one of its two motors functioning.*

Another arrived at the naval air base of Key West. A third bomber landed in another country—it does not say which—*different from where the three airplanes*—listen—*originally had planned to go, according to reliable local Cuban sources. There are unconfirmed reports of another airplane that crashed in the see near the Tortuga Island. The United States Navy is investigating the case. The pilots asked that their identities not be released... They exited their planes dressed in their military uniforms, and they immediately solicited asylum in the United States.*

Edward Ahrens, Director of Immigration Services in Miami, declared that the solicitudes are under consideration. The mustached aviator that landed in Miami expressed to immigration officials that he and the other three pilots of the Cuban air force had been planning for months to escape from Castro's Cuba. He added that the reason for the betrayal of Galo was that he and two of the other pilots had resolved to teach a lesson with the bombing and machine gunning of the air base installations on their way to freedom. He stated that he attacked his own base, in San Antonio de los Baños, and that the other pilots attacked others. The pilot demonstrated willingness to talk with journalists, but when photographers tried to take pictures, he inclined his head and put on sunglasses.

He explained that—listen well to such a lie and something so absurd—he explained that he and the other pilots had left family in Cuba and he feared reprisal by Castro against his relatives. So they affirm that they robbed the airplanes, that they deserted, and that they do not say their names in order that the names of those that robbed the airplanes and that deserted would not be known. They were air force pilots, they say. It is indisputable that the American who wrote this was completely drunk yesterday morning.

Miami, UPI. *The bomber pilot who landed in Miami explained that he was one of twelve B-26 pilots that remained in the Cuban air force after the desertion of Díaz Lanz[3] and the suppression that followed. Díaz Lanz was the chief of the air force of Castro, but he deserted at the beginning of 1959, shortly after Castro took charge of the government. He added that today he had been assigned to a routine patrol mission in the area of his base, and that the other two pilots, stationed in Campo Libertad on the outskirts, took off with excuses; one that he had to make a flight to Santiago de Cuba, and the other that he wanted to test his altimeter. He was in the air five minutes after 6:00 in the morning. My comrades, he added, took off earlier in order to attack the airfields that they wanted to punish. Later, and due to the fact that my fuel was running out, I had to head toward Miami, because I was not able to arrive to our agreed destination. It is possible that the others went to machine-gun another field before getting away, perhaps the beach of Baracoa where Fidel has his helicopter. The aviator did not reveal what was the agreed destination.*

From AP cables:

> Miami, April 15. AP—what they have said to the world—, *Three Cuban bomber pilots, fearing being betrayed in their plans to escape the government of Fidel Castro, fled today to the United States after machine-gunning and bombing airports in Santiago and Havana.*
>
> *One of the two twin-engine bombers, of the Second World War era, landed at the international airport in Miami, with a lieutenant in the cockpit. He told of the way that he and three others of the twelve pilots of B-26 airplanes,*

---

3 See glossary.

who are those that remain in the Cuban air force, planned for months to flee Cuba.

The other airplane, with two men aboard, landed in the naval air station at Key West. The names of the pilots were not released. Immigration authorities placed the Cubans in custody and confiscated the airplanes.

Approximately 100 Cuban refugees congregated in the airport cheered and applauded when the pilot was taken to customs and later transported to an unknown place.

Look at this one: *Edgard Ahrens, district director of immigration services of the United States, made public*—the Director of Immigration of Miami made public—*the following declaration made by the pilot of the Cuban air force.* That is, they not only state that he is Cuban, they have the nerve to declare that they are not providing his name, and that they are not releasing his name in order that it would not be known who they are.

...

Says the pilot—look at the story that they release for publicity, in order to cover all the news with details, in order to make the trick complete, with all the details, look at the story that they invent—:

I am one of the twelve pilots of B-26 airplanes that remained in Castro's air force after the desertion of Díaz Lanz, ex-chief of the Cuban air force, and the purges that followed. Three of my companion pilots and I had planned for months to escape the Cuba of Castro. The day before yesterday I realized that one of the three, Lieutenant Álvaro Galo—even a name, they take the name of one of the aviators of the FAR [Revolutionary Armed Forces], they provide a name; they arrive to such an extreme of cynicism and nerve!—*the day before yesterday I realized that one of the three, Lieutenant Álvaro Galo, who is pilot of B-26 airplane number FAR-915*—it happens that the pilot is precisely in Santiago, since it just so happens that he is stationed in Santiago—, *had been conversing with an agent Ramiro Valdés,[4] the chief of G-2. I alerted the other two, and we decided then that probably Álvaro Galo, since he had always acted something like a coward, had betrayed us. We then decided to take immediate action. Yesterday in the morning they assigned me to a routine patrol from my base, San Antonio de los Baños, over a section of Pinar del Río, and around the Isla de Pinos. I advised my friends in Campo Libertad, and they were in agreement that we ought to act. One of them had to fly toward Santiago; and the other presented as an excuse that he desired to check his altimeter; they were going to take-off from Campo Libertad at*

---

4 See glossary.

6:00—in Campo Libertad there was no B-26 plane, there were damaged airplanes.

I was in the air at 6:05. Due to the betrayal of Álvaro Galo, we had agreed to give a lesson, so I flew back to San Antonio, where his airplane is stationed, and I made two machine-gun passes over his plane, and over three more stationed nearby. On withdrawing, I was hit by short firearms, and then I adopted an evasive action. My comrades already had left previously to attack airfields that we had agreed ought to be attacked. Later, being low on gasoline, I had to enter Miami, due to the fact that I was not able to arrive to our destination, as we had agreed. It could be that they headed to machine-gun other fields before withdrawing, such as the beach of Baracoa, where Fidel guards his helicopter.

This is what they have said to the world. Not only do UPI and AP break the news of "Cuban airplanes," that "they took off with the airplanes and bombed," but in addition, they distributed this cartoon story throughout the world. And what do you think tens of millions of persons had read and have heard yesterday in the world, published by thousands and thousands of different newspapers and radio and television stations? What do you think that have said in Europe, in many places in Latin America, in many parts of the world? Not only have they stated the thing in such a manner, but they have provided a complete story, with details and names, and how everything was conceived. Even Hollywood has never gone so far.

Well, that is what UPI declares, it is what AP declares, and it is what the mercenaries declare. It is the declaration that the director of immigration issues, while he says that they do not release the name in order that they will not be discovered, after stating that they had just taken the airplane.

Does it end there? No, it does not end there; it follows a sequence. Now, there are declarations of Miró Cardona.[5] But before reading the declarations of Miró Cardona, I am going to give an example of a cable published in Mexico, which the AP of Mexico emitted, as proof of what they are distributing in all the world, what they have published in the majority of the newspapers, the reactionary newspapers in Mexico, in order that you will see how the apparatus of the lie and the international swindle functions:

Mexico D.F., 15. AP. The bombing of Cuban bases by defecting Cuban airplanes was received here with displays of delight by the majority of the daily newspapers, which joined with Cuban exile groups in saying that the bombing was the beginning of a movement of liberation from communism. The government maintained silence, while groups of Leftist and communist students supported the declaration of the Cuban ambassador, José Antonio Portuondo, who stated that the air

---

5 See glossary.

attacks were cowardly and desperate attacks by the imperialists. Among the Cuban exiles, much activity was observed. A Cuban source commented that the new Cuban government in exile will be translated to Cuba shortly after the first wave of invasion against the Cuban regime of Fidel Castro, in order to establish a provisional government, what is expected to be recognized rapidly by many anti-Castro Latin American countries. Amado Hernández Valdés, of the Cuban Democratic Revolutionary Front here, said that the moment of liberation is approaching; he declared that four Cuban bases were attacked by the three Cuban airplanes that deserted: Campo Libertad, new Havana, San Antonio de los Baños, Centro Aéreo de Santiago, and Guanito, Pinar del Río.

...

Declarations of Miró Cardona, in order that all will be exposed, what class of character and what class of *gusanos*[6] are these gentlemen, in order that you will see what kind of elements these parasites are.

Both agencies released the following.

A declaration emitted by Doctor Miró Cardona—this is from AP and UPI—*a heroic strike in favor of Cuban liberty was dealt this morning by a certain number of Cuban air force officials. Before flying with their airplanes to freedom, these true revolutionaries tried to destroy the greatest possible number of military airplanes of Castro. The Revolutionary Council is proud to announce that their plans were realized with success, and that the council has had contact with them and has applauded these brave pilots. Their action is another example of the desperation that patriots of all social layers can be led under the implacable tyranny of Castro. While Castro and his supporters try to convince the world*—listen well—, *while Castro and his supporters try to convince the world that Cuba has been threatened with a foreign invasion, this blow in favor of liberty, like others previously, was struck by Cuban residents in Cuba who decided to struggle against tyranny and oppression, or die in the attempt. For reasons of security, more details will not be announced.*

Miró Cardona was precisely the head of the provisional government that the United States sent together with baggage to an airplane that would be ready to land in Playa Girón as soon as the beachhead would be secured.

...

---

6 As noted above, in Cuba, the word "*gusano*," which literally means "worm," commonly was used to refer to a person of Cuban nationality who acts in opposition to the Cuban revolutionary government—Translator's note.

But, however, it does not end there. Now we are going to finish unmasking that fraud of imperialism in the United Nations, in which posed a distinguished man, liberal, of the Left, etc., etc., Mr. Adlai Stevenson, who is another perfect scoundrel.

...

The accumulation of lies was not yet sufficient.

The distinguished delegate ... arrives in the United Nations. *The US Ambassador Adlai Stevenson rejected the affirmations of Roa[7] and reiterated the declaration of President John F. Kennedy that under no circumstance—I repeat—in no circumstance will there be an intervention by the armed forces of the United States in Cuba. Stevenson showed the commission photographs of United Press International that show two airplanes that landed today in Florida after having participated in strikes against three Cuban cities.*

Then Stevenson says, It has the mark of the air force of Castro on its tail—he expressed, pointing to one of them—it has the Cuban star and initials; they are clearly visible. With pleasure I will exhibit this photo. Stevenson added that the two airplanes in question were piloted by officers of the Cuban air force, with a crew composed of men that deserted the Castro regime. No personnel of the United States participated in today's incident, and they were not airplanes of the United States, he stressed—they were Castro's own planes that took off from his own fields.

The Cuban minster said that 'the raids of this early morning undoubtedly are the prelude to an attempted invasion of the large scale, organized, supplied, and financed by Washington. The government of Cuba,' said Roa, 'formally accuse the government of the United States in this commission and before world public opinion of intending to use force in order to settle its differences with member states.'

Here we have, as rarely has had any people, the opportunity of knowing from within and without, sideways, and from above and below, what imperialism is. Here we have the opportunity to appreciate how its financial, propaganda, and political apparatus, and its mercenaries, secret bodies, and functionaries, function with such tranquility and in an unprecedented manner to deceive the world.

Now imagine, how can we know what is happening in the world? In what manner are we able to know what is happening in the world, if this is the version and the explanation, which they have made to believe who knows how many persons in the world.

---

7   Raúl Roa García, Minister of Foreign Relations of the Cuban Revolutionary Government. See glossary.

That is, they organize the attack, they prepare the attack, they train the mercenaries, they deliver the planes, they deliver the arms, they prepared the airports, everyone knows it; the attack occurs, and they declare tranquilly before the world. If the world knew, it would rise up with indignation before a violation so monstrous, so cowardly, so violating of the rights of the peoples, so violating of peace!

...

These are the crimes of imperialism. These are the lies of imperialism. And afterward arrive the archbishops to bless the lie! ("Out!"). Afterwards arrive the reactionary clerics to sanctify the lies!

...

But, however, is it possible to deceive the world in this manner? I imagine that the President of the United States has an ounce of decency, and if the President of the United States has an ounce of decency, the Revolutionary Government of Cuba calls upon him before the world, the Revolutionary Government of Cuba calls upon him before the world, if he has an ounce of decency, to present before the United Nations the pilots and the airplanes that he says left from the national territory!

Cuba will demand before the United Nations that they present there the airplanes and the pilots that they say deserted from the air force. We are going to see if they can continue hiding their faces!

If they do not present them, why do they not present them? Naturally, the President of the United States has the right to not be called a liar. Well, if the President of the United States desires that no one call him a liar, he ought to present before the United Nations the two pilots and the airplanes!

...

The imperialist government of the United States does not have any option but to confess that the planes were theirs, that the bombs were theirs, that the bullets were theirs, that the mercenaries were organized, trained, and paid by them, that the bases were in Guatemala; and that from there they departed to attack our territory; and that those that were not shut down went there to save themselves in the coasts of the United States, where they received shelter. Because, how can the government of the United States maintain that lie?

I ask UPI and AP that they have the amiability to tell Mr. Kennedy that we are saying that, if he does not present before the United Nations these those two pilots, then we say with total right that he is a gentleman that lies. If he is not a gentleman that lies, then why does he not present the pilots?

Do they believe by any chance that they are going to be able to hide before the world? No. Cuba has a radio installation that today already is transmitting to Latin America, and innumerable brothers of Latin America and the entire world are hearing it.

No! We are not in the era of the stagecoach but in the era of the radio. The truths of a country can be carried very far. Besides that, in case it has been forgotten, Mr. Imperialists, we are in the era of space travel, although that type of travel is not a trip for Yankees.[8]

What the imperialists cannot forgive is that we are here. What the imperialists cannot forgive is the dignity, integrity, courage, ideological firmness, spirit of sacrifice, and revolutionary spirit of the Cuban people (APPLAUSE). What they cannot forgive is that we are in their faces, and that we have made a socialist Revolution right under the nose of the United States! And that socialist Revolution we defend with these arms! That socialist Revolution we defend with the courage with which yesterday our anti-aircraft guns riddled the attacking airplanes with bullets. (EXCLAMATIONS OF: *"Venceremos!,"* "Fidel, Khrushchev, we are with both," and other revolutionary slogans).

That Revolution, that Revolution we defend not with mercenaries; that revolution we defend with the men and women of the people.

...

Compañeros workers and peasants, this is the socialist and democratic Revolution of the humble, with the humble, and for the humble. For this Revolution of the humble, by the humble, and for the humble, we are willing to sacrifice our life.

Workers and peasants, humble man and women of the nation, do you swear to defend to the last drop of blood this Revolution of the humble, by the humble, and for the humble? (PROCLAMATIONS OF: *"sí!"*) *Compañeros* workers and peasants of the nation, yesterday's attack was the prelude to an aggression by the mercenaries. Yesterday's attack cost seven heroic lives. Its purpose was to destroy our airplanes on the ground; it failed, they destroyed only three planes, and the majority of the enemy airplanes were damaged or shot down.

Here, in front of the tomb of fallen *compañeros*; here, next to the remains of heroic youth, sons of workers and sons of humble families, we reaffirm our resolve, just as they exposed themselves to bullets, just as they gave their lives, we all, proud of our Revolution, proud to defend this Revolution of the humble, by the humble, and for the humble, we will not waver, whenever the mercenaries come, no matter who comes, in defending it to our last drop of blood.

Viva the working class! (*"Viva!"*)

Viva the peasants! (*"Viva!"*)

---

8   Fidel refers to the fact that the Soviet Union had launched the first cosmonaut, Yuri Gagarin, and the USA had not yet launched its first astronaut into space.

Viva the humble! ("*Viva!*")
Viva the martyrs of the nation! ("*Viva!*")
Viva eternally the heroes of the country! ("*Viva!*")
Viva the socialist Revolution! ("*Viva!*")
Viva free Cuba! ("*Viva!*")
Patria o Muerte!
Venceremos.

To combat! Let us sing the National Anthem, *compañeros*. (Those present sing the National Anthem).

Compañeros, all the units ought to head toward the headquarters of their respective battalions, in view of the mobilization ordered in order the maintain the country in a state of alert, given the imminent aggression of the mercenaries, deducing from all the events of the last weeks and from yesterday's cowardly attack. Let us march to the houses of the militias, let us form the battalions and be ready to confront the enemy, with the National Anthem, with the stanzas of the National Anthem, with the shout of "to combat," with the conviction that "to die for the country is to live" and that "to live in chains is to live in dishonor and submerged in affronts." Let us march to our respective battalions, and there await orders, *compañeros*.

Communiques from the Battle at Playa Girón

The Country Will Resist and Remain Standing Firm[1,2]

At six in the morning today, April 15, 1961, B-26 planes of North American fabrication bombarded simultaneously points located in the city of Havana, San Antonios de los Baños, and Santiago de Cuba, according to reports received until now.

Our antiaircraft batteries opened fire on the attacking planes, hitting various, one of which withdrew enveloped in flames. Airplanes of the Revolutionary Armed Forces (FAR) took off immediately in persecution of the enemy.

Up to the moment of the writing of this report, numerous explosions continue to be heard, as a consequence of the fact that a munitions deposit near the air field of FAR remains enveloped in flames. Deaths have not been reported as of the moment, although numerous wounded have been reported.

The attack was carried out in a surprising and cowardly form. Our country is the victim of a criminal imperialist aggression that violates all the norms of international law.

The Cuban delegation in the United Nations has received instructions to directly accuse the government of the United States with being guilty of this aggression against Cuba.

The order for the mobilization of all the combat units of the Rebel Army and the Revolutionary National Militias has been given. All the commands have been placed on a state of alert.

If this air attack is the prelude to an invasion, the country will stand in resistance and will destroy with an iron hand any force that attempts to disembark in our land.

The people will be amply informed of all developments. Each Cuban ought to occupy the post that corresponds to the military units and centers of work without interrupting production, nor the illiteracy campaign, nor a single work of the revolution.

The country will resist firmly and calmly any enemy attack, sure of victory.
Patria o Muerte
Venceremos.
Fidel Castro Ruz

---

1 See footnote 1 (of the year 1961).
2 This comuniqué of April 15, 1961 was publsihed in *Bohemia*, año 53, número 57, pág. 63. April 23, 1961.

Declaration of State of Alert[3]

The Commander in Chief and Prime Minister of the Government of the Republic, declares the country to be in a State of Alert, and
ORDERS:

> The Rebel Army, the Militias, and all the forces of security to increase vigilance and to proceed without contemplation against suspicious persons committing or trying to commit acts of sabotage, shootings, or attacks.
>
> The Committees for the Defense of the Revolution to redouble their activities of vigilance, discovery, and denunciation of counterrevolutionaries and their activities.

EXHORTS:

> Workers, peasants, and intellectuals, all the working people to maintain their posts and to redouble their efforts in production and teaching.
>
> All the population to maintain order and the most strict discipline and to cooperate in squashing the mercenaries, the fifth columnists,[4] saboteurs, and counterrevolutionaries in general.
>
> Everyone to action for Cuba Free and Sovereign.
>
> Everyone to action for the first Revolution of redemption for the humble, the patriotic, democratic and socialist Revolution of Cuba, with the slogan of
> PATRIA O MUERTE! VENCEREMOS!
> FIDEL CASTRO RUZ, Commander in Chief, Prime Minister

Viva Free Cuba[5]

Disembarking troops, but sea and by air, are attacking various points of the national territory in the south of the province of Las Villas, supported by planes and warships.

The Glorious Soldiers of the Rebel Army and of the Revolutionary National Militias already have engaged the enemy in combat in all points of the

---

3 Published in *Bohemia*, Año 53, No. 17, pág. 66, April 23, 1961.
4 Term that emerged from the Spanish Civil War of 1936–1939, referring to fascists living in Republican-controlled areas that engaged in sabotage, the spreading of rumors, and other activities against the Republican cause.
5 Published in *Bohemia*, año 53, número 17, pág. 64. April 23, 1961.

disembarkation. They are in combat in defense of the sacred nation and the Revolution against the mercenary attack organized by the imperialist government of the United States.

Already our troops advance over the enemy, sure of their victory.

Already the People are mobilized, fulfilling orders to defend the country and maintain production.

Carry on, Cubans! To answer with iron and fire the barbarians that look down on us and that intend to make us return to slavery.

They come to take from us the land that the Revolution delivered to peasants and cooperatives; we combat to defend the land of the peasants and the cooperatives.

They come to take from us again the factories of the people, the sugar cane factories of the people, the mines of the people. We fight to defend our factories, our sugar cane factories, our mines.

They come to take from our sons, from our young peasant women, the schools that the Revolution has opened everywhere; we defends the schools of the children and the peasants.

They come to take from the Black men and women the dignity that the Revolution has returned to them; we struggle to maintain for all the people that supreme dignity of the human person.

They come to take from the workers their new jobs; we combat for a liberated Cuba with employment for each man and woman worker.

They come to destroy the nation, and we defend the nation.

Onward Cubans, all to their posts of combat and work.

Onward Cubans, that the Revolution be invincible, and against it and against the heroic people that defends it, all enemies will be smashed.

We shout now with more ardor and firmness than ever, when already there are Cubans mobilized in combat:

VIVA FREE CUBA!
PATRIA O MUERTE!
VENCEREMOS!
Fidel Castro Ruz

Peoples of America and the World![6]

United States imperialism has launched its announced and cowardly aggression against Cuba. Its mercenaries and adventurers have disembarked at a

---
6 Published in *Bohemia*, Año 53, No. 17, pág. 66, April 23, 1961.

point in the country. The revolutionary people of Cuba are defeating them with courage and heroism and are sure of smashing them.

Nevertheless, we appeal for the solidarity of the peoples of America and the world. We especially ask our Latin American brothers that they make the North American imperialists feel the invincible force of their action. That the world know that the peoples, workers, students, intellectuals, and peasants of Latin America are with Cuba, with its patriotic, democratic Revolution of the humble, and with its Revolutionary Governments. To strengthen the struggle against the principal enemy of humanity: Yankee imperialism.

The whole of Cuba is standing with the slogan *"PATRA O MUERTE."* Our battle is your battle. *VENCEREMOS*!

OSVALDO DORTICÓS TORRADO,
President of the Republic

FIDEL CASTRO RUZ
Prime Minister

To the People of Cuba[7]

The Revolutionary Government announces to the Cuban people that the armed forces of the revolution continue to struggle heroically against the enemy forces in the southwest zone of the province of Las Villas, where the mercenaries have landed with imperialist support. In the next hours, details will be given to the people of the successes obtained by the Rebel Army, the Revolutionary Air Force, and the Revolutionary National Militias in the sacred defense of the sovereignty of our nation and the achievements of the Revolution.

Fidel Castro Ruz
Commander in Chief
Prime Minister of the Revolutionary Government

Proof of the Participation of the United States

North American participation in the aggression that was carried out against Cuba has been demonstrated dramatically this morning, when our antiaircraft

---

7 "Castro Reports Las Villas Fighting," Havana Domestic SVD, April 18, 1946.

batteries shot down a North American military airplane piloted by a North American aviator, which bombed the civilian population and our infantry forces on the zone of the sugar cane factory Australia.

The attacking North American pilot, whose corpse is in the hands of the revolutionary forces, was LEO FRANCIS BERLISS. The revolutionary forces took possession of documents that indicated Flight License 08323-IM, with expiration date of December 24, 1962. The Social Security Card lists the number 014-07-6921. The motor-vehicle Registration indicates 100 Nassau Street, Boston 14, Mass. The registered address of the Yankee pilot is 48 Beacon Street, Boston. Height: 5 feet, 6 inches.

Documents of the mission of the attacking flight over our country also were found in the clothes of the Yankee pilot.

This is one of the four enemy military planes shot down this morning, bringing to nine the apparatuses shot down since the mercenary attack was initiated by the Peninsula de Zapata. The total liquidation of the mercenaries already is a question of hours.

General Staff of the Revolutionary Armed Forces

Victory[8]

Forces of the Rebel Army and the Revolutionary National Militias have captured by assault the last positions of the invading mercenary forces that had occupied national territory. Playa Girón, which was the last point of the mercenaries, fell at 5:30 in the afternoon.

The revolution has been victorious, although it paid with a high number of courageous lives of revolutionary combatants that faced the invaders and attacked incessantly and relentlessly, thereby destroying in less than 72 hours the army the U.S. imperialist government had organized for many months.

The enemy has suffered a crushing defeat. Part of the mercenaries tried to leave for abroad in several ships that were sunk by the Rebel Air Force. The rest of the mercenary forces, after having suffered many killed and wounded, dispersed completely in a swampy area from which none can possibly escape.

A large quantity of U.S.-made weapons was captured, including several heavy Sherman tanks. A complete count of the captured war material has not

---

8 "CASTRO COMMUNIQUE ANNOUNCES VICTORY," Havana Union Radio, April 20, 1961

yet been made. In the coming hours the Revolutionary Government will give a complete report of the events.

Fidel Castro Ruz
Commander in Chief of the Revolutionary Armed Forces
April 19, 1961
Year of Education

At Playa Girón, the Country for All Has Triumphed

Distinguished visitors from Latin America and from the entire world;[1] combatants of the Armed Forces of the people; Workers:

We have marched for fourteen and a half hours. I believe that only a people filled with infinite enthusiasm is capable of enduring such a test.

...

I believe that today we ought to sketch the guidelines to follow, to analyze what we have done up to today, in what point in the process of our history we find ourselves, and what lies ahead.

We all have been able to witness what has marched by here, and perhaps we who are on this platform are able to see better than you who are in the plaza, perhaps even better than those of you that have marched.

This May 1 says a great deal about what the Revolution here has been, it says a great deal about what the Revolution has attained up to today, and perhaps it does not say it to ourselves as much as to our visitors.

...

This May 1 march is different from previous ones, above all because previously this date was the occasion in which each worker sector expressed its demands, its desires for improvement, in front of those were completely deaf to the interests of their class.... Those marches were a day of expression of the complaints and the protest of the workers.

But how different this march of today has been, how different even from the first marches after the triumph of the Revolution. This march today shows us how much we have advanced.

...

Everywhere we see the fruits of the Revolution. The first that marched today were the children of the Camilo Cienfuegos School City.[2]

And we have seen the pioneers[3] march by here, with smiles of hope, confidence, and affection;

we have seen the Young Rebels[4] march;

---

1 Selections from a speech of May 1, 1961, in the Plaza of the Revolution. *Obra Revolucionaria* No. 16, La Habana 1961, pp. 10–20.
2 See glossary.
3 The pioneers are the members of the José Martí Organization of Pioneers, the mass organization of students of the first to the ninth grades.
4 The Association of Rebel Youth was the first political organization of revolutionary youth formed after the triumph of the Revolution.

we have seen the women of the Federation[5] march;

we have seen a great number of schools created by the Revolution march;

we have seen students of agricultural engineering march, who are studying in the capital of the Republic, one thousand in number from 600 sugar cane cooperatives;

we have seen humble youths of the people march, with their uniforms of the school center where they are preparing to be diplomatic representatives in the future of our country;

we have seen students of the schools for young peasants and peasants in Ciénaga de Zapata, the exact place that the mercenaries chose to attack our country;

we have seen thousands and thousands of peasant women march, who also are studying in the capital, proceeding from the most isolated places of our island, from the mountains of Oriente or Las Villas, or from the sugar cane cooperatives or the farms of the people;

we have seen the students that are studying to be workers in day care centers.

...

From where do those forces come and where are they going? They come from the people, and they are going toward the people. Those youths are sons of the people. When we saw them today writing with their formations a "LPV,"[6] or the inscriptions, "*Viva* our socialist revolution!" "We are socialists, onward, onward; whoever does not like it should take a laxative!." We thought: How difficult all of this would have been without a revolution! How difficult it would have been for any of those children from the mountains to have marched by here today! How difficult it would have been for any of these youths from our countryside, any of these young men and women of the most humble families, to experience the capital of the Republic, to study in any of those schools, to march with the happiness and pride with which they marched by here today, to be amazed at everything, to be amazed at our visitors, and to march with that faith in the future with which they march today.

...

It is truly astonishing that today more than 20,000 athletes and gymnasts have marched (APPLAUSE), if it is taken into account that we are just beginning. And we have not yet mentioned the most marvelous thing that we have

---

5 The Cuban Federation of Women, a mass organization founded in August 1960.
6 *Listo Para Vencer* (Ready For Victory).

had an opportunity to contemplate today, which is that armed and united people that has been present in this celebration of May 1.

...

One could explain to anyone why our people have emerged victorious from any test. We were observing the abundant presence of the women in the ranks of the federations; and it is that, simply. The men were in the artillery, cannon, mortar, antiaircraft units, or in the militia battalions that marched later; those women were the wives, sisters, mothers, and girlfriends of the militia members that marched in the battalions. And the young men that marched by here from the basic secondary schools, the pioneers, or among the athletes, are simply their sons.

...

From this nation, from this young and fighting nation, from this enthusiastic and fervent nation, Who did not march here today? Who was not able to march here today? Simply, the parasites. By here marched today the working people; by here marched today all those that work and that produce with their labor or with their intelligence, manual work or intellectual work, but producer of material goods or provider of services for the society and for the people. And that is the true people.

...

Those who live as a parasite, or want to live as a parasite, do not really pertain to the people. Only the invalid, the sick, the elderly, the child has the right to live without working. They have the right that we work for them, that we care for them, and that they can benefit from the work of all.

...

Our national community has arrived to understand what the Revolution is and in what the Revolution consists; it has arrived to understand with absolute clarity that the Revolution saves the country from the parasites outside and also the parasites within (APPLAUSE).

We remember that as a result of the nationalization of the largest industries of the country, in which initially the North American factories were nationalized, some asked, "But said factory was not Cuban?" With the second law [of nationalization], the question emerged, "How to nationalize a factory that was Cuban?" Well, that factory was not Cuban. That factory was of a gentleman, and it did not pertain to the people; it did not pertain to the nation. So it is correct to call it nationalizing the factory, meaning that it passes from the hands of Mr. so-and-so to the people, that is, to the nation.

Here a succession of gentlemen were accustomed to speaking of the nation, but they had a very limited concept of what the nation is or ought to be. They were constantly speaking of the nation, and establishing the duty of defending the nation.

But which nation? The nation of the few? The nation of a handful of privileged? The nation in which a gentleman has 1000 *caballerías*[7] of land and has three houses, while others live in a miserable hut on the dirt road of a sugar plantation? ... The nation of property for a few, with the denial of opportunity and benefits for the rest of the country; or the nation of today, where we have gained the right to direct our own destiny, where we have gained the right to construct the future that of necessity will be better than the present?

...

Now we are indeed able to speak of the nation; now we have a true concept of the nation, because when we say we defend the nation and are ready to die for the nation, we are ready to die for a nation that is not of a few, but is of all Cubans! (*"Patria o Muerte!"*)

What morality, what morality, what morality and what reason; what morality, and what reason, and what right, as if it were not the right imposed by a dominating and exploiting class! What right do they have to draft[8] a black man of the U.S. South—whom they deny all rights, they obligate to sit in a segregated seat in a public bus, they prohibit to enter many places—what right do they have to draft that black man, poor, without millions, without monopoly, deprived of all rights, to go to die in defense of the millions, the monopolies, the large estates, the mines, and the factories of the dominant class? What right do they have to draft that Puerto Rican—whose country has been systematically denied the least opportunity to be a sovereign and independent country—what right do they have, that Puerto Rican of Latin blood and tradition and of Latin origins, of sending him to die in the fields of battle in defense of the policy of the millionaires and the magnates of big finance and industry?

...

That is the concept that the dominant, privileged, and exploiting classes have of the nation.

...

The Revolution can attract the people with their infinite fervor and their infinite enthusiasm! The Revolution can gather the people, with their intelligence,

---

7 A *caballería* is unit of measure for agrarian land surface, equivalent to 134,300 square meters—Translator's note.
8 The United States at the time had a military draft, or obligatory military service, for men nineteen years of age, with deferments for university studies or defense-related employment, and exemptions for physical incapacity—Translator's note.

energy, and spirit of struggle and creation, and carry them toward the road of wellbeing and progress!

This people of today is the same skeptical people of yesterday. This enthusiastic people of today, this people that today has been on their feet for fifteen and sixteen hours, men and women equally, young and old, is the same people of yesterday, that was not capable of being on their feet for an hour to go together to a public act with those who were obligating them to go to an act, or that paid them to go to an act! This enthusiastic, heroic, and courageous people of today was the indifferent people of yesterday, with only a single difference: yesterday they worked for others, yesterday their sweat, their energy, and their blood was for others; and today their sweat, their energy, and their blood are for themselves!

...

What would have become of those young antiaircraft artillerymen or the artillerymen of antitank guns or of long-range guns? What would have become of those battalions, gallant and martial, and of our workers, who marched today by this plaza, well armed, well trained, and already with some experience? What would have become of the working-class leaders? What would have become of the workers and the members of the militias? What would have become of the wives, children, and sisters, and of their factories? What would have become of them, if imperialism had established even a beachhead in our territory?

...

We do not speak of what would have become of the happiness of the people and of the hope of the people, if imperialism had be able to conquer the revolution, because there is no more terrible spectacle in the history of humanity than a revolution vanquished.... The history of the Paris Commune, with an appalling number of workers murdered, gives us an idea of what happens when a revolution is conquered. History teaches that the vanquished revolutions have to pay an extraordinarily high price in blood to the conquering reaction, to the conquering dominant classes, because they charge for all the uneasiness with which they have had to live, for all their interests that were affected or threatened. And they not only collect a payment for the present debt; they also want to collect a payment in blood for future debts, trying to exterminate the revolution at its roots.

Of course, given certain circumstances, it is impossible to crush a revolution. I speak of revolutions that were conquered before taking power. What has never happened in history is that a revolutionary people that had really taken power has been conquered.

...

Therefore, we were thinking of all that we owe to those who sacrificed their lives; we were thinking that each smile of today was a tribute to those who made possible this happy day of hope.

...

The blood of the workers, the blood of the peasants, the blood of the humble was what the nation shed, struggling against the mercenaries of imperialism.

...

We have the right to say here to the people, above all to our visitors, that at the same instant that three of our airports were bombed simultaneously by airplanes of Yankee fabrication, with Yankee bombs and shrapnel, the Yankee agencies distributed to the world the story that our airports had been attacked by planes of our own Air Force, with pilots that had deserted that same day.

With cold blood, they carried out an act that was a true outrage, a violation of all international norms and of all moral norms: they launched a surprise attack at dawn against the airports of a country from foreign bases. But in addition to that, they deceived the world, communicating to the world through their [news] agencies, the agencies of imperialism, that the bombing was carried out by Cuban pilots that had deserted with Cuban planes, bombings that had been conceived in cold blood, with airplanes on which they painted the same insignias and colors of our airplanes.

If other reasons and other facts are not enough, this fact alone ought to be enough to make clear how criminal, how awful, how cynical, and how low and despicable are the actions of imperialism. It ought to be enough to enable us to conceptualize what Yankee imperialism is morally, what its news agencies are, and what its newspapers are, everywhere in the world, newspapers by nature reactionary, that make a game of all these lies. It is possible that tens of millions of persons in the world have not received any news of the facts other than the news that Cuban planes piloted by deserting pilots had attacked our airports.

...

Today we do not need to put forward proofs. A partial confession makes proofs unnecessary. The governing circles of the United States have confessed publicly, without giving to the world an explanation. It owes to the world an explanation of all the things that it previously said, of the declarations of the President of the United States, to the effect that they would not intervene in Cuban questions, of the affirmations that their own delegate to the United Nations made, saying that the bombing of our airports had been carried out by Cuban airplanes.

On confessing without any explanation to the world with respect to the previous reports and lies, they relieve us of having to look for proofs. But it is a fact that they attempted the attack, they launched the attack, and that attack costs the destruction of wealth and the loss of lives. That attack cost the blood of workers and peasants.

Who were those that fought against those workers and peasants? We are going to explain. Of the first 1,000 mercenaries captured... We ought to say that at this moment, the revolutionary forces have in their control nearly 1,100 mercenary prisoners, not including crewmembers of the boats. Making an analysis of the social composition of 1,000 of them, we find the following: 800, approximately 800, were of well-to-do families; among these 800, a part of them together owned 27,556 *caballerías*[9] of land that was affected by the Revolution; 9,666 houses; seventy industries; ten sugar cane factories; two banks, and five mines. In addition, more than 200 of these 800 were members of the most exclusive and aristocratic social clubs of Havana. Of the remaining 200 of the 1000, 135 were ex-military men of Batista's army, and the rest, 65, were lumpen or declassed individuals.

...

This is the social composition of the invaders: 27,556 *caballerías* of land; 9,666 buildings and houses; 70 industries; 10 sugar cane factories; two banks, and five mines.

We can be sure that if we were to ask all those meeting here how many are owners of sugar cane factories, there is not a single one; how many owners of banks, there is not a single one; how many were owners of large estates, there is not a single one.

...

Some of these shameless individuals said that they came to struggle for ideals, they came to fight for the free market. Let some idiot stop by here at this moment to say that he comes to struggle for the free market, as if this people does not know full well what that free market meant,

that free market meant impoverished neighborhoods, like *las Yaguas, llega y Pon, Cuevan del Humo*, and dozens of poor neighborhoods that surround this capital;

that free market meant unemployment for 500,000 Cubans;

that free market meant hundreds of families or thousands of families living along the dirt roads of plantations;

---

9 27,556 *caballerías* are equal to 3,700,770,800 square meters—Translator's note.

that free market meant more than 100,000 peasant families working the land in order to deliver a considerable part of their production to absentee landholders that had not seen even a single seed being planted on those lands;

as if the free market had not meant discrimination, injustice, outrages for the workers and peasants, peasants evicted from their huts, murders of workers' leaders, mujalism,[10] smuggling, cabarets, that is, gambling casinos, vice, exploitation, ignorance, illiteracy, and misery for our people.

How are they going to speak of free market to a people where there were nearly half a million unemployed, a million and a half illiterates, a country where there were half a million children without schools; in addition, a country where one had to stand in lines to go to the hospitals, and besides, where one had to seek the help of a politician in exchange for having to give him the voter registration card;[11] how are they going to speak of free market to a people that knows that free market meant aristocratic clubs for some thousands of families, and hungry and barefoot children begging in the streets, swimming in El Morro or next to the sewage water, because they could not go to the beach, because the beaches were closed, the beaches were for private use, the beaches were for the aristocrats, the beaches were for the fortunate, privileged, beneficiaries of the free market; nor could they even dream of going to Varadero, because Varadero was for a few moneyed families;

nor could the people even dream that their son study for a degree, because the universities were for the privileged of the free market; nor could they dream that their son one day would go to Europe to study languages, because going to Europe was for the sons of the privileged of the free market;

nor could a construction worker or worker of limited income dream that his son would be able to study in an institute, if he did not have an institute of capital;

nor could a sugar worker dream that his son would become a university graduate, or that his son could be a doctor or an engineer, because if the son of a worker was able to study, it was because he was a worker of capital, who was able to send—perhaps, the possibilities were limited—his son to an institute; but 90% of the sons of the workers… or if not 90%, at least 75% of the sons of the workers, who live in places where there were not centers of secondary education, and they were not able to dispose of resources for paying for stay in the

---

10   See the Introduction to the Year 1959 as well as Eusebio Mujal in the glossary.
11   In exchange for a favor from a politician, a citizen had to surrender his or her voter registration card to the politician, so that the politician could submit the electoral vote in his favor.

city, 75% of the sons of workers did not have opportunity to study. That opportunity was held exclusively by the beneficiaries of the free market.

Nor could they dream that the daughters of cart drivers or the daughters of cane cutters would have been able to march by here, dancing a tap dance, displaying elegant and beautiful dresses; nor was the son of a peasant able to dream of studying agriculture in the Soviet Union; nor could the people dream of the opportunity for the sons of humble families to study diplomatic law, to study physics, to study any profession, because these opportunities, in general, with some exceptions, were had only by the sons of the fortunate families.

How is this rich young man, ignorant of what work is, or what sweat is, or what it is to suffer, going to come here to say that he came to murder peasants, that he came to assassinate workers, that he came to shed the blood of the people in order to defend his free market?

And not only his free market, or the free market of his daddy, but the free market of the United Fruit Company, the free market of the Yankee monopoly company of electricity, the free market of the company that here controlled the telephones; the free market of the companies that controlled the refineries. That was not even a free market, because they were something more than free market enterprises, they were monopolies, and as monopolies, they virtually had suppressed the competition.

So, these gentlemen that came here, armed by imperialism, when they say that they were defending the free market, what they were defending really was the monopoly that actually is against the free market, because it controls the entire industry; its prices, its resources, and its methods seek precisely to ruin all the others. They were not even defending the free market in the liberal sense of the word.

...

In addition, they say that they came to defend the Constitution of 1940.[12]

It is curious that when the Constitution of 1940 was smashed by the Batista tyranny and was destroyed by the military *coup* of March 10 [1952], there was the complicity, first, of the Yankee embassy, secondly, of the reactionary clergy, thirdly, or rather first together with the others, of the dominant economic classes, of the monopolistic companies and of the rich people in our country; and the complicity of a judicial branch corrupted to the marrow of its bones, as well as the complicity of a great many corrupt politicians.

It is truly cynical that a young gentleman from these sectors, who comes in the company of politicians and abusers of authority of the era of Batista, of the

---

12   See glossary.

Batista that trampled on and destroyed that Constitution, and smashed it to pieces; who comes with the complicity of imperialism and with the complicity of the dominant classes to which these young gentlemen pertain, tied to hundreds of ex-military men that defended that tyranny of Batista, and linked with a bunch of criminals, torturers, and linked with a bunch of politicians; say to this people that they came to defend the Constitution of 1940.

In what the Constitution of 1940 advanced, and in what it had that was revolutionary, the Revolutionary Government is the only government that has respected it, complied with it, and carried it forward. That Constitution said that *"the large estate is proscribed,"* and *"for the purpose of its elimination*—the Constitution said "its elimination"—*the law would establish the maximum property of lands that any type of agricultural or industrial enterprise would be able to possess."* Clearly, this constitutional law never was fulfilled. Why? Because there had to be enacted a later law in the Congress, and who was in the Congress? The politicians, the lawyers of the Yankee monopolies, the owners of the large estates, the millionaires, and the rich. As an exception, there was a handful, a small number of workers' leaders, of humble men of the people, in that House and that Senate, where they were condemned to remain in the minority, because all the newspapers, all the radio and television stations, which pertained precisely to the same dominant economic sectors, had the control and the monopoly of the means of dissemination of ideas, and they drowned with the systematic lie any attempt in favor of the peasants.

...

So those in the Congress that had to enact the complementary laws of the Constitution were precisely the large estate owners, the millionaires, and the lawyers of the Yankee monopolies; therefore, there never was an Agrarian Reform law. A Yankee company had 17,000 *caballerías* of land, in spite of the fact that the law said, "the large estate is proscribed." And in spite of the fact that another precept of the law stated that "the law would dictate the adequate norms for the return of the land to Cuban hands," in spite of the fact that the Constitution, which was approved nineteen years ago and has had vibrancy since 1940, stated that the land had to return to Cuban hands, in those nineteen years there had not been a single law that took a single *caballeria* from a Yankee monopoly that had 17,000.

Another monopoly had 15,000, and another had 10,000 *caballerías*. For the benefit of those visitors who do not understand well what a *caballeria* is: ten thousand *caballerías* is approximately 140,000 hectares. There were companies that had here more than 200,000 hectares of land, of the best lands of Cuba. A constitutional law stated that the large estate is proscribed, and a law should be enacted that would put a maximum limit on the size of the land; a constitutional law stated that the land ought to revert to Cuban hands. The law never was fulfilled.

Similarly, that law stated that the state shall exhaust all means at its disposal to provide work to every manual or intellectual worker. For example, a teacher. The Revolution found more than 10,000 teachers without classroom, without work, and immediately it gave them work, because, at the same time, there were half a million children that needed schools. How? Well, simply: "the state shall exhaust all means at its disposal to provide for every manual or intellectual worker a decent life." And that was what the Revolution did. It exhausted all the means at its disposal to that end. And if it had not exhausted all means, it would be ready to exhaust all necessary means to give them work, yes, work, because that Constitution ordered it.

Those were fundamental principles that the Constitution established, and they would have resolved the problem of hundreds of thousands of peasants, the problem of hundreds of thousands of persons without work, and they never were fulfilled.

...

Those gentlemen did not have any political worry. What problem could they have? They did not have the problem of the worker or the peasant; they lived very well.

On the other hand, now, when the aristocratic clubs were ended; when parasitism was ended; when idleness was ended; when the good life at the cost of the workers and at the cost of the peasants was ended, then yes, they went away to the United States, and they found a Yankee government disposed to give them tanks, to give them bazookas, and to give them canons so that they could come here to shed the blood of workers and peasants.

Those gentlemen spoke of elections. What elections did they want? Those elections of politicians who bought votes, who had dozens of agents that were dedicated to corrupting consciences?

Those elections in virtue of which an unfortunate man or women of the people had to surrender their voter registration card in order that they be given work in a hospital or public works project, or in order that they be given employment; and all the teachers had to go there, all the professionals had to go, everyone, in order to beg favor of the politicians that they be given employment?

Those false elections, in which all prostituted themselves, that did not represent anything other than a procedure through which the exploiting classes, by means of their lawyers and their politicians, maintained themselves in power, and maintained the power of that regime of misery and hunger over the people?

Those elections of politicians of this kind, which we have had when there were not military coups, as frequently has happened in Latin America?

The Revolution is the direct expression of the will of the people, not an election every four years, but an election every day, a constant process of listening to the needs of the people and being connected to the people, a constant meeting with the people. Meetings like these, which surpass all the votes bought by the party politicians, who never would have been able to attain such a number of men and women that spontaneously and enthusiastically have come today to back the Revolution.

The Revolution is a profound change, not a farce or a deceit. The Revolution is a profound change and not a waste of time. What is it that these gentlemen want? Politicking, electoral posters, government posts filled by those scoundrels with panama hats and cigars, giving an image of being important?

Elections like those, no. Elections like those will not be held. Why? Because the Revolution simply has changed the concept of false democracy. As the facts show, it has gone from pseudo-democracy as the means for exploitation by the dominant classes, to a system of direct government of the people, by the people and for the people. Because, In addition, there has to pass a period of time, during which the privileges that oppress the people have to be abolished, have to be destroyed. Do the people have access to the time for occupying themselves in elections now, elections of this type?

What were the political parties? The political parties simply were the expression of class interests. Well here in Cuba, there is a class with interests. Do you know what it is? The humble class, the class of those that produce, the class of those that work, the intellectual workers and the manual workers.

That class is in power. It does not have an interest in or aspiration for the taking of power from an exploiting and privileged minority, since it already is in power. The Revolution knows that the previously dominant class would not be able to attain any backing in some elections that were by the people, simply because it does not know where to begin to combat the Revolution. But the Revolution does not have time to lose in these stupidities. The Revolution does not consider it remotely possible for the oppressing class to recover power; the oppressing and exploiting class never will recover power in our country.

The Revolution knows, and the people know, the people know that the Revolution is the expression of its will. The Revolution did not arrive to power with Yankee bazookas, nor with Yankee tanks, nor with Yankee recoilless guns. The Revolution arrived to power with the support of the people, in virtue of the sacrifices that the people made, of the struggles of the people, of the heroism of the people. Struggling precisely against the Yankee planes, arms, tanks, and cannons. Thus arrived the Revolution to power, with the full backing of the people. It has been in power and has governed with the people, and it is maintaining itself in power with the people.

And the people, what interest has the people now? The interest of the people is that the Revolution continue advancing without losing a minute, continue advancing without taking a single step back, not even to gather momentum, as the posters of the people say.

...

Can any government of America boast of being more democratic than the Cuban revolutionary government? Of greater support of the people than the Cuban Revolutionary government? Can a form of democracy more direct than this be conceived?

Why does democracy have to be the false and pedantic democracy of politicking and the buying of votes? Why cannot democracy be, on the other hand, this direct expression of the will of the people, expressed a thousand times, every day, constantly and in all aspects of life? Not going to an electoral college to scratch the name of a politician, but going to die, as went to die the men of the people, the humble men of the people, combatting against the Yankee tanks and arms?

The Revolution, the Revolution has given to the people, has given to the people something more than a vote to each citizen, it has given something more: it has given to each citizen a rifle, a cannon, an antiaircraft gun, a bazooka, a powerful arm to each humble man of the people that presented himself in the militias.

As they ask the question: We know that you have the majority, why do you not have elections? Well, sir, we are not going to do it as a favor to you or to please you. Because it is not in our interests to be distracted by such things. The people do not have an interest in pleasing idiots, the people do not have an interest in pleasing fools, the people to not have an interest in pleasing brainless young gentlemen.

The people have an interest simply in carrying forward its work. The people cannot waste time, because there is much work to do, and here no one rests, neither of the government nor of the people. The people has a very hard task ahead, carrying forward a revolution in the face of imperialism, in the face of the economic blockade of imperialism, the economic aggressions, and even the military aggressions.

...

We are not a war-like country, nor war loving. We are a country that simply see ourselves obligated to invest human energy and resources [in self-defense] for the fault of the imperialists.... The recent facts of imperialist aggression prove how right the Cuban people were to arm themselves and to prepare its workers and its peasants.... There is no doubt that if our people were not armed, then it would not have been able to smash the mercenaries that brought equipment as modern as that that the mercenaries brought. And if we were not well armed, the aggressive circles of imperialism already would have launched [an attack] some time ago against our country, if they had believed that they were going to find a people that was not going to defend itself.

...

It is inconceivable that there are governments so malicious that at the basis of this aggression of imperialism—which cost many lives, lives of great worth of workers and peasants—there are lackey governments so malicious, and so traitorous to the sentiment of America, that they even have initiated a policy of breaking [diplomatic relations] with Cuba. Instead of breaking with [the government of Nicaragua] of Somoza, from where the expedition departed; instead of breaking with the reactionary and immoral government of Guatemala, from where the expedition was organized; instead of breaking with the government of the United States, which paid for the airplanes and delivered the airplanes, tanks, and arms, in order to come here to murder workers and peasants.

They are breaking with the victim, the country that has been attacked, which is Cuba, with various pretexts, and some of them as stated by Costa Rica: simply, that if the mercenaries were shot. Among those mercenaries, there are criminals like Calviño,[13] who as you know, cut short dozens of lives here. There are murderers and torturers of all types. Of course, that government of imperialism has demanded that they break with us. Clearly, it wants to find a fig leaf; but that government does not find a fig leaf.

...

In an insolent act of interference in our internal affairs, that government expressed its disposition to break with us if we shot any of the mercenaries. Not break with imperialism; not break with Kennedy, who organized the aggression; not break with Nicaragua; not break with Guatemala. They put forward the idea of breaking with our people.

What was our attitude? To break with them? No. We responded in an energetic manner, leaving them with the historic responsibility. We are not breaking relations with the countries of Latin America, because we consider that they are our fraternal peoples. We feel united to them, as they, the peoples, have felt united to us against the aggression.

...

---

13 See glossary.

To those that speak to us of the Constitution of 1940, we say to them that the Constitution of 1940 is already too antiquated and too old for us.

...

We have to speak of a new constitution, yes, a new constitution, but not a bourgeois constitution, not a constitution corresponding to the dominion of the exploiting class over other classes, but corresponding to a new social system, without the exploitation of man by man. This new social system is called socialism, and that constitution will be, therefore, a socialist constitution.[14]

If Mr. Kennedy does not like socialism, well, we do not like imperialism, we do not like capitalism. We have as much right to protest the existence of an imperialist and capitalist regime ninety miles from our shores, as he considers himself with the right to protest the existence of a socialist regime ninety miles from his shores.

...

Rights are not given by size; rights are not given to a people that is larger than another. That is not important! We do not have but a small territory, a small people, but our rights deserve as much respect as those of any country, whatever be its size.

...

To whom did these things occur before Kennedy? To Hitler, to Mussolini. Hitler and Mussolini preached their rights to establish in neighboring countries the government that they considered appropriate. Hitler and Mussolini spoke with that language of force; they spoke of the strong, saying that, "the weak will disappear."

...

They say that a socialist regime here is a threat to their security. No, what threatens the security of the people of the United States is the aggressive policy of the warmongers of the United States; what threatens the security of the family and the people of the United States are those extremist commentaries, that aggressive policy, that policy that does not recognize the sovereignty and the rights of the other peoples.

...

It is absurd to pretend that a government that is dedicated to working for its people, and to creating wealth and service goods for the people; that a

---

14   The Revolution did indeed develop a new Constitution in 1976, in a historic moment in which the conflict with U.S. imperialism was less intense. The new Constitution institutionalized an alternative concept and alternative political structures of popular democracy, in accordance with the formulation in this speech that the Revolution is substituting false democracy or pseudo-democracy with direct democracy.

government that has been dedicated to struggling with all honesty, with total energy, and with determination in the face of all the aggression and in the face of all the obstacles that imperialism has placed on us, is placing in danger the life of a single North American.

...

They are indeed concerned with security. They know they lie when they say that Cuba constitutes a danger for the security of the United States. They know that Cuba has put in danger the security of the monopolies, not because we are going to order to promote revolutions or to make revolutions outside of here, no, but because the example of Cuba is a contagious example.

They do not have an interest even in recovering what they have lost here, the hundreds of millions; in the final analysis, that is nothing for them. They would give much more than that to destroy the example of the Cuban Revolution. They would give much more than that so that this Revolution would fail. Why? In order that it would not serve as a contagious example for the other peoples of Latin America.

...

So capitalism is good, monopolies are good, a free market and that lie is good! Then why do they want to destroy the Cuban Revolution? Why do we not want to destroy them? In the first place, because their system of government does not interest us; in the second place, because we know that they are going to destroy themselves, that its own contradictions are going to cause the system to collapse.

...

Here everyone is ready to wait for what comes with a smile and with complete tranquility. We are convinced that we have much less fear than they; we are convinced that we have less fear than they.

...

However, we declare that we are ready to discuss. In the interests of world peace, we are prepared to discuss and to find formulas for reducing tension. In addition, we are prepared to discuss because we do not have an interest in imperialism attacking us, we do not have an interest that imperialism commits suicide at our expense, as we have said many times.

...

Therefore, for world peace, for the interests that all the peoples have in peace, because we have an interest in peace, we are not on an insolent plan like them, nor an arrogant plan. In accordance with our right, we are disposed to talk.

Ah! What do they say? That economic questions can be discussed, but communism ninety miles from our shores is not a subject of discussion? Well, who has said to them that we accept, in any manner, discussion of questions that pertain to our internal affairs and to the social system that we Cubans want to establish here?

...

In reply to that question, the Cuban people have but one thing to say: that the Cuban people is the owner of its destiny, that the Cuban people is sovereign, and that the Cuban people is at liberty to establish here the social, economic, and political regime that it considers appropriate; and that it does not accept discussion of that particular question with the government of the United States.

...

The things that they want to discuss of an economic order, of any type, we are disposed to discuss. We offer that in the interest of world peace; we offer that in the accordance with the interest of our people and the American people themselves.

In a word: that they drop the phobia of the Revolution and the hatred of the Revolution, and that they discuss with us all the themes that they want to discuss, with respect to which we are reasonable and moral.

...

We have just inflicted a defeat on imperialism; no moment is better than this. But our view is not that the world should be made according to our whims; we do not believe that it has to be our will. We are disposed to adjust to the norms of civilized and peaceful coexistence with other countries. We have no reservations in saying that we are disposed to discuss and that we would be interested in discussion.

...

Of that we do not have any doubt; of that our people do have any doubt.

...

With the same calmness with which we are disposed to discuss, with that same serenity and that same security, we are going to defend our land to the last inch and until the last drop of blood, in a war for which we have arms, arms to defend ourselves, bullets to defend ourselves, in the city, in the countryside, everywhere, and above all we have a people.

...

Every man and woman must know what his or her duty is. And we know how to fulfill that duty in a simple manner, in a natural manner, as the peoples struggle when they have a big reason for struggle, as the peoples struggle when they have to defend the things that we have to defend.

...

While they were trying by all methods to deprive us of our foreign currency income, in order that we would have not anything with which to buy bread, they spent millions of pesos arming mercenaries, giving them airplanes, giving them ships, in order that they could come here to murder our workers and our peasants.

...

And who accompanied them in that shameful enterprise? Already you have seen, as I told you, the social composition of these gentlemen, the rich men that came here, the lands that they had; the war criminals that came here. And there was not lacking the habitual priest in the criminal aggression against our country, and in fact there was not one priest, but three. Three priests came with the invading brigade. Were the three priests Cuban? No, none was Cuban. They were nothing less than three Spanish priests, three Falangist[15] priests. When they were asked what they came to do, they said that they came for purely spiritual functions, to attend to their parishioners, to the attend to their good and noble and human and generous parishioners, their idealist parishioners of the 27,000 *caballerías*, of the 10,000 houses, their Calviño, their Soler Puig, their King,[16] assassins of solders. But they said that they came in a mission purely evangelical, purely Christian, purely spiritual.

However, reviewing the notebooks of these gentlemen, we find here: "*Call written by the priest Ismale de Lugo in his notebook. Call to the people...*," and I am going to read to you the call that he made to the people, this priest that came here in functions purely spiritual. He said, *The chief of the ecclesiastic services of the assault brigade...*—assault yes, but assault on the wealth of the country, and assault of the palace of Sports—*Reverend Father Ismael de Lugo, Capuchino, speaks to the Catholic people of Cuba in his own name and in the name of the other chaplains. Attention, attention, Cuban Catholics: the liberating force has landed on Cuban beaches; we come in the name of God*—so Calviño came in the name of God, so Soler Puig and King came in the name of God, so the owners of the cabarets and the gambling casinos came in the name of God, so the malicious exploiters that came here came in the name of God—*in the name of justice and democracy, to reestablish the law violated, the liberty trampled, and the religion defamed.* All this ought to be a lie, a slander.

We come not for hate but for love...—and there are the photographs of the women and girls murdered by the Yankee planes. I understand that many of you will have had an opportunity to see these appalling photos of women and girls murdered by the Yankee planes. *We come not for hate but for love, we come*

---

15 The Spanish Falangist Movement, a reactionary Spanish social and political movement promoting the disappearance of political parties and the protection of religious tradition—Translator's note.

16 See Calviño, Soler Puig, and King in the glossary.

to bring peace—and what do hundreds of families say that today have wounded sons in hospitals or are in mourning—*even when we have to make war in order to attain them.*

...

The assault brigade is constituted by thousands of Cubans—the first lie of this priest gentleman, because they had some 1500—, *that are in their totality*—listen well—*Christians and Catholics.* For example, Calviño, Soler Puig, King, etcetera, are in their totality Christians and Catholics! 27,000 *caballerías* of land, 10,000 houses, seventy industries, five mines, two bands, two hundred and some members of aristocratic clubs where no black Cuban would be able to go, ten sugar cane factories.

Its morality is the morality of the Crusades—with the difference that these crusaders did not come to regain the temple of the Lord, but to regain their large estates and their sugar cane factories—*they came to reestablish the Beatitudes that the Master taught in the Sermon on the Mount. Before landing, all have attended Mass and have received the Holy Sacraments. They know why they fight. They want that the Black Virgin, our patron saint, la Caridad del Cobre, does not suffer more contemplating from her sanctuary so much impiety, so much secularism, and so much communism.*

In these moments, we need the help of all Catholics of Cuba. We ask for prayers for our triumph, divine protection of our soldiers, civic cooperation, not leaving from your homes and praying to the gods of the armies,—see how he refers to the gods of the armies, as if it were a question of any pagan—*that the struggle be brief in order that the least amount of blood possible be shed, fraternal and Cuban blood*—he does not have a drop of Cuban blood, this Spanish Falangist priest speaking of the shedding of Cuban blood.

Our struggle is of those that believe in God against the atheists, of the spiritual values against materialism—spiritual values, and they came looking for their millions of pesos, they came looking for their Cadillacs, they came looking for their succulent lunch and dinner plates, they came looking for their clubs, they came looking for their sugar cane factories, their mines, their banks, their large estates; and they come speaking of spiritual values. *The struggle of democracy against communism*—the imperialist democracy of Kennedy. *The ideologies are defeated only by another superior ideology, and the only ideology capable of defeating the communist ideology is the Christian ideology. For that, we come; and for that, we struggle.*

Catholic Cubans, our military force is overwhelming and invincible, and greater still is the force of our morality and our faith in God and in His protection and aid. Catholic Cubans, I send an embrace in the name of the soldiers of the liberating army—Calviño, Soler Puig, King, etcetera—*to all family members, relatives, and friends; soon you will be together. Have faith that the victory is ours, because God is with us, and la Virgen de la Caridad cannot abandon her children. Catholics, long live free, democratic, and Catholic Cuba; long live Christ the King; long live our glorious patron saint. God bless you*—blessings, after all the crafty comments that he threw out—*Father Ismael de Lugo, chief of ecclesiastic services of the brigade.*

It is even more indignant when we recall that this gentleman is not Cuban and is nothing less than a Spanish Falangist, who could have used all this warlike spirit to call the Spanish people to struggle against the Moorish Guard of Francisco Franco. He well would have been able to have used this spirit.

...

So, what is happening? Have Spanish Falangist and fascist priests come here to make war against the Revolution?

Well very good. We are going to announce here to the people that the Revolutionary Government in the coming days will decree a law that will declare null and void all permissions to remain in the national territory to all foreign priests that there are in our country ("Good riddance, good riddance!").

That law will not have more than one exception. ¿Do you know for whom? Any foreign priest will be able to remain, with special permission, who in the view of the Government has not been combatting the Cuban Revolution, that is, has not maintained an attitude against the Revolution.

That is to say, will there be exceptions? Yes: a priest that has been honest, that has not been fighting the Revolution, that has not been making counterrevolution, can solicit permission, and the Government, if it considers it appropriate, can grant it, because there are some foreign priests, some, as exceptions, that have not had an attitude against the Revolution, but that has not been the general rule.

...

Is that the only counterrevolutionary activity that they have been carrying out? No.

They have been conducting counterrevolution in religious schools also, openly, filling the heads of the youths that they have under their influence with the poison of the counterrevolution; they have been doing it because they find an easy fertile soil in those schools, where in general go the sons of the wealthy families.

...

Therefore, we announce here that in the next days the Revolutionary Government will decree a law nationalizing the private schools.

That law cannot be a law for one sector. That law will have a general character. That is, all the private schools will be nationalized. Of course, not small schools where there is one teacher, but the private schools that have several teachers.

Now, have the directors of the private schools of the privileged and the directors of other private schools all had the same counterrevolutionary conduct? No, their behavior has varied. There are many directors of secular private schools, as well as some private non-Catholic religious schools, that have had a different attitude, and they have not been instilling the poison of the counterrevolution.

The State considers that it has the duty, the Revolution considers that is has the duty of organizing and establishing the principle of free education for all citizens of the country. And the people considers that it has the duty of forming the future generations in a spirit of love of the country, of true love of neighbor, of love for their fellow man, of love for their people, love for justice, love for the Revolution!

Now, what will be done with the private schools that have not had a counterrevolutionary conduct? Well, simply, the Revolutionary Government will compensate those directors or owners of schools that have not had a counterrevolutionary attitude, but to the contrary, have had a favorable attitude toward the Revolution. The Revolution will not compensate any teaching staff whose directors have been making counterrevolutionary campaigns, have been against the Revolution! But there will be compensation for those teaching staffs that have maintained a patriotic attitude and a respectable attitude toward the Revolution. They will be compensated, and their directors will be invited to work with the Revolutionary Government in the direction of that staff or another staff, so those directors will be called to help in teaching, in addition to being compensated. The professors and employees of all those secular schools will be given work and will have their work assured. The pupils of the schools will continue going to those schools, and the educational level will even be elevated. But in addition, they will have to pay absolutely nothing to go to those schools.

...

Ah, they will say that this "godless" government is against religious teaching! No sir, what we oppose is what these shameless scoundrels have been doing and the crime that they have been committing against our country! No Sir! Can they teach religion? Yes, they can teach religion in the churches, the priests that do not conduct counterrevolutionary campaigns, because religion is one thing, and politics is another.

...

Can the churches remain open? Yes, the churches will be able to remain open, and they will be able to teach religion there in the churches. Would it not be much better if, instead of declaring war against the Revolution, the Churches would focus on teachings of a religious type?

...

If the Churches desire peace with the Revolution, they can have it. If they were to give the Government and the revolutionary people the respect that they are due, the Revolutionary Government and revolutionary people will practice the same policy of respect and consideration toward them.

...

These are the facts, and we have been speaking as always with total clarity, and this does not mean anything but that we are ready to defend our Revolution, to continue ahead, convinced that our cause is right, and that justice is present with us.

...

We have spoken of our socialist Revolution.

Does this mean that the small merchant or the small industrialist has to worry? No.

The basic industries, the mines, the combustibles, the sugar cane factories, the banking function, and the commerce of importation and exportation, that is, the fundamental volume and the essential of the national economy, are in the hands of the people, through which the Cuban people, who have the foundation and have sufficient resources, can carry forward a full program of development of the economy of our country. Therefore, the Revolution can coexist with the small industrialist and the small merchant.

The Revolution always has taken into account the interests of those sectors of small property holders. The best proof is the Urban Reform. The Urban Reform affected 105,000 property holders. My understanding is that this month there will be between 100,000 and 105,000 owners of small property, that is, all the small property holders, will be collecting payments [from the state]. There was in the past month already 75,000 [small property holders] collecting payments in the [state] banks; the property holders did not have to bother the tenant. Before [the Urban Reform], if the tenant did not pay them, they received nothing.

With the fund that the Revolution has made, by means of the collection of all rent payments that surpass the sum of 600 pesos monthly, a fund has been made that guarantees that the small property holder receives payments [from state banks] for what he charges in rent, which in many situations before he was not able to collect. Of course, the Revolution does this through the collection of all rents that surpass 600 pesos. In this manner, the Revolution has this year, and will have for various years, a fund of nearly 80 million pesos for investment in construction every year, and in addition, to pay to all those owners that charged less than 600 pesos, and that was a total of 100,000 to 105,000 small property holders.

In addition, the Agrarian Reform law establishes that when that income of the small property holder is his only income, when it be his only income, the government will change it into a pension when the tenant has finished paying for the house. Why? Because we understand that the society ought to help the invalid, the child, and the elderly. It is in accordance with the principles of the Revolution that if a family does not have any other income, if an elderly person does not have any other income than the rent of a house for 80 or 100 pesos, and at the end of five years, for example, the tenant has completed payments,[17] in that case the society ought to continue helping that person.

This is the manner in which it was established by the law established, and it is the manner in which it is being implemented.

The socialist revolution does not mean that the interests of determined social sectors are eliminated without some reflection. The Revolution eliminated without any deliberation the interests of the great landowners, the large estate owners, the banks, the big industrialists. And the Revolutionary Government on the occasion of that nationalization of the large national companies, and of the banks, and of the Urban Reform, established, declared, that no other social interest of the middle sectors of the population would be affected without due consideration, without taking into account their interests.

And the Revolution has complied with its word. The Revolution has fulfilled the Urban Reform Law in all aspects related to the small property holder. The Revolution will fulfill its word and its declaration that no middle interest will be affected without taking into account its interests. Whereas previously the small merchant was exploited by the large wholesaler, today the small merchant has credit, as does the small industrialist.

The Revolution does not have interest in nationalizing or socializing these small industries and small commerce—nor middle industry and commerce—because the Revolution has ample tasks with all the centers of production and the sources of wealth with which today it is counting on to carry forward this program.

The Revolution understands that there can be collaboration by the small industrialist and the small merchant with the Revolution, and it understands that their interests can coincide with the interests of the Revolution.

---

17   In the Urban Reform Law, the tenants made rent payments to the state banks, at levels previously established by the owner. When the tenant's payments to the state had accumulated to the value of the property of the house, the tenants became owners of the house, and they were given certificates of home ownership.

At specific moments, the counterrevolution has wanted to make it appear that a hair salon was going to be nationalized, that the taxis were going to be nationalized; well, even the fried food stands were going to be nationalized. All those fried food stands: Blessed be all those fried food stands that often provide for the people who cannot go to an elegant restaurant!

The fruit stands, small commerce and small interests can coincide. The Revolution does not think about these cases, and it understands that the solution of these issues will be the result of a long process of evolution, it will be the result of a long process of evolution.

There still remain some interests that in truth are truly damaging to the people. There are times in which a tomato is sold here in the city at a price five times more than what is paid to the peasant; a pineapple is sold at a price five times higher. There still is a small plague of intermediaries that are truly sucking from the economy of the people and that really restrict consumption.

The Revolution still has to take some measures with the goal of making possible the breaking of the blockade of certain parasitic plagues that make extraordinarily expensive agricultural products, making the people pay very high prices for those products, while paying a pittance to the peasant. The Revolution has to take measures that would break that blockade and would enable the people to consume the most possible, favoring the development of agriculture.

So some measures remain to be taken. I make this warning so that none is confused, so that everyone knows what to abide by.

But fundamentally, the measures of the Revolution are taken; no one has to worry. What is more, this is a victorious moment of the Revolution that ought to serve as evidence for all those that have been doubtful or vacillating. Why deprive yourself of this privilege that our people have of participating in a process such as this in which we are living? Why deprive yourself of this happiness?

When we see the enthusiasm of the people, the unity of the people, the gigantic mass that marched in front of this platform, we were thinking: Why are there still Cubans whom this happiness pains? Why are they incapable of understanding that this happiness can be theirs? It is no more than a question of adaptation.

I ask you to reconsider before the invincible force of the Revolution, the overwhelming force of a Revolution that nothing or no one will be able to destroy, and reflecting on that, adapting yourself to it. So that tomorrow you also can see your sons marching in this manner with the sons of workers, and doing gymnastic exercises, and entering contests and winning awards, so that you can see them enjoying the same happiness.

...

In these days of aggression, the Revolution of necessity had to adopt measures against possible enemies, and it of necessity had to impede the action of the Fifth Column; and in these measures, possibly many persons, for distinct reasons, have been detained. Members of the team of ministers were sent to these same persons to speak with them. There are hundreds of persons at this moment who are going to converse with them, with all those that were detained.

The Revolution does not desire to make use of force. The Revolution repudiates the use of force, even against a minority. The Revolution prefers to make use of reason; the Revolution prefers to make use of persuasion. When there is a mistaken Cuban, but capable of rectifying and capable of understanding, we want to get that that Cuban to understand, to get that Cuban to rectify.

We are not so egoist that we want only for ourselves all this happiness, all the emotion, and all this glory, which is not the glory of us the ministers or functionaries of the Revolutionary Government, but is, above all, the glory of the people.

The Revolution does not have fear. The Revolution is too strong to have fear, the Revolution has too much backing for it to have fear.

...

After today these words are, sincerely, words that we say to those that, for having been born in the past, for having been educated in many of the lies of the past, have been incapable of understanding until today.

But also we have known of many cases of men and women of the people that were vacillating some months ago, who even had dollars put away, and anonymously they have sent them [to the revolutionary government] after this invasion. Above all after they saw what the mercenaries declared, after they saw their lack of reason, their lack of morality, their lack of logic, their lack of sense in coming to shed blood on this land. And above all, after they saw—by the confession of the Yankee imperialists themselves—, that that expedition was organized by the Central Service of Intelligence, ordered by Kennedy, discussed with the chiefs of the repressive organs of the General Staff, with the chief of the American squad. That is, it was an expedition clearly foreign against our country, such that the members of that expedition committed a crime of high treason against the country.

We with all frankness express that, in our opinion, we ought not to reduce the significance of our victory with sanctions that could appear too severe. The victorious peoples are generous peoples. Therefore, we propose that our people ought to take this into account, that our people ought not tarnish or reduce our victory with a severe sanction, massive, against all; which could serve, in addition, as a weapon of the enemies of the Revolution. Our Revolution will never lose on knowing, in the hour of victory, to keep under control all just indignation, all perfectly logical infuriation, occasioned by the injustice and the crime committed against our people.

We express this, as we believe that we ought to express all that we sincerely think is advisable for the Revolution and advisable for the people.

We have attained a crushing victory over the invaders, and also a moral victory even more overwhelming in the eyes of the people and in the eyes of the world.

...

What do we have ahead? We have ahead the risks of imperialist aggression; we have ahead great tasks. We have arrived to the point that we ought to express with all responsibility that the hour has arrived of making a greater effort; the hour has arrived of making the maximum effort.

The coming months are months are great importance, in which we have to strive hard, as much in the field of military preparation as in the field of production, as in the field of organization, as in the field of revolutionary and political work. In all of the areas, none of us has the right to rest; in all the areas, we have the obligation to do to the maximum, learning the lesson of this day of today.

...

Before ending, when we were speaking of the theme, over all this problem of the free market and all that series of problems, our opinion over this, we wanted to recall what we had said in this regard during the trial of Moncada.[18] And here there is a paragraph from that occasion, which says:

> The future of the nation and the solution of its problems cannot continue to depend on the egoistic interest of a dozen financiers, nor on the cold calculations over profits that ten or twelve magnates trace from their air-conditioned offices. The country ought not remain on its knees imploring miracles of various golden calves that, like those of the Old Testament, do not make miracles of any kind.
>
> The problems of the republic will have solution only if we dedicate ourselves to struggle for it with the same energy, honor, and patriotism

---

18   Fidel refers to his speech of self-defense on October 16, 1953, during the trial for his organization and leadership of the attack on Moncada military garrison in Santiago de Cuba on July 26, 1953. Subsequently distributed clandestinely under the name of *History Will Absolve Me*, the speech functioned as a manifesto and a platform of the July 26 Movement led by Fidel.

that our liberators invested in order to create it. And not with statesmen of the style of Carlos Saladrigas,[19] whose statesmanship consisted in leaving everything as it is and passing life mumbling nonsense about "absolute liberty for the market," "guarantees to investment capital," and the "law of supply and demand," as if they would resolve such problems. In a mansion on Fifth Avenue[20] these ministers can chat happily until there no longer remains not even the dust of the bones of those that today demand urgent solutions. And in the present world, no social problem is resolved by spontaneous generation.

Remembering the arguments of the invading mercenaries over "supply and demand," "guarantees to foreign capital," and the "free market," we again review what we thought then, how we thought when we were not in the Revolutionary Government, but when we were before a group of judges, prisoners of the tyranny that was going to judge us, and we spoke with complete clarity concerning how we thought over that theme, how we thought then and how we think with much more reason today, when we have acquired a long and fruitful experience in all these years of struggle.

The Revolution has been advancing in accordance with the revolutionary ideas that we have, which have played an important role in this struggle, and it has been advancing to the same measure that we all have been advancing. The Revolution has been developing to the same measure that our revolutionary ideas and the revolutionary ideas of the people have been developing.

Accordingly, on the occasion in which a million Cubans met to proclaim the Declaration of Havana,[21] the thought that constitutes the essence of Revolution, of our socialist Revolution, was expressed. That general assembly declared that it,

> *Condemns the large estate, source of misery for the peasant and a backward and inhumane system of agricultural production;*
>
> *Condemns the starvation wages and the dreadful exploitation of human work by illegitimate and privileged interests;*
>
> *Condemns illiteracy, the lack of teachers, schools, doctors, and hospitals, the lack of protection of the aged that prevails in the countries of America;*

---

19 See glossary.
20 An avenue of expensive houses in the Miramar section of Havana.
21 On September 2, 1960, a mass assembly in the Civic Plaza (today the Plaza of the Revolution), constituting the National General Assembly of the People of Cuba, approved the First Declaration of Havana.

Condemns the discrimination against the Black and the Indian;

Condemns the inequality and the exploitation of women;

Condemns the military and political oligarchies that maintain our peoples in poverty, impede their democratic development and the full exercise of their sovereignty;

Condemns the concession of natural resources of our countries to the foreign monopolies as a submissive policy that betrays the interests of the peoples;

Condemns the governments that do not listen to the sentiments of their people in order to comply with the mandates of Washington;

Condemns the systematic deceit of the peoples by agencies of dissemination that respond to the interest of the oligarchies and to the policy of oppressive imperialism;

Condemns the monopoly of the news by Yankee agencies, instruments of the North American trusts and agents of Washington;

Condemns the repressive laws that prevent workers, peasants, students, and intellectuals, the great majority in each country, from organizing and struggling for their social and patriotic demands;

Condemns the monopolies and the imperialist companies that systematically plunder our resources, exploit our workers and peasants, bleed and keep backward our economies, and force the politics of Latin America to submit to their designs and interests.

The Cuban People's National General Assembly condemn, in sum, the exploitation of man by man, and the exploitation of the underdeveloped countries by imperialist finance capital.

Therefore, the Cuban People's National General Assembly proclaim before America:

The right of peasants to the land;

The right of workers to the fruit of their labor;

The right of children to education;

The right of the sick to medical attention and hospital care;

The right of the youth to work;

The right of students to free, experiential and scientific education;

The right of Blacks and Indians to 'the full dignity of man';

The right of the woman to civil, social, and political equality;

The right of the elderly to a secure old age;

The right of intellectuals, artists, and scientists to struggle, with their works, for a better world;

The right of States to the nationalization of the imperialist monopolies, thereby rescuing national wealth and resources;

The right of nations to their full sovereignty;

The right of the peoples to convert their military fortresses into schools, and to arm their workers, their peasants, their students, their intellectuals, the black, the Indian, the woman, the young person, the old person, and all the oppressed and exploited, in order that they can defend, by themselves, their rights and their destinies.

The Cuban People's National General Assembly proposes:

The duty of workers, peasants, students, intellectuals, blacks, Indians, youth, women, the elderly, to struggle for their economic, political, and social demands;

The duty of the oppressed and exploited nations to struggle for their liberation;

The duty of each people to solidarity with all the oppressed, colonized, exploited, and attacked peoples of the world, regardless of where they are and the geographical distance from them. All the peoples of the world are brothers! (APPLAUSE)

This is the program and the essence of the thought of our socialist Revolution, that today I repeat on this day of triumph, and of success and hope for the working class of our country.

Viva the Cuban working class! (*"Viva!"*)
   Viva the brother peoples of Latin America! (*"Viva!"*)
   Viva the liberation of Latin America! (*"Viva!"*)
   Viva the redemption of man! (*"Viva!"*)
   Viva America! (*"Viva!"*)
   Viva the nation! (*"Viva!"*)
   Patria o Muerte!
   Venceremos!

Glossary

Agramonte Loynaz, Ignacio. Major General of the Cuban Liberator Army. Known as "The Major." Was one of the most outstanding leaders of the War of Ten Years (1868–1878). Died in combat in 1873.

Almeida Bosque, Juan. Participant in the attack on the Moncada military barracks of July 26, 1953 and a member of the *Granma* expeditionary force that disembarked on December 2, 1956. During the revolutionary war of 1956–1958, he was named *comandante* and head of the Mario Muñoz Third Front. After the triumph of the revolution, he held posts of high responsibility in the government and in the Communist Party of Cuba. He was the first president of the Association of Combatants of the Cuban Revolution, established on December 2, 1993. He was awarded the honors *Comandante de la Revolución y Héroe de la República de Cuba.*

Ameijeiras Delgado, Efigenio. Became involved in revolutionary activities after the *coup d'état* of March 10, 1952 and was imprisoned. Was a member of the *Granma* expeditionary force that disembarked on December 2, 1956. During the revolutionary war, he was a member of Column No. 1 of the José Martí First Front, and later was named head of Column No. 6 of the Frank País Second Front. He attained the rank of *comandante* in the Rebel Army. After the triumph of the Revolution, he was head of the Revolutionary National Police and combatant at the Bay of Pigs, and he fulfilled risky international missions, among them in Algeria and Angola. He is brigadier general of the Revolutionary Armed Forces. He was awarded the honor of *Héroe de la República de Cuba*.

Bandung Conference. Held in 1955, it is the antecedent of the Non-Aligned Movement. Twenty-nine chiefs of state met. They were of the first generation of postcolonial leaders of Asia and Africa. The host of the conference was President Ahmed Sukarno of Indonesia.

Batista Zaldívar, Fulgencio. Entered the Army in 1921. Until 1933, worked as a stenographer in different military garrisons and camps, and was promoted to Sergeant Major. In the midst of political instability following the fall of the dictator Gerardo Machado, Batista joined a group of rebellious Army sergeants and soldiers that seized control of Columbia military base on September 4, 1933 and that, joined with the University Student Directorate, declared a Provisional Revolutionary Government of Cuba. Batista took control of the *coup d'état*, was promoted to coronel, and formed a part of the new government. He rapidly became the real power behind the governments that were formed. He carried out a bloody repression of the revolutionary general strike of 1935. In the context of an antifascist international situation, he was elected president of the republic in 1940. Following the electoral defeat of his party in 1944, he voluntarily exiled himself to Miami, from where he continued influencing the policy of the island. He returned to Cuba to seek again the presidency in the elections of 1952, but shortly before the elections, he led a *coup d'état* with the blessings of the United States, and subsequently submerged Cuba in a sea of blood and pain. On January 1, 1959, he fled Cuba for the Dominican Republic, taking with him millions of pesos from the national treasury as well as his most notorious henchmen and followers. He died in Spain in 1973.

Bohemia. The most important and oldest of the Cuban literary magazines, founded in 1908. Has played an important role in the political and social life of the country.

Bureau of Investigations. Located on 23rd Street on the corner of 32nd Street. There were carried out numerous tortures, abuses, and murders of combatants of the clandestine resistance. It was demolished by the Revolution, and in its place a beautiful park was erected. Today it is called *Parque de la Clandestinidad*.

Cabaña—San Carlos de la Cabaña Fortress. So-called in honor of the Spanish King Charles III. Construction was begun in 1763, on the high bank of the Havana Bay, an area that had been defenseless until that moment. At the time of its completion in 1774, it was the largest Spanish fortress constructed in America.

Calviño Ínsua, Ramón. A member of the July 26 Movement, he was captured and imprisoned in the Police Station, where he was coopted by the notorious chief of the station, Estaban Ventura. He subsequently informed on and tortured a large part of the clandestine resistance in Havana. With the triumph of the Revolution, he left the country; and he returned in 1961 with the invading force at the Bay of Pigs. He was captured, tried, and executed.

Cantillo Porras, Eulogio. Was chief of the Air Corps at the time of the *coup d'état* of March 10, 1952. Although he did not participate in the *coup*, he accepted it and continued in the Army. He was promoted, eventually becoming Chief of the Joint Staff. In December 1958, before the imminent defeat of the armed forces by the Rebel Army, he negotiated with Fidel Castro the terms for the ending of the war, but he ignored the agreement, returning to Havana and devising a *coup d'état* that enabled Batista to escape. Detained after the triumph of the revolution, he was tried and sentenced to fifteen years in prison. Upon being freed, he went into exile in the United States, where he died.

Carratalá Ugalde, Conrado. A simple police guard, he earned promotions by means of tortures and crimes perpetuated against the clandestine resistance in opposition to the Batista dictatorship. He arrived to become a police coronel in his meteoric career of murders and depredations.

Castilla Más, Belarmino "Aníbal". Participated in the student struggle against Batista and in the clandestine resistance as Action Chief of the July 26 Movement in Santiago de Cuba. He commanded the José Tey Column of the Second Front, becoming its second-in-command. Following the triumph of the Revolution, he play important roles in the Revolutionary Armed Forces, the government, and the Communist Party of Cuba. Is Doctor of Historic Sciences, and has published various books on the insurrectional struggle.

Castro Ruz, Raúl. Was incorporated at a very young age into the anti-imperialist struggle, and after the March 10 *coup d'état* was a participant in all the battles against it: the attack on the Moncada military barracks of July 26, 1953; the *Granma* expeditionary force that disembarked on December 2, 1956; and the guerrilla struggle of 1957–1958, in which he was head of the Frank País Second Eastern Front. Following the triumph of the Revolution, he was military chief of the then province of *Oriente*, and later Minister of the Revolutionary Armed Forces, in which he demonstrated organizational capacities, converting the revolutionary armed forces into a high-quality military body, experienced in various internationalist conflicts. In his positions as Vice Prime Minister and as First Vice President of the Councils of State and of Ministers, he worked ceaselessly for the Cuban socialist transition. From 2009 to 2018, as President of the Council of State and of Ministers, he directed the destiny of the country. In his second term (2014–2018), he propelled a process of structural changes, with the intention of eliminating profound bottlenecks, insufficiencies, and deficiencies left by the crisis of the 1990s; and of promoting the reinsertion of Cuba into an increasingly complex international context. He continues to serve as First Secretary of the Communist Party of Cuba.

Chaviano del Río, Alberto. Initiated his military career as a soldier in 1933. Joined the *coup d'état* of September 4, 1933, and Batista compensated him with a promotion to colonel, assigned to the Moncada Barracks in Santiago de Cuba. He had direct responsibility for the murders, tortures, and other crimes unleashed in Santiago following the assault against the Moncada Barracks directed by Fidel Castro and members of the July 26 Movement in 1953.

Chibás Ribas, Eduardo René. Struggled against the dictatorship of Machado; combatted Batista during his first military dictatorship in the 1930s; was member of the Constitutional Assembly of 1940; and Senator of the Republic between 1944 and 1950. Became the head of the Party of the Cuban People (Orthodox) in 1947. Combatted political and administrative corruption from all platforms, especially the radio, from which he contributed to the raising of consciousness among the people and to generating a popular movement. On August 16, 1951, in his Sunday radio program, after again accusing the then Minister of Education and not being able to prove it, he committed suicide.

Cienfuegos Gorriarán, Camilo (1932, Havana -1959). After the March 10, 1952 *coup d'état*, he left for the United States, but was deported. He returned to Cuba, became involved in the student movement, and was detained and tortured. He returned to the United States, and from there traveled to Mexico, where he joined the July 26 Movement. He was a member of the *Granma* expeditionary force that disembarked on December 2, 1956. During the revolutionary war of 1957–1958, he distinguished himself, attaining the rank of *comandante*. As the head of Antonio Maceo Column No. 2, he was charged with bringing the war to the western provinces, but because of the needs of the revolutionary struggle, he remained in the central province of Las Villas. With the flight of Batista and the maneuvers to frustrate the revolutionary triumph, acting on the orders of Fidel Castro, he proceeded to Havana to take the Columbia military garrison. With the triumph of the Revolution, he was named Chief of General Staff of the new revolutionary army. In October 1959, returning from Camagüey after impeding the counterrevolutionary action of Huber Matos, the small aircraft in which he was traveling disappeared in the sea.

Cienfuegos Gorriarán, Osmany. Member of the July 26 Movement, he combatted the dictatorship and was an officer in the Rebel Army. He occupied various positions of high responsibility in the government and the Party. He was the first General Secretary of the Organization for the Solidarity of the Peoples of Asia, Africa, and Latin America, founded in 1966, with headquarters in Havana.

Camilio Cienfuegos School City. The first great educational work constructed by the Revolution. Located in the mountainous town of Bartolomé Masó in the province of Granma, it was inaugurated on July 26, 1959.

Clandestine resistance. The covert struggle that was organized in the cities during the dictatorship of Fulgencio Batista. Those involved carried out daring tasks, including promoting the revolution, collection of funds for the revolutionary movement, acts of sabotage, execution of henchmen and informers, carrying messages, preparation of supplies for the Rebel Army, aid to families of combatants imprisoned or missing, public denunciation of assassinations of revolutionaries, among others. A heroic struggle that cost thousands of lives of great worth.

Columbia. Military camp/base/headquarters, located in the zone called *Los Quemados*, near the settlement of *Marianao* in Havana. Construction began in 1899, by orders of the U.S. government of occupation. It was called *Columbia*, because the first troops that were lodged there proceeded from the District of Columbia, the capital of the United States. In 1908, the camp was headquarters of the General Staff of the Permanent Army. After September 4, 1933, it was called Columbia Military City. On March 10, 1952, Batista arrived there in the early morning, escorted by a group of police cars, whose chief was Rafael Salas Cañizares. There the *coup d'état* began. In 1957, Batista organized the Joint Staff of the Armed Forces, locating it in Columbia Military City.

Confederación de Trabajadores de Cuba (Confederation of Workers of Cuba). In 1939, labor organizations were restructured as the first unitary national organization of the working class by the First Cuban Communist Party, which controlled some of the most combative workers' federations, such as that of the sugar industry. However, the Confederation became an instrument for forcing the working class to submit to capital. With the revolutionary triumph of January 1, 1959, the worker masses removed their Baltistan and reformist management, and the Confederation incorporated itself into the tasks of the construction of the new society. Since 1961, it has been known as *Central de Trabajadores de Cuba* (CTC: Worker's Union of Cuba).

Constitution of 1940. A bourgeois democratic constitution, considered in its time to be the most advanced constitution of America. It gave expression to rights that had been struggled for in Cuba since the nineteenth century, and to progressive measures derived from the revolutionary activity of the 1930s. One of its articles declared the banning of the large estate. However, regulatory laws were not developed, leaving most of its precepts unimplemented. It was therefore a frustrated Constitution, although it inaugurated an important process for the development of political institutions. With the 1952 *coup d'état*, Batista abolished it and imposed what he called Constitutional Statutes.

Cowley Gallegos, Fermín. Coronel, chief of the military district of Holguín. Notorious assassin of the northern zone of the then province of Oriente. Directed the assassination of dozens of revolutionaries during Christmas 1956, the so-called "Bloody Christmas." Was executed by the July 26 Movement in a commando action of November 23, 1957.

Díaz Lanz, Pedro Luis. Was chief of the Revolutionary Air Forces from January to June of 1959, when he was dismissed because of his verified ties with the CIA agent Frank Sturgis or Fiorini, and because of irregularities in his headquarters. He fled to the United States, where he was received as a hero. He did not waver in carrying out armed actions against his people, like that of October 1959, coinciding with the betrayal of Huber Matos in Camagüey.

Dorticós Torrado, Osvaldo. Lawyer and president of the Bar Association of Cienfuegos. In 1933, he combatted the Machado dictatorship. Following the *coup d'état* of March 10, 1952, he joined the struggle against the dictatorship, incorporating himself in the July 26 Movement of Cienfuegos, in which he became regional coordinator. Detained on several occasions, he was expelled from the country at the end of 1958. Immediately following the triumph of the Revolution, he was named minister in charge of the legal analysis of proposed revolutionary laws. He was President of the Republic of Cuba from July 1959, when Urrutia resigned; to 1976, when the organs of Popular Power were established. He was a member of the national direction of the Communist Party of Cuba and its antecedents (Revolutionary Integrated Organizations, United Party of the Socialist Revolution), in which he occupied high responsibilities.

Echeverría Bianchi, José Antonio. Entered the University of Havana in 1950, where he stood out for his student political activities. Was elected President of the Association of Architectural Students, and in 1954, General Secretary of the University Student Federation (FEU). His actions of opposition to the dictatorship led to high support among the student body, and he was elected President of FEU on April 19, 1955 and again the following year, on June 13, 1956. At the end of 1955, joined with other *compañeros*, he founded the Revolutionary Directory, an armed branch the University Student Federation. On March 13, 1957, he directed the command that from *Radio Reloj* was to announce that the tyranny had been overthrown. With the failure of this plan, attempting to return to the university, he was confronted by the police, and he was shot and killed in the street.

Espín Guillois, Vilma. Was incorporated into the July 26 Movement at its establishment, and was a member of its national direction. Her activities in the clandestine resistance in Santiago de Cuba were of great importance, as a result of which she was included in the most wanted list by the police forces of the dictatorship. In July 1958, she was incorporated into the Rebel Army, in the Frank País Second Eastern Front. Following the triumph of the Revolution, she was entrusted with the responsibility of integrating the various women's organizations into the Federation of Cuban Women, and she was elected its president. She was a member of international women's associations, from which she worked for the empowerment of women. She was incorporated into the Central Committee of the Communist Party of Cuba in 1965, and was deputy of the National Assembly and member of the Council of State in representation of the Federation of Cuban Women from 1976 until her death in 2007. She was granted the honor of *Heroína de la República de Cuba*.

Escalona Alonso, Derminio. *Comandante* in the Rebel Army. Was designated to open a guerrilla front in *la Cordillera de los Órganos*, in the western province of Pinar del Río, in May 1958.

Estrada Palma, Tomás. First president of the Republic of Cuba from 1902 to 1906. Participated in the founding of the Cuban Revolutionary Party in 1892. Governed with honesty, but with absolute servility to U.S. interests. Near the end of his term, he decided to seek reelection, for which he made use of force and fraud. This caused a popular rebellion that threatened to overthrow him;

he preferred to solicit the government of the United States for a military intervention. A short time later, he resigned the presidency in order to facilitate the delivery of the destiny of the country to the interveners, for the second time.

Fernández Álvarez, José Ramón. Graduated from the School of Cadets and Artillery of Cuba in 1947. Following the March 10, 1952 *coup d'état*, he participated in conspiracies against the Batista tyranny with different political and military groups until 1956, when he was detained upon being discovered in the conspiracy of the so-called "Pure Ones." He was tried in a summary council of war and sentenced to prison in the Isle of Pines, where he remained until the triumph of the Revolution. In prison, he maintained contact with political prisoners, and participated in conspiratorial activities. After the triumph of the Revolution, he was incorporated in the Revolutionary Armed Forces. He commanded one of the principal groups of troops in the struggle against the mercenary landing in the Bay of Pigs, where he was wounded. He occupied positions of high responsibility in the government and the Communist Party of Cuba. From 1997 to 2018, he was President of the Cuban Olympic Committee.

Fifth Police Station. Located on Celascoaín Street, on the corner of Peñalver Street, in the municipality of Central Havana. One of its chiefs was Esteban Ventura Novo, who with his henchmen engaged in numerous acts of torture, with the intention of ending the clandestine revolutionary movement.

Figueres Ferrer, José. Costa Rican political figure, leader of the National Liberation Party. Was president of the Republic on two occasions, from 1953 to 1958, and from 1970 to 1974. He visited Cuba in March of 1959, when he expressed criticisms before a mass assembly of the anti-imperialist positions of the Cuban Revolution, which were refuted courteously but firmly by Fidel Castro. He returned to Cuba in 1982, and later made declarations of respect toward the Cuban Revolution.

Franqui Mesa, Carlos. Journalist. Member of the Popular Socialist Party (the first Communist Party of Cuba) in the 1940s. He was incorporated into the Rebel Army, connected to *Radio Rebelde*. In January of 1959, he was named director of the newspaper *Revolución* until 1965, when he became director of the Office of Historic Affairs. In 1968, he abandoned the country, and subsequently began to write against the Revolution.

García Íñiguez, Calixto. Combatant for Cuban Independence since 1868. In 1898, when the Cuban Liberator Army had defeated the Spanish Army, he supported the landing of the troops of the United States. Indignant at the decision of the North Americans to impede the entrance of the victorious Cuban Army to Santiago de Cuba, he renounced his charge. His July 17 letter of resignation to the chief of the U.S. forces, William Shafter, thoroughly revealed the true intentions of the occupation of the country.

García García, Pilar. Cuban military official during the dictatorship of Fulgencio Batista who stood out for being one of the principal oppressors of the Batista regime. It was said of him that he had the name of a woman and the soul of an assassin.

Gómez Ochoa, Delio "Marcos". Combatant in the Rebel Army, was second-in-command of Column 1 of the José Martí First Front. Promoted to *comandante* in April of 1958. Chief of the Simon Bolivar Fourth Front.

Guevara de la Serna, Ernesto Che. His youthful political and social concerns brought him to become involved in the July 26 Movement and in the *Granma* expedition as a doctor. However, during the war of liberation, he distinguished himself as a combatant, the first to be promoted to *comandante*. At the head of the Ciro Redondo Column 8, he directed the invasion toward the southern zone of Las Villas. He directed the victory in the battle of Santa Clara, which was one of the most decisive blows to the dictatorship. After the triumph of the Revolution, he was one of the most outstanding members of the Cuban revolutionary vanguard, serving as Minster of Industries, in which capacity he made theoretical and practical contributions concerning the socialist transition. He organized and directed a Latin American detachment that proposed to begin a regional revolutionary struggle from Bolivia. In the midst of very adverse circumstances for the guerrilla troop, he was wounded, captured in la *Quebrada del Yuro*, and assassinated in school house of *La Higuera*.

Guiteras Holmes, Antonio. Initiated studies in the University of Havana, where he was opposed to the dictatorship of Machado. He led an armed struggle in the province of *Oriente*, in which he was involved at the time of the fall of the Machado regime. During the so-called "Government of 100 Days," he was Secretary of Government, War, and Navy, from which position he propelled popular and revolutionary laws. With the fall of the government, he turned to clandestine resistance. He founded an anti-imperialist organization, *Joven Cuba*, to oppose the oligarchical power. He was killed in combat in *El Morrillo*, in the province of Matanzas, when he was attempting to leave the country in order to return with an armed expedition.

Grajales Coello, Mariana. Mother of the Maceo brothers, heroic generals of the Liberator Army in the three wars of independence. Collaborated in the wars, and cultivated in all her sons the love for a free Cuba. Cubans consider her the Mother of the Country.

Ichaso Macías, Francisco. Author of various books of essays and biographies. Ambassador of Cuba in the United Nations, he held positions in various administrations during the neocolonial republic. After the triumph of the Cuban Revolution, he abandoned the country and relocated to Mexico, where he was a journalist and was active in counterrevolutionary groups.

King Yung, Jorge. In the middle of the 1960s, he murdered the soldier Raúl Pupo, in front of his wife and minor children, enabling him to rob one of the vessels, in which he fled to Florida, carrying with him as hostages the wife and children of the victim. He was received by U.S. authorities and was enlisted to participate in the invasion at the Bay of Pigs, in which he was captured, tried, and condemned to death.

Llanusa Gobel, José. Was a prize-winning sportsman. He competed in the Olympic Games in London in 1948, and obtained a silver medal in the Pan-American Games in Guatemala in 1950. He was incorporated into the struggle against the Batista dictatorship, and after the triumph of the Revolution, was director of the Institute for Physical Education, Sports, and Recreation (INDER). He occupied important responsibilities, such as Minister of Education, member of the first Central Committee of the Communist Party of Cuba, and deputy to the National Assembly. He died in 2007.

Machado Morales, Gerardo. Elected president of Cuba in 1925. During his term, first with a hard hand and later by means of a dictatorship, he imposed a regime of terror, of administrative and political corruption, and of delivering U.S. interests. His regime fell on August 12, 1933, after a national general strike.

Mambises. Popular name for the members of the Liberator Army in the three wars of independence in Cuba against the Spanish colonialism.

Mariátegui, José Carlos. Member of the Peruvian political Left. Among the leaders in the founding of the Socialist Party, the literary magazines *Labor* and *Amauta*, and the Confederation of Workers of Peru. Connected Marxism to Peruvian and Latin American reality, not only utilizing its theoretical tools, but also intending to integrate it with the political and cultural traditions of the country, fundamentally with the communitarian traditions of the indigenous peasantry.

Martí Pérez, José Julián. Is the Apostle of Cuban independence. Organized the Cuban Revolutionary Party in order to carry out the "necessary war" against Spanish colonialism, and then, in peacetime, to direct the establishment of a Republic "with all and for the good of all." He lived exiled for fifteen years in the United States; he identified the essence of what we today call imperialism, and he was capable of warning of the danger that lied ahead for Cuban independence, because of the voracity of its neighbor to the North. He dedicated his brief and worthy life to that objective of Cuban independence. He pointed out the evils that persisted in the Latin American governments of his time. He designated the Latin American region as "Our America," and he called for an arrival to the era of its second independence. He died in combat a few days after having entered Cuba to direct the war that he had organized. He left a magnificent heritage of a vast work, an organic body of ideas concerning political themes, among many others, in which he expresses his love for the human being and for his country; ideas that have guided Cuban revolutionaries until today. His political thought has great validity, not only in Cuba, but in Latin America. After the triumph of the Revolution, he was designated *Héroe Nacional*.

Masferrer Rojas, Rolando. One of the most bloodthirsty thugs in the service of the Batista tyranny. Ringleader of the paramilitary group *Los Tigres*, he participated in the harassment, torture, and murder of numerous revolutionaries. With the triumph of the Revolution, he fled to the United States, and he became active in the counterrevolutionary groups. He died as a consequence of an attack carried out by a rival gang.

Mathews, Herbert L. Journalist of the United States; correspondent of *The New York Times*. He attained an interview with Fidel Castro on the farm of the peasant Epifanio Díaz on February 17, 1957, which was published on February 24. The interview had a great impact, nationally as well as internationally.

Matos Benítez, Huber. Was *comandante* and head of Antonio Guiteras Column 9 of the Mario Muñoz Third Front, and after the triumph of the Revolution of January 1, 1959, was designated as provisional chief of the Rebel Army in Camagüey. Detained in October of 1959 for seditious activities against the Revolution; he was sentenced to twenty years in prison. After serving the sentence, he left Cuba, and he became one of the ringleaders of the counterrevolution.

Mella MacFarland, Julio Antonio. Cuban revolutionary. During the 1920s, he founded the University Student Federation and cofounded the first Communist Party of Cuba, among many other organizations. His short life was characterized by feverish revolutionary activity, which converted him into a leader of international stature. He was one of the first Cuban intellectuals to bring to light the revolutionary thought of José Martí. He was assassinated in Mexico by the hired assassins of Machado at 26 years of age.

Miró Cardona, José. Lawyer, professor of the University of Havana, president of the Bar Association of Havana, and legal advisor of the most important U.S. companies. Criticized the Batista dictatorship and formed part of the civic opposition to the regime. Went into exile in 1958. After the triumph of the Revolution, he was Prime Minister in the initial cabinet of the revolutionary government, until February of 1959, when he as substituted by Fidel Castro. He was named ambassador to Spain. He relocated to Miami, and there he joined the counterrevolution. He was designated president of the "Cuban Revolutionary Council," a group of Cuban exiles that worked with the Central Intelligence Agency (CIA) to organize the Bay of Pigs invasion of 1961. In April of 1963, he resigned from the "Council" in a public letter, taking into account that President Kennedy had established communication with the revolutionary government, which he considered a betrayal.

Moncada Barracks. The second most important military center of the country, located in the city of Santiago de Cuba. On July 26, 1953, it was assaulted by a group of attackers, led by Fidel Castro, with the intention of obtaining arms and to begin the revolutionary armed struggle against Batista from the nearly mountains of the *Sierra Maestra*. The action failed, but from a political point of view, it was a success, because it resulted in the awakening of the consciousness of the people. In the trial for his leadership of the attack, Fidel's self-defense, known as *History Will Absolve Me*, was distributed clandestinely. Moncada Barracks was named for the General of the Liberator Army Guillermón Moncada.

Mora Pérez, Víctor. Was incorporated in the Rebel Army in April of 1957. Became *comandante* and chief of the Camagüey Front. Abandoned the revolutionary struggle.

Mujal Barniol, Eusebio. Born in Cataluña, Spain. In 1936, he began to direct the Worker Commission of the Cuban Revolutionary Party (Authentic), which party he represented in the Constitutional Assembly of 1940. Through the same party, he was a member of the House of Representatives and of the Senate of the Republic of Cuba. He obtained the position of Secretary General of the Confederation of Workers of Cuba (CTC) in 1949, and he was confirmed in that post in 1951. From the beginnings of his mandate, he instituted a obligatory union membership fee, which gained for him and his associates more than a little profit, which was supplemented by robbery and fraud of all types. He made a pact with Batista to conserve his charge in the CTC, which he maintained during the entire time of the dictatorship, and to collaborate in the repression of the worker movement.

Núñez Jiménez, Antonio. Cuban geographer and speleologist. First President of the Academy of Sciences of Cuba, and Founding President of the Speleological Federation of Latin America and the Caribbean. Participated in the founding of diverse national and international scientific societies. He joined the revolutionary struggle and was incorporated into Ciro Redondo Column 8 in 1958, in which he was named Captain of the Rebel Army at the order of *comandante* Ernesto Che Guevara. He wrote numerous books.

Operation Peter Pan. One of the most secret and sinister operations of ideological and political subversion organized by the Department of State of the United States, the hierarchy of the Catholic Church in Miami, the CIA, and the counterrevolutionary organizations, in their struggle against the Cuban Revolution in the 1960s. They stimulated what appeared to be a spontaneous migration, by manipulating the theme of the *Patria Potestad*, or the right of parents to custody of their children, generating the fear that the revolutionary government was going to violate this right by sending the children to the Soviet Union. Based on the promise of providing temporary shelter for the children in the

United States, a total of 14,048 children left from Cuba, many of whom never again saw their parents. The principal executor, in coordination with the government of the United States, was the priest of Irish origin Bryan O. Walsh.

Pedraza Cabrera, José Eleuterio. Cuban military officer. From his position as a military officer, he enriched himself by means of fraud and abuses. Batista returned him to active duty in 1958, in order to try to stop the advance of the Rebel Army in the central province of Las Villas, but he failed in the mission. He fled with Batista on January 1, 1959. He was tied to the principal plans of aggression against the Cuban Revolution. He died outside of Cuba.

Piedra Piedra, Carlos Manuel. Cuban lawyer. On January 1, 1959, he was designated president of the Republic in a spurious manner by the counterrevolutionary movement led by the general Cantillo. Not only did the Supreme Court refuse to administer the oath, but in addition, being rejected by Fidel Castro and the Rebel Army, he renounced the proposal a few hours later. He lived in Cuba until his death.

Platt Amendment. An appendix to a bill for the Budget of the U.S. Army, it was approved by the Congress of the United States and imposed as part of the text of the first Constitution of the Republic of Cuba in 1901, under the threat that if it were not accepted by the Cuban Constitutional Assembly, Cuba would continue being occupied militarily. It existed until 1934.

Prío Socarrás, Carlos. Constitutional president of the Republic of Cuba from 1948 to 1952. His government was characterized by servility to the interests by U.S. imperialism, political and administrative corruption, and gangsterism. He was overthrown by the Batista *coup d'état*. He abandoned the government without offering resistance, taking refuge in the embassy of Mexico, where he enjoyed a comfortable exile. After the triumph of the Revolution, he came back to Cuba, but he later returned to the United States, where he died.

Radio Swan. First radio station employed by the government of the United States against the Cuban Revolution in an organized and regular form. So named for having been installed on a small island of that name in the southern Caribbean.

Ray Rivero, Manuel. During the resurrection against Batista, he was Secretary of Foreign Relations of the Movement of Civic Resistance, and its Secretary General in Havana. After the triumph of the Revolution, he was designated Minister of Public Works. He very quickly deserted the revolutionary process, and in the United States, he was incorporated into the counterrevolution.

Rego Rubido, José María. A Cuban career military officer. He was in command of the Moncada military barracks at the time of the overthrow of the dictatorship of Fulgencio Batista on January 1, 1959. Carrying out what was agreed with Fidel Castro a short time previously, he surrendered the military fortress to *comandante* Raúl Castro, who occupied it with his troops. On January 19, Rego Rubido was designated military attaché at the Cuban embassy in Brazil.

Revolutionary tribunals. In response to the popular demand to try and punish the criminals of the dictatorship, the Revolution proceeded to establish revolutionary tribunals, with procedures based on previous penal laws. In a period of 114 days, from February 1 to May 25, 1959, 346 ordinary courts of war were carried out in La Cabaña. Of three thousand persons detained, 777 were brought to trial following investigations. The accused had all the guarantees of due process: defense lawyer, visits from religious representatives, public viewing, and complete access of the press. Seventy-seven of the accused were sentenced to the death penalty, for the magnitude of their crimes. All appealed to the Superior Court of War, which modified the sentences in twenty-six cases and ratified the remaining fifty-one. A slanderous campaign was undertaken from the United States, designed to present Cuba as a savage nation submerged in an orgy of blood. In response, Cuba developed Operation Truth, which included a popular demonstration in support of the revolutionary tribunals, and on the following day, a meeting of Fidel Castro with nearly 400 foreign journalists.

Roa García, Raúl. Intellectual and professor of the University of Havana. Participated in the revolutionary struggles since the 1920s. With the *coup d'état* by Batista, he departed for exile. With the triumph of the Revolution, he was designated Minister of Foreign Relations, from which position he made a valuable contribution to Cuban diplomacy. He was among the founders of the Communist Party of Cuba, member of the Central Committee of the Party, and Vice-President of the National Assembly.

La Rosa Blanca. Terrorist organization founded in January 1959 by Batista ministers and henchmen who fled Cuba at the triumph of the Revolution. It is considered as the "mother organization" of the counterrevolution and terrorism directed toward Cuba from the United States.

Salas Cañizares, Rafael. Was one of the architects of the March 10 *coup d'état* and "restorer" of the National Police. Countless abuses were committed under his command. Accompanied by a group of his oppressors, he illegally burst into the embassy of Haiti, with the intention of liquidating ten members of the clandestine resistance that had taken refuge there. The only one of them that carried a pistol was able to wound Salas, who died after various days.

Saladrigas Zayas, Carlos. Cuban politician known for his conservative ideas since the struggles against the Machado tyranny. After the *coup d'état*, Batista named him president of the so-called Consultative Council as well as other governmental charges. He was a person of limited national prestige.

Salvador Manso, David "Mario". Labor leader from the ranks of the Orthodox Party. He struggled against Batista in the July 26 Movement and directed its labor section. He was imprisoned in the *Castillo del Principe*, where he received word of the revolutionary triumph. In 1959, he was designated General Secretary of the Confederation of Cuban Workers (CTC), from which charge he was expelled for betraying the working class and the country.

Sánchez Mosquera, Ángel. Lieutenant coronel in the Army of Batista, chief of operations in the Sierra Maestra. As chief of Batallion 11, he was considered one of the most daring of the Army officers, but at the same time, one of the most criminal and crooked. He was wounded in combat and was left paralyzed. Batista took him with him in his flight.

Sardiñas Menéndez, Guillermo. Catholic priest and lawyer. Was chaplain of the Rebel Army, with the rank of *comandante*. After the triumph of the Revolution, he was an officer in the Revolutionary Armed Forces and Chief of Section of the Ministry of the Revolutionary Armed Forces.

Service of Military Intelligence. Founded by Fulgencio Batista, its original objective was to maintain vigilance within the Army, but it gradually reoriented its activities toward civil society. Its principal seat was in *Columbia*. Beginning in 1951, it counted officially on U.S. consultancy. Its members were selected by and enjoyed the confidence of Batista; his personal guard belonged to it. It was one of the most repressive Army institutions of the regime.

Soler Puig, Emilio. Known as "The Death," he was responsible for the assassination of the dockworker labor leader Aracelio Iglesias, in 1948, and of the exiled Dominican leader Pipi Hernández, in 1955. Sentenced, he escaped from prison in *La Cabaña*, taking refuge in the United States. He enlisted to participate in the Bay of Pigs invasion. He was captured, tried, and condemned to death.

Sosa Blanco, Jesús. One of the most notorious war criminals during the dictatorship of Fulgencio Batista, responsible for the assassination of dozens of peasants, the torching of entire hamlets, robberies, tortures, and abuses, perpetuated in the zone of the eastern province of *Oriente*, where he was military chief. He was captured after the triumph of the Revolution and condemned to death for his crimes on February 18, 1959.

Tabernilla Dolz, Francisco. Began his military career in 1918. Participated in the March 10 *coup d'état*, and was designated Chief of Staff of the Army with the rank of Major General. He enriched himself through contraband merchandising, gambling, and other illicit businesses. He was the perpetuator of dozens of crimes, tortures, and peasant evictions. In November of 1957, he was given the leadership of the newly created Joint Staff, which unified the three branches of the Army, Navy, and Police, with the intention of better organizing the popular repression. He fled from Cuba with Batista and died in the United States.

Trejo González, Rafael. Cuban student leader, assassinated by the police of the dictator Gerardo Machado during a popular demonstrations on September 30, 1930.

Trujillo, Rafael Leónidas. Dictator of the Dominican Republic. First governed from 1930 to 1934, and was the *de facto* ruler from 1934 until his assassination in 1961. Known for his exaggerated fondness for decorations and his excessive lechery, his dictatorship was characterized by anticommunism, the repression of all opposition, and the cult of the personality. Trujillo organized a conspiracy to overthrow the revolutionary government of Cuba. Planes with arms for Cuban counterrevolutionaries landed on August 13, 1959, but the revolutionary government had previous information, and it took possession of the planes and the arms. The conspirators included Cuban counterrevolutionaries that had emigrated from Cuba; military elements from the previous regime of Fulgencio Batista, some retired and others active in the Rebel Army; and chiefs of the Second National Front of Escambray.

Urrutia Lleó, Manuel. A lawyer who attained fame when he emitted a dissenting vote of not guilty in Cause 67, which was being pursued against the revolutionaries involved in the uprising of November 30, 1956, and against the expeditionaries of the *Granma*. Because of this gesture, he was proposed by the July 26 Movement to occupy the provisional presidency of the Republic. In a short time, his opposition to the radical direction of the Cuban Revolution caused him to enter into contradictions with the then Prime Minister, Fidel Castro. When Fidel resigned from his charge of Prime Minister, Urrutia, under great popular pressure, resigned from the presidency in July of 1959. In 1963, he was given safe conduct to leave the country. He settled in the United States, where he maintained a counterrevolutionary posture.

Valdés Menéndez, Ramiro. Participant in the attack on Moncada Barracks on July 26, 1953 and in the *Granma* disembarking of December 2, 1958. Promoted to *comandante* in March 1958, and named second-in-command of Column No. 8, which invaded the central provinces under the command of Che Guevara. Since the triumph of the Revolution, he has occupied various charges of great responsibility in the government and the Party. Valdés has been awarded the honors of *Comandante de la Revolución* and *Héroe de la República de Cuba*.

Ventura Novo, Esteban. Lieutenant of the national police at the time of the *coup d'état* of 1952. He was surrounded by unscrupulous elements, and for several years, he used traitors of the revolutionary movement as informers. He was chief of the Fifth Station, the headquarters for innumerable acts of terror, through which he sought to bring to an end the clandestine revolutionary movement. On January 1, he fled to the Dominican Republic with the dictator, and later he went to Miami, where he lived in complete comfort.

Bibliography

Academia de las FAR "Máximo Gómez." 1983. *La Revolución cubana 1953–1980, 2T*. La Habana: Ministerio de Educación Superior.
Almeida, Juan. 2002. *¡Atención¡ ¡Recuento¡* La Habana: Ediciones Verde Olivo.
Almeida, Juan. 2008. *La sierra y más allá*. La Habana: Casa Editorial Verde Olivo.
Álvarez Tabío, Pedro. 2003. *Celia ensayo para una biografía*. La Habana: Oficina de Publicaciones del Consejo de Estado.
Álvarez Tabío, Pedro. 2010. *Diario de la Guerra 1*. La Habana: Oficina de publicaciones del Consejo de Estado.
Álvarez Tabío, P. y Guillermo Alonso Fiel. 1993. *Fidel Castro, La historia me absolverá, Edición Anotada*. La Habana: Oficina de Publicaciones del Consejo de Estado.
Álvarez, Gregorio. 1983. III *Frente: a las puertas de Santiago*. La Habana: Editorial Letras Cubanas.
Álvarez, Martha. 2007. *Epopeya de libertad. Historia del Segundo Frente "Frank País"*. La Habana: Casa Editorial Verde Olivo.
Álvarez, Martha V. y Sergio Ravelo. 2008. *El renacer de la esperanza*. La Habana: Editora política.
Álvarez, Martha V. y Sergio Ravelo. 2009. *La victoria de la esperanza*. La Habana: Editora política.
Álvarez, Rolando. 1999. *Un día de abril de 1958*. La Habana: Editorial Letras Cubanas.
Alzugaray, Carlos: *Crónica de un fracaso imperial*, Editorial de Ciencias Sociales, La Habana, 2000.
Ameijeiras, Efigenio. 1984. *Más allá de nosotros*. Santiago de Cuba: Editorial Oriente.
Ameijeiras, Efigenio. 1986. *Un año tremendo*. La Habana: Editora Abril.
Anillo, René. 2011. *Que nuestra sangre señale el camino*. La Habana: Casa Editora Abril.
Bell, José. 2006. *Fase insurreccional de la revolución cubana*. La Habana: Editorial de Ciencias sociales.
Bell, José, Delia L. López y Tania Caram. 2006. *Documentos de la Revolución Cubana, 1959*. La Habana: Editora de Ciencias Sociales.
Bell, José, Delia L. López y Tania Caram. 2007. *Documentos de la Revolución Cubana, 1960*. La Habana: Editora de Ciencias Sociales.
Bell, José, Delia L. López y Tania Caram. 2008. *Documentos de la Revolución Cubana, 1961*. La Habana: Editora de Ciencias Sociales.
Bell, José, Delia L. López y Tania Caram. 2012. *Cuba: las mujeres en la insurrección, 1952–1961*. La Habana: Editorial Félix Varela.
Bell, José, Delia L. López y Tania Caram. 2013. *Cuba: la generación revolucionaria, 1952–1961*, Segunda edición. La Habana: Editorial Félix Varela.

Berdayes, Hilda, Ed. 2006. *Papeles del Presidente. Documentos y discursos de José Antonio Echeverría Bianchi.* La Habana: Casa Editora Abril.

Buch, Luis y Reynaldo Suárez. 1999. *Gobierno Revolucionario Cubano: Génesis y primeros pasos.* La Habana: Editorial de Ciencias Sociales.

Buch, Luis y Reynaldo Suárez. 2004. *Gobierno Revolucionario Cubano: Primeros pasos.* La Habana: Editorial de Ciencias Sociales.

Cabrera, Olga. 1974. *Guiteras, la época, el hombre.* La Habana: Editorial Arte y Literatura.

Cárdenas, Harold. 2010. "La primavera de los herejes. Política cultural en los primeros años de la revolución (1959–1961)," *Revista Cubana de Filosofía* (Edición digital No. 23, Enero–Junio).

Casa de las Américas. 1961. *La sierra y el Llano.* La Habana: Casa de las Américas.

Castillo, Andrés. 2000. *Cuando esta guerra acabe. De las montañas al llano.* La Habana: Editorial de Ciencias Sociales.

Castro Porta, Carmen, et al. 2010. *La lección del Maestro*, Segunda edición corregida y aumentada. La Habana: Editorial de Ciencias Sociales.

Castro, Fidel. 1967. *La historia me absolverá.* La Habana: Ediciones Políticas, Instituto del Libro.

Castro, Fidel. 1993. *La historia me absolverá*, Edición Anotada. La Habana: Oficina de Publicaciones del Consejo de Estado.

Castro, Fidel. 2007. *Selección de documentos y artículos (1952–1956).* La Habana: Editora Política.

Castro, Fidel. 2010. *La contraofensiva estratégica.* La Habana: Oficina de Publicaciones del Consejo de Estado.

Castro, Fidel. 2010. *La victoria estratégica.* La Habana: Oficina de Publicaciones del Consejo de Estado.

Castro, Raúl. 1961. "VIII aniversario del 26 de julio," *Fundamentos* (Año XXI, No. 175).

Chang, Federico. 1981. *El ejército nacional en la República neocolonial, 1899–1933.* La Habana: Editorial de Ciencias Sociales.

Chomón, Faure. 1969. *El asalto al Palacio Presidencial.* La Habana: Editorial de Ciencias Sociales.

Conde, Antonio del. 2004. *Memorias del Yate Granma.* México: np.

Cruz, Reynaldo y Rafael Borges, Eds. 2006. *Santiago insurreccional.* Santiago de Cuba: Ediciones Santiago.

Cuesta, José M. 1997. *La resistencia cívica en la guerra de liberación de Cuba.* La Habana: Editorial de Ciencias Sociales.

Dávila, Rolando. 2011. *Lucharemos hasta el final.* La Habana: Oficina de Publicaciones del Consejo de Estado.

Díaz, Fernando. 1989. *Camilo por los montes surcados.* Santiago de Cuba: Editorial Oriente.

Espín, Vilma, Asela de los Santos y Martha Álvarez. 2011. *Contra todo obstáculo*. La Habana: Casa Editorial *Verde Olivo*.

Gálvez, William. 1991. *Frank entre el sol y la montaña*, 2 T. La Habana: Ediciones Unión.

García, Manuel. 1981. *Sierra Maestra en la clandestinidad*. Santiago de Cuba: Editorial Oriente.

García Oliveras, Julio. 2003. *Los estudiantes cubanos*. La Habana: Casa Editora Abril.

García Oliveras, Julio. 2006. *Contra Batista*. La Habana: Editorial de Ciencias Sociales.

García Pérez, Gladys (Marel). 2005. *Crónicas guerrilleras de occidente*. La Habana: Editorial de Ciencias Sociales.

García Pérez, Gladys (Marel). 2006. *Insurrección y Revolución*. La Habana: Ediciones Unión.

González Lanuza, Gaspar. 2000. *Clandestinos. Héroes vivos y muertos*. La Habana: Editorial de Ciencias Sociales.

Graña, Manuel. 2008. *Clandestinos en prisión*. La Habana: Editorial de Ciencias Sociales.

Guanche, Julio César. 2004. *La imaginación contra la norma. Ocho enfoques sobre la República de 1900*. La Habana: Ediciones La Memoria, Centro Pablo de la Torriente Brau.

Guanche, Julio César. 2009. *1959: una rebelión contra las oligarquías y contra los dogmas revolucionarios*. La Habana: Ruth Casa Editorial and Centro Juan Marinello.

Guerra, Ramiro, et al. 1952. *Historia de la Nación Cubana,* Tomos VIII y IX. La Habana: Editorial de la Nación Cubana.

Guevara, Ernesto Che. 1970. *Obras 1957–1967,* 2 tomos. La Habana: Casa de las Américas.

Guevara, Ernesto Che. 2000. *Pasajes de la Guerra Revolucionaria, Cuba 1956–1959. Edición Anotada*. La Habana: Editora Política.

Guevara, Ernesto Che. 2005. *El socialismo y el hombre en Cuba*. La Habana: Editora Abril.

Guevara, Ernesto Che. 2011. *Diario de un combatiente. De la Sierra Maestra a Santa Clara, 1956–1958*. La Habana: Editorial de Ciencias Sociales.

Hart, Armando. 1997. *Aldabonazo*, Segunda edición. La Habana: Editorial Letras Cubanas.

Ibarra, Jorge. 1995. *Cuba, 1898–1958: Estructura y procesos sociales*. La Habana: Editorial de Ciencias Sociales.

Ibarra, Jorge. 2000. *El fracaso de los moderados*. La Habana: Editora Política.

Ibarra, Jorge. 2003. *Sociedad de Amigos de la República: Historia de una mediación, 1952–1958*. La Habana: Editorial de Ciencias Sociales.

Infante, Enzo. 2007. "La reunión de Alto de Mompié" en Enrique Oltuski, Héctor Rodríguez Llompart y Eduardo Torres Cuevas, Eds., *Memorias de la Revolución*. La Habana: Ediciones Imagen Contemporánea.

Infante Urivazo, R. 2011. *Frank País, Leyenda sin mitos*. La Habana: Editorial de Ciencias Sociales.
Instituto de Historia. 1983. *El pensamiento de Fidel Castro: Selección temática*, Tomo I, 2 vols. La Habana: Editora Política.
Instituto de Historia de Cuba. 2004. *La neocolonia: Organización y crisis desde 1899 hasta 1940*. La Habana: Editorial Félix Varela.
Le Riverend, Julio. 1971. *La República*. La Habana: Editorial de Ciencias Sociales.
Leyva, Georgina. 2009. *Historia de una gesta libertadora, 1952–1958*. La Habana: Editorial de Ciencias Sociales.
López, Francisca, Oscar Loyola y Arnaldo Silva. 2003. *Cuba y su historia*. La Habana: Editorial Félix Varela.
Martínez, Ricardo. 1978. *7RR: La historia de Radio Rebelde*. La Habana: Editorial de Ciencias Sociales.
Martínez Heredia, Fernando. 1987. "Transición socialista y democracia: El caso cubano." La Habana: *Cuadernos de Nuestra América*, Centro de Estudios sobre América.
Masetti, Jorge R. 1969. *Los que luchan y los que lloran*. Buenos Aires: Editorial Jorge Álvarez.
Mencía, Mario. 1988. *El grito del Moncada*. La Habana: Editora Política.
Menéndez Tomassevich, Tomás y José A. Gárcia. 1996. *Refugio y combate*. Santiago de Cuba: Editorial Oriente.
Miranda, Caridad: *Trazos para el perfil de un combatiente*, Editorial Oriente, Santiago de Cuba, 1983.
Norman, Heberto. 2005. *La palabra empeñada*, 2 Tomos. La Habana: Oficina de Publicaciones del Consejo de Estado.
Norman, Heberto y Pedro Álvarez Tabío. 2010. *Diario de la guerra 2*. La Habana: Oficina de Publicaciones del Consejo de Estado.
Nuiry, Juan. 2000. *Presente. Apuntes para la historia del movimiento estudiantil cubano*. La Habana: Editora Política.
Nuiry, Juan. 2007. *Tradición y combate: Una década en la memoria*. La Habana: Editorial Imagen Contemporánea y Editorial Félix Varela.
Núñez, Antonio. 1959. *Geografía de Cuba*. La Habana: Editorial LEX.
Núñez, Antonio. 2002. *En marcha con Fidel 1959*. La Habana: Editorial de Ciencias Sociales.
Núñez, Antonio. 2003. *En marcha con Fidel 1960*. La Habana: Editorial de Ciencias sociales.
Núñez, Antonio. 2004. *En marcha con Fidel 1961*. La Habana: Editorial de Ciencias sociales.
Oficina de Asuntos Históricos del Consejo de Estado. 2013–2014. *Revolución* (Boletines digitales).
Oltuski, Enrique. 2000. *Gente del Llano*. La Habana: Ediciones Imagen Contemporánea.

Oltuski, Enrique. 2007. "La revolución toma el poder" en *Memorias de la Revolución*. La Habana: Ediciones Imagen Contemporánea.
Ortiz, Fernando. 1969. "La decadencia republicana" en Pichardo, 1969.
Pérez, Ramón. 2012. *De palacio hasta Las Villas*. La Habana: Editorial de Ciencias Sociales.
Pérez, Roberto. 2003. *Desventuras de un ejército*. Santiago de Cuba: Editorial Oriente.
Pérez, Roberto. 2006. *La guerra de liberación nacional*. Santiago de Cuba: Editorial Oriente.
Pichardo, Hortensia. 1963. *Documentos para la Historia de Cuba*, Tomo I. La Habana: Editorial de Ciencias Sociales.
Pichardo, Hortensia. 1969. *Documentos para la Historia de Cuba*, Tomo II. La Habana: Editorial de Ciencias Sociales.
Pichardo, Hortensia. 1973. *Documentos para la Historia de Cuba*, Tomo III. La Habana: Editorial de Ciencias Sociales.
Pichardo, Hortensia. 1980. *Documentos para la Historia de Cuba*, Tomo IV. La Habana: Editorial de Ciencias Sociales.
Pino Santos, Oscar. 1973. *El imperialismo norteamericano en la economía de Cuba*. La Habana: Editorial de Ciencias Sociales.
Portuondo, Yolanda. 1986. *30 de noviembre*. Santiago de Cuba, Editorial Oriente.
Remos, J.J. 1952. "La Guerra hispanoamericana" en Ramiro Guerra, et al., *Historia de la Nación Cubana*. Tomo VI. La Habana: Editorial La Nación Cubana.
Rensoli Medina, Rolando J. 2010. "República de Cuba, ¿continuidad o ruptura?" *Revista Calibán*, No. 6 (www.revistacaliban.cu).
Revista Santiago. 1975. N° 18–19, junio-septiembre, Universidad de Oriente, Santiago de Cuba.
Roa, Raúl. 1977. *Retorno a la Alborada*. La Habana: Editorial de Ciencias Sociales.
Rodríguez, Lino. 2009. *Claves para la victoria*. Santiago de Cuba: Editorial Oriente.
Rodríguez, Nicolás. 2009. *Episodios de la lucha clandestina en La Habana (1955–1958)*. La Habana: Editorial de Ciencias sociales.
Rojas, Marta. 1973. *La generación del centenario en el juicio del Moncada*. La Habana: Editorial de Ciencias Sociales.
Rosado, Luis y Felipa Suárez. 1999. *Una mancha azul hacía el occidente*. La Habana: Ediciones Verde Olivo.
Suárez, Eugenio y Acela A. Caner. 2006. *Fidel: De Cinco Palmas a Santiago*. La Habana: Editorial Verde Olivo.
Suárez, Reynaldo y Oscar Puig. 2010. *La complejidad de la rebeldía*. La Habana: Ediciones La Memoria, Centro Cultural Pablo de la Torriente Brau.
Tabares del Real, José. 1973. *Guiteras*. La Habana: Editorial de Ciencias Sociales.
Torreira, Ramón y José Buajasán. 2000. *Operación Peter Pan: Un caso de guerra psicológica contra Cuba*. La Habana: Editora Política.

Trutié, Teudy. 2011. *Guantánamo y el Segundo Frente Oriental "Frank País" (1952–1958)*. La Habana: Editorial de Ciencias Sociales.

Valdés, Servando. 2008. *La elite militar en Cuba (1952–1958)*. La Habana: Editorial de Ciencias Sociales.

Vecino, Fernando. 2004. *Rebelde testimonio de un combatiente*. La Habana: Editorial de Ciencias Sociales.

Waters, Mary Alice. 2005. *Nuestra historia aún se está escribiendo*. New York: Pathfinder Press.

Zanetti, Oscar. 2003. *Cautivos de la reciprocidad*. La Habana: Editorial de Ciencias Sociales.

Zito, Miriam. 2001. *Asalto*. La Habana: Casa Editora Abril.

Index

abandonment 48
absentee land-holders 254
absolute amplitude 185
absolute clarity 53, 249
absolute majority 30, 48
abstract terms 108
abuses 140, 144–45, 164, 278, 288–90
   great 217
abyss 3, 41
Academy of Sciences 129, 287
Acción Encubierta 124
accusations 60–61, 67, 71, 92, 94–95, 145, 200, 230
   official 67
actions
   armed 7, 27, 281
   commando 281
   counterrevolutionary 280
   decisive 9
   denigrate revolutionary 18
   evasive 235
   following 123
   indiscriminate terrorist 216
   maximum 99
   military 4, 213
   repressive 17
activist 195
   political 195
activities
   conspiratorial 283
   counterrevolutionary 215, 266
   destabilizing 213
   economic 123
   political 282
   seditious 286
acts 32, 38, 46, 51, 53, 73, 75, 79, 81, 84–85, 90, 103, 131, 133–34, 158, 168, 178, 215–16, 223, 226–27, 229–30, 234, 236, 251–52
   despicable 209
   destructive 138
   developed 216
   erroneous 73
   hidden 231
   innumerable 292
   insolent 260
   last 169
   least 69
   numerous 283
   premeditated 73
   public 251
   scandalous 69
   terrorist 215
   unfriendly 178
acts of hostility 84, 178
Adams, John 175
administrations 6, 36, 215, 284
   public 35–37, 50, 111
Admiral Harley Burke 187–88
adventurers thirsty 105
adversaries, powerful 147
Aeroviz 167
affected commercial centers 215
affirmations 155, 191, 237, 252
   last 75
Africa 9, 190, 192–93, 277, 280
age 117, 224, 232, 250, 286
   average 224
   old 171, 206, 274
   young 279
agencies 90, 171, 207, 218, 231, 236, 252, 274
   cable 42
agents 77, 123, 222, 257
   foreign 68
   intelligence security 223
agents-conspirators 223
aggression 44, 70, 86, 92, 95, 124, 137, 139–40, 144–47, 149–50, 155, 158, 161, 183, 189, 199, 209, 213, 215–16, 225–28, 230–31, 239–41, 243–44, 260, 262, 271, 288
   armed 147, 214
   constant 154
   criminal 168, 264
   economic 149–50, 158, 182–83, 259
   imperialist 123, 214–15, 225, 259, 272
   justifying 164
   political 155, 183
   self-inflicted 187
   surprise 230
   worst 218
aggressive circles 260

aggressiveness, increasing 187
aggressors 149, 195
Agramonte, Ignacio 277
agrarian land surface 46, 116, 142, 250
Agrarian Law 45
agrarian reform 35, 39, 47–49, 51, 65, 67, 80, 86, 90–91, 94, 110, 121, 123, 146, 179–80, 182, 203, 220, 256, 269
Agrarian Reform Law 16, 35, 45, 47–48, 50, 179–80
agrarian structure 123
agreement 21–22, 37, 61–62, 95, 103–4, 109, 116, 124, 161, 179, 234, 278
   commercial 43, 125
   direct 143
   international radio 186
   old military 179
   present 179
agriculturalists, small 177, 202
agricultural producers 158
agricultural workers 124
   precarious 111
agriculture 47, 63, 184, 202, 255, 270
Ahrens, Edward 232
aid 8, 132, 140, 150, 165, 178–79, 184, 265, 280
   band 42
   country soliciting 108
   received generous 179
   technical 111
   unsolicited 168
air attacks 95, 241
air base installations 233
air bombers 228, 231
Air Corps 278
aircraft, small 93, 280
air fields 191, 231, 241
air fleet 133
air incursions 139, 183, 227
   international 233
air space 231
Alert 3, 242
Algeria 192, 277
Almeida, Juan 96, 154, 277
Alonso, Eduardo Héctor 51, 54–55, 60, 72, 76, 80, 84–85
Amauta 285
ambassador 145, 176, 284
   named 286

ambition 24, 28, 30, 73, 105, 109, 144
   noble 106
   personal 34, 72
Ameijeiras, Efigenio 277
America 25, 32, 42, 110, 125, 148, 152–56, 161–62, 167–69, 171, 175, 179, 190, 218, 220, 227, 259–60, 274, 278, 281
   brother peoples of 89, 148
   countries of 170, 207, 273
   first trench of 150
   flog 106
   free territory of 167, 172
   our 285
   peoples of 164, 231, 243–44
American Embassy 208, 222–23
Americans 9, 154, 167, 233, 263
American squad 271
American States 66, 85, 123, 144, 161, 213
Angola 277
animal breeding 116, 118, 204
annexationists 4
Anniversary, First 50
Antarctica 193
anthem 192
   national 87, 96, 107, 154, 198, 240
antiaircraft 244
antiaircraft batteries 241
antiaircraft defenses 45
anti-aircraft guns 239
Antonio Guiteras Column 286
Antonio Maceo Column 280
AP 159, 181, 233, 235–36, 238
Apostle 50, 119, 162, 285
Arabic world 193
Arbenz Guzmán, Jacobo 146, 157
archbishops 238
architectural students 282
Argentina 59, 167
armed forces 15, 20, 24, 26, 31, 71, 79, 237, 244, 247, 278–79, 281
   regular 32
armed struggle 4, 166, 284, 287
arms 9, 22, 26, 31–32, 90, 102, 139–40, 142–44, 146, 153, 159–60, 171–72, 178, 199, 206, 215, 222, 224, 226, 238–39, 258–60, 263, 275, 291
   atomic 189
   brotherly 162

INDEX   301

clandestine 30
favorite 61
hiding 31
high-quality 159
nuclear 193
obtaining 226, 287
smuggling 31
storing 31
arms races 191, 193
army 15–16, 19, 23–24, 27, 30, 37, 100, 106, 178, 206, 219, 223, 245, 265, 277–78, 288, 290–91
   mercenary 231
   neocolonial 7
   numerous 219
   political 32
   private 32
   professional 153
   professional mercenary 153
   regular 37
   single 92
   victorious Cuban 283
   well-armed 144
army officers 23, 290
artillery 249, 283
   anti-aircraft 232
   anti-tank 224
artillerymen 251
   young antiaircraft 251
Ascunce, Manuel 216
Asia 9, 190, 277, 280
Asian countries 124
aspirations 5, 17, 55, 90, 93, 143, 180, 192, 194, 206, 258
   common 172
   legitimate economic 190
assassinations 77, 280–81, 290–91
   indiscriminate 216
assassins 264, 281, 284
   hired 286
   principal 19
assault 93–94, 106, 245, 264, 279
   legendary 7
assault brigade 264–65
assemblies, great 139, 194
assembly 95, 97, 103, 168, 173, 189, 194–96
Atomic Energy Commission 169
atomic weapons 188–89

attack 21–23, 56, 66, 70, 82, 92–95, 113, 133, 145, 164, 167, 187–89, 201, 227–31, 233, 236, 238–42, 248, 253, 260, 272, 277, 279, 286–87, 291
   desperate 236
   direct 213
   enemy 241
   imperialist 229
   mercenary 243, 245
   pirate 231
   simultaneous 227–28, 231
   terrorist 226
attitude 23, 61, 71, 73, 78–79, 85, 97, 154–55, 160, 181, 260, 266–67
   appropriate 54
   counterrevolutionary 24, 267
   patriotic 23, 267
Attorney General Mario Hernández 77–78
Authentic Party 17
authorities 24, 26, 29, 56, 174, 178, 183, 255, 285
   appropriate 154–55
   civil 26
   hierarchical 34
   high 55
   highest 183
   legal 81
   legislative 176

B-26 bombers 232–235, 241
Baghdad Pact 9
Bandung Conference 9, 277
banks 118, 159, 178, 253, 265, 268–69
   foreign 107
   high 278
Baracoa 233, 235
Baraguá Industrial Corporation of New York 156
Bar Association 281, 286
barracks 31–32, 82, 126–27
barrels 198
   floating 63–64
Bartolomé Masó 280
base 25, 43, 49, 111, 125, 187–90, 215, 217, 222, 233–34, 238
   air 231
   atomic 189

base (cont.)
  foreign   252
  important   188
  military   43, 193
  naval   176, 187, 228
  naval air   232
Batista, Fulgencio   4, 6–7, 11, 16, 19, 21–24, 66, 69, 85, 87, 105–7, 158, 179, 181, 192, 198, 255–56, 277, 279–81, 290–91
  dictator   28, 36, 44, 63, 79, 280, 284, 288, 290
  enabled   278
  flight of   15–16, 280
Batista Armed Forces   16
Batista coup   5, 102, 288
Batista tyranny   179, 181, 256, 283, 286
battalions   159, 240, 249, 251
  militia   10, 199, 249
  respective   240
Battleship Maine   8
Bay of Pigs   214, 277–78, 283, 285
Belize   59, 105
Berliss, Leo Francis   245
betrayal   17, 126, 232, 235, 281, 286
  great   110
  presidential   17
Black Panther Party   9
Black Power Movement   9
Blacks   143, 160, 169–72, 175, 206–7, 274–75
  discriminated   192
  lynched   168
Blacks and Indians   170–71, 206–7, 274
Blacks of Harlem   174
Blanca, Rosa   79, 101, 289
blockade   215, 270
  economic   259
blood   19, 22–23, 132, 138, 144, 159, 178, 230, 239, 251–52, 255, 263, 265, 289
  cold   252
  courageous   231
  human   132
  sea of   41, 278
  shed   271
blood of Cuban workers   138
Bloody Christmas   281
Bogotá   184
Bohemia   108–9, 133, 241–43, 278
Bolívar   167

Bolivia   167, 284
bombings   68, 93, 133, 226, 233, 235, 252
bombs   28, 62, 94–95, 132–33, 192, 198, 221–22, 224, 227–28, 231, 238
  atom   198
  atomic   43, 169
  dropped   198
  hundred pound   133
  launched incendiary   215
  little   198–99
  nuclear   136
  single hydrogen   43
  small   198
bourgeois constitution   261
bourgeois democracy   5
bourgeoisie   5
  local   15
  local dominant   5
bourgeois law   7
bourgeois republic   4
  neocolonial   3, 7
boycott   155
  tourist   108
Bravo, Nicolás   51, 53, 61, 77, 79, 83–84
Brazil   289
bread   107, 114, 141, 263
Burma   9
businesses   90, 110, 194
  illicit   290
  lucrative   4, 222

Cabaña   15, 30–31, 87, 278, 289–90
Cadillacs   265
calculation   188
  conservative   47
Calviño, Ramón   260, 264–65, 278
Camagüey   30–31, 59, 280–81, 286
Camagüey Front   287
Camilio Cienfuegos School City   247, 280
campaigns   19, 23, 39–40, 42, 59, 68, 71, 77, 79, 89–90, 93, 108, 199, 208, 219
  comprehensive   215
  conduct counterrevolutionary   267
  defamation   175
  disinformation   59, 213
  great   61
  ideological   216
  illiteracy   241

INDEX 303

international 170
last military 8
making counterrevolutionary 267
malicious 70
permanent international discrediting 60
slanderous 289
subversive 183
systematic 227
campaigns accusing 68
Campo Libertad 233–36
camps 277, 280
    counterrevolutionary 125
Canada 59, 93
Canadian Pacific Steamship 108
Cantillo, Eulogio. 15–16, 20–22, 278
capacity 1, 16, 35–36, 81, 100, 221, 284
    defensive 125
    demonstrated organizational 279
capital 5–6, 15–16, 20–21, 27, 31, 39, 90–91, 157–58, 171, 185, 207, 224, 248, 253–54, 274, 280–81
    dead 39
    financial 3, 5
    guarantees to foreign 273
    imperialist 155
    inactive 118
    invested 190
    investment 118, 204, 273
    monopoly 5
    national 39
    new 20
    passive 39
    provisional 20
capital accumulation 5
capital demand 116
capitalism 5, 9, 261–62
    dependent 6
    underdeveloped 7
Carratalá, Conrado 41, 278
Carreras, Julio 4
casino games 67
caste 28, 229
Castilla, Belarmino "Aníbal" 279
Castro, Raul 83, 147, 153, 279, 289
Catholic Church 69, 87, 287
Catholics 264–66
cattle ranchers, large 98
caudillo 71–72

classic 71
Central America 11, 231
Central Committee 11, 282, 285, 289
Central Cunagua 156
Central Intelligence Agency 216, 226, 286
Céspedes Barracks 7
change 5, 7–9, 21, 37–38, 60, 108, 188, 191, 269
    initiating revolutionary 17
    minimal 2
    peaceful 191
    profound 258
    radical 108
    social 3
    socio-political 5
    structural 279
chaos 49, 105, 182
chaplains 264, 290
character
    affluent 117
    fundamental social 56
    general 266
    international 135
    radical anti-neocolonial 16
    socialist 10, 213–14, 216, 226
    unilateral 186
Chaviano del Río, Alberto 23, 41, 279
Che Guevara, Ernesto 8, 284, 287
chemical substances, highly-effective 222
Chibacista masses 112
Chibás, Eduardo R. 6, 112
Chile 51, 167
China 124, 164, 169, 194–95
churches 68–69, 267–68
Ciénaga 248
Cienfuegos, Camilo 15, 30–31, 66, 247, 280
Cienfuegos, Camilio, School City 247, 280
Cienfuegos, Osmany 280
Cinematographic Industries 10
Ciro Redondo Column 284, 287
cities 4, 6, 8–9, 20–21, 27, 93, 108, 116, 119, 125, 127, 132, 158, 174, 177, 199, 203, 205, 222, 227–28, 241, 255, 263, 270, 280, 287
    children's 111
    first 111
    principal 15

citizens 34, 36, 40, 64, 74, 88, 90–91, 95, 108, 110, 125, 132, 135, 139, 141–43, 160, 170, 175, 221, 254, 259, 267
Civic Front 76
civic kind 54
Civic Plaza 70, 139, 167, 217, 273
Civic Resistance 288
class 102, 236, 247, 258, 261
  dominant 218, 250–51, 256, 258
  dominant economic 255
  exploiting 250, 257–58, 261
  lower 172
  oppressing 258
  powerless 102
  professional 202
  reactionary 220
class composition 216
  mixed social 15
class interests 258
classrooms 115, 205, 214, 257
  primary school 124
class struggle, profound 1
claws 98, 150
  brutal 156
Clipper Line 108
clubs
  aristocratic 254, 257, 265
  aristocratic social 253
CMQ News 51
coexistence, peaceful 263
coincidence 65–66, 146, 184
Cold War 9, 170
collective revolutionary watch 197, 199
Colombia 167
Colón cemetery 226
colonialism 191
colonialists 194, 200
colonies 3, 5, 175–76, 191–93
colonization 4
  new 176
Columbia City 15–16, 19, 22–23, 27, 30–31, 105, 205, 280, 290
Columbia coup 23
Columbia military garrison 16, 22, 24, 27, 205, 277, 286
Columbus 119
columns 21, 140, 145, 277, 284, 291
  armored 21

combat 21, 26, 44, 95–96, 125, 163, 165–66, 197, 199, 219, 240, 242–43, 258, 277, 284–85, 290
combatants 28, 37, 111, 139, 166, 214, 247, 277–78, 280, 284
  male 166
  rebel 37
combative spirit 163
combat planes 95, 213
commerce 178, 194, 268–69
  clandestine 110
  free 206
  small 269–70
Commercial Pension Fund 66
communism 61, 66, 68, 85, 94, 190, 235, 262, 265
communist ideology 265
communist infiltration 86
Communist Party 5, 11, 67, 169, 195, 277, 279, 282–83, 285, 289
  first 125, 283, 286
communists 17, 67–70, 76–77, 94, 101, 179–81
Compañía Azucarera Atlántica 156
Compañía Azucarera Céspedes 156
Compañía Azucarera Soledad 157
Compañía Azucarera Vertientes Camagüey 156
Compañía Central Altagracia 156
Compañía Cubana 156
companies 108, 117, 140, 152, 154–56, 158, 180, 255–56, 286
  electric 157, 177, 180
  foreign 10, 48
  landowning 47
  large 10
  large national 269
  monopolistic 190, 255
  nationalized 208
  operating 156
  petroleum 155
  single militia 140
  telephone 157, 177, 179–80, 202
  tourist 108
compatriots 27, 29, 50, 70, 88, 95, 109, 174
concessions 170, 176, 179, 181, 207, 274
  commercial 176
  obtained profitable 179

onerous   10
untransferable   111
Confederation of Workers of Cuba   281, 287
Confederation of Workers of Peru   285
conflicts   16, 43, 218–19, 261
   atomic   187
   first   179
   international   187
   internationalist   279
   personal   83
   provokes   56
   second   179
   social   9
Congo   191–92
Conrado Benítez Brigades   213, 216
consciousness   102, 106, 230, 279, 287
   moral   221
conspiracies   25, 71, 90, 283, 291
   conscious   70
   hatching   25
   indecent   98
conspirators   291
Constitution   1, 3, 5, 47, 56, 62, 105–6, 115, 117, 176, 255–57, 261, 281
   advanced   281
   democratic   281
   first   288
   frustrated   281
   new   5, 261
Constitutional Assembly   5, 176, 279, 287
Consultative Council   289
contradictions   11, 16, 54, 262, 291
control   17, 19, 153, 155–56, 158, 221, 228, 253, 256, 272, 277
   direct   3, 5
   monopolistic   153
   remote   83
   seized   277
conviction   38, 225, 240
   absolute   46
   democratic   34
cooperation   226
   civic   265
cooperatives   49–50, 124, 165, 198, 243
   agricultural   204
   large consumer   49
corruption   4, 6, 17, 143–44, 159, 201, 223
   administrative   279, 288

political   6, 285
prior   221
Costa Rica   43, 167, 183, 195–96, 260, 283
Council of Ministers   34, 37–38, 53, 56, 59–62, 66, 71, 73–74, 80–82, 84–86, 95, 147, 157, 224
counterrevolution   25, 86, 102, 126, 146, 208, 216, 219–21, 223, 266–67, 270, 286, 288–89
   making   266
counterrevolutionaries   62, 126, 182, 221–24, 242
coup   6, 15–17, 19, 21–22, 28, 70, 89, 105–6, 152, 158, 277–81, 283, 289–91
   criminal   98
   inopportune   106
   reactionary   98
   rigged   23
   treacherous   20
coup leaders   15
Cowley, Fermín   40, 281
crimes   19, 23, 29, 40, 61–62, 80, 89, 97, 108, 127, 140, 144, 163–64, 169, 178, 197, 219, 228–29, 232, 238, 267, 271–72, 278–79, 289–90
criminal imperialist aggression   241
criminals   22–23, 40–41, 77, 87, 89–90, 93, 132, 178, 222, 229–30, 252, 256, 260, 289–90
criminal sanctions   85
criminal submission   153
crisis   9, 53, 60, 62, 66, 80, 84, 114, 187, 279
   constitutional   81
   grave   66
   institutional   81
   national   86
   permanent   6
   present   58
Crusades   265
Cuban air force   213, 232–34, 237
Cuban air force officials   236
Cuban airplanes   235–36, 252
Cuban American Sugar Mill   156
Cuban Catholics   264
Cuban Confederation of Workers   10
Cuban Constitution   5
Cuban Constitutional Assembly   107, 288
Cuban Democratic Revolutionary Front   236

Cuban exile groups   235–6, 286
Cuban Federation of Women   248
Cuban Independence   283, 285
Cuban Liberator Army   8, 277, 283
Cuban Olympic Committee   283
Cuban People's National General
    Assembly   170–72, 207, 274–75
Cuban Revolutionary Party   5–6, 282, 285, 287
Cuban revolutionary vanguard   284
Cuban Telephone Company   155
Cuban territory   11, 214
Cuban Trading Company   156
Cunard Tourist American   108

dangers   20, 30, 32, 43–44, 71, 73–74, 86, 136, 146, 169, 173, 187, 189, 193–94, 200, 262, 285
  grave   74
  greatest   44
  multiple   123
  red   181
day laborers   114
death penalty   40, 62, 216, 224, 289
debts   36, 62, 114, 251
  present   251
  public   107
deceit   258
  systematic   171, 207, 274
Declaration of Havana   125, 167, 169, 171–72, 195–96, 206, 209, 273
defeat   8–9, 74, 137, 146, 149, 215, 245, 263, 278
  electoral   278
  first great   213
defecting Cuban airplanes   235
defense   7, 10, 56, 83, 123, 125, 139, 144, 154, 157–58, 179, 183, 216, 219, 229, 242–43, 250
  civil   43
  legitimate   155
  popular   10
  sacred   244
demagoguery   30, 97
democracy   7, 19, 88–89, 91, 108, 132, 139, 141–43, 145, 147, 158, 169–70, 190, 259, 264–65
  direct   143, 261
  honest   143
  imperialist   265

indisputable   143
  lost   8
  pedantic   259
  political   115
  popular   261
  rare   141
  real   143
  strange   141
demonstrations   4, 42, 53–54, 84, 88, 113
  generous   88
  largest   154, 158
  popular   289, 291
denial   194–95, 250
  systematic   169
Department of State   146, 174, 287
dependency   3, 5, 11, 123, 134, 181
destiny   25, 27, 29–30, 41, 44, 52, 55, 72, 79, 106–7, 110, 140, 145, 158, 170–71, 189, 200, 207, 219, 225, 250, 263, 275, 279, 283
destruction   161, 181, 193, 220, 222, 225, 227, 253
detractors   89, 94, 144
development   1, 9, 21, 48, 81, 137, 155, 180, 184–85, 190–91, 193, 200, 208, 215, 241, 268, 270, 281
  agrarian   59
  agricultural   180
  democratic   170, 207, 274
  economic   178–79, 184
  industrial   47, 118
  integral   155
  social   184
Díaz Lanz, Pedro   67–68, 70, 77, 79, 85, 233–34, 281
  traitor   69
dictatorship   7–8, 15–17, 19, 25, 27–28, 30–31, 35, 37, 43, 49, 62, 89, 111, 113, 127, 280–82, 284–85, 287, 289, 291
  bloody   89
  inhumane   8
  oppressive   7
  second   4
Dien Bien Phu   9
diplomatic relations   124, 145, 169, 185, 260
  establishing   169
diplomatic steps, first   226
discipline   24, 53–54, 84

INDEX

exemplary 82
strict 242
discrimination 166, 169–70, 207, 254, 274
sex 111
District of Columbia 280
documents 1–2, 16, 107, 113, 124, 154, 167, 179, 201, 206, 245
fundamental 206
important 17, 216
new 206
original 1, 168
worn 179
domination 168, 176, 220
bourgeois neocolonial 10
economic 177
foreign 4
oligarchical 4
Dominican Republic 113, 278, 291–92
Dominicans 25
Dorticós, Osvaldo 157, 281
dreams 16, 40, 43–44, 91, 119, 138, 147, 201, 254–55
idealistic 40
limited income 254
sugar worker 254
duty 3, 24–26, 29, 34, 52–55, 59–60, 65–66, 69, 71, 73, 75, 80, 88, 95, 102, 104, 119, 138, 144, 147–48, 155, 162, 172–73, 188, 193, 195, 201, 206–7, 250, 263, 267, 275
active 288
first 27, 29, 31, 33, 54
granted preferential customs 3
painful 135, 137
sacred 71
dysfunctionality 16

Eastern socialist countries 124
Echeverría, José Antonio 282
economic interests 149, 224
foreign 177
economic opportunism 137
economic strangulation 93
economic structure 6
weak 134
economy 36, 48, 91, 107, 123–24, 134, 149, 155, 158, 161, 164, 171–72, 177, 181–82, 201–2, 207–8, 228, 268, 270, 274
independent 220

national 155, 157, 268
strong 134
weak 134
Ecuador 167
education 10, 115, 119, 123, 126–27, 153, 171, 202–6, 208, 211, 214, 218, 246, 274, 279, 285
free 267
integral 111
scientific 171, 206, 274
secondary 129, 254
system of 10, 116
year of 213, 215
efforts
enormous 58
extraordinary 218
little 154
long 106
supreme 111
Egypt 9
Eisenhower, Dwight D. 186, 193
elections 81, 144, 257–59, 278
fair 106
false 257
fraudulent 144
partial 7, 107
presidential 6
sham 36
Electricity Company 202
El Morrillo 284
El Morro 254
Emergency Tribunals 111
empire 153, 161, 197, 200
exploiting 162
financial 168
powerful 200, 220
enemies 30, 32, 38, 53, 61, 71–73, 77, 89–90, 99, 101, 103, 110, 113–14, 138, 142, 144–45, 147, 150, 178, 182, 194–95, 197, 218, 221, 226, 240–43, 245, 272
conscious 130
external 17
foreign 32
imperialist 208
possible 271
powerful 220
principal 244
reactionary 101

enemies (cont.)
  rooted 218
  small 220
  worst 90
enemy action 148
energy 40, 69, 118, 149, 204, 209, 251, 272
  extraordinary 140
  human 259
English imperialism 200
enterprises 130, 157, 264
  agricultural 118, 204
  industrial 256
  mining 124
enthusiasm 41, 49, 92, 163, 166, 224, 270
  extraordinary 92
  finite 250
  infinite 247
errors 22, 24, 29, 53, 63, 66, 71, 106, 130, 148, 150, 195
  grave 119
  great 99
  political 29
Escalante, Anibal 11
Escalona, Derminio 282
Escambray 29, 216, 291
Espín, Vilma 282
Estrada, Tomás 4, 282
Europe 116, 180, 192, 235, 254
evangelical 264
eviction 115, 174, 203
evil 89, 126, 131, 225, 230, 285
exclamations 147, 153–54, 157, 159, 197–98, 221–24, 229, 239
  prolonged 144
executions 40, 61–62, 170, 215, 222, 280
Executive Committee 79
existence 16, 69, 111, 114, 169, 193, 218, 261
  miserable 110
  modern 64
exploitation 5, 44, 107, 137, 140, 153, 159, 161, 167, 170–71, 176, 191, 197, 207, 217, 229, 254, 258, 261, 274
  agricultural 115
  capitalist 125
  dreadful 170, 207, 273
  formal 5
  historic forms of 5
  real 5
explosion 8, 132, 136, 146, 198, 231
  nuclear 136

explosives 93, 136, 224
  high-powered 222

fabrication 133, 197
factories 19, 102, 116, 158, 160, 172, 198, 202, 243, 249–51
  operating 133
  sugarcane 109
faculties 34, 66
  constitutional 74
failure 41, 226, 282
faith 24, 34, 56–57, 72, 85–86, 90, 104, 148, 150, 172, 248, 265–66
  absolute 52
  awakening of 57, 91
  good 73, 114
Falangist priests 264
false democracy 143, 258
  substituting 261
families 4, 10, 47, 50, 109, 111, 116–17, 119, 138, 142, 145, 164–65, 179, 184, 203, 205–7, 224, 253–54, 261, 269, 280
  hundreds of 110, 253, 265
  poor 142
  wealthy 266
  well-to-do 253
family dwelling units, multiple 110, 116, 203
family income 177
farce 42, 258
  electoral 36
farmers, small 10, 115, 118, 203–4
fear 31–32, 34, 44, 48, 92–96, 98, 109–10, 114, 135–36, 149–50, 209, 221, 262, 271, 287
  dictators 25
Federation of Cuban Women 10, 125, 163–64, 166, 282
Federation of Cuban Workers 105, 149, 163
Fernández, José Ramón 283
FEU 125, 282
Figueres, José 42, 283
firmness 243
  ideological 239
First Congress 152
First Cuban Communist Party 281
First Declaration of Havana 167, 273
Flagler theatre 109
Florida Industrial Corporation of New York 156
food industries 116
  canned 116

INDEX

fools   176, 184, 259
forces   17, 29, 31, 48, 71–72, 74, 80–81, 85, 89,
    105–6, 110, 115, 123, 139–42, 153, 163–64,
    166, 171, 176–77, 187–91, 202, 207–8, 216,
    218–20, 224, 241–42, 245, 248, 261, 265,
    270, 274, 283
  air   232, 238, 252
  foreign reactionary   220
  great imperialist   220
  interventionist   191
foreign currencies   57, 263
foreign hands   115, 142, 149–50, 203
foreign interests   94, 140, 153, 156, 201
foreign monopolies   170, 202, 207, 274
  great   220
foreign policy   124
  independent   10
Foreign Relations   237, 288–89
Formosa   169
fortresses   20, 142, 202
  best   20
  converting   129
  largest Spanish   278
  principal   15
Foster Dulles, John   160
foundations   3, 175, 189, 217, 268
  legal   3
France   138, 192
Francisco Sugar Company   156
Frank País Second Eastern Front   279, 282
Franqui, Carlos   64, 96, 283
fraud   89, 126, 143, 237, 282, 287–88
freedom   16, 19, 30, 91, 107–8, 112, 115, 135, 162,
    164, 175, 190, 202, 233, 236
Freedom School City   205
free market   253–55, 262, 272–73
Free Officers Movement   9
French army   192
French colonialism   9
French workers   138
functions   3, 19, 26, 31, 36, 79, 124, 208, 237,
    264
  banking   268
  international swindle   235
  spiritual   264

Gaceta Oficial   60–61, 154
Galo, Álvaro   232, 234–35
gambling   110, 219, 290
gambling casinos   254, 264

gangs   97, 140, 178
  armed   213
  counterrevolutionary   215
  rival   286
  worst   127
gangsters   4, 79, 168, 288
Garand rifles   159
García, Calixto   8, 283
García, Pilar   284
General Advisory Council   169
General Assembly   167–69, 173, 175, 177, 179,
    181, 183, 185–87, 189, 191, 193–96, 213, 273
General Secretary   282
  designated   290
  first   280
General Shafter   8, 283
General Sugar States   156
generations   7, 40, 46, 73, 91, 108, 114, 119, 128,
    147, 205, 267
  first   277
  mockery   7, 114
  spontaneous   118, 204, 273
Ghana   193
Giron Beach   214
glory   24, 85, 271
Goliath   220
Gómez, Delio "Marcos"   284
government   4–5, 7, 15–17, 20, 34, 36, 50–51,
    55–60, 66, 75, 77, 79–80, 88–89, 110–11,
    126, 128, 134, 141–44, 146, 154–55, 161,
    168–71, 175–87, 189–90, 194–95, 197,
    207–8, 220, 226–29, 231–33, 235, 237–38,
    241–42, 259–63, 266, 268–69, 277,
    279–80, 283–84, 288
  bad   110
  colonial   192
  colonialist   228
  corrupt   178
  democratic   146
  destructive   228
  dictatorial   7
  difficult   58
  direct   258
  exploiting   228
  godless   267
  imperialist   187, 189, 228, 230, 238, 243,
    245
  lackey   231, 260
  legal   23
  municipal   165

government (cont.)
  neutral 110
  past 48
  post-insurrectionary 16
  provisional 214, 236
  reactionary incumbent 213
  red 181
  short-lived 5
  tyrannical 179
  worse 173
Grace Line 108
Grajales, Mariana 26, 163, 284
Granma 27, 29, 56, 65, 99, 105, 280, 284, 291
Granma expeditionary force 277, 279–80
great revolutions 218–19
  first 138
Grau, Enrique 51, 73
Guanabacoa 59
Guanacahabibes 59
Guantanamo 187–88
Guantánamo Sugar Company 157
Guatemala 145–46, 157, 160, 180, 238, 260, 285
  invade 145
Guevara, Ernesto Che 8, 15, 284, 287, 291
Guiteras, Antonio 107, 284
gusanos 223, 236

Hair Salon Workers 149
Haiti 167, 289
happiness 25, 27, 115, 147, 163, 165, 202, 248, 251, 270–71
  extraordinary 126
  unrestrained 126
harassment 181, 227, 286
  incessant 182
  systematic 227
Harlem 174–75, 197
hate 25, 38, 46, 75, 105, 120, 199, 219, 264
Havana 1, 8, 15–16, 19, 21–22, 27, 30, 32, 58, 64, 70, 87, 92, 108–9, 118, 125, 132, 159, 167, 169, 171–72, 195–96, 206, 209, 216, 228, 233, 241, 253, 273, 278, 280, 282, 284, 286, 288–89
Havana Bay 278
Havana Union Radio 245
headquarters 93, 174, 240, 280–81, 292

heart 46, 54, 60, 70, 99, 103, 106, 114, 138, 187, 197
heart disease 44
hemisphere 169
  peaceful 182
henchmen 106, 162, 208, 219, 278, 280, 283, 289
Hernández Valdés, Amado 236
Hidalgo 167
Hiroshima 169
historic truth 190
history 1, 7, 18, 27, 42, 56, 65, 104, 113, 115, 119–20, 125, 127, 131, 150–51, 153, 163, 166–67, 193, 206, 217, 219–20, 225, 228, 230, 247, 251, 272, 287
  incomplete 9
  making 84
  modern 138
history will absolve me 113, 201, 206
Hitler, Adolf 261
Holguín 281
Holland 180, 190
Holland American 108
Hollywood 235
Honduras 186
honesty 38, 55, 73, 118, 181, 204, 262, 282
  complete 84
  strict administrative 47
horrors 110, 127, 170
  worst 127
hospitality 195, 197
hospitals 6, 117, 170, 184, 202, 207, 254, 257, 265, 273
House of Representatives 287
houses 10, 23, 31, 43, 46, 50, 62–65, 78, 93, 102, 111, 116, 118–19, 142, 184, 198, 205, 222–25, 240, 250, 253, 256, 264–65, 269
  expensive 118, 273
  little 63–65
  making 184
  small 63–64
housing 6, 10, 39, 111, 114–16, 118, 184, 202–3, 205, 208
  construction of 39, 119, 205
  decent 111, 119, 205–7
housing rents 10, 177, 179
  reduced 223

humanity   138, 164, 191, 193–94, 200, 225, 244
   destiny of   194, 225
   history of   218, 251
humble classes   145, 258
hunger   44, 111, 115, 134, 141, 170, 180, 257
huts   46, 65, 110–11, 116, 177, 202–3, 254
   miserable   114, 145, 250

Ichaso, Francisco.   109, 284
idealism   28
ideals   29, 48, 71, 105, 110, 147, 221
   high   123
ideas   42, 54, 70, 114, 153, 201, 218, 285–86
   conservative   289
   dissemination of   218, 256
   false   30
   free   70
ideologies   265
   superior   265
   ultraconservative   4
   varied   4
imperialism   9, 123–24, 156, 169, 191, 198–200, 208, 213, 216, 220–22, 230, 232, 237–38, 251–52, 255–56, 259–63, 288
   arrogant   200
   barbarous   200
   modern   219
   oppressive   171, 207, 274
   resist   206
imperialists   4, 16, 171, 198–99, 207, 214, 226–27, 229–31, 233, 235–37, 239, 259, 261, 274
impunity   69, 109, 112, 182, 222
   total   208
incomes   6, 47, 111, 116, 179, 203, 263, 269
   crude   177
independence   4, 9, 15, 48, 50, 116, 134, 163, 167, 175–77, 192
   economic   134, 155, 192
   political   192
   real   11
   second   285
   wars of   4, 284–85
Independent Front   209
India   9
Indian peoples   171
Indians   119, 170–72, 206–7, 274–75

indigenous communities   4
Indonesia   9, 277
industrialization   111, 115–16, 184, 203, 208
industries   39, 47, 59, 116, 215, 250, 253, 255, 284
   basic   268
   chemical   116
   important   178
   largest   249
   metallurgical   116
   national   39
   new   39
   oil   116
   principal   6
   seventy   253, 265
   small   269
   textile   116
inequality   170, 207, 274
   social   170
infant mortality rate   177
Iñiguez, Alberto   51
injustices   7, 39, 43, 114, 132, 137, 144–45, 153, 169, 217, 225, 254, 272
   inconceivable   218
insignias   213, 252
insinuations   97, 135
insolent plan   262
institutions   2, 36, 54, 118, 123–24, 204
   all-powerful   146
   civic   59, 85, 202
   established   165
   first   165
   non-public   36
   political   281
   religious   69
   repressive Army   290
   scientific   129
instructions   75, 119, 174
   received   241
instruments   90, 159, 161, 171, 177, 185, 199, 207, 274, 281
   modern   222
insubordination   74
insufficiencies   279
insurrection   8, 15–16, 74, 223
   armed   8
insurrectional plans   109

insurrectional struggle 279
Integrated Revolutionary Organizations 11, 214
intellectuals 4, 125, 162, 170–72, 195, 206–7, 242, 244, 274–75
   first Cuban 286
   persecuted 168
intelligence 74, 81, 129–30, 139, 181, 249–50, 271
   political 79
intention 1, 8, 10, 18–19, 22, 28, 35, 37, 62, 83, 92–93, 114, 144, 158, 168, 190, 279, 283, 287, 289, 291
   imperialist 215
   noble 28
   presumed 90
interest rate 47, 49
interests 30, 35–38, 45–48, 52, 55, 57, 75, 79, 81, 84, 94, 108–9, 112, 130–32, 141, 143–45, 149–50, 153, 155, 157, 159–60, 168, 170–71, 173, 179–81, 183, 186, 192, 195, 200, 207, 219–20, 222–24, 258–59, 262–63, 268–70, 274, 282, 285, 288
   despicable 155
   egoistic 204, 272
   enemy 89
   established 109–10, 206
   financial 190
   fundamental 154
   great 29, 218
   illegitimate 194
   legitimate 75
   material 197
   monopoly 44, 134, 190
   national 154
   personal 78, 131
   popular 10
   powerful 115, 133, 181
   predominant 156
   privileged 170, 207, 273
   sacred 196
   selfish 117, 132
   social 269
   special 55
   strong 53, 81
interference 168, 183, 260
   foreign 80
   political 156
intermediaries 47, 270

international cables 68
international law 186, 189, 241
   regional 182
international problems 178
   complex 42
international scientific societies 287
international women's associations 282
International Workers' Day 139
interventions 15, 59, 69, 86, 167, 237
   irrefutable 168
invaders 147, 215, 245, 253, 272
invasion 146, 155, 215, 236–37, 241, 271, 284–85
   backed 10
   foreign 236
   mercenary 213, 215
investments 39, 181, 185, 191, 193, 268
   appropriate 184
   foreign 193
   industrial 39
   public 185
Iran 190
Iraq 9, 190
iron 243
   twisted 136
iron hand 241
island 8, 119, 129, 174, 187, 189, 205, 248, 278
   small 288

jail 109, 117
Japan 228
Japanese airplanes 228
José Martí First Front 277, 284
José Martí Organization 247
jubilation 27, 91, 166
   extraordinary 88
   infinite 91
judgment 70
   common 169
judicial branch 8, 255
Judicial Power 3, 78, 111
July Movement 111–13, 214
jurisdiction 31, 61
   civil 61–62
justice 22, 25, 40, 61, 71, 80, 109, 112, 130, 135, 144–45, 153, 162, 164, 229, 264, 267–68
   ancestral aspirations of 7, 114
   social 123

Keesel, Pedro Alomá 109
Kennedy, John F. 189, 237–8, 260–61, 265, 271
Key West 232, 234
Khrushchev, Nikita S. 188, 239
King, Jorge 264–5
knowledge 1, 98, 118, 129–31, 205, 227
Ku Klux Klan 169

labor 4–5, 51, 171, 206, 228, 232, 249, 274, 281, 290
lack of protection 170, 207, 273
lack of teachers 170, 207, 273
La Coubre 132, 226
land 31, 35, 39, 46–49, 72, 95, 107, 110–12, 114–16, 118, 124, 136, 142, 146, 149, 171, 174, 177, 180–81, 202–4, 206, 215, 220, 222, 231, 236, 241, 243, 250, 253–54, 256–57, 263–64, 271, 274
  agricultural 176
  appropriated unused 146
  beautiful 119
  best 155, 178, 256
  caballerías of 146, 203, 253, 256, 265
  country regains 49
  cultivated 47
  foreign 95
  idle 47
  inch of 114, 119
  maximum extension of 115, 118, 204
  meter of 115, 203
  native 112
  noble 148
  productive 115–16, 203
  promised 114
  rented 47
  sheathed 172
  swamp 118, 204
  usurped 118, 204
landings 62, 135
  armed 187
landing strip 215
landowners 5, 10, 88, 98, 107, 112, 115
  large 132
large estate owners 170, 201, 253, 256, 269
large estates 47, 59, 111, 115, 134, 170, 180, 207, 250, 253, 256, 265, 273, 281
large-scale voluntary work 214

Las Villas 8, 30, 242, 244, 248, 280, 284, 288
Las Yaguas 253
Latin America 7, 25, 43, 48, 61, 88, 119, 123, 139, 146, 150, 152–55, 157, 159–62, 168–69, 171–72, 182, 184, 190, 195, 207, 213, 235, 239, 244, 247, 258, 260, 274–75, 280, 286–87
  liberated 172
  peoples of 150, 155, 161, 167, 169, 184, 213, 262
law 16, 24, 36, 39–40, 45–49, 60–62, 66, 72, 74, 80, 83, 90, 94–95, 106, 115, 117, 119, 134, 154–57, 174, 176, 179, 182–83, 189, 201, 203, 220, 224, 256–57, 264, 266, 269
  complementary 256
  constitutional 256–57
  continental 161
  dictating 105
  diplomatic 255
  expansive 35
  first 25
  inadmissible 181
  inevitable 179
  infallible 217
  mining 181
  necessary 179
  new 176
  penal 65, 68, 80, 289
  regulatory 281
  repressive 171, 207, 274
  second 249
  single 256
  third 179
  universal 182
Law of July 157
lawyers 4, 112, 115, 117, 256–57, 281, 286, 290–91
leaders 38, 54, 69, 79, 91, 98, 101, 109, 112, 123, 144, 148, 192–93, 200, 206, 216, 226, 254, 256, 277, 283, 285–86
  assassinating 91
  governmental 98
  local 4
  maximum 51
  new 123
  postcolonial 277
  principal 99
  public 54

leaders (cont.)
    spontaneous   76
    supposed   17
    union   54
    working-class   251
leadership   17, 101, 103, 112–13, 123, 125, 201, 272, 287, 290
    national   81
    political   215
League of American Writers   195
Lebanon   9
leftist   170, 235
Leónidas, Rafael   291
lesson   219, 233, 235, 272
    great   140
letter   21, 60, 64–65, 67–69, 131, 283
    public   286
    single   141
    supposed   68
liberal representative democracy   3
Liberals   4
liberation   8, 13, 150, 172, 193, 200, 235–36, 275, 284
    definitive   7
    economic   194
    final   156
    year of   15, 17
    year of the   51
Liberator Army   4, 8, 284–85, 287
liberators   9, 118, 204, 273
liberty   74, 79–80, 84, 108, 113, 137–38, 144, 153, 172, 236, 263–64
Liberty School City   27, 87, 105
life   7, 25, 28–29, 36–37, 45, 52–53, 73, 79, 99, 106–7, 112, 114, 124, 129, 132, 135, 148, 177, 195, 221–22, 239, 259, 262, 285
    decent   111, 115, 257
    economic   45, 111
    given artificial   192
    good   257
    independent political   220
    national   141
    short   286
    social   108, 123, 278
    urban   119
light aircraft   215
Lions Club   59
literacy campaign   216

nation-wide   213
Llaguno, Lincoln   83
Llanusa, José   285
local Cuban sources, reliable   232
long-term high interest   39
Los Quemados   280
    social   219
Lumumba, Patrice   192

Macareño Industrial Corporation of New York   156
Maceo, Antonio   23, 280, 284
Machado, Gerardo   4, 7, 279, 284–86, 289
machetes   90, 148
machine guns   31, 228, 232–33
Mambi Army   8, 285
management   118–19, 204
    professional   118, 204
    reformist   281
Manatí Sugar Company   156
maneuver   15, 73, 75, 78, 81, 146, 164
Manhattan   174
Manhattan Project   169
manifestos   56, 107–8, 111, 201, 272
manipulations, multiple   18
mansions   28, 118, 204, 273
Manso, Salvador   290
Manzanilla   105
Marianao   280
Mariátegui, José Carlos   2, 285
marines   135, 167, 186, 188, 199
Mario Muñoz Third Front   277, 286
markets   4, 39, 119, 181, 185, 228
    absolute liberty for the   273
    domestic   39, 47
    new   94, 182
Martí, José   6, 24, 40, 50, 119, 167–8, 201, 227, 285
Martín, San   167
Martínez Sanchez, Augusto   83
martyrs   19, 169, 240
Marx, Karl   5
Marxism-Leninism   214
Marxist battle   109
Masferrer, Rolando   41, 101, 286
mass assembly   192, 273, 283
mass demonstrations   4, 6, 17, 133

INDEX 315

masses   32, 102, 114, 123, 145, 199, 229, 245, 265
   gigantic   270
   great   6, 199, 218–19, 221, 229
   unredeemed   7
mass funeral   213
mass gatherings   33
mass literacy campaign   213
mass media   18, 197
mass meeting   59, 91–92, 167, 196
   great   92
   multitudinous   109
mass mobilizations   4
mass murder   117
mass organizations   247
masters   7, 106, 113, 200, 265
   despotic   172
   foreign   134, 155
Matanzas   30–31, 284
   northern   59
Mathews, Herbert L.   67
Matos, Huber   17, 105, 280–81, 286
Máximo Gómez   23
May Day   139
measures
   aggressive   155
   anti-capitalist   123
   avoiding extreme   222
   contemplated military   124
   exceptional   173
   extreme   66
   first   38, 63
   improvising   49
   legal   111
   necessary   75, 155
   progressive   281
   radical   216
   third   179
   unit of   46, 116, 142, 157, 250
measures of reprisal   134
mechanics   77
   operating   232
mechanism
   constitutional   76
media   90, 153, 218
   international   153
medicines   44, 110, 117, 184
   saving   184
medium, happy   41, 104

meeting   23, 56, 59, 80, 83, 86, 91, 98, 140, 152, 154, 161, 163, 172, 183–84, 202, 253, 258, 289
   constant   258
   official   81
   public   163
Mella, Julio   106–7, 286
members   4, 11, 15, 26, 34, 37, 48, 61, 101, 129, 139, 163, 169, 188, 199, 224, 247, 251, 253, 265, 271, 277–80, 282–85, 287, 289–90
   family   265
   good   131
   last party   56
   militia   199, 249
   passive   157
mercenaries   44, 133, 140, 232, 235, 237–40, 242–45, 248, 252–53, 260, 271, 283
   invading   273
   pesos arming   263
mercenary forces   213, 245
   invading   245
merchant marine   94
merchants   4, 114
   small   114, 268–69
Mexico   160, 167, 195, 235, 280, 284, 286, 288
Miami   81, 92, 232–35, 278, 286–87, 292
Miami International Airport   232
Middle East   190
military   21, 61, 170, 207, 230, 274
   detest   140
military academy   87
military aggressions   150, 183, 215–16, 259
military fortresses   171, 206, 275, 289
military garrisons   19–20, 277
Military Intelligence   131, 290
military operations   15, 227–28
military prison   87
military techniques   125
   mastered modern   214
   modern   215
military uprising   42
militias   136, 139–40, 148, 158–59, 199, 215, 224, 240, 242, 251, 259
   peasant women   158
   popular   125
millionaire generals   107
millionaires   117, 229, 250, 256
minerals   181, 232

mines   176, 243, 250, 265, 268
　five   253, 265
　principal   181
　tin   172
Minister of Defense   83
Minister of Education   279, 285
Minister of Foreign Relations   237
Minister of National Defense   83
ministers   28, 32, 34, 37–38, 53, 55–57, 59–63, 66, 68, 71, 73–74, 78, 80–86, 95, 97, 118, 147, 157, 204, 224, 271, 273, 279
　designated   288–89
　foreign   51, 161, 215
miracles   107, 114, 117, 119, 183, 204, 272
Miramar   118, 273
Miranda Sugar Estates   156
Miró, José   235–36, 286
Moa Bay   181
Mobutu Sese Seko   192
Moncada   7, 29, 56, 99, 113, 201, 277, 279, 287, 291
Moncada Program   201, 203, 205, 207, 209
money   25, 36, 39, 47, 63, 77, 95, 105, 107, 117, 132, 159, 197
　shame against   6
monoculture   134
　agricultural   134
monopolies   10, 42, 132, 134, 153, 156, 159, 171, 177, 179, 181, 184, 190–91, 193, 197, 207, 250, 255–56, 262, 274
　exploiting   155
　imperialist   171, 190, 206, 274
　powerful   197
monopolists   160, 181, 201
Monroe Doctrine   168, 190
Moorish Guard   266
morality   5, 29, 250, 265, 271
moral principles   55
　inflexible   55
Mora, Víctor   287
mortar   249
　heavy   224
Moses   114
mothers   42, 100, 112, 163–64, 249, 284
　working   165
mountains   190, 248, 287
　highest   45

movement   4, 17, 21–22, 27, 29–30, 32, 71, 77, 81, 87, 99, 101–2, 107, 111, 125, 235, 272, 278–82, 284, 290–91
　counterrevolutionary   23, 288
　first   29
　mass   4
　political   5, 264
　popular   4–5, 279
　progressive military   9
　revolutionary military   23
　safe   21
　student   280
　subversive   186
　worker's   125, 214, 287
Movement of Cienfuegos   281
Movement of Civic Resistance   288
Mujal, Eusebio   17, 19, 99, 101, 125, 254
mujalism   103, 254
multiple family dwellings   114, 118, 205
　filthy   111
multiple story buildings, modern   118, 205
murderers   112, 127, 136, 145, 219, 254, 260
murders   40, 89, 117, 133, 254, 264, 278–79, 286
Mussolini, Benito   261

Nagasaki   169
Nasser, Gamal Abdel   193
nation   7–8, 11, 31, 37, 45–47, 49, 52, 58, 73, 76, 88, 92–93, 95, 107, 110–14, 116–18, 124–25, 155, 159, 161, 164, 171, 177, 191, 204, 206, 219–21, 224–25, 229, 239–40, 243–44, 249–50, 252, 272, 275
　exploited   172, 275
　fervent   249
　fighting   249
　independent   9
　revolutionary   95
　sacred   243
　savage   289
National Air Federation   167
National Assembly   285, 289
National Bank   57, 118
National Capitol   51
National Federation of Barbershop and Hair Salon Workers   149
National General Assembly   167–69, 171, 206–7, 273

INDEX

nationalization   111, 152, 154, 156, 158, 171,
    192–193, 198, 203, 206, 249, 269, 274
national liberation movements   124
National Liberation Party   283
National Security Council   124
national territory   156, 187, 189, 228, 231, 238,
    242, 266
    occupied   245
Nazism   228
negotiations   185–86
    diplomatic   185
    diplomatic channels   185
neocolonialism   3
Nepotism   66
news agencies   214, 252
    large international   42
    transnational   213
newspapers   51, 62, 64, 69, 96, 101, 145, 153,
    159–60, 197, 231–32, 235, 252, 256
    daily   235
    oligarchy-owned   213
    reactionary   235
New Tuinicú Sugar Company   156
Niagara sugarcane factory   93
Nicaragua   167, 260
Niquero   59
Nkrumah, Kwame   193
nobility   46, 116
Non-Aligned Movement   277
normalization   61
norms   4, 32, 241, 256, 263
    international   252
    moral   252
    promoted socialist   214
North America   155–56, 185–86, 197
North American   74, 93, 108, 116, 132–34, 152,
    155, 160, 167–69, 171–72, 176–82, 187–88,
    190, 195, 207, 228–30, 244–45, 249, 274,
    283
nucleus   165
    dangerous counter-revolutionary   216
Núñez, Antonio   131, 287

OAS   66, 85, 123, 161, 164, 166, 183, 189, 213–14
oath   34–35, 96, 288
Obra Revolucionaria   247
occupation   125, 176, 280, 283
officers   23–24, 178, 214, 237, 280, 290
officials   25, 35–36, 80, 92

immigration   232
important   56
venal   118, 204
O'Higgins, Bernardo   167
Old Testament   117, 204, 272
oligarchies   10, 171, 207, 274
    exploiting   143
    financial   169
    political   170, 207, 274
Olympic Games   285
Operation Peter Pan   216, 287
operations   21, 68, 156, 215–16, 226–28, 290
    largest covert   11
    naval   187
    offensive   135
    particular   28
    psychological   216
    sinister   287
    surgical   42
Operation Truth   289
Oppenheimer, Robert   169
opposition   109–10, 172, 191, 236, 278, 282,
    291
    civic   286
    counterrevolutionary   124
    first   191
    natural   45
    second   191
oppresses   106, 143, 258
oppression   7, 18, 89, 106–7, 113, 140, 236
    political   115
oppressors   98, 106, 289
    principal   284
optimism   27, 149, 163
order   19, 23, 30, 35–38, 40, 52–53, 57, 60, 64,
    70–71, 83, 86, 93–94, 100, 102–3, 112, 115,
    119, 126, 129, 133, 136, 140, 142, 146–47,
    158–59, 164–66, 168, 171, 176, 199, 202,
    222, 231, 233–36, 240, 242–43, 257,
    262–65, 280
    constitution   118, 204
    economic   263
    legal   155
    maintaining   109
    social   217
Ordinary Tribunals   62
organisms   74, 208
    new governmental   10
    powerful   227

organization   5, 9–11, 17, 30, 32, 101, 103, 111,
    146, 153, 161, 186, 199, 213, 215, 272, 280,
    286
  anti-imperialist   284
  counterrevolutionary   215, 287
  first political   247
  formidable   140
  international   168, 183
  mass   10, 125, 163, 248
  mother   289
  national   281
  official   158
  political   125
  single unified labor   5
  technical   49
  terrorist   289
  women's   282
Organization of American States   66, 85, 123,
    144, 161, 213
Organization of Pioneers of Cuba   10
organs   51, 74, 90, 215, 282
  governmental   109
  official   167
  repressive   271
Oriente   30–31, 105, 115, 203, 248, 279, 281,
    284, 290
orphanage   76
Orthodox Party   6, 112, 290
owners   5, 90, 109, 116, 118, 146, 149, 158,
    203–5, 253, 256, 263–64, 267–69
  estate   160
  large sugar estate   112
  plantation   4, 46
  real estate   115

P-51 planes   43
Pacific   228–29
Palm Garden of New York   108
Panama Canal   167
Pan-American Games in Guatemala   285
parasites   28, 107, 110, 115, 117, 177, 219, 236,
    249
  large   219
  satellite   219
  small   219
parasitic plagues   270
Parque Céspedes   20
participation   49, 154–55, 214–15, 244

  active   163
  combative   213
  decisive   8
patriotism   48, 57, 118, 135, 151, 204, 272
patriots   105, 167, 236
  fellow   20
patron saint   265
  glorious   266
payments   37–38, 178, 180, 251, 268
  charged   25
  charging   24–25
  collecting   268
  completed   269
  prompt   180
  tenant's   269
peace   27, 29–31, 43, 80, 108, 138, 164, 169,
    173–75, 191, 225, 238, 262, 265, 268
Pearl Harbor   228–30
peasant families   46, 88, 115, 118–119, 139–40,
    146, 153, 165, 177, 203–5, 254, 290
  indigenous   285
peasants   24, 35, 39, 47, 49, 57, 72, 86, 88,
    90–92, 95, 101, 107, 110–12, 116, 119, 124,
    129–30, 139, 141–43, 145–46, 148, 162–63,
    170–72, 202, 206–7, 214, 221–22, 229, 239,
    242–44, 248, 252–57, 260, 264, 270,
    273–75, 290
  defenseless   178
  landless   152
  murder   255
  unfortunate   23
  young   248
peasant women   165
  young   243
Pedraza, José   288
penalties   62, 224
  established new   61
pensions   62, 114, 269
Pentagon   162, 222
peoples   1, 20, 42, 58, 90, 92, 99, 104–7, 109,
    111, 113, 115, 117, 119, 127, 132, 149–53, 156,
    159, 167–73, 179, 186, 190–92, 194, 196,
    206–7, 214, 219–20, 227–28, 230, 232,
    238, 243–44, 260–62, 274–75
  attacked   172, 275
  brother   148, 150, 167, 275
  exploited   152, 162
  foreign   218

INDEX   319

fraternal   150, 156, 260
generous   271
liberated   162
sister   146, 218
underdeveloped   156, 195
people's farms   124
peoples of Asia   280
peoples of Asia and Africa   9
people's stores   124
peoples struggle   263
persecution   29, 108, 169, 241
personnel   216, 237
   diplomatic   216
   human   165
Peru   285
pesos   22, 25, 36, 39, 49, 63, 65, 76–77, 86, 91, 107, 268–69
   millions of   22, 108, 265, 278
petroleum   94, 124–25, 178, 190, 198, 232
Philippines   9, 176, 190
Piedra, Carlos Manuel   22, 288
pilots   95, 232–34, 238, 252
   air force   233
   attacking North American   245
   bomber   233
   brave   236
   companion   234
   deserting   252
Pinar del Río   29–31, 93, 234, 236, 282
pirate airplanes   182–83, 227
plague   115, 140, 223
   small   270
planes   44, 93, 95–96, 135, 190, 228, 232, 235, 237–39, 242, 252, 291
   attacking   241
   small   133
Platt Amendment   3–5, 155, 187, 288
   economic   134
Playa Colorada   58
Playa Girón   214–16, 236, 241, 243, 245, 247, 249, 251, 253, 255, 257, 259, 261, 263, 265, 267, 269, 271, 273, 275
plunder   140–43, 171, 184, 197, 207, 274
poison   32, 168, 266–67
police   23, 136, 282, 291
   national   289, 291
   repressive political   153

policy   24, 103–4, 106, 111, 124, 134, 169, 171, 207, 216, 250, 260–61, 268, 274, 278
   aggressive   261
   submissive   170, 207, 274
   unrestrained   108
   warlike   187
political maneuvering   89, 105, 110, 140, 201
political parties   4, 8, 24, 111, 258, 264
politicians   109–10, 118, 184, 189, 220, 254–57, 259
   corrupt   184, 255
   elections of   257–58
   professional   170
   false   144
Pope Pius   170
popular consciousness   8
popularity   55, 57
Popular Socialist Party   11, 125, 214, 283
population   10, 116, 119, 123, 129, 163, 177, 203, 213, 215, 229, 242, 269
   civilian   245
   rural   124
   rural child   177
   total   177
   urban   116, 203
poverty   6, 89, 117, 119, 137, 145, 170, 207, 274
   generalized   6
   sharing   114
power   4, 10, 19, 24, 28, 34, 43, 57, 72, 74, 77–78, 80–82, 85, 89, 105–6, 109, 117, 123, 125, 144, 155–56, 159–60, 177–78, 182, 200, 218, 251, 257–59
   concentration of   76
   destructive   228
   exceptional   154–55
   inalienable   167
   invincible   172
   legal   76
   legislative   8
   oligarchical   284
   persuasive   84
   political   218
   real   277
   recover   258
   taking   144, 251
prejudice   26, 90, 94, 142, 181, 186

president   20, 22, 24, 31–32, 34, 37, 53–56, 59–63, 65–69, 71–76, 79–84, 86, 96, 134, 147, 154–55, 157, 173–75, 182, 191, 193, 238, 244, 252, 279, 281–83, 286, 289
   designated   286, 288
   elected   277, 282, 285
   first   277, 282, 287
Presidential Palace   34, 42, 67, 76, 80–81, 83, 86–87, 90, 92, 197
pressure   67, 84
   great popular   291
prestige   54, 56, 58, 69, 72, 99, 104
   limited national   289
   moral   104
pretexts   32, 147, 174, 187, 260
   hackneyed   94
   possible   94
price   10, 77, 141, 147, 157–58, 179, 255, 270
   charging monopoly   155
   high   251, 270
   low   110
   subsidized   124
pride   31, 48, 52, 96, 225, 248
priests   264, 266–67, 288
   fascist   266
   foreign   266
Prime Minister   27, 34, 42, 51, 58, 64–66, 68–74, 76, 78, 88–89, 92, 96–99, 104–5, 119, 132–33, 147, 149, 152, 157–58, 173, 226, 242, 244, 286, 291
   charge of   16–17, 58, 63, 72, 291
   office of   34, 55, 88
   position of   16–17, 84
   post of   55, 84, 88
principles   34, 47, 55, 86, 106, 110, 114, 196, 206, 209, 267, 269
   basic   167
   fundamental   55–56, 257
   human   229
   unmovable   222
   unquestionable   35
Prío, Carlos   17, 78, 105–6, 288
prison   25, 109, 145, 278, 283, 286, 290
prisoners   30, 170, 273
   mercenary   253
   political   283
   torturing   178
privileges   28, 53, 90, 107, 110, 130, 140, 142–44, 151, 159, 161, 201, 217, 219, 224, 258, 270

   foreign   94
   national   153
   perpetuate   155
problems   24, 35–36, 39, 46, 57–62, 64, 66–70, 74, 76–86, 88, 92, 103, 105, 109, 115, 117–19, 130, 135, 149–50, 160–61, 165, 173–76, 178–80, 184–87, 189–95, 201–5, 209, 219, 257, 272–73
   difficult   75, 85
   discuss   185
   economic   47, 93
   enormous   58
   food   59
   moral   78
   new   175
   political   57, 176
   unique   78
process   3, 5, 7, 11, 57, 66, 84, 123, 125, 185, 214, 247, 270, 279, 289
   complex   1
   constant   258
   convulsive   217
   democratic   144
   electoral   144
   extraordinary   41
   important   281
   institutional   124
   insurrectional   1, 15
   long   27, 270
   momentous   99
   political   3
   tranquil   217
procommunist position   69
production   5, 47, 49–50, 124, 182, 242–43, 254, 269, 272
   agricultural   170, 182, 207, 273
   ingenious   183
   interrupting   241
products   111, 114, 119, 144, 164, 182, 218, 270
   expensive agricultural   270
   general consumer   124
   industrial   39
professionals   139, 257
   young   115
profit calculations, cold   117, 204
profits   5, 36, 38, 116, 197, 272
   little   287
promises   7, 50, 57, 105, 107, 109–11, 113–15, 117, 119, 138, 203, 205, 287

INDEX 321

false 115, 202
promotion 1, 84, 278–79
proofs 40, 58, 74, 133, 158, 232, 235, 244, 252–53
   best 26, 268
   forward 252
propaganda 124, 197, 237
   demagogic 106
   dropped 227
   false 197
   subversive 216
property 25, 49, 65, 111–12, 124, 154–56, 158, 177–78, 181, 184, 203, 250, 269
   maximum 256
   small 268
property holders 4, 39, 46–47, 111, 177, 268
   small 268–69
protection 39, 118, 155, 170, 179, 205, 207, 264–65, 273
   divine 265
   given 222
protectorate 3
protests 7, 9, 92, 139, 153, 170, 247, 261
   public 4
Provisional Revolutionary Government of Cuba 277
pseudo-democracy 143, 258, 261
Puerto Rico 167, 176, 208, 250
Punta Alegre Sugar Sales Company 156

Quebrada del Yuro 284
question
   bad 82
   basic 53
   central 101
   economic 262
   first 51, 88, 180
   fundamental 101
   identical 85
   important 92
   metaphysical 58
   particular 263
quotas 158, 161

radicalization 16
   progressive 16
radio 22, 59, 83, 86, 153, 232, 235, 239, 256, 279
Radio Rebelde 19, 45, 283

Radio Reloj 282
Radio Swan 288
rage 67, 102
raids 237
   pirate air 231
ranks 4, 23–24, 32, 56, 98, 101, 249, 290
   close 112, 148
raw materials 4, 116, 228
Ray, Manuel
rays 91, 231288
reaction 54, 86, 100, 103, 148, 220, 228
   conquering 251
   extreme 104
   first 64
   international 42
   logical 109
   maximum 99
   national 42
   unfavorable 108
reactionaries 102, 105–6, 260, 264
   defeated 220
   international 220
reactionary clergy 255
reactionary clerics 238
reactionary interests, great 219
reactionary oligarchies 42
reactionary press 42, 219
realization 112, 123, 185
reasons, cold 85
Rebel Air Force 245
Rebel Army 8, 15–16, 19–20, 27, 30–31, 35, 37, 70, 74, 93, 111, 123, 139, 148, 215, 226, 241–42, 244–45, 277–78, 280, 282–84, 287–88, 290–91
Rebel Army in April 287
Rebel Army in Camagüey 286
rebel columns 20
rebellion 4, 9, 29, 106, 144, 153
   popular 282
rebelliousness 200
rebellious spirit 2
rebels 9, 20–22, 24, 37, 123
Rebel Youth 8, 247
refineries 202, 208, 227, 231, 255
reforestation 118, 204
reform 62, 119, 124
   educational 124
   integral 10, 119, 203, 205
   preliminary 111

reform (cont.)
  profound Agrarian   10
  radical agrarian   180
  year of agrarian   123, 125
regime   7–8, 132, 159, 195, 257, 285–86, 290–91
  capitalist   261
  humane   132
  inhumane   132
  political   263
  puppet   169
  socialist   261
region   7, 92–93, 105, 199, 213
  isolated   49
  remote   76
Rego, José María   22–23
relations   5, 35, 51, 55, 169, 186, 199
  breaking   260
  commercial   181
  international   59
  labor-capital   5
  reestablished   124
  social   123
  traditional   186
René, Eduardo   279
rent payments   268–69
rents   72, 111, 116, 118, 174, 177, 203–4, 223, 268–69
  exorbitant   110
  high level of   116, 203
  paying   47, 115, 203
  reducing   118, 205
representation   63, 74, 159, 168, 192, 282
  diplomatic   223
  official   172
representatives   25, 98, 107, 111, 152, 160, 164, 173–74, 180–81, 188, 194–95, 202, 214, 287
  diplomatic   248
  religious   289
repression   287, 291
  popular   291
reprisals   134–35
  economic   137
  feared   233
Republic   1, 3–4, 9, 20, 23–26, 30–32, 37, 40, 48, 53–56, 59–63, 65–69, 71–73, 75–77, 79, 81–84, 90, 96, 103, 106, 108, 112, 117, 126, 134, 147, 154, 157, 176, 179, 204–5, 242, 244, 248, 272, 278–79, 282–83, 285, 287–88, 291
  centralized   3
  democratic   5
  independent   176
  modern   3
  neighboring   180
  neocolonial   5–6, 125, 284
  oligarchical   5
  unfortunate   110
resign   52–53, 55, 72–75, 80–81, 83
resignation   51, 53, 58, 72–74, 77, 79, 81, 83, 283
resistance   26, 98, 110, 241, 288
  armed   56
  clandestine   125, 278–80, 282, 284, 289
  plan of   198
  prolonged   225
resources   5, 47, 49, 77, 91, 117–18, 130, 137, 149, 164, 171, 184, 204–7, 209, 221, 254–55, 259, 268, 274
  limited   165
  little   4
  national   224
  natural   170, 176, 185, 190, 192–93, 207, 228–29, 274
  technical   227
response   21, 81, 83, 85, 119, 144, 149, 169, 174, 186, 188, 195–96, 289
  dignified   164
  eloquent   164
responsibility   27, 32, 34, 50, 69, 79, 103, 123, 159, 180, 193, 215, 272, 282
Revolución Cubana Revista Verde Olivo   8
revolutionaries   4, 19, 23, 27–29, 31, 33–34, 37, 55, 65, 72, 101, 103, 109, 112, 114, 125, 139, 152, 166, 195, 199, 205, 223, 236, 256, 272, 277, 279–81, 287, 291
Revolutionary Air Forces   244, 281
Revolutionary Armed Forces   56, 68, 139, 234, 241, 245–46, 277, 279, 283, 290
Revolutionary Armed Forces and Chief   290
Revolutionary Council   236
  fictitious Cuban   215
Revolutionary General Strike   19
Revolutionary Government   10, 15–16, 46–47, 68, 71, 87, 89, 92, 94, 97, 99, 118–19, 126, 133–35, 139, 143, 146, 148, 155, 157, 159–60, 163, 178–79, 181, 183–87, 189, 196–97, 201, 204–5, 208, 223, 226, 238, 244, 246, 266–69, 271, 273, 286–87, 291

revolutionary history   35
revolutionary ideas   273
revolutionary impulse   19
revolutionary institutionality   123
revolutionary justice   61, 90
revolutionary laws   25, 40, 56, 58, 79, 89, 94, 99, 115, 154, 199, 282, 284
    enacting   57
    first   65
revolutionary leaders   20, 79, 88, 101
revolutionary leadership   1, 15
    reconquer   102
revolutionary measures   38, 45, 57, 94–95, 149
    single   56
revolutionary militias   10, 139
revolutionary mission   10
revolutionary movement   19–20, 23, 107, 109, 111, 152, 280, 292
    clandestine   283, 292
Revolutionary National Militias   226, 241–42, 244–45
Revolutionary National Police and combatant   277
revolutionary organizations   11, 22, 29, 31, 112
revolutionary origin   73
revolutionary principles   54
revolutionary process   1, 3, 16–17, 52, 58, 69, 99, 104, 123, 125, 143–44, 155, 217, 219, 288
    magnificent   93
revolutionary proclamation   21
revolutionary program   201
Revolutionary Provisional Government   40
revolutionary slogans   239
revolutionary spirit   239
    extraordinary   163
revolutionary stage   58, 99, 166
revolutionary strategy   8
revolutionary struggle   15, 76, 113, 137, 202, 280, 287
    regional   284
revolutionary tasks   125
revolutionary thought   70, 286
revolutionary tribunals   95, 222–224, 289
revolutionary triumph   17, 280–81, 290
revolutionary war   35–36, 50, 58, 105, 144, 277, 280
revolutionary watch committee   199
riches   150

national   155
natural   161
rifles   26, 82, 100, 106, 136, 143, 148, 259
rights   26, 30, 56, 134, 141–43, 156–57, 171, 206–7, 229, 238, 250, 261, 275, 281
    civil   9
    human   7
    legitimate   186
    political   36
risks   35, 56–58, 97, 125, 187, 222, 272
    moral   99
    real   97
    running   97
Rivero, Ray   288
road   2, 20, 24, 34, 41, 54–55, 85, 93, 115, 120, 129, 131, 137, 150, 193, 200, 251
    anguished   202
    dirt   142, 145, 250, 253
    disastrous   150
    political   109
Roa García, Raul   73, 86, 237, 289
robbery   31, 65, 79, 117, 140, 197, 201, 287, 290
    unjustified   31
Robeson, Paul   170
rockets   168, 188, 228, 231
role   1, 7, 23, 56, 82, 85, 130, 150–51, 163, 208
    central   123
    decisive   18
    difficult   123
    important   9, 273, 278–79
    political   102
roots   48, 60, 101, 103, 158, 175, 251
    cultural   175
Rosenberg, Ethel   170
Rosenberg, Julius   170
Rubido, Rego   288–89
ruin   28, 115, 182, 188, 255
    economic   58
Russia   188

sabotage   132–33, 213, 215, 222, 224, 226, 231, 242
    acts of   226, 242, 280
    economic   216
    international   227
saboteurs   224, 242
sacrifice positions   103
sacrifices   24, 29, 31–32, 34, 37, 43, 52, 63, 65, 80, 88, 91, 103, 107, 132, 141, 144, 147, 159, 239, 258

sacrifices (cont.)
  greatest   50
  sincere   34
  spirit of   28–29, 37, 63, 239
Saladrigas, Carlos   118, 204, 273, 289
salaries   36–39, 62–63, 65–66, 76, 117
  fabulous   208
  high   39, 208
  reduced   65, 107
  reducing   63
  regular   38
Salvador, David "Mario"   103–4, 290
Sánchez Mosquera, Ángel   290
sanctions   62, 117, 271
Sandino, César Augusto   172
Santa Clara   31, 199, 284
Santiago   7–9, 16, 20–23, 27, 227–28, 233–34, 236, 241, 272, 279, 282–83, 287
Santo Domingo   22, 25, 44, 167
Sardiñas, Guillermo   290
Saudi Arabia   190
School of Cadets and Artillery of Cuba   283
schools   6, 50, 55, 72, 86, 110, 118, 124, 126–27, 129–30, 141–42, 165, 170–71, 184, 198, 202, 206–7, 221, 243, 248, 254, 257, 266–67, 273, 275
  agricultural   116
  industrial   116
  old   71
  private   266–67
  religious   266–67
  secular   267
  small   129
scientists   129, 170–71, 206, 274
  removed   169
Second National Front of Escambray   291
Second World War   9, 233
Secretary General   174, 287–88
sectors   6, 36, 46–47, 85, 107, 142, 145, 178, 202, 255, 266, 268
  conservative   7, 113
  determined social   269
  dominant economic   256
  exploited   145
  popular   9
  producing   124
  reactionary   177
  social   46
  socioeconomic   7

suffering   145
women's   163–64
security   47, 90, 169, 174, 189, 215, 236, 242, 261–63
  social   10
security agent   222
security protection   84
seeding cassava   145
seeds   106, 129
seeing   56, 90–91, 94, 126, 130, 224
Sekou Touré, Ahmed   193
self-defense   113, 201, 206, 259, 272
selfishness   44, 48, 130, 194
Senate   68, 79, 85, 145, 188, 256, 287
  foreign   69
Senate Armed Forces Committee   188
Senator Platt   176
sentiments   9, 23, 45, 70, 86, 90–91, 95, 159, 171, 183, 207, 225, 260, 274
  religious   68
Sergeant Major   277
services   17, 24, 39, 110, 125, 131, 139, 153, 162, 191, 208, 221, 249, 286, 290
  customs   92
  ecclesiastic   264, 266
  educational   6
  electric   177
  lending   72, 81
  obligatory military   250
  public   107, 111, 149, 176–77, 220
  telephone   10, 179
servility   288
  absolute   282
Seventh Fleet   195
sewage water   254
Shafter, William   283
shame   99, 149, 153, 189, 197
sharecroppers   47, 111, 114, 203
shelter   43, 45, 65, 111
  received   238
  temporary   287
  underground   95
ships   29, 68, 108, 132–33, 136, 146, 169, 226–28, 230, 245, 264
  burning   136
  pirate   146, 227
Sierra Maestra   20, 29–30, 35–36, 45, 49, 65, 70, 74, 91, 99, 125, 145, 158–59, 166, 198, 208, 287, 290

silver medal   285
Simon Bolivar Fourth Front   284
Sinclair Cuba Oil Company   156
situation   8, 17, 46, 58, 66, 68, 72–77, 80–81, 85–86, 100, 102, 109, 134, 187, 200, 227, 268
   bad   99
   common   6
   complex   17
   dangerous   57
   difficult   75–76, 79, 98
   economic   46
   false   86
   international   9, 277
slander   90, 93–94, 139, 218, 264
   rain vile   106
   unimaginable   90
slavery   243
   white   219
slaves   4, 106, 137, 193, 200
slogan   70, 91, 132, 148–49, 151, 197, 225, 242, 244
   central anti-corruption   6
   foreign   70
smuggling   219, 254
socialist Revolution   11, 239–40, 242, 268–69, 273, 275, 282
   first   3
socialists   239, 248
socialist transition   1, 284
social problems   36, 107, 110, 118, 130, 184, 204, 273
   reducing   36
Social security and government unemployment insurance   111
Social Security Card   245
society   10, 110, 117, 141, 161, 214, 217, 249, 269
   civil   5, 290
   colonized   3
   independent   3
   new   281
soil   93, 98, 167
   fertile   266
soldiers   26–27, 37, 56, 79, 135–36, 138–39, 142, 145, 148, 198, 226–27, 265, 277, 279
   best   26
   good   26
   murdered   222

rebel   133, 139
   wounded   30
Soler, Emilio   264–5, 290
solidarity   9, 43, 97, 148, 162, 168, 172, 180, 244, 275, 280
   awakened human   221
solution   22, 39, 47, 71–73, 78, 81, 85, 117–18, 184–86, 201, 204, 270, 272–73
   harmonic   101
   national   21, 113
Somoza, Anastasia   43, 260
sons   49, 100, 112, 119, 151, 159, 162–64, 218, 221, 239, 243, 248–49, 254–55, 266, 284
   wounded   265
Sosa Blanco, Jesús   23, 40, 290
   crimes of   40
South Africa   192
sovereignty   11, 26, 79–80, 90, 133–34, 138, 155–57, 164, 167–71, 186, 189, 200, 206–7, 244, 261, 274–75
   national   10
Soviet Union   124, 168–70, 181–83, 190–91, 239, 255, 287
Spain   8, 15, 167, 175, 195, 278, 286–87
Spanish Civil War   242
Spanish colonialism   152, 175, 285
Spanish Falangist   265–66
Spanish King Charles   278
Spanish priests   264
species   43
   human   43
spectacle   46, 68, 83, 100
   disgraceful   97
   terrible   251
Speleological Society   129, 131, 287
spheres   32, 123
   economic   128
   national   42
   productive   5
   technical   128
squad   26, 40
   firing   95, 221
stagnation   5, 48
Standard Oil   156
starvation wages   110, 170, 207, 273
state   35–37, 39, 48–49, 56, 66, 73–74, 77–78, 81, 93, 107–9, 111, 115–18, 125–26, 145–46, 165, 171, 180, 187, 191, 193, 203–4, 206, 208, 240–42, 257, 267–69, 274, 277, 279, 282

state (cont.)
   democratic   144
   economic   77
   member   237
   modern   3
   powerful foreign   144
state apparatus   37, 214
   new   10
State Department   160
state lands   124
station   278
   naval air   234
   sinister police   127
Stevenson, Adlai   237
students   1, 4, 54, 92, 95, 125–26, 139–40, 142–43, 148, 162, 171–72, 206–7, 244, 247–48, 274–75, 282, 279
   communist   235
   veterinary   49
subversion   186–87
   political   287
sugar   5–6, 124–25, 133, 157–58, 182
   quantity of   43, 125
sugar cane cooperatives   248
sugar cane factories   157–58, 243, 253, 265, 268
   largest   160
   principal   158
sugar cane factory Australia   245
sugar cane harvest   57, 59, 214, 231
sugar cane processing plants   172
Sugar Companies   155
Sugar Law   154
sugar plantations   142, 215, 250
sugar production   178
sugar quota   43, 93, 134, 182–83
suicide   43, 225, 262
   committed   6, 279
Sukarno, Ahmed   277
Superior Court of War   289
supply and demand   273
   law of   118, 204, 273
Supreme Court   7, 22, 78, 288
surprise attack   81, 228–30, 252
surrender   8, 16, 22, 158, 198, 254, 257
   total   15
   unconditional   19
Swan Islands   186
symbols   8, 43, 65, 91, 103, 127, 140, 163, 228

   highest   167
Syria   9
system   3, 5, 10, 152, 199, 218, 229, 258, 262
   best   129
   colonial   9
   fiscal   111
   inhumane   170, 207, 273
   national   10
   political   4
system of collective revolutionary watch   197, 199

Tabernilla, Francisco   21–22290
tanks   21, 81, 85, 105, 159, 178, 215, 257–58, 260
tasks   20, 31–32, 34, 42, 56, 63, 69, 71, 89, 102–3, 106, 119, 127–28, 147, 165–66, 208–9, 214, 269, 281
   daring   280
   difficult   31, 34
   fulfilled   216
   fundamental   144
   great   128, 146, 165, 213, 272
   hard   259
   primary   165
   principal   1, 143–44
taxes   36, 111, 118, 181, 205, 270
teachers   6, 114, 117, 129, 142, 170, 177, 184, 202, 207, 214, 216, 221, 257, 267, 273
   voluntary   166, 205, 223
   young Black   216
teacher's associations   59
technicians   49, 65, 118, 127, 133, 204, 208–9
technology   116, 135
tenant farmers, small   111
Tenth Congress   17, 97
territory   168, 176, 182–83, 186–87, 189, 192, 222, 238, 251
   foreign   92
   liberated   26, 35
   occupied   167
   small   261
terror   7, 93, 285, 292
   inspired   100
terrorism   222–24, 289
   act of   224
   liquidate   224
Texaco   157
Texas   167
Texas Company West Indian   156

textile workers 107
  supported 195
threat 6, 134–35, 146, 188–89, 261, 288
  perennial 115, 203
  removed 86
titles 49, 72
  free 203
  legal 47
tobacco growers 4
tombs 33, 112, 114, 135, 138, 239
tonight 97, 100
  expressed 82
  speaking 27
Tortuga Island 232
tragedy 43, 108, 116, 133
  appalling 115
traitors 68, 80, 91–92, 131, 167, 208–9, 222, 292
transformation 1, 123, 213
  great 130
  major social 11
  profound 123
  profound anti-capitalist 3
  radical 124
  sound 7, 114
transition 5
  national liberation and socialist 1
treachery 16, 66, 228
treason 68, 73, 79, 95, 232
  high 271
Treasure Lagoon 64
Trejo, Rafael 291
trials 40, 56, 61–62, 74, 105, 113, 201, 272, 287, 289
  celebrated 17
triumph 1, 5, 8–9, 15, 19, 21, 25, 30, 37, 41, 56, 104, 110, 118, 132, 150, 202, 222, 247, 265, 275, 277–86, 288–91
  popular 16
troops 21, 23, 78, 82, 135–36, 145, 243, 283, 289
  disembarking 242
  first 280
  foreign 136
  guerrilla 284
truce 113
  prolonged indefinite 21
Trujillo, Rafael 66, 79, 106, 291
trusts 35, 42, 44, 72, 75, 85, 159–60

foreign 107, 110
international mining 181
truth 23, 27, 29, 31–33, 36, 43, 65, 68, 81, 89–90, 98, 102, 105–6, 127, 131, 135–36, 149, 153, 162, 178, 192, 197, 199, 202, 218, 231, 239, 270
tuberculosis 177, 180
twin-engine bombers 233
tyranny 8, 25, 29, 40, 98, 105–6, 109, 127, 169, 178, 184, 199, 236, 255, 273, 282
  atrocious 132
  bloody 108, 177
  despicable 163
  implacable 236

unconstitutionality 7
underdeveloped countries 5–6, 134, 171, 178–79, 184–5, 191–93, 207, 274
unemployment 6, 115, 119, 203, 253
  high 36
unions 19, 98, 102, 192, 214
  federated 17
  intimate 143
  Mujalist 19
United Fruit Company 115, 146, 157, 160, 181, 203, 255
United Nations 9, 124, 167, 169, 173–75, 177, 179, 181, 183, 185–87, 189, 191, 193–95, 197, 214–15, 237–38, 241, 252, 284
United Party 11, 282
United Press International 232, 237
United States 3–5, 7–9, 11, 15, 17, 43, 85, 123–24, 133, 143, 146, 152, 157, 160–62, 168–70, 175–91, 193–95, 208, 213–15, 222–23, 225–34, 236–39, 241, 243–44, 250, 252, 257, 260–63, 278, 280–81, 283, 285–91
unity 5, 80, 86, 90, 101, 139, 151, 164, 169, 270
  continental 169
  precarious 214
University of Havana 1, 282, 284, 286, 289
University Student Directorate 277
University Student Federation 10, 125, 282, 286
unselfishness 28, 37, 52, 88
  absolute 37
unspeakable crime 109
untransferable ownership 203
UPI 92, 159, 181, 188, 232–33, 235–36, 238

Urban Reform Law 10, 201, 223, 268–69
Urrutia, Manuel 56, 73, 77, 81, 83, 282, 291
use of atomic weapons 188–89

Valdés, Ramiro 234, 291
validity 24
　given 58
　great 286
value 52, 103, 132, 155, 157, 191, 214, 219, 269
　solid 47
　spiritual 265
　total 184
Varadero 254
Vázquez, Euclides 51, 54, 73
Venezuela 167
Ventura, Esteban 283, 291
veterinarians 115
victims 39, 66, 69, 72, 74, 90, 132–33, 136, 139, 160, 165, 191, 213, 216, 226–27, 231, 241, 260, 285
victory 16, 25, 45, 92, 150, 163, 214, 241, 243, 248, 266, 271–72, 284
　moral 272
　robbing 19
　total 15, 19
Vietnam 9
virtue 42, 176, 179, 182, 187, 257–58
voter registration card 254, 257
votes 31, 36, 106, 110, 117, 159–60, 164, 168, 208, 257–59
　dissenting 291
　electoral 170, 254

war 8–9, 19, 27, 30, 40, 43, 49, 65, 80, 95, 97, 100, 126, 144, 169, 174–75, 182, 191, 193–94, 225, 227–28, 263, 265–66, 268, 277–78, 280, 283–85, 289
　atomic 193
　civil 41, 195, 227
　dangers of 43, 194
　economic 124
　endured 43
　necessary 285
　nuclear 193
war criminals 25, 40, 61, 97, 133, 174, 186, 264, 290
Washington 133, 161–62, 168, 171, 185, 207, 216, 237, 274
　agents of 171, 207, 274

watchfulness, collective 199
wealth 107, 116, 141, 172, 184, 191, 227, 253, 261, 264, 269
　national 171, 206, 274
　ostentatious 6
weapons 98, 154, 209, 245, 272
　anti-air 224
　economic 183
West Indian 115, 203
women 26, 44, 131, 143, 163, 165–67, 171–72, 214, 218, 221, 224, 239, 243, 248–49, 251, 257–58, 264, 271, 274–75, 282
　ban 165
　great 163
　young 165
Women's Combat Units 166
work 1, 5, 32, 35, 37, 40–41, 43, 45, 49, 52–53, 59, 63, 67, 80, 82, 88–89, 107, 109–10, 112, 114–15, 117, 126–28, 133, 138–39, 141–42, 144, 147, 160–61, 164–66, 171–72, 174–75, 177, 180, 202, 206–9, 229, 249, 255, 257–59, 267
　centers of 19, 241
　creative 40
　daily 80
　difficult 126
　forced 40
　given 257, 267
　great 41, 147, 208
　human 170, 273
　important 165
　intellectual 249
　long 208
　manual 249
　perennial 114
　political 272
　professional politicians 114
　revolutionary 57, 205
　single 241
Worker Commission 287
workers 5, 10, 17, 19, 57, 63, 79, 92, 95, 97–101, 103, 107, 110–11, 114, 116, 125–26, 132–33, 135–36, 138–43, 148, 153, 158–59, 162–63, 168, 171, 202, 206–7, 224, 228–29, 239, 242–44, 247–48, 251–54, 256–57, 260, 264, 274–75, 281, 285, 287
　agricultural sugar 142
　assassinate 255
　combative 281

INDEX 329

construction 254
dozens of 133
duty of 172, 275
exploited 152
hundred 226
industrial 114, 202
intellectual 115, 141, 257–58
manual 258
murder 260
new 199
privileged 6
railroad 107
rural 124
salaried low-income 6
single 139
sons of 239, 255, 270
workers and peasants 35, 111, 171, 207, 239, 253–54, 260, 274
   blood of 253, 257
working class 17, 97–104, 112, 239, 275, 281, 290
   organized 98
world 3, 24, 27, 30, 37, 40, 43, 67, 71, 88, 90, 135, 138–39, 147–48, 150, 152, 156, 160, 162, 168–70, 172–73, 175–79, 181, 188–91, 193–95, 200, 202, 206, 208–9, 219–20, 225, 227–28, 230–33, 235–39, 243–44, 247, 252–53, 262–63, 272, 275
   better 171, 206, 274
   new 123, 218
   old 218
   present 118, 204, 273
   underdeveloped 123
world market 158
world opinion 176

World War I 195
World War II 169, 232

Yankee agencies 171, 207, 232, 252, 274
Yankee arms 232
Yankee bank 198
Yankee bazookas 258
Yankee imperialism 152, 161, 200, 244, 252
Yankee monopolies 168, 256
youth brigades 205, 224
   women's 165
youth congress 160
youth movement 125
youths 6–7, 37, 116–17, 125, 148, 152–53, 162, 171–72, 206, 232, 239, 248, 266, 274–75
   assassinated 108
   inexperienced 50
   murdered 145
Yung, King 285

Zapata 172, 245, 248
Zapata's Swamp 59, 63–65
zone 39, 59, 65, 82, 133, 136, 167, 191, 199, 245, 280, 290
   costal 64
   frontier 160
   geographical 8, 215
   mountainous 213, 215
   northern 281
   poorest 49
   reserving 118, 204
   rich 167
   rural 109
   southern 284
   southwest 244

www.ingramcontent.com/pod-product-compliance
Lightning Source LLC
Chambersburg PA
CBHW071332080526
44587CB00017B/2810